By the hard work of others, we are led
to the most beautiful things that have been dragged
out of darkness and into the light.
Everyone is invited to experience the light
of every age and every people.
So, let us walk hand in hand with those from every age.
Let us turn from this brief and transient time
and offer our minds and hearts to the past,
which is long and eternal.

      —Seneca, *On the Shortness of Life*

THE CLASSICS CAVE
Sugar Land

THE CLASSICS CAVE

the earliest light for a brighter life

www.theclassicscave.com

ARE YOU looking for the best books ever? Or new ways to read and benefit from them? To practice what you've read? To learn and grow a little? Let the Cave be your guide!

THE CLASSICS CAVE (the Cave) is an educational* organization centered on the classics of Greek and Roman antiquity, with an emphasis on the best of ancient Greek literature.

OUR MISSION is to shine the light of the past into the present for a brighter life today.

OUR GOAL is practice—the application of ancient wisdom and ways to our contemporary lives.

WE publish books, develop and provide online content, organize and do outreach, and produce and distribute a variety of print and other media intended to entertain and educate, inspire, encourage, and cultivate.

VISIT THE CAVE online (www.theclassicscave.com) to support our mission and to access a growing catalog of engaging books and other beneficial content designed for individuals, educators, groups, and all others interested in benefiting from ancient literature.

SUPPORT THE CAVE by telling others about our work and by leaving a positive review online. You may also wish to buy a book or join The BAGL Club or the AAGS (to adopt an ancient Greek). Or sponsor the BAGL. Or partner with us by giving a donation. Thanks!

With GRATITUDE, we thank our readers, members, sponsors, donors, and all participants in Cave content—you who make the work and outreach of the Cave possible. Without you, the Cave would not exist!

*For the Cave, **education** is that happy transition from ignorance to knowledge; from foolishness to wisdom; and from mediocrity or vice to excellence or virtue, culminating in good habits and character.

In praise & Recognition of the Stoics & Stoicism

"No kind of philosophy is more profitable . . . than the philosophy of the Stoics." —Thomas James

"The words of the Stoics are for the most part those of men arguing with wisdom and insight." —Cicero

"[Stoicism is] the greatest system of organized thought which the mind of man had built up for itself in the Greco-Roman world before the coming of Christianity. . . . I believe that it represents a way of looking at the world and the practical problems of life which possesses still a permanent interest for humankind, and a permanent power of inspiration." —Gilbert Murray

"Stoic Cosmopolitanism . . . extends beyond self-love in the narrow sense to embrace all that belongs to the individual, family, friends, fellow citizens and, finally, the whole of humanity."
                                        —Frederick Copleston

"The Stoics commonly hold up internal calm and peace of mind as that which is finally to be desired." —W.J. Oates

"You [Stoics] who are acquainted with the Stoic Porch, you have committed to your divine books the best of teachings, that virtue of the soul is the only good." —Athenaeus the epigrammatist

"The Stoics, who place man's highest good in the rational soul, live according to the spirit." —Augustine of Hippo

"Readily I follow [the early Stoics] Zeno of Citium, Cleanthes of Assos, and Chrysippus of Soli." —Annaeus Serenus

"Zeno of Citium has for many years been devoted to philosophy in the city and has continued to be a good man in all other respects, exhorting to virtue and moderation those of the youth who come to him to be taught, directing them to what is most excellent, offering to all in his own manner of living a pattern for imitation in perfect conformity with his teaching." —Athenian decree

"You, O Zeno, made self-sufficiency your rule, letting go of empty riches. . . . With foresight you contended by means of a deliberate plan, the mother of fearless liberty." —Zenodotus the Stoic

"Whenever you are about to meet with someone, particularly if he is one of those who are judged 'outstanding,' ask yourself, 'What would . . . Zeno the Stoic do in this situation?'" —Epictetus

"Zeno of Citium, who scaled high Olympus, . . . his path was a path to the stars—the way of moderation alone." —Antipater of Sidon

"If you wish to know the principal teaching of the philosophers, which is in itself short, read Zeno the Stoic. . . . Keep the words of [the early Stoic] Cleanthes ready at hand." —Epictetus

"I admire Chrysippus, the leader of the Stoics, for many things . . . Chrysippus, who was himself a genuine philosopher and an archetypical man in every way." —Athenaeus of Naucratis

"My Stoic studies were my health and deliverance. . . . Zeno of Citium and Chrysippus of Soli have done greater things than they would have if they had led armies, held high office, and passed laws." —Seneca

"It was a wise and useful provision of the ancients to transmit their thoughts to posterity by recording them in collections. . . . If they had not done so, we would not know what . . . Zeno the Stoic and other philosophers set down for the conduct of human life."

—Vitruvius

THE BEST OF THE
EARLY STOICS

THE BEST OF THE
EARLY STOICS

The Lives, Writings & Teachings
of the Early Stoics

The Best Parts in Translation
with
a Narrative Summary of the Rest

selected, introduced, and edited by
The Classics Cave

CAVE BEST OF SERIES
the best of the classics for today

THE CLASSICS CAVE
Sugar Land

The Best of the Early Stoics:
The Lives, Writings & Teachings of the Early Stoics

Copyright © 2023 by Tim J. Young

ISBN 978-1-943915-36-1

Published in the United States by
The Classics Cave
P.O. Box 19038
Sugar Land, TX 77496
contact@theclassicscave.com
www.theclassicscave.com

The Classics Cave (the Cave) is an educational organization centered on the classics of Greek and Roman antiquity, with an emphasis on the best of ancient Greek literature. Our mission is to shine the light of the past into the present for a brighter life today. Our goal is practice—the application of ancient wisdom and ways to our contemporary lives. We publish books, develop and provide online content, organize and do outreach, and produce and distribute a variety of print and other media intended to entertain and educate, inspire, encourage, and cultivate.

Visit the Cave online (www.theclassicscave.com) to support our mission and to access a growing catalog of engaging books and other beneficial content designed for individuals, educators, groups, and all others interested in benefiting from ancient literature.

For the one entering this great work . . .
Pause for a moment before its door.

Such is the holy gift the Muses give to human beings.
—Hesiod, *Theogony*

CONTENTS

PART 3
Stoic Logic, Physics & Ethics in Cicero's Works

PART 4
Stoic Logic, Physics & Ethics in Other Ancient Authors

POINTS OF WISDOM & WAYS OF PRACTICE
from the Early Stoics

OTHER MATTERS OF INTEREST
Related to the Early Stoics

Cave Best of Series
Introduction
the best of the classics for today

Have you ever considered how many excellent works of ancient Greek and Latin literature there are to read? Think of all the significant works of poetry and prose—of all the epics, tragedies, comedies, histories, philosophies, orations, biographies, and more!

The problem, of course, is in the approach. How should you read them all? It is The Classics Cave's goal to offer a possible solution—and so the Cave Best of Series, which presents the best of an author, title, or group of authors.

Take the author, title, or group you have in hand. Of the available versions of the work, the Cave Best of Series version is unique for a few reasons. One, it is much shorter than most renditions of the work—oftentimes the number of pages totals anywhere from one-third to one-half of other versions.* Consequently, if you are pressed for time or do not know how many hours you would like to invest in reading the work, then the Cave Best of Series version may be for you.

That is not to say you will not get the whole work—the whole story or discourse or whatever the work centers on. Rather, you will get it in two forms—another unique feature of the Cave Best of Series presentation of a work. Whereas most versions offer either the whole or parts of a work (without any significant explanation of what happens in between each part), the Cave Best of Series version gives you the best or most significant parts in translation, along with a narrative summary of the rest that will tell you exactly what is going on in between. This means you will get the full content, feel, and experience of the work without missing out on anything essential.

And that's important. Unlike study guide versions that offer summary outlines alone, you will have extensive passages and narrative summaries of the whole work that will allow you to judge for yourself what is happening, what characters are central, what themes are significant, what the arguments are and whether they succeed or not, and the like—all depending on the work itself.

This is what the Cave Best of Series offers: the whole work in translated and narrative summary form, making for a relatively quick read that will let you come to terms with the work by yourself.

Not only that but there is also an information-packed introduction that is meant to draw the reader into and answer the most significant questions about the author and the work. Why should we care about *this* author and *this* work? What are the essential facts we should know? What are the work's most important ideas and themes? There is always a full exploration of these points that references the work itself as well as any pertinent scholarship.

Toward the end, there is a section presenting a "Plan of Life" (or something similar), "Points of Wisdom," and "Ways of Practice" related to the author. The latter "Ways" consist of workbook or journal-like prompts and exercises intended to motivate the reader to feel, think, and act in beneficial ways according to the author's "Points of Wisdom" (just as ancient readers or auditors would).

Finally, there is a unique section called, "Other Matters of Interest Related to [the Author]." It offers additional information about the author, whether a summary of the work, a cast of characters found therein, maps, a glossary of relevant Greek terms, suggestions for further reading, and so on.

In the end, when you read the work as presented in the Cave Best of Series, you will be entertained, educated, and, we at The Classics Cave hope, motivated to practice—to act in an intentional, specific manner toward a better life. With this in mind, welcome to the . . .

Cave Best of Series
the best of the classics for today

---

* Even so, whole, or mostly whole, works are sometimes included in the Cave Best of Series if the work is particularly short.

INTRODUCTION

Stoicism represents a way of looking at the world and the practical prob-
lems of life which possesses still a permanent interest for humankind, and
a permanent power of inspiration. —Gilbert Murray

A SK A GROUP of your friends to describe what a "stoic" is, and
you are likely to get answers like this: "A stoic is someone who
isn't very emotional." Or, "A stoic likes to appear strong and
tough." Or, "A stoic is someone who doesn't express his feelings."
And tacking on to the last, another may say, "That's right, a stoic
doesn't smile very often, and he certainly doesn't cry."

For others in your group, this shortage of emotions or lack of
expression of feelings may indicate something far more severe. "A
stoic is someone who *represses* his feelings."

Depending on your assembly of friends, the latter description
may trigger memories of Psychology 101, Sigmund Freud, and his
notion of "repression," where "threatening or painful thoughts or
feelings are excluded from awareness." Freud held that repression
"is the basis of many other ego defenses and neurotic disorders."[1]

Meaning? *Not good!*

Even worse than repression, for one or two among your friends,
the term stoic and such characterizations may sound the alarm of
"toxic masculinity," a concept that has been around for decades but
has only recently figured into some heated exchanges after the American Psychological Association released its *APA Guidelines for Psycho-*
logical Practice with Boys and Men a few years ago. Many have equated
toxic masculinity with what the APA calls "traditional masculinity,"
a phenomenon—or "ideology," as they put it—that, among other elements, includes "emotional stoicism," "some men shy[ing] away
from directly expressing their vulnerable feelings," the "eschewal of
the appearance of weakness," as well as strong notions of self-reli-
ance and a "reluctance to seek psychological help."[2]

Armed with the APA's assertions, one of your group offers, "A stoic is one who has bought into the whole ideology of traditional masculinity."

"Toxic masculinity," quips another.

The first pivots, "A stoic is any one of Dwayne 'the Rock' Johnson's movie characters—or Arnold Schwarzenegger's."

"Don't forget John Wayne," another says, going old school, "or Clint Eastwood. They play the ultimate stoic characters." And quoting dirty Harry with a raspy voice, he mouths, "Go ahead, make my day."[3]

Of course, after hearing these different portrayals of what a stoic is, descriptions that are not far off from dictionary definitions, you may want to know how much *this* stoicism aligns with ancient Stoicism—that is, the philosophy developed in the third century BC.[4] The short answer is a great deal *and* very little. While the ancient Stoics wished to curb their emotional lives according to what they judged to be the skillful guidance of reason, they were interested in far more. They wanted to think well, to explore the nature of reality, and to align their lives with that reality—all, most importantly, to be happy.

WHY SHOULD WE CARE ABOUT THE EARLY STOICS & STOICISM?

In the year 155 BC, Diogenes of Babylon, the head of the Stoic school, was in Rome with the skeptic Carneades, the head of the Academy, and Critolaus of Phaselis, the leader of the Peripatetics.[5] The three men had travelled there in order to negotiate with the Romans— really to beg remission of a fine of nearly five hundred talents imposed on Athens for sacking Oropos, a Greek town some twenty miles distant. When the philosopher-ambassadors were brought before the senate to make their case, they spoke through an interpreter, one of the senators, Gaius Acilius. The second-century AD writer Aulus Gellius reports that Diogenes of Babylon spoke *modesta et sobria*, which is to say, "with due measure and sobriety."[6]

Both characteristics of speaking were pleasing to the Romans. Not only that but many were attracted to Diogenes' teaching when he later lectured on the Stoic philosophy and way of life. Professor David Sedley explains that these "packed lectures" given by Diogenes

and the other philosophers produced "shock waves among the Roman establishment."[7] From that moment on, Romans were interested in philosophy as they had not been before—an interest that included Stoic philosophy.

Founded by Zeno of Citium (c. 335-263 BC), Stoicism was a force in Greek and Roman history from its launch in Athens sometime around 300 BC to well into the third century AD and beyond. And though Stoicism's organization and influence was uneven during this long stretch of time, what is clear is that many—both men and women—deeply cared about and benefited from it.

This is the first reason why we should care about Stoicism. For half a millennium—from the time when Zeno of Citium's student Cleanthes of Assos "wrote down Zeno's sayings on oyster shells and the shoulder blades of oxen"[8] because they meant so much to him, to when the second-century AD Roman emperor Marcus Aurelius wrote his Stoic-inspired journal of meditations, *To Himself*—Stoicism mapped out an understanding and way of life that strengthened and directed many amid the vicissitudes of human existence.

This was true not only in terms of time but also in terms of place. Practicing Stoics lived in a wide area of the ancient world from Babylon in Mesopotamia, the ruins of which are in Iraq today; to Tarsus in Cilicia, in modern Turkey, the home of St. Paul, who was likely familiar with if not influenced by Stoic teaching;[9] to Rhodes, an island just off Turkey and at one point a major outpost of the Stoic school; to Athens, Rome, and beyond, following the northwestern expansion of the Roman Empire to Spain, France, and the British Isles.

We see the significance Stoicism had for Athens in the decree that was set up in honor of Zeno of Citium to recognize the good he had done for the city and the education of its youth.

> Zeno of Citium, the son of Mnaseas, has for many years been devoted to philosophy in the city and has continued to be a good man in all other respects, exhorting to virtue and moderation those of the youth who come to him to be taught, directing them to what is most excellent, offering to all in his own manner of living a pattern for imitation in perfect conformity with his teaching.[10]

Diogenes Laertius further reports that the Athenians paid homage to Zeno by entrusting him with the keys of the city, giving him "a golden crown," and setting up "a bronze statue" of him.[11]

We can also assume that at least some of the people of Macedonia were trained in Stoicism—if, that is, we accept the word of Antigonus, the king of Macedonia, who, we are told, "favored Zeno" and "listened to him lecture whenever he came to Athens," attending as well the lectures of the Stoic Cleanthes.[12] At one point, Antigonus requested that Zeno visit him in order to instruct him in Stoicism. In the letter of invitation, the king makes the following argument for why the philosopher should meet with him: Understand, he writes, "that you will not only be instructing me but all the Macedonians together." Though Zeno declined to go due to his old age, he did send two men in his place. One of them, Persaeus of Citium, travelled to Macedonia, teaching Antigonus' son Halcyoneus and doubtlessly other Macedonians before eventually dying in the king's service at Corinth.[13]

Much later, it was common for wealthier Romans to send their sons to study philosophy with the Stoic Epictetus (mid-first to second century AD) in Nicopolis. We get some idea of what the experience was like from Epictetus himself. "The school of a philosopher is like an operating room in a hospital," he declares in one of his discourses. "You should not leave it feeling pleasure or delight but suffering pain. For you do not come there in health," he reflects, but with various disorders. "Am I, then, to sit there uttering pretty, trifling thoughts, and little exclamations" so that you may go away with your disorders? "Is it for this that young men travel away from home?" Is it for this that "they leave their parents, their friends, their relations, and their estates?" His emphatic answer: "No!"[14] Young men travelled to him, then, to undergo surgery and gain health. And when better, these in turn went home and spread the benefits of Stoicism to the family and friends they had left behind.

As for other individuals, we may observe with the examples of both men and women how significant and helpful Stoicism was in the ancient world. Diogenes Laertius tells us, for instance, that Cleanthes, a one-time boxer, "intensely studied philosophy" with

Zeno, "sticking with [Zeno's] teachings."[15] Cleanthes eventually became the second head of the school. The Roman Stoic Seneca reports that Cleanthes morphed into the Stoic that he became thanks to the fact that he had lived and studied with Zeno. "Cleanthes could not have been the image of Zeno if he had merely heard him teach; rather, he lived with him, observing him in private, watching to see if he lived in accord with his own principles."[16]

Much later there was Hierocles "the Stoic," who wrote the *Elements of Ethics* sometime prior to 150 AD, a work that deals with, among other matters, our natural relationship to ourselves, and our relationship and duty to others.[17] Hierocles was, according to the second-century AD Roman author Aulus Gellius, "a righteous and venerable" man—though that is about all we know of his character and life.[18]

Turning to Rome, we may note with Anthony Gottlieb that "for a time, Stoic ethics was more or less the official philosophy of the upper classes in the Roman Empire."[19] We've already witnessed this phenomenon with the young Roman men who travelled to study with Epictetus.

One of the earliest Roman Stoics, and perhaps the most archetypical *Roman* Stoic, was Marcus Cato (the Younger) (95-46 BC). Scholar of Hellenistic philosophy A. A. Long judges that "the life and death of Cato the Younger showed what it might mean to be a Roman and a Stoic." Cato, he goes on, "undoubtedly helped to popularize Stoicism among Roman aristocrats during the first century AD."[20] The statesman, orator, and writer Cicero, who was himself strongly influenced by Stoicism even though he counted himself an Academic skeptic, judged that "Cato, in my view, is a perfect specimen of a Stoic."[21] A century later, Seneca described Cato in Stoic terms as "a brave man" who lived "in defiance of Fortune." He was "a living image of the virtues." As Seneca notes in his treatise *On Anger*, Cato was also a man who knew how to check his anger with various strategies, including humor.[22]

Seneca himself, the tutor of and advisor to the emperor Nero, also exemplified how a Roman could benefit from Stoicism. In one letter he testifies how "my Stoic studies were my health and deliverance."

It was his conviction that "Zeno and Chrysippus"—the first and third heads of the Stoic school—"have done greater things than they would have if they had led armies, held high office, and passed laws." In fact, he concludes, "they did pass laws—though not for one single community of citizens but for the whole of humankind." Finally, though words not claimed directly for himself, he certainly would echo the speech he puts in the mouth of his friend Serenus. "Readily," he says, "I follow Zeno, Cleanthes, and Chrysippus."[23]

In his *Consolation to Marcia*, Seneca offers the addressee the example of Marcia's friend Livia (a.k.a., Julia Augusta), the wife of Augustus, the first Roman emperor. When Livia was experiencing a particularly intense grief after the loss of her son, she gave herself "to the consolation of Arius," the Stoic philosopher Arius Didymus, who was "her husband's teacher in philosophy." As for Marcia, the point is clear: Livia is a woman, Seneca announces, "who calls on you to follow her example," witnessing to the fact that adhering to the way of Arius' Stoicism "did her much good."[24]

Though we have little sure or direct evidence, the same was surely true for other women in antiquity—that is, they learned and benefitted from Stoicism just as Livia and Marcia did by means of Arius Didymus' "classic of emotional therapy," as David Sedley labels it. What we know with certainty is that the Stoics believed that women *should* benefit from their philosophy. This is not surprising given the fact that the early Cynic Antisthenes, an important influence on early Stoicism, held that "virtue is the same for a woman as it is for a man."[25] Later, the Stoic Cleanthes wrote a work titled, *On the Notion that Virtue Is the Same for Men and Women*. Similarly, the first-century AD Stoic philosopher and teacher Musonius Rufus taught in his lectures that "women have received from the gods the same reasoning power as men" and so "women should study philosophy." For him it followed that "a desire for virtue and an affinity for it belong by nature not only to men but also to women." He went on: "Since this is so, why would it be appropriate for men but not women to seek to live honorably and consider how to do so, which is what studying philosophy is?" There must, he concluded, be "female philosophers." In one lecture answering the question "whether daughters should get the same education as sons" (the answer is yes), he observed that "it is obvious that there is not one type of virtue for a man and another for a woman." He averred that both men and women need good sense, justice, self-control, moderation, and sobriety. As he saw it, the point is clear: "The same virtues [require] the same lessons."[26] Given this evidence, we may accept the conclusion that the Stoics presented their philosophy and way of life both to men and women, urging everyone universally to pursue a life in accord with nature, reason, and virtue.

As for specific examples of women benefiting form Stoicism, there are unfortunately only a few. And our evidence is indirect, gleaned solely from each woman's family relations to Stoic men and the ancient reports of each woman's Stoic-like virtue. With that understood, there are three women worth mentioning. One is Porcia Catonis, the daughter of the above-mentioned Stoic Marcus Cato, and the second wife of Brutus, who led the conspiracy that resulted in Julius Caesar's assassination.[27] Another is Fannia, the daughter of Clodius Thrasea Paetus, who was a Stoic and "renowned for his uprightness." She was the second wife of Helvidius Priscus, who, according to the ancient Roman historian Tacitus, "followed those teachers of wisdom"—the Stoics—"who hold that the honorable alone is good, the base alone is evil, and things such as power and high birth and the rest, anything external to the mind, they count as neither good nor evil."[28] A final is Annia Cornificia Faustina Minor, the daughter of Marcus Aurelius, the Roman emperor known for his Stoic meditations.

With the mention of Marcus Aurelius, who ruled from 161-180 AD, we come to the end of Stoicism's prevalence as a philosophy and way of life. Still, we may note the impact of Stoicism from the late second century to our own time. *This is the second reason why we should care about Stoicism*—for its long-term influence.

We've already observed the profound guidance that Greek Stoicism gave to various Romans from the time of the Roman Republic on. As we've seen with the examples of Julia Augusta, Seneca, Musonius Rufus, Marcus Aurelius, and others, the impact continued into the imperial period. A. A. Long remarks, "In the Roman world during the first two Christian centuries Stoicism was the dominant philosophy among educated pagans."[29] Professor Christopher Gill notes that "as well as being the dominant philosophical movement in the period, Stoicism was also strongly embedded in Greco-Roman culture and, to some extent, in political life, and the idea of living a properly Stoic life remained powerful."[30]

The ongoing power of Stoicism persisted for two major reasons, one having to do with pagan or non-Christian philosophy, the other with Christian philosophy or theology. As for the former, both Middle Platonism and Neoplatonism "absorb[ed] Stoic themes and language" into their own philosophical teachings.[31] A. A. Long explains, for example, that the Neoplatonist Plotinus "incorporated Stoic and Aristotelian concepts in his new interpretation of the Platonic tradition."[32] Christopher Gill writes that Plotinus "shared with Stoicism the idea that a rational force unifies and organizes matter." He further comments that "the tendency of Platonism to absorb Stoic themes and language leads to the appearance of these in works of popular philosophizing with (broadly) Platonic roots, such as the *Dialexeis* (lectures) of Maximus of Tyre (second century AD) and the *Tablet of Cebes* (first century BC or AD)."[33]

There is nothing surprising in this use of Stoicism or even, as one scholar describes it, the "pill[aging] by eclectics," since it was common during this period for the different schools of philosophy to learn from one another and adapt ideas and terminology for their own uses. In fact, Stoicism was sometimes judged to be merely an amalgamation of earlier philosophies. It was a common criticism of Zeno of Citium to suggest that his philosophy was nothing new, that it was only novel in its use of language. Cicero, for example, judges that "Zeno, the founder of Stoicism, was actually an inventor of new terms rather than a discoverer of new ideas."[34] However that may be, the charge (though why should it be something negative to use the wisdom of another?) may be made against most philosophers and schools after the initial creative phase of Greek philosophy.

As for Christians thinkers, since they were educated in the same schools and manner as the pagan philosophers, it is no surprise that they responded to and made use of Stoicism in a similar way, whether favorably or critically or both.[35] "It was the [Christian] Church," writes A. A. Long, "which helped above all to keep Stoic ideas in circulation, and Stoicism in its turn had an important influence on the Christian Fathers."[36] It is an influence that is, however challenging to detect, evident among both eastern and western Christians, including Clement of Alexandria, Origen, Tertullian, Lactantius, Augustine, and Boethius.

More specifically, we encounter the favorable reception and use of Stoicism within the realm of ethics.[37] Mark Morford explains that "Many of [Stoicism's] ethical doctrines were attractive to early Christians, who appropriated them."[38] A. A. Long adds that they oftentimes did so "without acknowledgement."[39] Meaning? There was among Christian writers no self-identification as a Stoic. Regardless, the significant point for us is that early Christians *were* influenced by Stoicism in terms of ethics. Mark Morford states, "Three doctrines of the Stoic system have significantly affected the [Christian] tradition: that happiness is the goal of rational action; that virtue is attained by living in accordance with nature; and that virtue, achieved through reason, is the only good."[40]

To give one example, in the *City of God*, Augustine of Hippo (fourth and fifth centuries) approvingly cites the beliefs of "the Stoics and other philosophers on the passions and disturbances of the soul." The Stoics, he notes, "stand on the side of the mind and reason against the tyranny of the passions." A few paragraphs later he clarifies that "scripture subjects the mind to God for his direction and assistance, and the passions to the mind for their moderation and bridling."[41] In stating such, Augustine subtly baptizes Stoic teaching in the waters of the Christian tradition, namely, sacred scripture and the notion that God is the sole or ultimate source of human well-being.

More broadly speaking, A. A. Long sums up early Christianity's positive relationship with Stoicism in the form of Clement of Alexandria (second to third centuries) in the following manner. Clement, he expounds,

> assimilates the Stoic *logos* to 'the word of God,' approves of the suppression of emotional impulses, and while teaching salvation as the basis of

ethics sees the life of the Christian as 'a collection of rational actions, that
is, the invarying practice of the teachings of the Word, which we call
faith.' . . . The sinner, like the Stoic 'fool', is ignorant. And we find Clement using a Stoic style of argument to prove that man is loved by God.
Clement was steeped in Greek literature, and the Stoic doctrines which
he refers to or incorporates are part of the orthodox tradition. Of all of the
Christian Fathers he is the most valuable as a source for Stoic theory.[42]

A negative or critical response to Stoicism is also readily discov-
erable in early Christian writing. Justin Martyr, for instance, dispar-
aged the Stoic teaching—or lack thereof—regarding God. "I
surrendered myself to a certain Stoic," he relates of his education in
his *Dialogue with Trypho*, "and having spent a considerable time
with him, when I had not acquired any further knowledge of God
(for he did not know himself, and said such instruction was unnecessary), I left him."[43] Christians were also critical of the thorough-
going materialism of the Stoics, as well as their permissible views
toward suicide. Further, as A. A. Long explains, "Some Stoic doctrines, such as the identification of God with fire and the denial of
the soul's immortality, were anathema to the early Fathers of the
Church, which helps to explain why no complete texts by any early
Stoic philosophers have survived."[44]

Despite the criticism, Stoicism and its ideas endured through the
centuries well beyond the period of the early Church, continuing
past the time when the Christian Byzantine emperor Justinian closed
the ancient schools of philosophy, including that of the Stoics, in Athens in 529.[45] Seneca was an important source for Stoicism in the west,
as well as Cicero's writings, whereas in the east, "Epictetus' *Manual*
[*Enchiridion* or *Handbook*] took the space of Seneca."[46] Mark Morford
reports, "Manuscripts of Seneca and Cicero were diffused from the
11th century onward, especially in France and Germany."[47]

Regarding Cicero, as A. A. Long urges, we should not "overlook
the importance of his earlier political writings, *De republica* and *De
legibus*, in which the Stoic concepts of natural law and justice are expounded. It was largely due to Cicero," he contends, "that such ideas
gained the support of Roman lawyers and the Roman Church

Fathers who gave them a new foundation in western culture."[48] And from them, these ideas passed to medieval theorists and jurists, including Albert the Great, Thomas Aquinas, and Marsilius of Padua.

At the beginning of the Renaissance, Petrarch (fourteenth century), who declared himself "Ciceronian" and labeled Cicero and Seneca "our philosophers," penned *On the Remedies of Good and Bad Fortune* from a largely Stoic point of view—that of Seneca and the presentation of Stoicism found in Cicero. In the work, reason responds to the misdirected expectations of various passions. Nevertheless, Petrarch "disagreed with the Stoics on the self-sufficiency of human beings to attain virtue through reason." Erasmus, who produced a critical edition of Seneca's works in 1529, brought up the same point, that "human beings were not the source of their own virtue."[49]

The point raises the fact of a number of ongoing criticisms of Stoicism that began in the early Christian period, continued through the Middle Ages, and lasted into the Renaissance. Although much was admired about Stoicism, and utilized, much was also censured—including the idea that everything is body or matter; the notion of an all-ruling fate; the rejection of the emotions or passions; the assertion of immanent divinity; and the view that suicide is sometimes acceptable, even right.

Still, there were many who judged Stoicism fundamentally compatible with Christianity. The Flemish humanist scholar Justus Lipsius (1547-1606) was one who had a tremendous long-term influence in Europe—so much so that "after the 17th century all philosophers had to take Stoicism into account, and some were strongly influenced by it, including David Hume . . . and Bishop Joseph Butler." Late in the sixteenth century, Justus Lipsius "developed the first systematic exposition of Stoicism since antiquity." His Stoicism, known as Neostoicism "was a practical philosophy for troubled times."[50] Of four works, Justus Lipsius' most significant was *On Constancy* (1584). Professor John Sellars explains that the book "outlines the way in which a Christian may, in times of trouble, draw upon a Stoic-inspired ethic of constancy (*constantia*) to help him to endure the evils of the world."[51]

There were many who engaged with Stoicism over the next few hundred years as the following examples demonstrate. The French essayist Michel de Montaigne was particularly inspired by Seneca, even though, in the end, he looked to "our Christian faith" rather than "Stoic virtue" for any true and "miraculous metamorphosis."[52] The German philologist and anti-Protestant controversialist Kaspar Schoppe wrote *Elements of Stoic Moral Philosophy*, a work that was, says Mark Morford, "didactically Christian." The Frenchman Guillaume du Vair published a translation of Epictetus, which included an essay that "sought to reconcile Neostoicism with Christianity."[53] In the dedicatory epistle that accompanied his English translation of Du Vair's *The Moral Philosophy of the Stoics*, Oxford librarian Thomas James declared, "Philosophy in general is profitable unto a Christian man, if it be well and rightly used. But no kind of philosophy is more profitable and nearer approaching unto Christianity than the philosophy of the Stoics."[54] In Spain, Francisco de Quevedo also hoped to square Stoicism with Christianity in like manner to Du Vair, Lipsius, and others. Though not explicit, Stoicism may be detected in Baruch Spinoza's theology and ethics.[55] Moving forward in time, the American transcendentalist and essayist Ralph Waldo Emerson and the German philologist and philosopher Friedrich Nietzsche were both influenced by Stoicism—Emerson relative to his notion of the Spirit present behind and throughout nature and "present to the soul of man," and Nietzsche in terms of the "eternal recurrence" or "eternal return" of all things.[56]

Stoicism's impact has been ongoing during the past hundred years in popular culture, philosophy, and psychotherapy or counseling. As for the first, we may briefly note its appearance in Tom Wolfe's 1998 novel, *A Man in Full*. Therein, the imprisoned Conrad Hensley reads from "THE STOICS. The complete extant writings of Epictetus, Marcus Aurelius, C. Musonius Rufus, and Zeno" (alas, a fictional volume). For Hensley, the book is the "word of Zeus," which is a means to freedom, confidence, and tranquility in life, and even an exhortation toward a kind of Stoic evangelistic mission.

Relative to philosophy, Stoicism has experienced serious attention in the form of critical study and is undergoing somewhat of a revival with the efforts of a variety of adherents and their works. One example is scientist and professor of philosophy Massimo Pigliucci. In his book *How to Be a Stoic*, he reveals why "I've become a Stoic," offering, among other reasons, that Stoicism is rational, science-friendly, and practical. More, it "speak[s] to us in plain language" and "speaks most directly and convincingly to the inevitability of death and how to prepare for it."[57] Another is professor of philosophy William B. Irvine. His "interest in Stoicism," he discloses, "is resolutely practical. My goal is to put this philosophy to work in my life"—a practice that he holds compatible with most religious beliefs.[58] A last example is professor emeritus of philosophy and ethicist Lawrence C. Becker, who has constructed what may be described as an updated form of the philosophy in *A New Stoicism*, originally published in 1998. In Becker's own words, the book "outlines a contemporary version of Stoic ethics, not a reconstruction of the ancient one." "We hold," he states (the "we" referring to contemporary Stoics, including himself), "that there is a single unifying aim in the life of every rational agent, and that aim, guided by the ultimate goal of a good life (happiness, eudaimonia), is virtue, achieved through the perfection of agency."[59]

As for psychotherapy or counseling, we may note with professor Sarah Marks that "the cognitive-behavior traditions have . . . situated themselves within Greek—and more specifically Stoical— thought."[60] The point holds true for the significant founders of the cognitive-behavior tradition, for both Albert Ellis (1913-2007), the developer of Rational Therapy, what came to be called Rational Emotive Behavior Therapy (REBT), and Aaron Beck (1921-2021), the originator of Cognitive Behavior Therapy (CBT). Ellis, for instance, in *Reason and Emotion in Psychotherapy*, reveals the following regarding the connection between REBT and Stoicism:

> I induced this principle of the ABCs of emotional disturbance [central to REBT] from working with hundreds of clients from 1943 to 1955. But I also took it over from many philosophers I studied from 1929 (when I was 16) onwards. . . . Clearest of all amongst the ancients were the Greek and Roman Stoics, especially Zeno of Citium (the founder of the school),

Chrysippus, Panaetius of Rhodes (who introduced Stoicism into Rome), Cicero, Seneca, Epictetus, and Marcus Aurelius. . . . I largely adapted REBT's ABC theory of emotional disturbance from Epictetus and other Stoics and . . . made Epictetus one of the patron saints of cognitive therapy.[61]

With this ongoing impact over the past hundred years, we come to this present moment, and so to *the third reason why we should care about Stoicism*. Briefly stated, as we have seen with the example of others, we too can benefit from the ancient philosophy that began with Zeno of Citium and persisted through time with adherents such as Cleanthes, Chrysippus, Seneca, Epictetus, and Marcus Aurelius.

The point is clear not only from the examples already cited (Pigliucci, Irvine, and Becker) but also from the testimony and activity of others. For instance, the scholar Gilbert Murray states, "I believe that [Stoicism] represents a way of looking at the world and the practical problems of life which possesses still a permanent interest for the human race, and a permanent power of inspiration."[62] Then there is Jim Stockdale's *Thoughts of a Philosophical Fighter Pilot*, in which he gives witness to the power of Stoicism, specifically in the form of Epictetus. "The Stoic philosopher Epictetus," he testifies, "was foremost among my consolations in the pressure cooker of Hanoi," where, after being shot down, he was in prison for eight years during the Vietnam War. From Epictetus and his writings, he received "comfort and strength."[63] Other examples include Donald Robertson's *Stoicism and the Art of Happiness*, Jonas Salzgeber's *The Little Book of Stoicism*, and Elen Buzaré's Stoic *Spiritual Exercises*, as well as online sites such as Daily Stoic (Ryan Holiday) and Modern Stoicism, which promote the practical effectiveness of Stoicism by means of annual conferences, courses, blogs, videos, and the like.[64]

But who were the Stoics? Although we've already caught glimpses, let's turn now to a few basic facts about this highly beneficial and influential group of ancient philosophers.

BASIC FACTS ABOUT THE EARLY STOICS & STOICISM

What was ancient Stoicism? Ancient Stoicism was a philosophical system oriented to practical living, which is to say, how to live well, with the ultimate goal of happiness (*eudaimonia*) always kept in mind. As such, Stoicism was about character, about human excellence or virtue, since virtue was judged sufficient for happiness.

For the Stoics, the three parts of philosophy—logic, physics or natural philosophy, and ethics—were closely related. Logic was aimed at physics, which was, in turn, aimed at ethics. In line with these three parts, the key imperatives of Stoicism, all oriented one to another as goals, were to . . .

- Think well (logic), to . . .
- Understand nature, or the way things are (physics), to . . .
- Live in harmony with nature (ethics), to . . .
- Live in conformity with reason (ethics), to . . .
- Live in accord with virtue (ethics), to . . .
- Have a good flow of life, or to be happy (ethics).

We will delve more extensively into each of these points and the three parts of Stoic philosophy in the next section, "The Big Themes & Ideas of the Early Stoics & Stoicism."

What was it like to practice the Stoic way of life? Although extraordinary both in its ideas and its demands, Stoicism was in many ways an ordinary affair in that it did not draw practitioners away from ordinary life—from your city, family, friends, or business. Rather, Stoicism counseled full engagement with ordinary life and offered advice about how to be so engaged. Well-known Stoics were manual laborers, businessmen, teachers, scholars, writers (poets, playwrights, satirists, essayists, textbook authors, expositors), librarians, heads of school, counselors, political advisors, statesmen, senators, consuls, and even emperors. To practice the Stoic way of life, then, was to practice a well-lived life precisely when and where you found yourself. For the Stoics, happiness was not *out there* somewhere apart from the present time and circumstances; rather, it was practiced right *here* and *now* in terms of duty or what was fitting. Generally speaking, duty was a matter of virtue—of living wisely, courageously, moderately, and justly. More specifically, it was about a person's present and ongoing circumstances—your family, for example, friends, work, and city-state.

What periods make up Stoic history? Stoic history is divided into three periods. The early Stoic period is called the "Early Stoa." It lasted from the founding of Stoicism (c. 300 BC) to the first half of the second century BC. The next was the "Middle Stoa," which lasted through the remainder of the second century to the end of the first century BC. The last was the "Late Stoa." It more or less coincided with the time of the Roman Empire (late first century BC to the last quarter of the fifth century AD).

Who were the major early, middle, and late Stoics? The three most significant early Stoics were Zeno of Citium, the founder of Stoicism; Cleanthes of Assos, Zeno's loyal follower and successor; and Chrysippus of Soli, the third head of the school, as well as its greatest and most prolific systematic thinker. Panaetius and Posidonius were both central to the Middle Stoa. They made significant adjustments to Stoicism, adapting it to their time and place. Finally, Seneca, Epictetus, and Marcus Aurelius were significant late Stoics. We have extensive writings from all three.[65]

What does the name "Stoic" mean? And how did the Stoics get their name? Originally called "Zenonians" after their founder, the followers of Zeno of Citium were eventually named Stoics after the *stoa* (a covered colonnade or portico) nearby the *agora* or marketplace in Athens that Zeno used to pace back and forth in while lecturing. Portrayed by Pausanias in his *Description of Greece*, this particular stoa, the so-called *Stoa Poikilē* (the Painted Colonnade), was a magnificently decorated space, with a bronze statue of Hermes, murals celebrating glorious moments in Athenian history and mythology, and shields taken in battle.[66]

How was early Stoicism related to Cynicism? And what about earlier Greek philosophy? Zeno of Citium initially read about philosophy and its goals in books, whether when he was young in Cyprus or, as Diogenes Laertius reports, after he first came to Athens. Either way, when he arrived in Athens, he was determined to meet and follow someone "like Socrates," the Athenian philosopher who had focused on how to live a good and happy life, "investigat[ing] ethical matters both in his workshop and in the marketplace."[67] Since Socrates had died decades earlier, Zeno settled for and gave his allegiance to Crates of Thebes, one of the early Cynic philosophers.

Crates was himself the follower of Diogenes of Sinope, who was inspired by Antisthenes of Athens, who was, along with Diogenes, credited with being the founder of Cynicism. We are told that Antisthenes learned "the art of endurance" from Socrates, his mentor and friend. As for Diogenes, Plato called him "a Socrates gone mad." According to later Stoics, "the Cynic philosophy and way of life [was] a shortcut to virtue." Whereas Stoicism was the steady-as-you-go climb up the mountain of virtue, Cynicism was the off-the-road, straight way up. The Cynic ideal was to follow nature so that they would be as simple and as shameless and, yes, as happy as dogs (from *kyōn*, or "dog," the source of the name "Cynic"). For Zeno of Citium, this shamelessness was a bit much, and so, after studying with others, he began to teach and eventually founded his own school.[68]

What are the major ancient sources for early Stoicism? Aside from fragments cited in both Stoic and non-Stoic literature, much of early Stoic writing has been lost. The most extensive collections come from the Late Stoa, including the essays, letters, and plays of Seneca, the *Handbook* and discourses of Epictetus (recorded by his student Arrian), and the *Meditations* or private journal *To Himself* of Marcus Aurelius. Other works from this period include the lectures or essays and sayings of Musonius Rufus (mostly found in Johannes Stobaeus' *Anthology*) and the *Elements of Ethics* and *On Appropriate Acts* of Hierocles the Stoic.

As for the Early Stoa, we have to rely on the third century AD biographer Diogenes Laertius and his *Lives and Opinions of Eminent Philosophers*, a work that provides the foundation for the volume you have in hand (Parts 1 and 2). Therein, Diogenes Laertius cites various Stoic works and views, as well as many other ancient writers.[69] We may note in passing that his work has been judged by scholars to be both reliable and not. The bottom line is that we must judiciously read the *Lives* in the light of other sources.

Otherwise, we know much about ancient (early) Stoicism from the writings of, among others, the Roman statesman, orator, and philosopher Cicero; the physician and Platonic philosopher Galen; the writer and biographer Plutarch; the physician and skeptic philosopher Sextus Empiricus; the Neoplatonist philosopher Plotinus; and a handful of early Christian writers (Clement of Alexandria, Origen, Tertullian, Lactantius, Eusebius, and Augustine of Hippo). This volume includes writings from Cicero, Sextus Empiricus, Plutarch, a number of early Christians, and many others.

What books did the early Stoics write? The early Stoics wrote many books on a variety of topics and sub-topics related to the three divisions of Stoic philosophy. Unfortunately, most of these are no longer extant except for a few quotations in other works. Nevertheless, to offer some idea of his some-27 books, Zeno of Citium wrote *On Life According to Nature*; *On Impulse*, or *Human Nature*; and *On the Whole Cosmos*. Apparently more prolific than Zeno, Cleanthes of Assos wrote *On Sensation*; *On Reason*; *On Good Counsel*; *On the Goal of Human Life*; *On Duty*; and *On Virtues*. Finally, Chrysippus, the most prolific of all the early Stoics at some-705 books, wrote with a focus on logic. To give a small fraction of his titles, there is *The Art of Logic and of Modes*; *On Inferences*; *On the Rules for Syllogisms*; *Definitions of the Good*; *Definitions of Things Neither Good Nor Bad*; *On Proverbs*; *On Habits*; *On the Kinds of Virtues*; and *Proofs that Pleasure Is Not the Good*.

THE BIG THEMES & IDEAS OF THE EARLY STOICS & STOICISM

The goal of life. Like most Greeks, and in agreement with Socrates and those who followed him in one way or another, Zeno and the Stoics judge that happiness is the end or goal (*telos*) of life.[70] As such, it shapes the path that Stoics resolve to follow.

But to follow the path, the Stoics figure they not only have to know *where* they are going but also the nature of the path and how it fits in with the surrounding landscape. In other words, they wish to know *what we must do* to achieve happiness, and how this *what* or path corresponds to the rest of human life and the whole of reality itself.

The three parts of Stoic philosophy. That question—What must we do to achieve happiness, the goal of life?—naturally involves Zeno and the Stoics in other questions and topics having to do with human knowledge, the nature of the world and the place of human beings within it, and, finally, the details of what had to be done in terms of a path to follow.

These questions and topics form the substance of the three parts of Stoic philosophy—logic, natural philosophy or physics, and ethics—three divisions we will explore in detail as we go along.

For now, let's briefly look at one analogy the Stoics give to explain the three parts. They liken philosophy to "a fertile, all-productive field," where logic "is the fence that goes around the field, ethics is the crop, and physics is the soil or the fruit tree."[71] In the analogy, logic is the science of knowing; it is the barrier that keeps falsehood out and the truth within the field. The field itself, with its soil and fruit trees, is natural philosophy, the part of philosophy that discovers "what is" in terms of the whole of reality and human life. Finally, ethics—the crop—is everything having to do with human flourishing, including the goal of life and the means by which we can attain the goal.

With that, let's turn to the Stoic system, exploring each of the three parts of philosophy. We'll begin with logic, move on to natural philosophy, and finish with ethics.

Stoic Logic or Knowing

The parts of the logical part of philosophy. Derived from *logos*, the Greek word *logikos*—as in the *logikos* part of philosophy—indicates not only that which is reason-based or intellectual but also that which is related to speaking or speech.[72] Accordingly, the logical part of Stoic philosophy includes dialectic, definition, canons and criteria, and rhetoric.

Dialectic.[73] The Stoics hold that dialectic (*dialektikos*) is "the science of correctly discussing subjects by means of question and answer." They define it as "the knowledge of truth and falsehood and that which is neither true nor false." More exactly, dialectic is the *scientific* knowledge—careful, subtle, and precise—of what is and what is not, having to do with, as Chrysippus put it, "things that signify" (things said or human utterance) and "things that are signified." Counted a virtue, dialectic and various allied virtues (earnestness, deliberateness, levelheadedness, irrefutability) strengthen the Stoic, providing a firm stance and steady habit in the form of knowledge.

Explaining why dialectic is a virtue, Cicero states that "it offers a method that guards us against giving assent to any falsehood or ever being tricked by deceptive probability. And it enables us to maintain and to defend the truths that we have learned about good and bad things." He further judges it "the art" that is able to remove "rashness and ignorance," as well as any kind of error, frivolity, or mere opinion. And this is important. According to Zeno of Citium, "the strongest point of the wise man is found in his avoiding being taken in and in his seeing that he is not deceived." It is the earnest practice of dialectic that enables the philosopher to avoid such a fate.

We read that Zeno himself was "an extremely subtle dialectician and a very acute thinker." His "inclination was toward searching and inquiry." He was "precise in everything." As for Chrysippus, we are told that his practice of dialectic was nearly divine. He "became so well-known for dialectic that most people supposed that the gods would adopt his system if dialectic ever existed among them."

Definition.[74] Part of the precision of dialectic has to do with definitions—another division, as we have noted, within logic. Cicero states that definition serves "to delimit [a] particular term"—an explanation that simply presents the literal meaning of the Greek word *horos* (limit, boundary, definition), a word observed in the English "horizon." In his book *On Definitions*, the Stoic Antipater explains that definition has to do with being precise, with breaking down a word into its constituent meanings, thus giving a careful and exact analysis. He writes that "a definition is an expressed statement in accord with a precise analysis or reduction." For Chrysippus, "a definition is an account of what is distinct." Taking these explanations together, a definition establishes the horizon or boundaries of a word, indicating what is within the limits of its meaning and, by implication, what is without. What is within is what is distinct about the word's meaning, its precisely analyzed meaning.

We may grasp the significance of definition for the Stoics by knowing the role definitions play in Stoic thought. In short, they help us to identify the truth. They are "the means of recognizing the truth," Diogenes Laertius states, "inasmuch as real things or objects are grasped by means of conceptions." And "concepts," relates Augustine of Hippo, are "those things which [the Stoics] expound by definition."

Canons and criteria.[75] We have observed so far that both dialectic and definition are used by the Stoics to get at truth. Another tool is what they termed "canons and criteria" *(s. kanōn and s. kritērion).* Like definitions, these are another "means of discovering the truth." They serve as the standard or measure of truth, the means by which we can judge or test something to see whether it is true. Included in the canons and criteria are things such as mind, right reason, preconception, sensation (a "measuring rod" of knowledge), and what the Stoics call an "apprehending presentation"—all things we will learn about in a moment when we come to the Stoic parts of knowing.

Rhetoric.[76] Finally, there is rhetoric, which is "the science of speaking well on matters set out in detailed narrative speeches or expository speeches." If truth is the goal of Stoic logic, including dialectic, definition, and criteria and canons, then we may view rhetoric as the art by which the Stoics discourse with success about the truth. So it is that they identify various parts of rhetoric, as well as a range of virtues and vices of discourse, aspects of the Stoic presentation of truth that need not deter us.

The parts of knowing. Seeing that the Stoics are interested in knowing the truth of things in order to live accordingly, we next turn to what they understood to be the process of knowing. So as to have a comprehensive view of this process and the various methods involved, we will first spend some time with what may be called *the parts of knowing,* that is, everything involved in the process, from the human knower to things known. Doing so, we will briefly survey each of the following: the human parts or powers of knowing; real things; presentations; the senses and sensation; preconceptions and conceptions or concepts; and, finally, the distinction between knowledge, grasp, opinion, and ignorance. After, we'll look at the parts of knowing together in order to view the Stoic process of knowing in a comprehensive manner.

The human parts or powers of knowing — the soul and its parts.[77] Generally speaking, it is the soul that knows. The soul is a "warm breath" or an "exhalation" — which is to say, it is that which we may feel with our own hands upon exhaling. The soul itself enables life and action. By it "we live and breathe, and by its influence we are set in motion." Relative to the process of knowing, the soul is able to sense things. In terms of its natural function, it is "a nature capable of sensation." As a sensing thing, the soul is that which is affected by real things external to it. In this way, it is impressed, altered, or modified by what the Stoics call impressions or presentations (on which, more in a moment).

The Stoics recognize eight parts of the soul. One is the generative or productive part by which the soul and body together reproduce itself. Five are the senses or sense faculties (sight, smell, hearing, taste, and touch). These five are the soul's "reporters" and "messengers" relative to the external world. Another is the vocal part by which the soul communicates itself. The eighth is the rational or intellectual part of the soul, the soul's leading part or leader, which organizes and directs every other part of the soul. In Greek it is called the *hēgemonikon*.[78] Situated in the highest part of the soul, it is identical with — or nearly so, anyway — the mind (*nous*) and the intellect (*dianoia*). As for its location relative to the body, some Stoics locate it in the head while others put it in the heart.

What does the *hēgemonikon* do? First, it serves as the source of motion in the soul, motion or activity that extends throughout the whole of human nature, body and soul. As such, it is the origin of the various powers exercised by the soul. "All the powers that are sent out into the parts of the whole are sent out from the leading part as from a fount or spring." As the source of these and the director of the soul, the *hēgemonikon* plays the leading role in sensation, apprehension, and cognition. The Stoics identify knowledge itself as "a particular state or condition of the leading part" of the soul. Finally, the leading part is the place "from which rational speech comes," —that is, the place from which we humans rationally articulate what we have come to know.

Real things. Humans come to know real things, objects that exist, things that *are*. Real things are *what is* in the cosmos—from what is dark or smooth, for instance, to individual elements, to rocks, trees, and horses, to humans, stars, and gods.

Most significantly, real things impact other real things; they produce effects. Relative to the process of knowing, they enable sensation, apprehension, and cognition, and they give rise to utterance or rational articulation. In short, together with the human parts or powers of knowing, real things make possible the whole process of knowing, including presentations, sensations, conceptions, and knowledge itself.

Presentations (phantasia).[79] Ancient sources tell us that a presentation is "an impression (*tupōsis*) on," or "an alteration (*alloiōsis*) of," or "a modification (*pathos*) that occurs in the soul."[80] As for it being an "impression," Diogenes Laertius relates that "the name is borrowed from the impress (*tupos*) made by the seal ring upon the wax." More precisely, he defines presentation as "that which comes from an existing or real thing, agrees with it, and has been stamped and impressed and sealed on the soul in a way that would not be the case if it came from a non-existing or unreal thing."

Said another way, real things give rise to presentations that correspond to the same real things in such a way that they provide accurate or matching information about the real things. Presentations, then, correspond to or agree with and thus reveal or *present* those real things that give rise to them.[81] In turn, this real-thing-corresponding information impacts the soul, impressing, altering, or modifying it in some manner.

The full explanation, however, is more complex. Some presentations, we learn, accurately present real things; others do not.

The Stoics call the first "apprehending presentations."[82] They arise from a real object, meaning that the apprehending presentation directly and actually apprehends or grasps something real. Conversely, it is the "existing thing itself" that impacts the soul through the apprehending presentation. As such, as accurately *presenting* a real thing, presentations are trustworthy, having, as Zeno of Citium judges, "an exposition or disclosure proper to themselves of the things presented." Zeno terms such trustworthy presentations "graspable," that is, presentations that one can truly get a hold of, "resembling things that are grasped by the hand." These are true presentations, distinct and clearly imprinted on the soul.

The second kind of presentation, a non-apprehending presentation, by contrast, "does not proceed from any existing thing or object—or, if it does, it fails to agree with the existing thing itself." Consequently, in terms of its purported source, it either relays faulty or inaccurate information about something real, or it somehow originates in unreality (whatever, precisely, *that* is), arising from something that does not even exist. Non-apprehending presentations are "neither distinct nor clearly imprinted" on the soul.

We may grasp the distinction between the two kinds of presentation if we look at the difference between dreams and waking reality. In the first, the visions we see do not immediately arise from anything real. Rather, they simply appear in our minds in a fleeting, phantom-like manner. Such visions the Stoics term "phantasms." They are, Diogenes Laertius explains, "an apparition (*dokēsis*)"—or a seeming—"in the intellect, the kind that may occur in sleep." By contrast, an apprehending presentation is an impact on the soul made by something real, something that is directly before us in some manner. Take a horse. If a black stallion is standing before us, there will be an apprehending presentation that imprints, alters, or modifies our souls. On the other hand, if later on in the day we think of the horse, this thinking is no longer an apprehending presentation but a "notion or thought-object" or a "phantasm in the intellect." Of course, such a notion is in some way related to a presentation (the prior one of the black stallion). But since the horse is not directly before us, the information presented is merely apparent rather than real. Diogenes Laertius states it this way: "A notion or thought-object is a phantasm in the intellect that is neither something real nor any quality; rather, it is an apparent thing and an apparent quality. For example, a mental image of a horse may come to be even though there is no horse present."

As for the more subjective basis of the presentation, there are three ways to classify presentations. One has to do with whether the presentation is sense-based or not. If it is sense-based, then it is grasped or "received by means of one or more of the senses or sense organs." If it is not sense-based, then the intellect is the means by which it is grasped. Another classification distinguishes the rational from the non-rational presentation. Rational presentations impact rational animals, whereas non-rational presentations impact non-rational animals. Finally, there are skill-based presentations and those that are not skill-based. In describing the difference, Diogenes Laertius explains that "a statue . . . is viewed differently by a trained and skilled craftsman in sculpting . . . than it is by one who is not trained and skilled."

The final point we must explore regarding presentations is how they work on the soul. According to Cleanthes, they do so in the manner of a signet ring impressing a soft wax seal. "Cleanthes understood 'impression' (*tupōsis*) as a thing that is both pressed in and standing out, similar to the impression made in wax by signet rings." Chrysippus, by contrast, judged that such impressions, one after another, would lead to muddled wax, which is to say a cluttered, confused, and incoherent soul or mind. This is why he suspected that Zeno of Citium used the term impression "in the sense of 'alteration'." If we think of "impression" in this way, he said, then "it is no longer absurd that, when many presentations coexist in us at one and the same time, the same body receives many alterations."

Why, for Chrysippus, was this the case? He explains with an illustration, one that is key not only for understanding how presentations work but also for grasping how sensation works. "It is just like the air when many people simultaneously speak," he says. When this occurs, the air "receives numerous and different blows and has many alterations. So will the leading part experience something analogous to this when it receives a variety of presentations." The Stoics hold that we hear thanks to sound waves. "We hear when the air between the sonant body and the organ of hearing suffers concussion, a vibration that spreads spherically and then forms waves and strikes upon the ears, just as the water in a reservoir forms wavy circles when a stone is thrown into it."[83] Presentations work upon the soul, then, as sound waves do in the air. Just as each sound or voice emits information in the form of waves impacting the air, so does each real thing emit, as it were, corresponding information that impacts the soul, altering it. Likewise—and significantly to the point—just as the information from each voice remains distinct, so too does each alteration of the soul remain distinct.

But how or in what way is the soul impacted or altered? The question brings us to the topic of sensation.

Senses and sensation.[84] For the Stoics, the senses and sensation are central to the process of knowing. The early Christian theologian and philosopher Origen comments that the Stoics "hold that all that we apprehend is apprehended through the senses, and that all knowledge comes through the senses."[85] So it is that everything—grasping things and knowledge itself—depends on the process of sensation.

But what is sensation? According to Diogenes Laertius, the Stoics apply the term sensation to the following four phenomena. First, "sensation" is used for "the equipment of the sense organs." These are the five bodily sense organs—the eyes, ears, nose, tongue, and skin. Second, "the operation of the sense organs is itself . . . called sensation." The operation is the proper activity of the sense organs, what they do according to their own function. Third, there is "the breath or current passing from the leading part of the soul to the senses." It is this breath or *pneuma* that is responsible for sensation, the medium through which, we might say, sensation occurs. Accordingly, each sensation is a breath extending from the sense organ to the leading part of the soul (*hēgemonikon*), or, as both Aetius and Diogenes Laertius put it, each sensation is a breath extending from the leading part to the sense organs. To give a few examples: "Sight," we learn, "is a breath extending from the leading part to the eyes." Or, "smell is a breath extending from the leading part to the nose."

Before we encounter the fourth way that the Stoics use the term sensation, let's note that sensation, as the Stoics understand it, involves both the body (in the form of the sense organs that are parts of the body) and the soul (in the form of the breath that extends from the sense organs to the leading part of the soul).

Finally, then, sensation is applied to "direct apprehension by means of the senses." Said another way, sensation is the moment when the soul directly apprehends a presentation, or, more exactly, an *apprehending* presentation. It is the moment when the soul has been impressed, altered, or modified by the presentation.

But there's more. The Stoics suggest there must be some kind of voluntary mental recognition of the apprehension, what they term "assent," for there truly to be sensation. As Cicero reports the matter, Zeno "proposed that sensation is a joining or combination of a kind of impulse or influence or impact presented from outside the individual sensing,"—the impact of the presentation itself—"and to these presentations received by the senses, Zeno joined the assent of the rational soul, which he located within us and declared a voluntary act." Sensation, therefore, is a combination of external impact and internal voluntary assent—an important point, as we will see.

When we recognize a friend walking down the street, we not only receive an apprehending presentation of our friend by means of our eyes or perhaps our ears as he or she calls out to us, but we also voluntarily agree with or assent to the presentation, giving rise to full-on sensation. "Yes, that's our friend," we realize and confirm. The same is true when we spot a white flower or hold a chunk of rough volcanic rock in our hands. Various presentations impact our senses as we voluntarily assent to them—or not.

We observe, then, that sensation is a process generally involving four things—five if sensation does not involve direct contact with the thing sensed.[86] The four are the external object, the sense organs, the soul or *pneuma* (breath or current), and the *hēgemonikon* or leading part of the soul. During the process of sensation, the external object gives off sense data or information in the form of an apprehending presentation. If there is no direct or immediate contact between the sense organ and the object sensed (as there is not with sight, hearing, and smell), the sense data travels through the medium of air (the fifth thing involved in sensation), presumably in some kind of wave-like manner.[87] The presentation impacts the soul by means of the sense organs. The sense organs then convey the sense data or information to the leading part of the soul by means of the medium of the soul itself, the *pneuma*, which is the breath or current that connects the sense organs with the leading part of the soul, the *hēgemonikon* or intellect.[88] Finally, the *hēgemonikon* voluntarily offers or withholds assent.

Preconceptions and conceptions or concepts.[89] Sensation is significant for the role it plays in concept formation. According to Augustine of Hippo, the Stoics held that "it was from the bodily senses that the mind conceives notions, called by them *ennoiai* or 'concepts'—that is, those things which they expound by definition."

How does the development of concept formation work? Aetius explains that it begins with the leading part of the soul, which is "like a sheet of paper that is easy to write on" when humans are born. It is upon the *hēgemonikon*—the easy-to-write-on sheet of paper—that each person "inscribes each one of his concepts." Here's where sensation enters the act. "The first manner of inscribing something on the *hēgemonikon* is by means of the senses." Sensing something leads to a memory of that thing. And multiple memories of similar things add up to an acquaintance with or experience of similar things. Aetius puts it this way: "When, for example, one senses something white, one has a memory of it after the thing departs. And when there occur many memories of a similar kind, then one is said to have 'an acquaintance with'—for 'an acquaintance with' is a multitude of memories of a similar kind."[90]

This experience of or acquaintance with many similar things is what the Stoics call a "preconception," which is a naturally occurring general conception of a thing, or, as Diogenes Laertius gives it, "a preconception is a *natural* conception of universals or general concepts." The "naturally occurring" aspect of preconceptions sets them apart from conceptions or concepts, which occur by means of teaching. A young child forms a preconception of the general concepts of "mother" or "horse" by encountering his own and other mothers and seeing many horses, whereas something such as the concepts of "soul" or "rational" are developed by teaching. Aetius expounds:

Some of these concepts come into being naturally according to the aforementioned way [that is, by sensation and memory formation culminating in an acquaintance with or experience] — and this without the art of teaching. Others, however, come into being through our instruction and care. These latter ones are alone called 'concepts' or 'conceptions,' whereas the others are called 'preconceptions.'

The Stoics judge that our minds or reason is "filled up with preconceptions in the first seven years" — that is, we naturally develop the stock of general notions (preconceptions) we will possess by our seventh birthday. From then on, and doubtlessly in some circumstances before, we learn new concepts by means of instruction.

How do we arrive at concepts — both natural (preconceptions) and learned (conceptions)? Aside from the general answer, "naturally . . . [and by means of] instruction and care," as Aetius puts it, we do so in various ways. Diogenes Laertius lists nine: direct experience, resemblance, analogy, transposition, combination, opposition, transition, nature, and deprivation. As for the first, "sense objects," he explains, "are thought about by means of direct experience." This is the "acquaintance with" mentioned by Aetius, that which consists of many memories of single instances of sensation — the many instances of sensing white liquid leading to the naturally formed preconception of milk.[91]

One final point. It is upon these preconceptions and conceptions that a whole system of philosophy may be built. Completing his explanation cited a moment ago, Augustine of Hippos states, "It is from this" — the various notions and concepts — that the Stoics "develop the whole system of their learning and teaching, and all the connections therein."

The use of reason versus sensation in concept formation. We sense or perceive various things by means of sensation and reason. Consequently, both are the means by which we form different kinds of concepts. "According to the Stoics, it is by sensation that we apprehend black and white, and rough and smooth, whereas it is by reason that we apprehend the conclusions of demonstrations — such as the existence of the gods, as well as their foreknowledge."[92] If we see many white tunics, flowers, and clouds, and if we feel many smooth chins, jars, and walls, we will naturally form the concepts (preconceptions) of "white" and "smooth." By contrast, since the gods or God usually cannot be sensed directly, we must know them, or various conceptions of them, indirectly through reason by means of various arguments or demonstrations.

Knowledge, grasp, opinion, and ignorance.[93] The Stoics commonly declare that a wise man will not hold "mere opinions." Why? Because thoughtless people opine. By contrast, sages possess knowledge.

A thoughtless man, for example, may see a coiled *thing* in a shadowy corner of his house and opine, "Ah, a snake!"[94] Not so a wise man. Instead, before assenting to the presentation that the coiled thing is a snake, — that is, before making the judgment that it is a snake rather than something else, — he will shine an oil lamp on it to determine what its real nature is. In doing so, he will see that it is a coiled rope rather than a snake. Even so, he may withhold assent for a moment while he further edges toward the object to get a better look and even pick it up and touch it with his own hands. And finally, giving his assent to the rope's presentation that has reached his mind by means of both sight and touch, such a man will have knowledge.

"Knowledge," the Stoics state, "is either a firm and direct apprehension or a habit that is, in the reception of presentations, unchangeable by argument." Cicero similarly defines knowledge as "a sensation that is grasped in such a way that it cannot be torn away by reason or an argument." In the case of the rope, no argument, no matter how subtle, will dislodge the conclusion, "This is a rope," from the mind once the rope has been clearly seen by the eyes and held and touched by the hands. The case similarly holds for less tangible realities or knowledge — say the existence of God.

Whereas knowledge is strong and sure, opinion "is weak and false assent" based on ignorance (the absence of knowledge), its source of weakness. Opinion, we are told, "shares attributes with what is false and what is unexamined." It is saying, "That's a snake!" before taking a closer look.

But what about that moment when the man first receives the presentation of the coiled thing before he has ascertained with full knowledge that it is a rope rather than a snake (or the other way around)? At that point he may grasp *a coiled thing*, realizing that it would be credible to judge it either a snake or a rope. Zeno counts such a "grasp" neither "correct nor incorrect but declares it to be only 'credible' or 'believable.'"

Including all states of mind relative to real things, then, we have four. There is *opinion* founded on ignorance ("It's a snake!"); there is a *grasp* ("It's a coiled thing that may be a snake or rope or something else."); there is *knowledge* (After verifying by means of sight and touch what it is, "It's a rope."); and, lastly, there is *ignorance*, which is simply the opposite of knowledge (for which one may say, "I don't know what it is" —an entirely appropriate response in many cases).

The Stoic process of knowing. Now that we have thoroughly explored the human parts and powers of knowing, we are in a position to briefly summarize what the Stoics held about the process of knowing. So here goes.

The process begins at birth. Within the first seven years, and thanks to the scribal powers of sensation as well as memory, the easy-to-write-on paper sheet of the soul (more specifically, the leading part of the soul—the *hēgemonikon*) gets filled up with preconceptions, which are natural concepts that arise from seeing and otherwise sensing similar things again and again. Doubtlessly— though we are not told in the source material we have—these similar things are labeled for the growing child: "Mommy," "ball," "white," "rope," "horse," and so on. By seven or eight, then, the developing child knows many real things by means of these naturally occurring preconceptions—what a ball, horse, and mother are, the color white, the feel of something smooth, what something "coiled" is, and the difference between a rope and a snake.

About this time, the child goes off to school.[95] This—and even before, perhaps—is the beginning of a life-long instruction in and concern with concepts (those learned). Building on naturally formed preconceptions, the child is taught all manner of new concepts until the intellect matures around the age of fourteen.[96]

At this point, the youth has all the tools necessary to know with wisdom and truth. He is ready to apply both preconceptions and conceptions, and all the methods he has learned regarding how one can know, to learning more about the world and living life well.

One night he is outside reclining beneath the stars. Sitting there, he considers many of the preconceptions he has learned over time. One is that of "star." When he looked up into the night sky as a young boy, he saw countless similar objects night after night. At some point, even though he already had a preconception of them, they were all labeled "star" by his father. So it was also with "dark," a preconception covering not only the night sky between the stars but the water deep in a well when he went to collect it or the rumbling clouds he observed during a succession of stormy days. So too with "light," which was applied to the stars at night and the sun during the day, as well as the fire his mother would light for cooking and the oil lamps they would light just as the sun was setting. And so on, preconception after preconception. Sensation worked in conjunction with memory to form the acquaintance with or experience of a thing. The process resulted in these various naturally occurring preconceptions.

Sitting there in the dark, he also thinks of his schooling and all the concepts he has learned, things built upon the foundation of preconceptions. He remembers Euclid's geometry and all its postulates and proofs. He recalls learning that the earth is round, as well as the whole cosmos. And peering into the sky, that the stars are fire. In fact, now that he is studying with the Stoics, he realizes that the stars are gods. And though he can hardly see the movement of the stars revolving in an orderly manner across the sky right at *this* moment, he knows they do, guided by the providential hand, as it were, of the gods—or God. He assents to the concept of providence thanks to various Stoic arguments, most moving from what is better known to something less clearly known, and finally from the ordered cosmos to the one or ones who order and go on ordering.

Whatever he knows, he knows thanks to real things external to himself. These real things give rise to presentations that reveal or *present* the real thing itself to the knower himself—the boy. The presentations impact his sense organs. His senses, in turn, performing their proper action or operation or function, communicate the information regarding the real thing to the leading part of his soul through or by means of his soul's substance, the breath or *pneuma* (even as air carries a vision of something seen or the sound of something heard to the viewer or hearer). It is at this point that he must either assent or withhold assent to the presentation's information that has entered his soul via sensation. Assuming assent, his leading part or intellect then converts the information into thoughts and things said or sayables. These, then, are communicated by means of the vocal organs (sent from his intellect or *hēgemonikon* to his vocal organs by the conduit of his soul's breath).

We see, then, that the process of knowing involves five things: the external object, the presentation, the senses and sensation, the breath or *pneuma*, and the leading part of the soul or the intellect.

Zeno, Cicero tells us, demonstrated what knowing or knowledge is like with a gesture:

> Before another man, he would show his hand with the fingers outstretched and say, "A presentation is like this." Next, he would draw in his fingers a little and say, "An assent is like this." Then, he would press his fingers closely together and make a fist, and say, "A grasp or comprehension is like this." And by this analogy, he introduced the name *katalēpsis* (grasp or comprehension), which was not used before. But then he would move his left hand to that fist in order to squeeze it tightly and with might. And he would say, "Such is knowledge," and that no one but a wise man was the master of knowledge.[97]

Methods of knowing. Now that we've explored the general process of knowing, let's turn to look at a few of the methods the Stoics used to gain knowledge.

Logical inference. One such method was dialectic itself, which, recall, is the means by which a wise person methodically asks questions and gives answers. Part of this questioning and answering is the more technical form of logic consisting of various kinds of arguments presented in the form of syllogisms. These lines of reasoning proceed by inference from "what is better grasped" to "something less clearly grasped."[98]

An example of an inferential argument is the Stoic argument demonstrating that the "cosmos is destructible or perishable, inasmuch as it is generated." Diogenes Laertius explains that the argument's conclusion "is based on the analogy of those things that are understood by the senses"—that is, things around us that are "better grasped." Given our ordinary experience of things, we observe that those things that are made up of perishable parts are perishable as a whole. Tree leaves fall brown to the ground; tree limbs dry up and snap in the wind; eaten by insects, trees as a whole eventually die. Taking this observation of ordinary things, we may conclude that "the cosmos [itself] is perishable" since its parts are perishable in that they "transform into one another."[99]

Cicero offers another example of "logical inference." It is by means of logical inference, he says, that we arrive at the concept or "the notion of good." Again, we move from things we know well or directly to things we know less well or indirectly. "The mind ascends by inference," Cicero says, "from those things in accord with nature until finally it arrives at the notion of good."[100] What are "those things in accord with nature"? They are things such as strength, health, and beauty, as well as all the virtues. From these, we are able to form an idea or notion of good.[101]

Truth from truth. With this movement toward truth by inference, we see that, as the Stoics put it, "a truth follows from a truth." The truth of the perishing of something on a large scale follows from the truth of the perishing of something on a smaller scale. Or the truth of the general nature of the good follows from the truth of the good of something in accord with nature. Or, to offer the example given by Diogenes Laertius, "'It is light' follows from 'It is day.'"[102]

The power of concepts. Each of these simple statements involves conceptions or preconceptions that convey meaning. "It is light" brings to mind certain concepts—most notably the preconception of "light"—as does "It is day." These concepts are significant for the Stoics methodologically because it is by them that real things are grasped. "Real things are grasped by means of conceptions."[103]

The sun with its light truly rolls across the sky in twelve hours, let's say (though, of course, we know it is the earth that is actually revolving). This occurs again and again, the occurrence which is termed "day." The term or concept "day," then, conveys and so enables us to grasp this regular appearance of the sun with its light. The term or concept "night," by contrast, signifies the absence of the sun and so the absence of light. Consequently, if it is light outside, then we can infer that it is day. Or if it is dark, night.

The benefit of training in the logical part of philosophy, and the imperative to study.[104] In writing to Antigonus, the king of Macedonia, Zeno of Citium acknowledges that learning is advantageous. "I welcome your love of learning," he writes, "inasmuch as you hold to the truth that stretches out toward advantage and not to that popular kind of instruction that tends only to the corruption of morals." The implication is that learning—studying, training—should be both intellectually and morally beneficial.

This intellectual and moral benefit, in short, is what Stoic training in the logical part is all about. It is not merely about becoming clever at argumentation, even though that occurs and is significant. Rather, it is training oriented toward truth about the reality of things in order to live a good life (the opposite of "the corruption of morals")—the advantage or benefit accruing to instruction.

Chrysippus, we learn, held that "we should no more use the power of reason or argumentation than we should the power of weapons for things that are not fitting." How should the power of reason or argumentation,—which is to say, logic,—be used? It "should be employed in the discovery of truths," he urged, "and for relating [truths] together—not for the contrary, though many do it."

The goal in training, then, is truth for the sake of moral advantage. This advantage is the overall Stoic goal in pursuing philosophy, and particularly logic.

But how exactly does training in logic benefit those of us who train? The first advantage is that we will not be thrown in life. "Without the study of dialectic," we're told, "the wise man cannot guard himself in argument so that, as in a wrestling match, he will never be thrown."[105] The wise man in the midst of argumentation—or let's say those of us who wish to be wise—is here compared to a wrestler in a wrestling match. If a wrestler's training with weights and so on helps him not to be thrown in a match, then study or training in dialectic or logic furnishes the wise man with the ability not to be thrown in argumentation, and surely in the whole of life as well, since all of life is related to thinking well. How is it that the wise man is not thrown? Diogenes Laertius explains: "The study of dialectic enables him to distinguish between truth and falsehood, and to judge well between what is plausible and what is ambiguously expressed, . . . [and to] methodically ask [well thought-out] questions and give [truthful] answers."[106] In the context of argumentation and life, falsehood, ambiguity, and a lack of method in asking and answering questions are liable to defeat us. So it is that in wrestling with reality, the study of dialectic or logic helps us not to be outmaneuvered and thrown.

Cicero makes a similar case for the Stoic position regarding training in dialectic. According to the Stoics, this study

> offers a method that guards us against giving assent to any falsehood or ever being tricked by deceptive probability. And it enables us to maintain and to defend the truths that we have learned about good and bad things. They hold that without the art of dialectic any man may be tricked and led away from what is true or actual toward what is false or deceptive.

In Cicero's *Academica*, Lucullus argues that ethical practice and the wisdom it is based on demands "our ability to perceive and grasp many things."

Significantly, the Stoics believe in the need to train relative to the reception of presentations. The reason for this training is straightforward: the way we receive and make judgments based on presentations—really the whole process of knowing—has a *real* or *actual* impact on what happens in our lives and consequently in the lives of those around us. Here's how Diogenes Laertius puts it: "Overhastiness in judgment affects the actual course of events, so that those who are untrained in presentations fall into disorder and a lack of purpose." To state it positively, the man who is trained in the reception of presentations will not draw false conclusions or make hasty judgments or decisions. Accordingly, his life will be ordered and have purpose since he knows what he is about and what he is doing. Such a man, the Stoics believe, is able both to argue and converse well, discussing subjects proposed by others and readily answering questions. "There is no other way," they judge, "that a wise man may show himself to be sharp, ready-witted, and generally skillful in argumentation."

Lastly, and more related to the modern conception of logic, the Stoics hold that "the study of syllogisms is very useful." With such a study, we come to know "what is demonstrative or what offers proof" relative to any question or inquiry. This in turn "contributes a good deal to the correction of judgments or opinions." When we know what may or may not be demonstrated, we know what we may or may not assent to. For instance, is it possible to demonstrate that a "coiled thing" in a shadowy corner of a room is a snake? If not, is it necessary to assent to fear? Put another way, is it necessary to allow fear to take the lead in making the following kind of argument or demonstration?—"There's a coiled thing in the corner; it must be a snake!" (The answer, of course, is no, it isn't necessary.) Finally, the "arrangement and retention in memory" of various syllogistic forms will "give a scientific character to our comprehension of things."

For all these reasons, the Stoics preach the imperative to study. The early Stoics themselves were paradigms of this study. Reports have it that Zeno was "very energetic in his approach to philosophy." His "inclination was toward searching and inquiry." Similarly, after Cleanthes approached Zeno, he "intensely studied philosophy" with him. Finally, we're told that "when someone reproached" Chrysippus "for not going with the multitude to hear" a popular speaker, his reply was, "If I had followed the multitude, I would not have studied philosophy."

As for how we should study, the simple answer is by listening and with humility and deliberate choice. Diogenes Laertius reports a conversation Zeno had with a young man who was "talking nonsense" —that is, he was making false conclusions and judgments. "The reason why we have two ears and only one mouth," Zeno quipped, "is so that we may listen more and talk less." To the Cynic philosopher Crates, his former teacher, Zeno remonstrated, "The

right way to seize a philosopher is by the ears." Zeno went so far as
to alter Hesiod's poetry to read, "Best of all is that man who is won
over by good advice," rather than as it originally went, "Best of all
is that man who thinks about everything himself."[107] As for humility, Zeno judged that "there is nothing as fatal as supposition or
self-conceit if we want to master the sciences." Lastly, deliberate
choice. In his letter to King Antigonus, Zeno acknowledges that the
very act of turning toward philosophy and "away from well-known
pleasure" indicates not only one's nature but one's "deliberate
choice." The implication is that all of us must make the well-considered choice to study philosophy and pursue the good life, studying "the truth that stretches out toward advantage."

Zeus the deliverer. Positively speaking, Stoic logic or knowing is
aimed at the benefit that knowledge renders us. Negatively put, we
wish to escape ignorance, that which is the opposite of knowledge,
that which proves harmful time and again. Fortunately, we have
Zeus (or God) to turn to in our endeavor—or so hold the Stoics.

According to the Stoics, we should turn to him—to God, the
great actor in the cosmos—for deliverance from our own ignorance.[108] If indeed we are ignorant, we may admit that we "neither
see the universal law of God, nor do [we] hear it." And with other
humans, we may pray, "Zeus, giver of all, shrouded in dark clouds,
ruler of the thunderbolt, deliver [us] human beings from mournful
ignorance, scatter it from [our] souls."[109]

If we docilely approach Zeus (or God) in this way—Zeus who
is, according to the Stoics, the reason or *logos* within the cosmos, the
divine mind (capital M), as we will see—then we will learn to reason well, and we will come to know the nature of the cosmos and
our relation to it and so how best to live.

So now, having made the prayer for the enlightenment of reason, we move on to the nature of things, to natural philosophy.

Stoic Natural Philosophy or Physics

Natural philosophy or physics.[110] Natural philosophy or physics (the
word comes from the Greek word for nature, *physis*) is the study of

what is, of everything that is. For the Stoics, this includes everything within the ordered reality of the cosmos[111] and everything without—things such as the basic principles, elements, and (the) void on the one hand, to the stars, sun, moon, and earth on the other. On earth it includes rocks, plants, animals, and humans, and relative to humans, the body and soul. In the heavens it includes the study of the one God, as well as the many gods.

Natural philosophy seeks to understand the nature of things in terms of substance, causes, genus and species, parts and wholes, qualities and characteristics. There are math- and nature-based questions. The former involve investigations into the revolution of the stars or the size of the sun—to give a few examples. The latter look at things such as matter and the various kinds of mixture, and whether the cosmos is living or not. Then there are investigations inspired by medical inquiry. These research the leading part of the soul (the *hēgemonikon*), as well as the originating seeds and like things. Otherwise, as do natural philosophers of other schools, the Stoics study various earth and sky phenomena such as comets, meteors, winds, hail, rain, snow, lighting and thunder, the rainbow, the seasons, and earthquakes.

The Stoics count natural philosophy as a virtue. According to Cicero, they do so "with good reason since he who is to live in accord with nature must base himself on the management and order of the entire cosmos." Such a man must not only understand the structure and organization of the whole cosmos but also how it is managed—by whom or by what means. "No man," Cicero continues, "can truly make judgments regarding good and bad things unless he knows about the whole plan of nature, and also about the life of the gods, and the answer to the question whether human nature is or is not in harmony with the whole—that is, with the cosmos."

Our ethical life, based as it is on judgment, as we will see, hinges on our understanding of natural philosophy. We see this, for instance, relative to ancient ethical maxims such as "nothing in excess." Excess relative to what, precisely? Natural philosophy answers the question. "Without natural philosophy, no one can consider the meaning of the ancient maxims of the wise—a meaning that is quite significant—that command us to 'submit to the right moment' and 'follow god' and 'know yourself' and 'nothing in excess.'" Finally: "this knowledge [natural philosophy] alone is able to convey the power of nature to cultivate justice and maintain friendship and the other kinds of love. Nor can we truly understand piety toward the gods nor the amount of gratitude we owe them without an explanation of nature."

Nature.[112] The Greek word for nature (again, *physis* or *phusis*) is related to the verb *phuō*, which means, among other things, "to produce" or "to generate." We see this meaning in the Stoic use of "nature" when they employ it to signify "that which causes terrestrial things to spring up." Nature, however, is more than that which produces things—though it is also that.

Diogenes Laertius provides the following definition of nature, which gives us a fuller idea of what the Stoics meant:

> Nature is a permanent state or condition moving from itself, producing and holding together all things that arise out of it at determined times and in accord with the generative principles, and effecting results homogenous with their sources.

There are three points to keep in mind in this definition. First, there is nature itself, something permanent or lasting (the Greek is *hexis*, a permanent state or condition) that is in motion in that it produces things, holds them together, and causes further things (results) to occur. The motion itself is self or nature generated.[113] Second, there are various things ("all things") that arise from nature, which is to say they originate in and are caused by nature, or, more specifically, by means of "generative principles." Third, there is a regularity in terms of "determined times." With these points, we note aspects of nature that the Stoics emphasized: permanency, motion, regularity.

According to Cicero, Zeno defined nature as "a craftsmanlike or skillful fire that proceeds methodically to the work of production or generation." Expanding on this definition, Cicero states that the "whole of nature . . . follows a specific way and adheres to a definite method." Nature is not merely *like* a craftsman, but it *is* "a craftsman," one that "cares and looks out for the benefit and time-liness of everything."[114] Cicero reports that "all things are subject to and dependent upon nature, by which they are produced and sustained in the most excellent manner."

Finally, nature supports all. We observe this not only in the whole of the cosmos but in its parts as well, such as the earth and things upon the earth.[115]

> If nature supports the earth and causes her to thrive, then the same conclusion applies to the rest of the cosmos. For a plant's roots cling to the earth. By contrast, animals are sustained by breathing air. And air itself sees with us and hears with us and speaks with us—for none of these functions can be performed without air.

The all and the whole. The Stoics distinguish between what they term "the all" (*to pan*) and "the whole" (*to holon*). The all or the totality of things is comprised of both the cosmos and the external void, whereas the whole or the entirety consists of the cosmos alone without the void.[116]

We will get to the cosmos and its nature in a moment. As for the external void, it is incorporeal and infinite or unlimited, the emptiness that is "spread around the outside of the cosmos." Significantly, the void is external to the cosmos, which is to say that "there is no emptiness or void within the cosmos."[117] We'll see what this means for the cosmos momentarily. For now, one final point. Though the void *can be* occupied with bodies, with corporeal things, in point of fact it is not.

The nature of the cosmos.[118] If the void is infinite or unlimited, incorporeal, and empty of things, the cosmos is, by contrast, finite or limited, corporeal, and full of things. Since there is no emptiness or void within the cosmos, it is fully united. Diogenes Laertius explains that this unity "necessarily follows from the sympathy and agreement or joined tension of heavenly things in relation to earthly things." In this way, the cosmos is a kind of continuum, one thing in contact with another, and that with another and another, from top to bottom, side to side, and all around.

Round and rotating, the cosmos takes on the form of a globe or sphere, a circle in three dimensions. The circle and sphere, we are told, are the most beautiful shapes or forms, excelling all others in terms of uniformity and compactness.[119] Not only that, but the sphere is the form that is "the most suitable for motion."

That the cosmos is in motion is significant. Motion points to the fact that it is not some static thing that has forever been as it is and forever will be. Rather, the cosmos was generated, is in a state of change or transformation, and will eventually perish in a massive act of self-destruction the Stoics call the great conflagration.[120]

Not only is the cosmos in motion but, more specifically, it is a living, rational animal—that is, a living being or thing (*zōon*). "It is an animal," we read, "in the sense that it is a substance that is alive and endowed with sensation." It is rational since it is pervaded by reason (*logos*) and managed by mind (*nous*). "The cosmos is managed by mind and providence inasmuch as mind pervades every part of it just as the soul pervades every part of us." But "there is a difference of degree" in terms of how mind extends through the cosmos. "Mind spreads through some parts as a permanent state or condition, as is the case with bones and sinews. But it spreads through other parts as mind itself, as is the case with the leading part of the soul."

Pervaded with mind, the cosmos is divine, which is to say it is God. The cosmos is "entirely perfect." This is so because it "includes everything." The cosmos lacks nothing—an attribute ("lacking nothing") that is commonly applied to God in the ancient Greek world.[121] "The cosmos is equipped in every way, perfect and full in terms of its measure and parts." This, the Stoics contend, is particularly true relative to virtue or excellence (*aretē*). "There is nothing in the cosmos better than excellence or virtue. Virtue, therefore, is an essential attribute of the cosmos since nothing is more complete than the cosmos."[122]

We may finish with the summation of the Stoic view of the cosmos given by the Christian historian Eusebius of Caesarea.[123] "The Stoics call the whole cosmos with all its parts God. They furthermore say that God alone is one, finite, living, eternal, and divine. All bodies are contained in God, and in him there is no void."

The two principles (s. archē)—a first look. "The Stoics hold that there are two principles of the whole cosmos."[124] There is one active and one passive principle, about which we will learn more shortly. For now, we need merely note and keep in mind the four chief characteristics of the two. Both are without beginning in time, indestructible, corporeal, and without form.[125] One last point: the two principles are different from the basic elements found in the cosmos.

The elements (s. stoicheion).[126] Like the two cosmic principles, the elements are corporeal. In contrast with the principles, however, they have a beginning, meaning they are generated. They are destructible or perishable, as well, since they are eventually destroyed in the great conflagration. Finally, if the principles are formless, the elements have form.

There are four elements. They are fire, air, water, and earth. In terms of their basic qualities, we read that "fire is the hot element, and water is the moist; air is the cold, earth the dry—though this last quality is also found in the air." We will return to these four again when we look at the generation and destruction of things within the cosmos.

For now it is important to understand that the elements are the things from which all other things within the cosmos arise and to which they return. "An element is that from which particular things first come to be at their birth and into which they are finally resolved."[127] The elements are like the letters of the alphabet, which are "the elements of speech." Marshalled together and spoken, the letters or alphabetic elements become speech. "C" and "A" and "T," each one an individual letter, form "CAT." Hence, "CAT" originates with or arises from C, A, and T, just as a cat within the cosmos arises from the four elements.

Though things arise from and return to the elements, we should keep in mind that, absolutely speaking, it is from and into the two principles (the passive and the active) that the cosmos is generated and perishes. Let's take a closer look at these principles.

The passive principle—substance (ousia) or matter (hulē).[128] Of the two principles of the cosmos, matter—identified as first or "primary matter"—is the passive principle. As such, matter is that in the cosmos which is acted upon by the active principle. Accordingly, it can be changed. It may be useful to think of a big lump of clay in terms of matter's passive capacity or potential for modification.

What is matter? It is "the substance of all existing things," we read, where substance itself is defined as "a body (*sōma*) that is finite."[129] To state it another way, substance is a limited corporeal thing. (Recall, both principles are corporeal.) In itself, matter has no form and no specified nature. It is "substance without quality." Finally, matter is both without beginning in time and indestructible.

What changes does matter undergo because of the activity of the active principle? The short answer is *every* change. Diogenes Laertius explains that "matter is that out of which or from which anything whatever is produced." As such, matter is the "from which" of all things. In other words, matter changes into all things, which is to say it undergoes every change that occurs in the cosmos.[130]

First and foremost matter is the "from which" of the four elements, which first emerge from matter when the things of the cosmos are produced. These elements are, in some sense, matter itself. We know this because we are told that the "four elements together constitute substance without quality, that is, matter." Yet, as we will see, in another sense they are not matter. "There is a difference between principles [including matter] and elements."

Relative to the whole cosmos, matter "neither increases nor diminishes." Relative to the various parts, however, it "both increases and diminishes." This simply means that as a whole, the finite quantity of matter is constant, but as a certain part—say a stone or a tree or a giraffe or a woman—it varies.

Most importantly, since matter is unable to be and do anything on its own, it must necessarily have the active principle within it in order to be or do anything—a point that brings us to the active principle itself.

The active principle—God, reason, mind.[131] "The active principle," Diogenes Laertius explains, "is the reason within the passive principle, which is to say, it is God." Further, he states that "God and mind and fate and Zeus are one thing." With these two remarks, we see that the active principle may be discussed under different labels—reason, God, Zeus, or fate. For the Stoics, these identifications allow them to relate Stoicism both to traditional Greek religion, albeit in a unique manner, and to the long tradition of Greek philosophy. As for us, they offer some basic starting points to understand the nature of the active principle.

First, the term "active." Hailing from the Greek verb *poieō* or *poiein*, it has a range of meanings. The "active" notion itself comes from the verb's meaning relative to *doing*. The active principle is that which does things. What does it do? It *makes* or *produces* things, as a poet uses the alphabet to make poems or a bronzesmith works with fire to produce things out of copper and tin. As maker or producer, it is *cause*—the cause of things. Finally, all these—doing, making, producing, causing—involve *motion*. Hence, the active principle is always in motion, doing things, producing things.

The active principle, we learn, is God. In a sense, God *is* the cosmos itself. "The Stoics call the whole cosmos with all its parts God."[132] This is true for the Stoics in the way that we might identify ourselves with certain aspects of ourselves, say the aware, active, or living aspects versus those that are more unaware and passive, or not exactly alive. When someone is living, we say, "There's Joe." When someone has died, we say, "Joe has passed," or, "Joes is gone"—that, even though the body remains. Before we cut our fingernails, we may call them "mine" as we care for them. And so we may consider them as ourselves. But when clipped and discarded in the trash, we don't exactly think of them as *ourselves*. This is what the Stoics are getting at when they identify God with the cosmos. It is not that God or the active part is matter or the passive part, but that when God is acting within the passive part, *that* is God.

What more can we say about the God of the Stoics? First, we may repeat what we've already stated regarding the two principles—that God is without beginning, indestructible, corporeal, and without form. Corresponding to the first two attributes, we may add that God is eternal and immortal. Finally, along with matter, God is the fundamental "from which" that everything comes and the final "to which" that everything will return—the origin and the end of things.

As for God's corporeality, the Stoics believe it follows from God's activity. Because God is active, God must be corporeal. This must be true, reasons Zeno, since "anything capable of acting on anything or being acted on by anything in any manner could not be incorporeal." God is the active, corporeal agent within the cosmos that acts upon matter, the passive substrate. Even so, we must recognize that God is not the same kind of body or corporeal nature as matter. Rather, Hippolytus tells us that the Stoic God is "a body of the utmost refinement."

Though corporeal, God is nevertheless without form. More specifically, "God's form is not human." That said, God is "called by many names" and identified with the various gods that do take on human form—Zeus, Athena, Hera, Hephaestus, Poseidon, and Demeter. Rather than pointing to the form of God, however, these names simply indicate how God pervades all things. God "is the maker of the whole cosmos, and he is, as it were, the father of all things, both in general and in that part of him that pervades everything, that which is called many names according to its various powers." For instance, "the name Athena is given since the leading part of God extends to the aether" or "Hephaestus since he spreads to the skillful fire."

In this way, in the way that God "pervades everything," the Stoics hold that the substance of God takes on the forms of everything God produces. "The Stoics define the substance of God this way," Aetius makes clear, "it is an intelligent and fiery breath [or spirit] that has no shape [or form] but changes into whatever it wishes, becoming like all things."[133] (That this breath is *fiery* is a point we will return to.) This transformation of God into all things is true not only of beautiful things but of ugly things as well. "The Stoics say that God is a pervading breath that pervades even ugly or putrid things."

The order of the cosmos comes about through God's activity. "The active principle is the reason (*logos*) within the passive principle, which is to say, God." Acting, God makes. God is "the maker of the cosmos"—"of the orderly arrangement of the cosmos"; he is "the maker of each thing throughout the whole." As we've already observed, God is "the father of all things." He is, as the *Hymn to Zeus* states, "the origin and leader of nature, guiding all things with law."

Along these lines, we know that God manages the cosmos. God takes "providential care of the cosmos and of the things in the cosmos." We read that "the cosmos is managed by mind and providence inasmuch as mind pervades every part of it, just as the soul pervades every part of us." God is "the one everlasting rational principle in all things." This reason or *logos* is the "law of nature."

Given God's *logos* nature, God is that which is the order or structure of the cosmos. Where there is law or measure or proportional relations, there is God. As such, God is the meaning of all, the most profound account or explanation that one can give of things. God is both the ground and limit of things, the ultimate definition of the cosmos as that which is most distinct (as the Stoics might put it given Chrysippus' understanding of definition—see above).

The preceding points bring us to the production or generation of the cosmos. Before we move on, though, let's log a few more points about God.

First, the Stoics hold that God is a living being (*zōon*). Consequently, when we consider the Stoic view of reality, we cannot exactly compare it to the kind of materialism in which living things emerge from non-living things or bits of matter (to put it simply). Rather, life (or Life)—a living principle, a living being—is the beginning point or the foundation of all reality. And recall: nature is a living thing. Therefore, where there is reality (nature, the cosmos), there is life. So it is that scholars avoid calling the Stoic view "materialist," but rather say it is "physicalist" or "corporealist" or, given the underlying life aspect of things, it is "vitalist" (from *vita*, the Latin for life).

Second, there is no evil or bad within God. "God . . . accept[s] nothing evil into himself." Stated positively, this means that there is only good within God. What God is and what God does is good— surely something having to do with the fact that God is *logos*, reason itself, not to mention God's many other attributes.[134]

It follows from the good within or the good that *is* God that God is perfectly or completely happy. Diogenes Laertius explains that because God accepts nothing evil into himself, he is "perfect in happiness."[135] The same is potentially true for human beings—since to be good is to be happy. But more on that in "Stoic Ethics."

For now, knowing that God without beginning and without end is the living, immortal, indestructible, rational, good, happy, and active principle that pervades matter, the passive principle, let's move on to the production or generation of the cosmos and all the things therein.

The production or generation of the cosmos.[136] The first point to gather about the generation of the cosmos is that it is part of a cycle—a vast cycle of rising and falling, generation and destruction. We learn that "at certain periods of time, God absorbs into himself the whole of substance and once again produces it from himself."

Of course this is somewhat paradoxical in that God *is* in some sense the cosmos and this substance (*ousia*).[137] One (imperfect) way to look at it might be a man who yo-yos in his personal fitness. There are times when he lets his body slide into a formless mass of fat and ill-formed muscle. There are other times, however, when he sets his mind to it—his mind that pervades his whole body—that he intentionally and mindfully exercises his body, skillfully shaping it relative to its quads, biceps, pectorals, and that six pack that was there all along. Then again there are other times when things reverse. And so on, repeatedly. Fitness enthusiast, couch potato; fitness enthusiast, couch potato—cycling again and again.

Whatever you make of the analogy, here's the description of the production or generation of the cosmos we have from the Stoics. First, the beginning. "In the beginning," we are told, "God was by himself."[138] This "God" is the active principle we have already encountered, and so he is everything we have already learned about God. One point we need to emphasize, though, is the fact that God at this moment (and always) is fire. This is not to say that he is fire in the sense that we know fire, as in a campfire or a candle flame. God is not the "fire" that is one of the four generated elements. Rather, God (in the beginning) is the primordial fire, God-as-fire, the "fiery breath" we've already encountered that becomes all things. This God-as-fire is "nature," as Zeno puts it, "a craftsmanlike or skillful fire that proceeds methodically to the work of production or generation." Along with fire, God is breath or spirit (*pneuma*), as in "fiery breath"—something remarkably similar to air, in that breath, our warm breath, is simply the air we inhale and exhale.

In the beginning, then, God-as-fire, the fiery breath, is by himself. Then God—or the substance of the cosmos, or matter (given our sources, it's hard to know with precision)—is "changed," we are told, "from fire into moisture." How does God do this? God "turn[s] all substance into water by means of air." So it is, therefore, that "the cosmos comes into being when its substance is changed from fire into moisture by means of air."

We may conclude from these few points that God—God-as-fire and God-as-air (breath)—becomes water (moisture). It is at this point that the Stoics compare cosmic generation to the generation or begetting of any animal:

> Just as in animal generation the seed (*sperma*) is surrounded by fluid, so in cosmic generation the generative principle (*spermatikos logos*) of the cosmos remains in the fluid [think of the water or moisture that has been produced by means of air] and makes the matter of the cosmos serviceable to God for the next stage of generation.

In animal generation it is the seed, the sperm (*sperma*), that actively carries the design and growth plan, as it were, of the generated animal. The female is the passive material—or so the ancients believed. Likewise, it is the active and rational generative principle (*spermatikos logos*, the rational seed or the seminal reason) that makes matter serviceable or good to work with.

Now that the rational, generative principle has been added to matter, we get the basic elements of the cosmos. "And so," we read, this principle "produce[s] the four elements, fire, water, air, and earth." These are the four elements we have already discussed above, the ones that are generated and will eventually perish. Recall, "fire is the hot element, and water is the moist; air is the cold, earth the dry." How does this production of the four elements occur? According to the Stoics, "the denser part of the moisture"—the initial fluid or water that is produced from fire by means of air—"condenses into earth, and the finer part is turned into air. And this process of rarefaction goes on more and more until it generates fire."

We must stop here and note that our sources seem to indicate two sets of elements. One set of three elements seems always to be present in or with or *as* God. God is fire; God is breath (air). Prior to or at the very beginning of the production of the cosmos, God transforms himself as fire into water or fluid by means of air (breath). Then comes the other set of four elements, the ones we are more or less familiar with in our daily lives—fire, air, water, and earth. The only element that seems to be lacking in or with or as God, therefore, is earth. Regardless, in order to grasp what the Stoics think about the production of the cosmos, we have to keep this distinction between the two sets of elements in mind—however unclear it is given our sources.[139]

So we have the four elements, the very things from which all other things within the cosmos arise and to which they return. To repeat: "An element is that from which particular things first come to be at their birth and into which they are finally resolved."

Next comes everything else, as the elements are the building blocks of all things. It is "from the mixture of these elements" that "plants and animals and the other general kinds of things" come.

That, in a few paragraphs, is the Stoic teaching regarding the genesis of the cosmos. In short, the cosmos' production is a transformation or change of God or matter or substance (or God-matter-substance) into the four elements, and from the mixture of these everything else comes, including human beings.[140]

One last but significant point. Cicero explains that "it is by means of our hands"—that is, our human hands—"that we strive to produce another nature, as it were, out of things found in nature" (nature, here, signifying the cosmos). We see, therefore, that there are two natures or cosmoses. There is the cosmos (the natural) produced by God, by divine reason, and there is within the cosmos the human world (the artificial) produced by human beings, by human reason and art, which participates in divine reason.

What more can we say?

The arrangement of the cosmos and the things therein.[141] As we have already seen, there is a certain orderly process in the production of the cosmos. One thing leads to another in a step-by-step way. The significance of this for the whole cosmos is that it is ordered, which is the literal meaning of the Greek word *kosmos* (order).

God, we learn, "is the maker of the orderly arrangement of the cosmos." Not only does the cosmos have the most suitable form for motion, the spherical form, but everything within it is arranged in the best possible manner. "The parts of the cosmos are arranged so that they could neither be more useful nor more beautiful in appearance"—a point we will return to in a moment.

What is this arrangement or structure? The answer comes in a few passages that address not only the elements themselves but where they are stationed in the cosmos:

[The Stoics] believe that the parts of the cosmos are arranged in the following manner. The earth is in the middle, located in the center. Next comes water, which is shaped like a sphere all around, concentric with the earth, so that the earth is within the water. After the water comes a spherical layer of air. There are five celestial circles.[142]

The stars are located in these five circles—all the stars, including the so-called wandering stars or planets.

But where is fire in this view of the cosmos? We discover the answer in another passage. It is right there with the stars. "Fire is the highest element. It is also called aether and is first generated in the sphere of the fixed stars." Then, as if going down the ladder of the Stoic cosmos, we read, "Next comes the sphere of the planets. Next to that is the air. Next is the water. And the lowest of all is the earth, which is at the center of all things."

So we have the ordered cosmos. At the center of the cosmic sphere are earth-based things—rocks, fields, hills, and mountains. Then there is water. Think of all the bodies of water upon the earth's surface—rivers, lakes, seas, and oceans—and all the water in the form of clouds just above the earth's surface. Next there is air, something that would have been known to the Stoics by the common experience of air at lower elevations or at the top of a mountain—air down here, air up there, air all the way up to the celestial sphere. Finally, the Stoics believe that the stars, including the sun, are fire.

A few more points about the stars while we are on them. One, they are living beings or animals. Two, they are divine, that is, gods. This includes not only stars as we conceive of them (fixed stars) but also planets (wandering stars). Two, as living beings and gods, the stars possess "sensation and intelligence." We know this, three, thanks to the "order and regularity" of the stars, their "rational and measured motion" through the heavens that indicates design rather than happenstance. As such, the "eternal regularity of the stars" reveal a "completely rational" order, pointing to the fact that "the stars move by their own free will and their own understanding and divinity."

The cosmos or world-structure is itself a continuum of the four elements or bodies marked by transformation or emergence. "Water rises up from earth," we gather, and "air from water, and aether [or fire] from air." And then the process is "reversed as air comes from aether, water comes from air, and earth, the lowest natural element, comes from water." Significantly, it is the motion of this transformation or emergence that keeps the various portions of the world or cosmos together. "The parts of the cosmos are held together by the ongoing passage up and down, and side to side, of these four bodies by which all things are composed."

As mentioned at the beginning of this section, "the parts of the cosmos are arranged so that they could neither be more useful nor more beautiful in appearance." This is not meant by the Stoics to be a kind of Panglossian declaration that this world is *actually* "the best of all possible worlds." Rather, it is merely intended to convey a simple point, that given the initial four existing elements and the conditions of the production of the cosmos, nothing better could actually be produced. As the Stoics put it, "Given the natural elements, the best that could be produced from them has been produced." The four words "that could be produced" are key. "Anyone who wishes to improve some part of the cosmos will either make it worse or"—in a violation of the conditions of production—"will be asking for something impossible given the nature of things."

Now that we've explored the Stoic belief in an excellently ordered cosmos, let's turn our attention to the hierarchy of nature, following it from the most rudimentary productions at bottom to the highest grade of being at top. We begin with plants, to which nature gives the powers of nourishment and growth. Next up are animals, upon whom nature bestows "sensation and motion, together with a kind of appetite or desire that draws them toward health-giving things and withdraws them from destructive things." Humans are like other animals in that we share in sensation, motion, and appetency or impulse. But to impulse, nature adds the gift of reason so that humans are higher up than other animals such as horses, dogs, or frogs. As for human nature, generally speaking, it consists of body and soul, which are both corporeal, though differing in degree of fineness. The soul, as we have seen, is a "warm breath"; it is a "nature capable of sensation." It has eight parts, the most important being the leading part of the soul (the *hēgemonikon*). The human mind is part of the cosmic mind. (For more on human nature, see *"The human parts or powers of knowing—the soul and its parts"* in "Stoic Logic or Knowing.") Finally, the gods are at the top of the hierarchy of nature. They are living, rational beings. They are "beings that are naturally good and wise. From the very beginning, these beings are born with right and consistent reason, which is superior to human reason."

How do we know that the gods exist? In short, we do, the Stoics argue, thanks to, one, our observation of the heavens that suggests intelligent design; two, the consensus of humankind in that all humans believe in the gods (or God) and always have; three, the recorded epiphanies of the gods, that they have appeared in bodily form to humans; four, the existence and utility of things such as divination, prophecy, divine signs, and the like; and, five, the absurd consequences that would follow from denying the existence of the divine—things such as piety, holiness, wisdom, and justice would vanish along with the gods (or God).[143]

Returning to humans: just as the gods are "joined together as citizens . . . in a community of friendship," so humans also join together in various forms of partnership. Cicero explains that "nature creates in parents a love and affection for their children. This love and affection is the source to which we trace the origin of the association of humankind in communities." Men and women unite together to form families. Families in turn join together to form communities, from villages to cities to city-states or nations. Not only do humans naturally relate to one another in community, but they are also joined with the gods. "There is a community that exists between the gods and men since they participate in reason, which is the law of nature."[144] By contrast, humans are not united in society with the other animals. There is "no justice . . . between human beings and animals." Consequently, "men can make use of animals for their own purposes without injustice."

The management of the cosmos and the things therein (the divine mind and providence).[145] We have seen that the Stoics identify the active principle as God, Zeus, reason, mind, and fate, all significant identifiers relative to the generation, arrangement, and management of the cosmos. The most important identification, though, is mind, because, on analogy with human beings, mind or intellect is the chief location of reason, that which (theoretically, anyway) directs humans to the good, both in terms of survival and flourishing. With its rational capabilities, the mind manages human life, foreseeing what will come and successfully meeting it with various provisions. In the Stoic view, the same is true for the cosmos as a whole. "The cosmos is managed by mind and providence inasmuch as mind pervades every part of it just as the soul pervades every part of us."[146] The divine mind, with its reason (*logos*) that knows and sees ahead and prepares the way for what will come, supplying whatever is necessary, extends through the whole of the cosmos, caring for each thing, large and small, by means of providence. That said, we learn that "there is a difference of degree" in terms of how far mind is present. "In some parts there is more of mind, in others less." Still, as a whole, "the cosmos and every part of the cosmos was formed from the beginning by the gods and is managed by the providence of the gods through all time."

Cleanthes' *Hymn to Zeus* is a celebration of God's management of the cosmos. Therein, we learn that the whole cosmos obeys Zeus, who rules everything. Zeus is the "leader of nature, guiding all things with law." He sets up natural limitations for things, determining what is suitable, and ordering the disordered. Nothing at all happens apart from God. By his thunderbolt—an element of the hymn that ties Stoicism to the traditional Greek myths and hymns—Zeus directs "the universal rational principle that moves through all things." In this way, the noble is joined with the ignoble "so that there is one everlasting rational principle in all things."

The management of the cosmos is performed not only by the one active principle, God or mind, but also by the many gods. "The cosmos is managed by the providence of the gods." But recall, the gods are the manifestation of God; they *are* God going by other names. As the maker and manager of the cosmos, God "is, as it were, the father of all things, both in general and in that part of him that pervades everything, that which is called many names according to its various powers"—Zeus, Athena, Hera, Hephaestus, Poseidon, and Demeter. "In addition to the sidereal divinities," we discover that "the natures of many other gods have been identified and named . . . from the great benefits they offer. . . . For [the Stoics] judged that whatever confers great utility on human beings must arise from divine goodness."

Against Epicureanism.[147] The idea—that the gods actively oversee the management of the cosmos—stands in direct opposition to Epicureanism, a philosophy that was elaborated by Epicurus about the same time that Zeno of Citium was developing Stoicism. For Epicurus, the "blessed and indestructible" gods are not concerned with the "troublesome business" of managing the cosmos. Rather, the management of things, if we may call it such, is left to chance collisions of atoms in the void. As for the gods, he declares that "the divine nature must be kept free from the task" of operating things and kept "in perfect bliss." The Stoics disagree. In contrast to Epicurus' invented "shadowy, do-nothing gods," the Stoics affirm "there is a multitude of gods," whose managerial work is easy. Still, "even though they are active, they do not have to pursue their endeavors by means of difficult and troublesome toil." The bottom line:

Is it possible for any sensible person to observe all the stars, arranged as they are, and the vast sky, so splendidly ornate, and yet to regard them as being produced from bodies [atoms] randomly falling here and there and quickly moving back and forth? Or could have any other nature devoid of mind and reason produced these effects, which not only demand reason to bring them into existence, but it is impossible to understand what kind of things they are without the most advanced reasonings and calculations.[148]

The point—that intelligence of a high order produces and orders all things—brings us to Stoic arguments for the divine management of the cosmos.

Arguments for divine providence and intelligent design.[149] For the Stoics, all things demonstrate the "rational design or purpose of an intelligent nature." We may observe this, they claim, in the magnificent arrangement of things—in the order and beauty of the stars progressing through the heavens, as well as in much smaller phenomena, such as the way cranes fly in triangular formation or the partnership of a certain muscle and shrimp in procuring food. "The parts of the cosmos are arranged so that they could neither be more useful nor more beautiful in appearance. . . . [They] could not possibly have been as they are if they were not ruled by an intelligent and divine providence." The conclusion? The arrangement of things is the result of "reason" and "deliberation" and "art" and, therefore, an "intelligent nature"; it is not "a matter of chance."

How, after all, the Stoics query, can anyone possibly believe that this clearly ordered cosmos is a product of chance? Think of it this way, they challenge:

When you look at a statue or a painting, you see at once the presence of art. Likewise, when you see a ship sailing along some course, you do not doubt that it is moved along by reason and art. Or when you observe a sundial or a water clock, you grasp that it declares the hour of the day by means of an art and not by means of chance. How, then, does it make sense to suppose that the cosmos, which includes these very works of art and the craftsmen who made them and everything else, has no share in deliberation or reason?

They further use the following analogy to argue for the deliberate and intelligent production of the cosmos versus any chance production (as Epicurus and his adherents believe):

> Must I not, at this point, express amazement that there are any men who persuade themselves that certain solid bodies they call atoms, which are carried along by the force of their own weight, produce, by the chance encounter of these bodies, this very well furnished and most beautiful cosmos? It seems that anyone who thinks that such a chance production is possible will also believe that, if we shake up and toss onto the ground a vast number of the letters of the alphabet . . . , it would be possible to produce the continuous text of the *Annals* of Ennius, all ready for us to read. As for me, I doubt whether chance would be able to produce even a single verse! How, then, can our Epicurean friends or anyone else assert that the cosmos is brought about by means of the random and chance collisions of tiny bodies? . . . If collisions of atoms are able to produce the cosmos, why can they not produce a colonnade or a temple or a house or a city? Relative to the cosmos, these are simple works and far easier to produce.[150]

The purpose of divine providence.[151] What is the point of all this cosmic order or the goal of all this divine, rational activity? In general terms, it is about excellence of construction toward the end of the long-term survival and fullness of the cosmos. "Providence," we are told, "is chiefly directed toward and occupied with, first, making sure the cosmos is the best constructed so that it will last, and, after that, making sure it lacks nothing—most importantly that it contains uncommon beauty and every adornment."

More specifically, however, the excellence of the cosmos "was made for those living beings that employ reason—that is, for the gods and for humans, who surpass all things in excellence since reason is the best thing of all." "So it makes sense to believe," the argument goes, "that the cosmos and everything within the cosmos was fashioned for the gods and human beings."

Relative to the hierarchy of nature, we see that everything is ultimately ordered to the benefit and activity of human beings. "The grain and fruits produced by the earth were created for the sake of animals, and animals for the sake of human beings. . . . Man himself, however, is born to contemplate and imitate the cosmos." As Eusebius of Caesarea puts the Stoic position, "We must suppose that the God who manages the whole takes into consideration humankind."

Fate. Recall that the Stoics not only call God mind and reason but "fate" as well. For them, God *is* fate. Consequently, in some manner, God's management of and providential care for the cosmos and everything therein occurs by means of fate, which is to say, by means of God himself. In short, then, the Stoics believe that everything is fated. As Chrysippus and others declare, "All things happen by fate." It is up to humans to respond well to this fate. For more, read the following lengthy endnote.[152]

The destruction of the cosmos in the great conflagration.[153] We have already encountered the Stoic conclusion that "the cosmos is destructible or perishable, inasmuch as it is generated." From this we know that at some point in its long duration the cosmos will begin to decline and return to its formless origin. The Stoics term this eventual return the "great conflagration" or "conversion into fire" (*ekpurōsis*).

We may call the *ekpurōsis* the "eventual" rather than the final or ultimate return because, for the Stoics, it is not anything permanent. Rather, in cyclical fashion, the return or end merely serves as the beginning point for another production. "At certain periods of time, God absorbs into himself the whole of substance and once again produces it from himself."

What happens so that God the active principle absorbs everything into himself? To answer, let's briefly review how the elements are generated. Initially, the divine, primordial fire (God-as-fire) is converted into water or moisture by means of the divine air (God-as-fire-breath). It is in this water that the rational, generative principle works to produce the four cosmic elements (matter). From the water comes earth (condensed water), air (rarefied water), and fire or aether (rarefied air). This water (whether the initial cosmic water or various forms of water found on earth in the guise of the sea and rivers and vapors rising therefrom) nourishes the realm of fire, that of the aether and the stars, doing so during the lengthy existence of the cosmos.

Vapors rise up, nourish the fiery stars (including the sun), and they in turn shed water upon the earth in a cycle (or a re-cycle) that is almost perfectly sustainable.

Except it's not. During every cycle, "a very small amount" of the moisture or water is lost to the fiery consumption of the stars and aether so that eventually the water is entirely used up. When this happens, the water will "neither be able to nourish the earth, nor will the air go up since it cannot rise after the water is gone. In this way," the Stoics conclude, "nothing will remain but fire."

But this fire is God—Zeus, mind, reason, fate, the active principle. And so the cosmos inevitably forms again since this is what God does. God is by definition the active principle. Acting as fire, God becomes matter—water, earth, air, and fire, and everything formed from and with these—until the water is all used up and everything resolves once again into fire in an ever-recurring cycle—what some have termed the "eternal recurrence."

The rational cosmos, human rationality, and the ethical imperative. We have learned that "the whole cosmos is a living and rational animal"; it is "rational and alive and endowed with sensation." This is so because the divine mind extends through the whole cosmos, the active reason or *logos* within passive matter.

As for humans, we are rational insofar as our minds and reason participate in the life of the divine mind and reason. As we will see in the next section, the ethical imperative is to do so—that is, we must live according to reason and so be rational in all we feel, think, say, and do.

Stoic Ethics

Ethics. We have come now to the goal of Stoic philosophy, that for which everything else is studied—everything in the logical part and everything in the portion dealing with natural philosophy.

For the Stoics, the whole of philosophy aims at living well. As such, it is not a dry, academic affair, separated from our day to day life. Nor is it merely about satisfying our curiosity. On the contrary, it is, as Zeno encouragingly writes to the Macedonian king

Antigonus, a matter of gaining some advantage: "I welcome your love of learning inasmuch as you hold to the truth that stretches out toward advantage"—that is, the truth that aims at ethical benefit, excellence of life, virtue. Logic is pursued *for* natural philosophy and ethics. And natural philosophy is explored *for* logic and ethics. But ethics is studied and practiced for itself alone—though surely goodness leads to greater knowledge and wisdom.

We see what the Stoics require and what the Stoic goal is in Cleanthes' *Hymn to Zeus*. The hymn acknowledges that people "neither see the universal law of God, nor do they hear it." If people did see and hear it, the hymn goes on, and "if they wisely obeyed it," then "they would have a noble life."

What, then, is required? First, we must learn to see and hear. Second, we must come to know the object of this seeing and hearing, the universal law of God, which is the mind and reason of God pervading the cosmos. Finally, we must obey this law. If we do so, we will have a noble life—or so the Stoics promise. This "noble life" is the goal of the whole philosophical endeavor from logic to physics to ethics.

But what more can be said about the Stoic understanding of the end or goal of life?

The end or goal (telos) of life.[154] Writing to Zeno of Citium, Antigonus of Macedonia acknowledged that Zeno had in his long life attained "perfect happiness." Diogenes of Laertius concurred: "Zeno surpassed everyone . . . in bliss." The Athenians recognized he was a remarkable man, "a good man," they observed—so much so that they passed a decree memorializing his service to the city in terms of his devotion to philosophy, his teaching, and the pattern of life he offered others. He exhorted the Athenians "to virtue," the decree announced, "directing them to what is most excellent."

In these fragmentary appraisals of Zeno's life, we detect the "noble life" the Stoics live for. In its essence, it has to do with being good, with living excellently or virtuously, and so with being happy, since happiness is, for the Stoics, the same as a good, virtuous life.

But let's back up. The end or goal of life for the Stoics is a triune unity, we might say, one goal made up of three ongoing acts. Put simply, the one goal is happiness. Epictetus, a much later Stoic, expresses it this way: "God made all human beings to be happy." If the one goal is happiness, the three ongoing acts are, one, to live in harmony with nature; two, to live in conformity with reason (to live a rational life); and, three, to live in accord with virtue.

It's important to understand that these three—life in accord with nature, reason, and virtue—are not merely the means to the end of happiness as if happiness were a separate goal. Rather, to live in such a manner is simultaneously *to be* happy and to flourish as a human being. To live naturally, therefore, is to be happy. To live rationally is to be happy. To live virtuously is to be happy.

Here's how Diogenes Laertius expresses the goal in the *Lives*:

> Our individual natures are portions of the whole of nature, which is to say the whole cosmos. This is why the goal of life is to live in conformity with nature—that is, with our own nature as well as with the nature of the whole cosmos. Accordingly, one holds back from every action forbidden by the law common to all things—that is to say, the right reason that pervades all things and is the same as Zeus, who leads the administration of every existing thing. This very thing is the virtue of the happy man and the good flow of life, when all actions promote the harmony of the divine power dwelling in each man with the will of the administrator of the whole cosmos.

The addition and role of impulse (hormē).[155] The Stoics maintain that nature provides for the preservation and thriving of each kind of being in the hierarchy of nature in distinct though not unrelated ways. At bottom, plants are given the powers of nourishment and growth. "Fixed by their roots in the earth," we read, plants are "nourished by means of their own roots," thereby growing and flourishing.[156] Therefore, the "general rule of nature" for plants is to go along with the regulation of nature by gaining nourishment and growing.

In addition to the powers of nourishment and growth, animals are given sensation, motion, and impulse or appetency. As for the latter, impulse (*hormē*) is that which sets an animal in motion, urging it on toward something. Without impulse, an animal would always rest inert like a stone rather than starting out for or beginning anything. Impulse is appetite, the eager desire an animal has for a thing. But toward what do animals naturally have an impulse? What is it that animals eagerly desire?

Epicureans judge that pleasure is the answer—that animals, including humans, naturally and first of all desire pleasure. In the *Letter to Menoeceus*, Epicurus declares, "We recognize that pleasure is our first good, present at birth, and that it is the beginning point of every choice and avoidance." As proof that pleasure is what humans and other animals naturally desire, he points "to the fact that living things, as soon as they are born, are quite satisfied with pleasure, whereas they are naturally upset with pain—and this without rational reflection."

The Stoics disagree. "The Stoics declare false the assertion—made by some—that the first urge or impulse of animals is directed toward pleasure." Rather, for them pleasure is merely a "byproduct that never comes until nature by itself has sought and taken those things suitable to the animal's constitution." As we'll see in a moment, the latter part—"things suitable to the animal's constitution"—is a significant part of the Stoic understanding of impulse.

For the Stoics, the first impulse of every animal "is to self-preservation." Generally speaking, this impulse causes an animal to seek what is beneficial and healthy and to reject what is harmful and unhealthy. This is so because "nature endears the animal to itself from the beginning," making it "so that it is near and dear to itself." In the words of Marcus Cato in Cicero's *On Ends*,

> a living being feels an attachment to itself from the very moment it is born. . . . From this moment on, it feels an impulse to preserve itself and to feel affection for its own constitution and for those things that tend to preserve that constitution. By contrast, it feels an aversion for destruction and for those things that appear to bring destruction.

Beyond the assertion, however, the Stoics offer proof in the form of babies or infants. Babies are not born immediately seeking out pleasure and dodging pain, they observe. Rather, as soon as they are born, they "desire healthy things and reject the opposite." What are these things? As for mammalian infants, they desire nourishment in the form of milk, protection-ensuring affection in the form of touch, various forms of care (changing wet or dirty clothes, for instance), and ongoing restoration and growth in the form of sleep. Babies desire these, the Stoics say, even "before they have experienced pleasure or pain."[157]

Epicureans, to be sure, counter that babies cry out for food, touch, care, and sleep precisely because they want the pleasure of these and to avoid the pain of not having them. Not so, the Stoics reply. The substance of what a baby wants is not the pleasure that may happen to result from gaining nourishment and so on, but the nourishment itself and all the other things that contribute to the baby's self-preservation. In fact, hunger is nature's warning system given to alert the baby to its need for sustenance. When the baby notices hunger, it is in some manner aware that *something* must be done. Consequently, it whimpers or cries. This hunger and crying out is impulse in action on behalf of the baby's integral being. The imperative desire is not, "Feed me! I want to avoid pain and experience pleasure," but "Feed me! I'm aware my body needs something to sustain itself!" So it is that the mother draws near, and the baby "is led by nature without any instruction to seek the teats of its mother's breasts in order to satisfy itself with their abundance."

The Stoics note evidence for the impulse toward self-preservation in other ways. One example has to do with animals seeking out their natural environment. A duck, for instance, even though it has been hatched and reared by a hen, will "leave its hen mother" and settle in "water, its natural home" whenever it has the opportunity to do so. Why? Because "the instinctual guard of self-preservation that nature has planted into animals" is so powerful. In the case of the duck, the instinct drives it to live where it is naturally and best able to move and sustain itself.

Another example is the fact that animals, including human beings, wish to preserve their bodies healthy and whole, limbs and all. Marcus Cato states that "there is no one who, given the choice, would not prefer to have all the parts of his body sound and whole, rather than maimed or distorted although equally serviceable."

Finally, there is the impulse toward self-preservation that is revealed in the fact that animals naturally yearn to "secure the perpetual preservation of their kind." We are told that there is an "extraordinary longing, in both males and females, to join their bodies together" toward the end of procreation. Not only that, but impulse continues beyond the act of procreation to the long-term love and care for offspring: "Observing the labor parents spend on bearing and rearing their young, we seem to be listening to the voice of nature itself. . . . It is apparent that we are driven by nature itself to love those whom we have begotten."

With the latter—the perpetuation of ourselves through others and the natural love and affection that occurs for our offspring—we should briefly note that the Stoic understanding of self-preservation very much stresses the tie between ourselves and others. This is particularly true for social animals, including human beings. For the Stoics, it is "important to understand that nature creates in parents a love and affection for their children. This love and affection is the source to which we trace the origin of the association of humankind in communities." So parental affection is the foundation of other human associations. "We are by nature equipped to form marital unions, assemblies, and cities or states." We read the same point in the later Stoic writer Hierocles the Stoic, who wrote the *Elements of Ethics* and *On Appropriate Acts* sometime prior to 150 AD. Therein, Hierocles writes about our natural duty in terms of ourselves, our relatives, our fellow citizens, and our fellow humans, that is, the "entire race of human beings."[158]

To conclude, impulse is nature's primary means of control or direction. By means of impulse, "nature has made the animal so that it is near and dear to itself. As such, it pushes away all that is harmful and pulls near all that is suitable and fitting."

For most animals, this "pushes away all that is harmful" and "pulls near all that is suitable and fitting" happens naturally. Consequently, "nature's rule for animals is to follow the direction of impulse." But what about humans? Do we simply follow impulse as other animals do? The short answer is both yes *and* no—but mostly no. Though we humans survive by impulse alone, we do not (always) flourish. For that we need something more.

The addition and role of reason.[159] The Stoics insist that humans are called to a life of reason. "For those beings we call rational"— in this case human beings—"the rational life correctly became the natural life when reason was given to them by means of a more perfect rule." What is the role of reason relative to that of impulse? "Reason was added to shape impulse as a skilled craftsman."

The point is fundamental. According to the Stoics, we humans are different from other animals in that we are rational. Significantly, this means we not only have impulse to guide us in the life-long activity of self-preservation. Rather, we also have a powerful tool or capacity—reason—that can and should help to direct and thus benefit us.

But the capacity of reason raises an important point. If impulse can be skillfully crafted or directed by reason, then there are multiple directions humans can go in any activity or pursuit. Not so with non-rational animals. Take squirrels, for instance. Squirrels go about surviving—self-preserving—in very ordinary, squirrel-like ways. By impulse they live in and under the cover of trees to get away from predators such as hawks swooping down from the sky. By impulse they forage for nuts and other edibles. By contrast, and thanks to reason, humans have many options. And so we see the various human solutions for these same ends (safety and nutrition) expressed in distinct building techniques and architectural styles, defensive measures, food gathering and production methods, culinary arts, and the like.

What's the significance? For the Stoics, as we'll see, this means we humans can be both wise or foolish, good or bad, virtuous or vicious, depending on how we use reason to shape impulse.

For now, let's repeat again that, for human beings, the rational life *is* the natural life. To say it another way, it is unnatural for humans to live by impulse alone. Impulse shouts, "Survive!" Reason calmly adds, "Wisely." Impulse gnaws, "Eat!" Reason steps in to advise, "Just enough." Impulse urges, "Copulate!" Reason counsels, "With your spouse alone for the sake of children." Impulse worries, "Supply yourself with what it takes to live!" Reason adjoins, "With whatever is just."

Notice how each impulse is necessary to get humans moving toward survival. But unlike other animals that respond to impulse in an instinctive manner that naturally leads them to what is best for them in terms of survival or self-preservation (including preservation of the species), we humans have the voice and power of reason that can lead us to the healthiest or best way to follow impulse rather than any way whatsoever. This best or excellent way is called virtue.

Virtue and vice.[160] We have already seen that, for the Stoics, the end or goal of life is to live in accord with virtue. This is because "happiness consists in virtue," which is to say that happiness *is* virtue.

What is virtue? For the Stoics, "virtue is in one sense the perfection of anything in general, say a statue." As such, it is excellence—the very best or height of that thing's being. In the case of human beings, virtue is "the fulfillment or perfection of a rational being *as* a rational being following nature." Accordingly, virtue is tied up with reason and nature in that living in accord with virtue is the same as living in accord with reason and in harmony with nature. Where one is (nature, reason, or virtue), there are the others. Therefore, if we want to know the virtuous thing to do, we must know the rational thing to do; and if we want to know that, we must know the natural thing to do—natural, that is, for a *rational* being rather than for any other animal living by impulse alone. In line with reason and nature, virtue is the ongoing and "harmonious disposition" of the soul "that tends to make the whole of life harmonious." Finally, virtue is chosen "for its own sake" rather than "from fear or hope or any external motive" such as the fear of getting caught or the hope of pleasure or some other benefit.[161]

Though the virtues are, according to the Stoics, the same for men and women, and though they are "inseparable from one another,"[162] there are nevertheless various divisions among the virtues that are important to note. One division has to do with what each virtue is centered on. For instance, practical wisdom is concerned with "what is to be done," whereas justice has to do with "the distribution of valuable things." Another involves the distinction between intellectual and non-intellectual virtues. The latter virtues are simply the perfection or excellence of something not directly related to the intellect, things such as health and strength. These virtues "do not require the mind's assent." By contrast, intellectual virtues are related to knowledge and so to the intellect. Take practical wisdom. It is the "knowledge of what one should do, and what one should not do, and neither" or the "knowledge of good things and bad things and of things that are neither." Courage, moderation, and justice are other virtues that involve knowledge—knowledge, respectively, of what is fearful, of what is to be chosen and avoided, and of proper distribution. Finally, the most important division is that between primary and secondary or subordinate virtues, a division that was taken over from earlier Greek philosophers. Primary virtues include practical wisdom, courage, moderation, and justice. Subordinate virtues follow on primary virtues. For example, good counsel and understanding follow on practical wisdom, just as good order and propriety do on moderation.

Vice is the opposite of virtue. Whereas virtue is knowledge, vice is ignorance. "The vices are ignorance of those things of which the virtues are the knowledge." So it is that vice is ignorance about what to do, what to choose, what to fear, the proper distribution, and so on. More, vice offers assent to something when no assent should be given. Primary vices are folly, cowardice, immoderation, and injustice. Secondary or subordinate vices include bad counsel, slow-mindedness, and a lack of self-control.

For the Stoics, there is no ground or space between vice and virtue in terms of happiness. Rather, those of us who are on the way to virtue are miserable until we are wholly virtuous.

> For just as a drowning man who is so close to the surface of the water that at any moment he might come up into the air is no more able to breathe than if he were actually at the bottom already, . . . similarly a man that has made some progress toward the state of virtue is no less in misery than the one who has made no progress at all.

Further, there are no degrees of virtue or vice. "The Stoics declare that just as a stick must be either straight or crooked, so a man must be either just or unjust. Neither are their degrees of justice and injustice. The same is the case for the other virtues." If a man is moderate, then he is moderate; if a woman is wise, then she is wise. The same goes for immoderation and foolishness. Following this, we learn that "all failures or sins are equal."

> For if one truth is not more true than another truth, then neither is one falsehood more false than another falsehood. In the same way, one deception is not more deceptive than another deception, nor is one failure or sin more of a failure or more sinful than another failure or sin. For the man who is one hundred stadia from Canopus and the man who is only one stadium away are equally not in Canopus. In this way, the man who commits the greater and the one who commits the smaller sin are equally behaving incorrectly.

Even though we have either wholly arrived at virtue or not, the Stoics nevertheless hold that virtue can be taught. In his letter to the Macedonian king Antigonus, Zeno writes, "If any man with a nature such as yours receives a reasonable amount of training, in terms of ungrudging instruction, he will easily reach perfect virtue." This is evident from the fact that base men really *do* become good. That virtue is possible is clear thanks to the examples of real men who were actually virtuous—men such as Socrates, the Cynics Antisthenes of Athens and Diogenes of Sinope, and Zeno of Citium himself, who lived in accord with virtue, treading "a path to the stars."

Unfortunately, if virtue can be gained through teaching and training, then it can also be lost—or so thought Chrysippus, who observed that virtue "can be lost through drunkenness and melancholy." Cleanthes, by contrast, held that virtue cannot be lost. Regardless, we must try to learn about virtue, train to be excellent, and make the attempt to maintain a virtuous life. It is our duty as rational humans following nature to do so.

Duty or what is fitting.[163] The early Stoic Archedemus declared that the goal of life is "to live while carrying out every duty, that is, whatever is appropriate." If we compare this to what else has been said about the end or goal of life, then we see that doing our duty or whatever is appropriate is related to living in harmony with nature and in conformity with reason.

In fact, we are told that duty "is a fitting action or activity in relation to nature's arrangements." As for reason, duty is "that which, when done, may be supported by a reasonable account." Reason is that which determines what is fitting or not and, accordingly, chooses to do such things.

Some things are duties in all circumstances, whereas others depend on the circumstances. Thus, we see that duty or what is fitting is not an absolute but something that involves deliberation or the use of reason.

The good, the bad, and the indifferent.[164] "Of existing things," Diogenes Laertius reports, "the Stoics declare that some are good, some are bad, and some are neither." The latter are "things indifferent."

Generally speaking, the good is that which is beneficial. The good both produces happiness and makes it complete insofar as it *is* happiness itself or a portion of it. The good is in step with nature and reason. More exactly, the good is virtue itself (the various virtues) and those things that participate in virtue, such as "excellent men" and virtue's "accompanying byproducts, joy and merriment and like things." Virtue is good in that it is, as we have noted, "the fulfillment or perfection of a rational being *as* a rational being following nature."[165] The good may be related to the soul or to external things (such as having an excellent friend) or neither. Otherwise, the good may either be an end or a means to an end. A virtuous friend who teaches and models virtue, helping us to be virtuous, serves as a good means (an example of virtue) to a good end (virtue). The good is both noble and beautiful — for a truly beautiful and noble thing *is* a good thing. Good things are all choiceworthy and equal. Lastly, as with virtue, the good does not admit of degrees. Either something is good or it is not.

Opposed to the good is the bad, which is harmful. The bad is vice or those things that participate in vice. Otherwise, we may extend the opposite of what we have said about the good to the bad.

The indifferent—things that are neither good nor bad—requires some discussion, though. Indifferent things may be categorized variously. First, something is indifferent if it excites neither desire or impulse nor aversion or disgust, things such as the number of blades of grass in a lawn. Second, something is indifferent if it contributes neither to happiness nor to unhappiness, things, according to the Stoics, such as reputation or bodily strength. This category includes everything but for the virtues or the vices since these alone contribute to happiness or unhappiness. Things that do no more benefit than harm are also indifferent. For the Stoics, money or wealth is such a thing. While money may benefit us in getting what we want, it may also be the cause of harm if someone robs or sues us because of it. Finally, there are those indifferent things that can be used well and badly. Again, money may be used to benefit or harm ourselves or others.

The Stoics further subdivide those indifferent things that neither contribute to happiness nor to unhappiness. Some, they teach, are chosen and some are not. "Regarding [these kind of] indifferent things, they say that some are preferred and some are not preferred—that is, they are rejected." We know the difference between the two categories thanks to what the Stoics term "value." "Those things that have value are preferred, while those that do not have value are rejected." Valuable things are those that exist in accord with nature; they are able to contribute to a harmonious life. In other words, they are a means to an end (a contribution to) rather than the end itself such as the good is. And yet even these means to an end may be further divided into those that are preferred for their own sake (such as natural ability or intelligence), those that are preferred for the sake of something else (such as money or a noble birth), and those that are preferred both for their own sake and for the sake of something else (such as strength or good eyesight).

The turning or perversion of the rational soul.[166] We have already learned that the Stoics hold that the cosmos is arranged in the best possible manner. In line with this "best," they hold that the initial impulses or "the starting-points offered by nature are incapable of turning aside or perversion." Said another way, nature leads well.

It follows, then, that we should expect to find actual human beings that are all virtuous as they rationally shape impulse and so live in accord with nature, reason, and virtue. But this is not what we find. Rather, we find that many, if not most, humans are far from virtuous. Wise or virtuous people are very few—if they exist at all. So what's going on? What has gone wrong? What's wrong with us humans?

Before looking for an answer from the human perspective, we need to rise up to a cosmic perspective. There we see that in some manner perfection includes imperfection. As the *Hymn to Zeus* declares, Zeus has "joined together all noble things with things ignoble, so that there is one everlasting principle in all things." And for Zeus, "what is unpleasant is pleasant."

In a similar though somewhat different way, the second-century Roman emperor Marcus Aurelius, who practiced Stoicism, notes in his journal of meditations, *To Himself*, how certain (apparent) imperfections in natural things are attractive and give rise to pleasure:

> We should observe that even the things that follow from the things that are produced according to nature contain something pleasing and attractive. For instance, when bread is baked, some parts are split at the surface, and these parts that are open in this way and have a certain appearance contrary to the purpose of the baker's art, are beautiful in a way, and in a certain way excite a desire to eat. And again, figs, when they are quite ripe, gape open. And in ripe olives the very circumstances of their being near to rottenness adds a peculiar beauty to the fruit. And the ears of wheat bending down, and the lion's eyebrows, and the foam that flows from the mouth of wild boars, and many other things—though they are far from being beautiful, if a man should examine them individually, still, because they follow things that are formed by nature, they help to adorn them and please the mind.

With this in mind, we turn to certain apparent imperfections in the (natural) cosmos. For one, there is the eventual exhaustion of fuel that will lead to the ultimate destruction of the cosmos in the great conflagration. The very perishability of the cosmos implies a certain imperfection.[167] Otherwise, we are told that there is a "tendency toward certain maladies in the body, such as the buildup of mucus and diarrhea." Similarly, we learn that just as there are the aforementioned tendencies in the body, "so with the soul there is a tendency to" various maladies such as "enviousness, pitifulness, and quarrelsomeness." And so, explaining the Stoic view, Diogenes Laertius states, "Just as we say that there are certain bodily illnesses or infirmities, for example, gout and arthritic disorders, so also are there soul illnesses, such as love of reputation and love of pleasure, and similar things."

We learned before that health is a non-intellectual virtue, one that does not require assent. By analogy, we can say that disease or unhealth is a non-intellectual vice. Disease is a naturally occurring imperfection that ultimately leads to the decline and destruction of the human body. Similarly, vices (unhealth of the soul) occur naturally. But why? The short answer, we may lament, is that the Stoics never quite get around to answering the question—at least in the sources we have. Still, we can tease out an answer having to do with reason.

"The wise man does everything well," we read, "in the same way that we say Ismenias plays everything well on the flute." The question: how is it that Ismenias plays everything so well? Was he born playing well? On the contrary, we must presume that Ismenias was taught how to play the flute. And that he trained hard, putting in hours and hours of practice before he was able to play everything well. Similarly, the wise man was not born wise. Instead, thanks to the gifts of nature, he was born with the components or faculties necessary to be wise and do everything well. But these—most importantly, the capacity of reason—had to be formed, educated, and exercised.

Consider that reason was given to humans to shape impulse well. What this means is that impulse in some sense actually requires shaping. This apparently is not the case with animals. Lions naturally eat antelopes. They copulate according to nature, at certain times and under certain conditions. And they rest beneath the shade of a tree. Humans are similar in that we have similar natural

impulses to eat, reproduce, find shelter, and so on. But in contrast
with animals such as lions, our impulses require shaping whereas
theirs do not.

The first point, then, is that human impulses—however natural and non-turning-aside they are—require shaping. The second
point has to do with reason itself. When we humans are born, reason itself requires formation or training. Recall: we become virtuous by means of teaching and training. Therefore, without such
teaching and training—without such formation, education, and
exercise—we will not be virtuous, which is to say, we will not live
in accord with reason and thus naturally. Consequently, we will
live in accord with something less than reason or knowledge—
something the Stoics term opinion (*doxa*). Hence, rather than rationally and skillfully shaping impulse, we will muddle along under the influence of opinion, which is little better than blindness.

This is the source of the problem for us human beings—the
source of the "turning" or "perversion" of the rational soul. "From
falsehood or error," we read, "there arises a distortion or perversion, which extends throughout the intellect." And, "when a rational being is turned aside or perverted, this is due to the
persuasiveness of external pursuits or sometimes to the influence
of acquaintances." The *Hymn to Zeus* similarly comments that
nothing on earth takes place apart from Zeus, nothing "but what
is done by bad men in their own folly" —"folly" being the same as
the turning, distortion, or perversion in the intellect.

So natural impulse is not the problem. The problem is a lack of
teaching and formation, as well as too little training of the intellect
and reason, which results in folly. Things go well when we humans form and educate one another; things go poorly when we
don't. "And from this distortion"—the perversion arising from
falsehood or error—"grow many passions or emotions, which are
responsible for much confusion and instability."[168]

The passions (bad and good).[169] A passion, according to the Stoics,
is a judgment or decision. A bad passion is unnatural and irrational in the sense that it is "disobedient to reason." (Bad passions
include grief or pain of mind, fear, desire, and pleasure, with

subordinate bad passions related to these.) Paradoxically, even though a bad passion is "disobedient to reason," it is in fact reason itself in the act of judging or deciding. As we have noted, the problem is found in the fact that reason judges based on opinion rather than knowledge. Thanks to this opinion-based judgment, a bad passion is "a motion or excessive impulse of the soul that is contrary to reason or nature." Where impulse requires the skillful shaping of reason for it to serve as a beneficial guide to action, reason fails to deliver. By contrast, a good passion is a sensible or reasonable elation of the soul. Put another way, a good passion is an impulse that has been skillfully shaped by reason. As such, it is a knowledge-based judgment. (Good passions include joy, caution, and willing, with subordinate good passions related to these.)

Let's look at an example, that of the good passion of "willing," defined as "reasonable appetite," versus the bad passion of "desire," which is "an appetite that is contrary to reason." Imagine we are at a feast. If, while eating from the plenty that is available, we shape the impulse of hunger (that moves us toward nourishment and thus survival) with the help of reason (the knowledge, for instance, that "moderation in all things" is best), we'll eat just enough to satisfy the requirements of nourishment and perhaps a little more since the meal is, after all, a feast or celebration. In such a case, we'll be moderate relative to the situation. Such a response to hunger illustrates the good passion of willing (again, "reasonable appetite"). By contrast, if we do not skillfully shape the impulse of hunger in the presence of platters full of food, we'll likely give in to impulse and eat immoderately, falsely judging according to opinion (the view that more is better, that excess food is more satisfying in terms of pleasure, which we mistakenly judge as something good; or the view that more or the most pleasure is better than some or a little pleasure). This illustrates the bad passion of "desire" (again, "an appetite that is contrary to reason").

The right judgment imperative.[170] From this one example, we see that it is absolutely imperative for humans to judge well when faced with various impulses. Again, it is not that these impulses are bad in themselves. Hunger is good insofar as it urges us on to eat in order to gain nourishment to survive and thrive. The impulse toward sex is also good for the reproduction of ourselves and the species, and for the intimacy and relationship building it entails. And so on with every other impulse.[171] But each of these natural impulses must be directed by reason informed with knowledge rather than reason perverted by opinion. Therefore, it is imperative that human beings are formed and educated from an early age, that human reason is trained and exercised to judge well. If we humans are able to reason well, and so, presumably, to judge well, then we will have the power to live well. And so we will, as it were, be able to play the flute well like Ismenias.

This is why the Stoics put so much stock in philosophy. It is philosophy, beginning with logic, that trains the intellect to reason well. As said at the beginning, this training and exercise of the intellect is ultimately oriented to ethics, toward living well, toward living wisely (rationally with knowledge) and being happy.

Let's finish this topic, then, with the Stoic observation that "wise men are genuinely earnest for and attentive to their own improvement." And with that, let's move with the Stoics toward the goal of life.

Stoic happiness.[172] We have already noted that the one goal of Stoic philosophy is happiness—though, keep in mind that the one goal is expressed in three ongoing acts (acts in accord with nature, reason, and, most importantly, virtue). As the late Stoic Epictetus expressed the goal, "God made all human beings to be happy."

What makes for happiness? According to both Zeno and Chrysippus, "virtue is sufficient in itself for happiness"—that is, virtue does not require anything in addition to itself for happiness. Again, "happiness consists in virtue, which is the state of the soul that tends to make the whole of life harmonious."

Zeno, we are told, lived accordingly, making "it his practice to place all the constituents of the happy life in virtue alone." From this point alone we know that Zeno made it his practice to live in conformity with reason and so in harmony with nature. In this he was wise and, we may assume, a happy man.[173]

The wise man. The Stoics usually did not make a practice of identifying wise human beings—those such as Socrates or Zeno of Citium.[174] Rather, as though portraying an ideal, they settled for detailing the nature of those who would be wise *if* such a wise man truly existed.

What are the wise like? What do they do? Most importantly, the wise live by reason so that natural impulse is skillfully shaped in all they do. Consequently, "the wise man is without passion."[175] So it is that the wise are truly free rather than slaves. Most importantly, the wise are happy: "Inasmuch . . . as the final good is to live in agreement and harmony with nature, it necessarily follows that all wise men at all times enjoy a happy, perfect, and fortunate life, free from all hindrance, interference, or want."[176]

LET'S GO!

As we see from the three parts of Stoic philosophy, Stoicism is emphatically oriented toward being and doing. Though thinking plays a vital role, the clear goal is to act in a certain manner and so to follow a certain path toward happiness—in harmony with nature, in conformity with reason, and in accord with virtue.

The Cave invites you to enter the Painted Colonnade of the ancient Stoics in order to learn from Zeno of Citium and the other early Stoics. Come and listen to what they have to say. Then train with them. Learn the path of nature; follow the lead of reason; experience the happiness of virtue.

As for the latter, you may wish to turn to "Points of Wisdom & Ways of Practice from the Early Stoics" where you will find "A Stoic Plan of Life" as well as three ways to practice Stoic philosophy.

Whatever you think and whatever you do, the Stoics ask you to keep in mind that the only human good is virtue.

So with that, let's go!

Let's skillfully shape impulse by means of reason—the divine and active principle in all things—in order to live well.

NOTES

[1] See Gerald Corey, *Theory and Practice of Counseling and Psychotherapy* (Belmont: Brooks/Cole Cengage Learning, 2013), 67.

[2] American Psychological Association, *APA Guidelines for Psychological Practice with Boys and Men* (Washington, DC: APA, 2018), 11, 3, 17.

[3] Such, yes, *masculine* characters—one could well protest and so leave out the tendentious "toxic" designation—are as old as the Spartan Dieneces, who appears in Herodotus' *Histories* (the fifth century BC account of the wars between the Persian Empire and the Greek city-states). When, just before the battle of Thermopylae (480 BC), Dieneces finds out that countless Persian arrows flying through the sky will hide the sun and thus darken its light, he insouciantly responds, "This is good news—then we shall have our fight in the shade." See Herodotus, *The Histories* 7.226. See also Cicero's *Tusculan Disputations* 1.101, where the author approvingly mentions the same event in the context of having a proper—dare we say stoic?—disdain for death.

[4] Here are two example entries for STOIC: *Webster's New College Dictionary* gives, "Apparently indifferent to or unaffected by pleasure or pain: impassive." And the *Cambridge English Dictionary* gives, "Not showing or not feeling any emotion, especially in a situation in which the expression of emotion is expected." In his book exploring Stoicism for modern life, William B. Irvine reveals, "Before I began my research on desire, Stoicism had been, for me, a nonstarter as a philosophy of life, but as I read the Stoics, I discovered that almost everything I thought I knew about them was wrong. To begin with, I knew that the dictionary defines a *stoic* as 'one who is seemingly indifferent to or unaffected by joy, grief, pleasure, or pain.' I therefore expected that the uppercase-*S* Stoics would be lowercase-*s* stoical—that they would be emotionally repressed individuals. I discovered, though, that the goal of the Stoics was not to banish emotion from life but to banish negative emotions. When I read the works of the Stoics, I encountered individuals who were cheerful and optimistic about life." See William B. Irvine, *A Guide to the Good Life: The Ancient Art of Stoic Joy* (Oxford: Oxford University Press, 2009), 7.

[5] Though it had changed significantly since his time, the Academy was the philosophical school founded by Plato (c. 427-347 BC). The Peripatetic philosophers followed in the line of Aristotle (384-322 BC), whose school was the Lyceum.

[6] Aulus Gellius, *Attic Nights* 6.14. The story of the sacking of Oropos and fine, which was ultimately reduced to 100 talents, is told in Pausanias, *Description of Greece* 7.11.4-5.

[7] David Sedley, "The School, from Zeno to Arius Didymus," in Brad Inwood, ed., *The Cambridge Companion to The Stoics* (Cambridge: Cambridge University Press, 2003), 20.

[8] Diogenes Laertius, *Lives and Opinions of Eminent Philosophers* 7.174 (from here

on *Lives*). Diogenes Laertius was a third century AD biographer of Greek philosophers, his work extending from the Presocratics to Epicurus. Assuming "Laertius" indicates where Diogenes was born, he was from Laertes, a seaport town in Caria or Cilicia (both in modern Turkey).

[9] To what extent and how directly Paul was acquainted with Stoicism has been debated for decades. See, for instance, Frederick Clifton Grant, "St. Paul and Stoicism," *The Biblical Word* 45, no. 5 (1915): 268-281, or N.T. Wright, *Paul: A Biography* (New York: Harper One, 2018).

[10] Diogenes Laertius, *Lives* 7.10.

[11] Ibid., 7.6.

[12] Ibid., 7.169.

[13] For the story, including the letter of Antigonus to Zeno and the latter's response, see ibid., 7.6-9. For Persaeus with Antigonus, see ibid., 7.36. For Persaeus' death in Corinth, see Pausanias, *Description of Greece* 2.8.4.

[14] Epictetus, *Discourse* 3.23.30. In the *Handbook* 48.2, Epictetus observes that "The one who is making progress in philosophy moves through life as one who is healing, careful not to disturb what is healing until it is fully healed." For more from Epictetus, pick up the Cave's forthcoming *The Handbook of Epictetus: Pocket Edition*.

[15] Diogenes Laertius, *Lives* 7.168.

[16] Seneca, *Epistle* 6.6.

[17] See *Hierocles the Stoic: "Elements of Ethics," Fragments, and Excerpts*, trans. David Konstan (Atlanta: Society of Biblical Literature, 2009).

[18] Aulus Gellius, *Attic Nights* 9.5.

[19] Anthony Gottlieb, *The Dream of Reason: A History of Western Philosophy from the Greeks to the Renaissance* (New York: W.W. Norton & Company, 2016), 300.

[20] A. A. Long, *Hellenistic Philosophy: Stoics, Epicureans, Sceptics*, 2nd ed. (London: Gerald Duckworth & Co., 1986), 233.

[21] See Cicero, *Stoic Paradoxes* 2. In Cicero's *On Ends* (3.10), Cato expresses disappointment in the fact that Cicero has not joined the Stoic school. Therein Cicero finds Cato "seated in the library" at the house of Lucullus. "He was surrounded by many books on Stoicism," he says. Cicero explains that Cato turned to him and declared, "How I wish that you had been inclined to the Stoics! You of all men might have been expected to count virtue as the only good."

[22] See Seneca, *Letter to Lucilius* 104.29; *On the Tranquility of the Mind* 16.1; and *On Anger* 2.32.2 and 3.38.2.

[23] Seneca, *Letter to Lucilius* 78.3; *On Leisure* 6.4; and *On the Tranquility of the Mind* 1.10.

[24] Seneca, *Consolation to Marcia* 4.1-2. Regarding Arius, David Sedley reports that two Stoics in particular had Augustus' ear. Of one, he writes, "Athenodorus . . . spent most of his career at Rome where, as the emperor's moral counselor, he is reported to have been held by him in high regard." Of the other, he relates, "Much the same can be said of Arius Didymus. Like

Athenodorus a Stoic, and like him a court philosopher who gained Augustus' confidence, he achieved eminence as an exponent of practical moral philosophy." See David Sedley, "The School, from Zeno to Arius Didymus," in *The Cambridge Companion to The Stoics*, 31-32.

25 Diogenes Laertius, *Lives* 6.12. For the Cynics, see the Cave's *The Best of the Cynics: The Lives, Writings & Teachings of the Ancient Cynics*.

26 *Musonius Rufus: Lectures and Sayings*, trans. Cynthia King, ed. William B. Irvine (CreateSpace, 2011).

27 It is worthwhile to note, since the information has infelicitously made rounds online, that John Dryden (seventeenth century) incorrectly translated Plutarch's descriptive *philostorgos* of Porcia as "addicted to philosophy" rather than what it should be, "affectionate" or "loving tenderly." See "Life of Marcus Brutus" 13 in *Plutarch's Lives: The Translation Called Dryden's* (Boston: Little, Brown and Company, 1865) — an edition that was "corrected from the Greek and revised by A.H. Clough."

28 See Simon Hornblower, Antony Spawforth, and Esther Eidinow, eds., *The Oxford Classical Dictionary* (Oxford: Oxford University Press, 2012), 337; and Cornelius Tacitus, *The History* 4.5.

29 A. A. Long, *Hellenistic Philosophy: Stoics, Epicureans, Sceptics*, 233.

30 Christopher Gill, "The School in the Roman Imperial Period," in Brad Inwood, ed., *The Cambridge Companion to The Stoics* (Cambridge: Cambridge University Press, 2003), 33.

31 Ibid., 55.

32 A. A. Long, *Hellenistic Philosophy: Stoics, Epicureans, Sceptics*, 235.

33 Christopher Gill, "The School in the Roman Imperial Period," in *The Cambridge Companion to The Stoics*, 55.

34 Cicero, *On Ends* 3.5.

35 To give a few examples of such an education, Justin Martyr (second century) studied with Stoic, Peripatetic (Aristotelian), and Pythagorean instructors before landing with a Platonist. L.W. Barnard states that "it was while a Platonist that Justin became a Christian." See Barnard's *Justin Martyr: His Life and Thought* (Cambridge: Cambridge University Press, 1967), 6-7. See also Justin Martyr, *Dialogue with Trypho* 2. Later in the fourth century, Basil of Caesarea and Gregory of Nazianzus, both immensely significant Christian theologians, studied philosophy in Athens.

36 A. A. Long, *Hellenistic Philosophy: Stoics, Epicureans, Sceptics*, 235.

37 Though Christians were in fact using Stoic ideas, at the time many Christians simply traced these ideas back to Christian (or Jewish) sources. Ambrose of Milan, for instance, has this to say: "We are told that the Stoics taught that all things that are produced on the earth are created for the use of men, but that men are born for the sake of men so that mutually one may be of advantage to another. But from where did they get such ideas if not from sacred scriptures?" He goes on to cite Moses and David. "So," he concludes, "these philosophers

have learned from our writings." See Ambrose of Milan, *On the Duties of the Clergy* 132-134. Other Christian thinkers, such as Ambrose's protégé Augustine of Hippo, saw parallels between the Christian and the Stoic approach to life and ethics. Both Christians and Stoics live according to the (Holy) Spirit, he observes. "The Stoics, who place man's highest good in the rational soul, live according to the spirit." See Augustine of Hippo, *City of God* 14.2.

[38] Mark Morford, "Stoicism," in Anthony Grafton, Glenn W. Most, and Salvatore Settis, eds., *The Classical Tradition* (Cambridge: The Belknap Press of Harvard University Press, 2010), 908.

[39] He states that "much that had been distinctively Stoic in origin was absorbed into the complex amalgam of Judaic [including that of Philo of Alexandria] and Greek teaching that became Christian theology and ethics. So Stoicism is a part, but a largely unacknowledged part, of the Christian tradition." A. A. Long, "Stoicism in the Philosophical Tradition: Spinoza, Lipsius, Butler," in *The Cambridge Companion to The Stoics*, 367.

[40] Mark Morford, "Stoicism," in Anthony Grafton, Glenn W. Most, and Salvatore Settis, eds., *The Classical Tradition*, 909.

[41] Augustine of Hippo, *City of God* 9.4-5.

[42] A. A. Long, *Hellenistic Philosophy: Stoics, Epicureans, Sceptics*, 235.

[43] Justin Martyr, *Dialogue with Trypho* 2.3.

[44] A. A. Long, "Stoicism in the Philosophical Tradition: Spinoza, Lipsius, Butler," in *The Cambridge Companion to The Stoics*, 367.

[45] What the precise nature of this closing was in Athens is uncertain. Regardless, other schools in Alexandria, Antioch, and Constantinople remained open. See James Hannam, *The Genesis of Science: How the Christian Middle Ages Launched the Scientific Revolution* (Washington D.C.: Regnery Publishing, 2011).

[46] A. A. Long, *Hellenistic Philosophy: Stoics, Epicureans, Sceptics*, 236. In his introduction to Justus Lipsius' *On Constancy* (Exeter: Bristol Phoenix Press, 2006), John Sellars relates, "Adaptations of Epictetus' *Enchiridion* made for use in monasteries (references to 'Socrates' being altered to 'St. Paul'), highlight the perceived affinity between Christian and the Stoic way of life" (1-2). To read Epictetus *Handbook* (*Enchiridion*), pick up the Cave's forthcoming *The Handbook of Epictetus: Pocket Edition*.

[47] Mark Morford, "Stoicism," in Anthony Grafton, Glenn W. Most, and Salvatore Settis, eds., *The Classical Tradition*, 909.

[48] A. A. Long, *Hellenistic Philosophy: Stoics, Epicureans, Sceptics*, 231.

[49] For Petrarch's disagreement with the Stoics and Erasmus' similar point, see Mark Morford, "Stoicism," in Anthony Grafton, Glenn W. Most, and Salvatore Settis, eds., *The Classical Tradition*, 909.

[50] Ibid., 910. Neostoicism is sometimes written Neo-Stoicism.

[51] John Sellars, introduction to Justus Lipsius, *On Constancy*, trans. Sir John Stradling (Exeter: Bristol Phoenix Press, 2006), 2.

[52] Michel de Montaigne, "Apology to Raymond Sebond" 2.12, cited in Mark

Morford, "Stoicism," in Anthony Grafton, Glenn W. Most, and Salvatore Settis, eds., *The Classical Tradition*, 911.

[53] For Schoppe and du Vair, see ibid., 911.

[54] Cited in John Sellars, introduction to Justus Lipsius, *On Constancy*, trans. Sir John Stradling (Exeter: Bristol Phoenix Press, 2006), 1 and 14. Thomas James' English has been modified to reflect a more modern usage.

[55] For analysis of Stoicism and Spinoza, see A. A. Long in *Hellenistic Philosophy: Stoics, Epicureans, Sceptics*, 208-209, and "Stoicism in the Philosophical Tradition: Spinoza, Lipsius, Butler," in *The Cambridge Companion to The Stoics*, 369-379. In the latter he observes, "The modern assessment of Spinoza's Stoic affinity is a curious record of extremes" —some writers leaving out any mention of Spinoza's debt to Stoicism, and others who "see Spinoza as heavily indebted to Stoicism and concerned to refashion it" (369). As for A. A. Long himself, he simply wishes to note the "conceptual similarity and difference" between Stoicism and Spinoza (370).

[56] See Ralph Waldo Emerson, *Nature*, Chapter 7, "Spirit." The notion of "eternal recurrence" appears in a few of Nietzsche's works, including *The Gay Science*, *Thus Spoke Zarathustra*, and the posthumous work, *The Eternal Return*. For a discussion relative to Stoicism, see Robert Hicks, *Stoic and Epicurean*, 24.

[57] Massimo Pigliucci, *How to Be a Stoic: Using Ancient Philosophy to Live a Modern Life* (New York: Basic Books, 2017), 2, 5-6. Otherwise, he states, "For all its uniqueness, Stoicism has numerous points of contact with other philosophies, with religions (Buddhism, Taoism, Judaism, and Christianity), and with modern movements such as secular humanism and ethical culture" (10).

[58] William B. Irvine, *A Guide to the Good Life: The Ancient Art of Stoic Joy* (Oxford: Oxford University Press, 2009), 5, 12. "The Stoic philosophy of life may be old," he acknowledges, "but it merits the attention of any modern individual who wishes to have a life that is both meaningful and fulfilling —who wishes, that is, to have a good life."

[59] Lawrence C. Becker, *A New Stoicism*, revised ed. (Princeton: Princeton University Press, 2017), 6, 22.

[60] Sarah Marks, "Psychotherapy in historical perspective," *History of the Human Sciences* 30, no. 2 (2017): 3-16. Note that the term "stoical" is simply used here as a synonym for "stoic" (or "Stoical" for "Stoic").

[61] Albert Ellis, *Reason and Emotion in Psychotherapy*, revised ed. (New York: Carol Publishing Group, 1994), 64-65. It should be noted that Albert Ellis nevertheless states that, "I am hardly a Stoic. I favor, in addition to Epictetus, Epicurus . . ." Epicurus was the founder of another major ancient Greek school of philosophy, Epicureanism. For more on Epicurus and Epicureanism, see the Cave's *The Best of Epicurus: The Life, Writings & Teachings of Epicurus the Greek Philosopher*. Regarding the "ABC theory of emotional disturbance," Gerald Corey, in *Theory and Practice of Counseling and Psychotherapy*, 293, states, "The A-B-C framework is central to REBT theory and practice. . . . A is the existence of

a fact, or activating event, or an inference about an event, an individual. C is the emotional and behavioral consequence or reaction to the individual; the reaction can either be healthy or unhealthy. A (the activating event) does not cause C (the emotional consequence). Instead, B, which is the person's belief about A, largely creates C, the emotional reaction."

[62] Gilbert Murray, *The Stoic Philosophy* (New York: The Knickerbocker Press, 1915), 2.

[63] Jim Stockdale, *Thoughts of a Philosophical Fighter Pilot* (Stanford: Hoover Institution Press, 1995), 20.

[64] In addition to these, see the various forthcoming offerings from the Cave: *The Wisdom & Way of the Early Stoics: Pocket Edition*, and *The Early Stoics Workbook & Journal: Ancient Greek Wisdom & Ways for Living Well & Aiming for Genuine Happiness*.

[65] For further detailed information about the Stoics, consult "The Cast of Significant Stoics" in "Other Matters of Interest Related to the Early Stoics." Though this book is called *The Best of the Early Stoics*, it would perhaps be more accurate to say "the Early and Middle Stoics." Here we take "Early" to include both.

[66] Pausanias, *Description of Greece* 1.15.

[67] For Zeno, see Diogenes Laertius, *Lives* 7.2-3. For Socrates, see ibid., 2.21.

[68] For more on ancient Cynicism and their teachings and practices, see the Cave's *The Best of the Cynics: The Lives, Writings & Teachings of the Ancient Cynics*. If you'd like to incorporate the teachings of the Cynics into your own life, carry the Cave's *The Wisdom & Way of the Cynics: Pocket Edition* with you. Finally, if you'd like to practice Cynic philosophy with the Cynics, see the Cave's *The Cynics Workbook & Journal: Ancient Cynic Wisdom & Ways for Living Well & Aiming for Genuine Happiness*.

[69] The *Lives* presents anecdotes about and the teachings of various Greek wise men—philosophers—and the major schools of Greek philosophy, beginning with Thales of Miletus and ending with Epicurus. Therein, Diogenes Laertius refers to the works and views of the Stoics Zeno of Citium, Cleanthes of Assos, Chrysippus of Soli, Persaeus of Citium, Ariston of Chios, Apollophanes of Antioch, Herillus of Carthage, Dionysius of Heraclea, Sphaerus of Bosporus, Zeno of Tarsus, Diogenes of Babylon, Antipater of Tarsus, Boethus of Sidon, Archedemus, Heraclides of Tarsus, Apollodorus of Athens, Apollodorus of Seleucia, Panaetius of Rhodes, Posidonius Apamea, Hecaton of Rhodes, Eudromus, and Crinis. "Other ancient writers" include Antigonus of Carystus, Diocles of Magnesia, Hippobotus, Demetrius of Magnesia, among others.

[70] For more on happiness being the end or goal of life, see the Cave's forthcoming *Happiness: What the Ancient Greeks Thought and Said about Happiness*.

[71] Diogenes Laertius, *Lives* 7.40.

[72] The Greek word *logos* is a rich word that signifies anything from "word," "speech," and "story," on the one hand, to "reason," "account," and "inward thought," on the other.

[73] For "*Dialectic*," see Diogenes Laertius, *Lives* 7.15, 42, 62, 180; Cicero, *On Ends* 3.72, and Cicero *Academica* 1.35, 42, and 2.66. Compare the definition of dialectic given by Sextus Empiricus: "The Stoics declare that dialectic is the knowledge of things true and things false and things neither" (*Against the Ethicists* 1.187).

[74] For "*Definition*," see Cicero, *On the Nature of the Gods* 2.147; Diogenes Laertius, *Lives* 7.42, 60-62; Augustine of Hippo, *City of God* 8.7.

[75] For "*Canons and criteria*," see Diogenes Laertius, *Lives* 7.42.

[76] For "*Rhetoric*," see ibid., 7.42.

[77] For "*The human parts or powers of knowing — the soul and its parts*," see ibid., 7.156, 157, 159. Eusebius of Caesarea similarly tells us that Zeno labeled the soul "an exhalation with sensation" (*Preparation for the Gospel* 15.18). In his *Meditations* (5.33), the late Stoic Marcus Aurelius says the soul is "an exhalation from blood." Contrary to other Greek philosophers who hold that the soul is an incorporeal reality, the Stoics judge that both the soul and body are corporeal. See also Sextus Empiricus, *Against the Physicists* 1.102 and *Against the Logicians* 1.39.

[78] *Hēgemonikon* (a form of *hēgemonikos*) is related to the Greek *hēgemōn*, "one who leads; a leader, commander, chief, sovereign; a guide," the source of the English "hegemony" and "hegemonic."

[79] For "*Presentations*," see Diogenes Laertius, *Lives* 7.45-46, 50-51, 61, 158. Cicero reports that "a 'presentation' . . . was, as Zeno defined it, an appearance impressed and formed from the thing from which it originated, with a constitution or nature that it could not have if it originated from a thing that was not the one it actually did originate from" (Cicero, *Academica* 2.18). See also Cicero, *Academica* 1.41, 2.77; Aetius 4.12; Sextus Empiricus, *Against the Logicians* 1.228, 230-231.

As for the translation "presentation" of the term *phantasia*, the classics scholar R.D. Hicks noted nearly a century ago (1925) that "the [Greek] word *phantasia* . . . is a technical term in Stoic logic for which no one English equivalent is as yet unanimously adopted." After parenthetically observing the word's basic significance as "appearance" or "appearing," Hicks went on to suggest that *phantasia* "denotes the immediate datum of consciousness or experience, whether presented to sense or in certain cases the mind. Hence," he concluded, "'presentation' is nearer than 'perception' or 'impression.'" It seems today that the matter of what term or "English equivalent" to adopt for *phantasia* is still not settled among scholars since some give "impression" rather than "presentation," or occasionally they use both interchangeably. Along with R.D. Hicks and others, the Cave will use "presentation" so that the reader will be clear what is behind the word when it is encountered.

[80] For each term, see Diogenes Laertius, *Lives* 7.45, 50; Sextus Empiricus, *Against Logicians* 1.228, 230; and Aetius 4.12.

[81] Zeno of Citium says that a presentation is impressed "from a real thing — just as the thing is" (Cicero, *Academica* 2.77). Aetius clarifies that a presentation "makes plain what made it" (4.12). More exactly, it is the presentation-caused "modification that occurs in the soul" that "makes plain" real things.

[82] Scholars oftentimes call these "cataleptic impressions" or "cataleptic presentations," the word "cataleptic" derived from the Greek *kataleptikos*, which refers to the "direct apprehension" or "grasping" or "comprehension" of an object.

[83] Cicero identifies air as "our partner" in sensation, that is, the medium through which sights, sounds, and smells pass. See note 87 below.

[84] For "*Senses and sensation*," see Origen, *Against Celsus* 7.37; Diogenes Laertius, *Lives* 7.52; Aetius 4.21; Cicero, *Academica* 1.40. For the five sense organs, see Aetius 4.21; for the eyes and ears, see Diogenes Laertius, *Lives* 7.157-158.

[85] Origen's point seems, however, to contradict the observation (above) that presentations may be directly grasped by the intellect. For more on the intellect, see "*The use of reason versus sensation in concept formation*" below.

[86] The fifth is air, which carries the presentation from the real thing or object to the person sensing the real thing.

[87] Keep in mind that, according to the Stoics, "We hear when the air between the sonant body and the organ of hearing suffers concussion, a vibration that spreads spherically and then forms waves and strikes upon the ears, just as the water in a reservoir forms wavy circles when a stone is thrown into it" (Diogenes Laertius, *Lives* 7.158). Elsewhere we learn that "air itself sees with us and hears with us and speaks with us—for none of these functions can be performed without air" (Cicero, *On the Nature of the Gods* 2.83).

[88] Recall, the soul itself, the soul's substance, is a "warm breath" (Diogenes Laertius, *Lives* 7.157); it "is a nature capable of sensation" (ibid., 7.1.156). Notice the parallel between the air that exists between the sense object and the senses and the breath-current or *pneuma* that exists between the senses and the *hegemonikon*. Interestingly, the Stoic understanding of *pneuma* seems to parallel the ancient Indian or Hindu understanding of *prana*. See, for instance, the discussion of *prana* in Swami Vivekananda, *Raja-Yoga* (New York: Ramakrishna-Vivekananda Center, 1982).

[89] For "*Preconceptions and conceptions or concepts*," see Augustine of Hippo, *City of God* 8.7; Aetius 4.11; Diogenes Laertius, *Lives* 7.54.

[90] The Greek term (*empeiria* or *empeiros*) means that one is experienced with a thing and thus comes to be acquainted with it. For example, in sensing milk and summer clouds and cotton, one comes to be acquainted with white things. Note the empirical (from experience, *empeiria*, or experienced or experience-based, *empeiros*) basis and thus nature of concepts.

[91] Regarding the other ways we arrive at concepts, Diogenes Laertius explains: "We think about things related to those things near at hand by means of resemblance—as when we think of Socrates from a statue of Socrates. We think about things by means of analogy in terms of increasing the size of the thing, as with the giant Tityus and the Cyclops, and in terms of decreasing its size, as with the pygmy. In this way, the center of the earth is thought about analogously in terms of smaller spheres. An example of transposition is when we think about a man having eyes on his chest. We think about things such as a centaur, a half-man

and half-horse creature, by means of combination. And things such as death by means of opposition. Moreover, by means of a kind of transition, we think about some things such as place and the meaning of words. Some conceptions such as justice and goodness come by means of nature. And some by means of deprivation, such as the man without hands" (*Lives* 7.52-53).

92 Diogenes Laertius, *Lives* 7.52.

93 For "*Knowledge, grasp, opinion, and ignorance*," see Diogenes Laertius, *Lives* 7.47, and Cicero, *Academica* 1.41, 42. Sextus Empiricus defines knowledge in similar terms: "Knowledge is a firm and certain direct apprehension unalterable by argument" (*Against Logicians* 1.151).

94 Though the example of the rope and the snake hails from Indian Advaita Vedanta (non-dual philosophy), it works perfectly well here. And it is apropos given the likely mutual influence of Greek and Indian philosophy. See Thomas McEvilley, *The Shape of Ancient Thought: Comparative Studies in Greek and Indian Philosophies* (New York: Allworth Press, 2002).

95 Incidentally, the Stoics judge that "the ordinary or general Greek education is useful" (Diogenes Laertius, *Lives* 7.129). For more on Greek education, see Raffaella Cribiore, *Gymnastics of the Mind: Greek Education in Hellenistic and Roman Egypt* (Princeton: Princeton University Press, 2001).

96 This, of course, does not mean that Stoics believe a fourteen year-old knows everything or will no longer develop. It seems only to mean that the intellect has come into its final state of development.

97 Cicero, *Academica* 2.145.

98 Diogenes Laertius, *Lives* 7.45.

99 For the argument, see ibid., 7.141. At the most basic level, this is true of the four elements (fire, air, water, earth) from which everything else arises in the cosmos and to which everything returns. These elements are constantly undergoing transformation, one into another and back again. For more, see the next section, "Stoic Natural Philosophy or Physics."

100 For the argument, see Cicero, *On Ends* 3.33.

101 Strictly speaking, according to the Stoics, the virtues are the only true goods in the list. That said, strength and the rest are counted as things that are in accord with nature, and so they are in some sense, however imperfect, goods. For an extended discussion, see "*Virtue and vice*" and "*The good, the bad, and the indifferent*" in "Stoic Ethics."

102 Diogenes Laertius, *Lives* 7.81.

103 Ibid., 7.42.

104 For "*The benefit of training in the logical part of philosophy, and the imperative to study*," see Plutarch, *On Stoic Self-Contradictions* 1037b; Cicero, *On Ends* 3.72 and *Academica* 2.23; Diogenes Laertius, *Lives* 7.3, 8, 15, 23-25, 45, 48, 168, 182.

105 The "wrestling match" is not literally mentioned; however, it is strongly implied by the Greek *aptōtos*, which, in reference to a wrestler, means "never thrown."

[106] Diogenes Laertius, *Lives* 7.47.

[107] See Hesiod, *Works and Days* 293-295. To read Hesiod's epic poems, see the Cave's *The Best of Hesiod's Theogony & Works and Days*.

[108] The Greek "Zeus" is related to the Proto-Indo-European *deiwos* or **dewos* (sky), the source of the Latin *deus*, meaning "god" or "God." Consequently, in a sense, to turn to Zeus is to turn to god or God, just as to turn to Allah (which comes from the Arabic meaning "the god" or "the God") is to turn to god or God. The Greek *theos* (god or God), by contrast, does not hail from the same source. See Mircea Eliade, *A History of Religious Ideas: From the Stone Age to the Eleusinian Mysteries*, vol. 1 (Chicago: The University of Chicago Press, 1978), 189.

[109] Cleanthes, *Hymn to Zeus* 24, 31-33.

[110] For "*Natural philosophy or physics*," see Diogenes Laertius, *Lives* 7.132-134; Cicero, *On Ends* 3.73.

[111] The Greek word *kosmos* means, among other things, "order."

[112] For "*Nature*," see Diogenes Laertius, *Lives* 7.148; Cicero, *On the Nature of the Gods* 2.57-58, 81-83, 86.

[113] Though Diogenes Laertius doesn't spell it out, the point is significant. That nature "moves from itself" means that it is, among other things, a soul or soul itself since soul is, according to a tradition going back at least to Plato (see *Phaedrus* 245e), self-motion or that which moves from or by means of itself rather than by means of something else. As such, Diogenes Laertius will note that it is thanks to soul that we humans "are set in motion" — that is, our own soul, instead of something external to us, is the cause of our movement (see *Lives* 7.157: "Zeno of Citium and Antipater, in their treatises *On the Soul*, and Posidonius, say that the soul is a warm breath. For by this we are alive and breathe, and by it we are set in motion").

[114] Cicero is actually speaking of the "reality of the cosmos" here, but given the fact that the remark comes right after his discussion of nature as "craftsmanlike" and so on, he is clearly referring to the cosmos *as* nature. See *On the Nature of the Gods* 2.58. It is worth noting something else Cicero says about the cosmos, something that offers additional insight into the nature or meaning of "nature." After stating that "Epicurus . . . divides the nature of all existing things into bodies, the void or emptiness, and their attributes," he continues, "By contrast, when we Stoics say that the cosmos exists in accord with and is managed by nature, we do not mean it in the manner of Epicurus, as if the cosmos is like a lump of earth or a piece of rock or anything else that does not have its own natural property of coherence. Instead, the cosmos is like a tree or an animal, in which nothing is accidental or arbitrary. Order is manifest, as well as something resembling art or craftsmanship" (*On the Nature of the Gods* 2.82).

[115] By the way, "earth" is not capitalized here or throughout the text (thought it could be as a proper noun) since it falls somewhere between an element ("earth") and our home planet ("the Earth"). Something like the same reasoning is behind the lack of capitalization for "sun" and "moon."

116 For the distinction, see Sextus Empiricus, *Against the Physicists* 1.332. Sometimes the distinction is encompassed by one term alone: "As Apollodorus says, the all or totality of things (*to pan*) means, in one sense, the cosmos. In another sense it means the system composed of the cosmos and the external void. So then, the cosmos is finite, and the void is infinite" (Diogenes Laertius, *Lives* 7.143).

117 Diogenes Laertius, *Lives* 7.140.

118 For "*The nature of the cosmos*," see Diogenes Laertius, *Lives* 7.138-139, 140, 143; Cicero, *On the Nature of the Gods* 2.30, 36-39, 45; Eusebius, *Preparation for the Gospel* 5.15.

119 Cicero, *On the Nature of the Gods* 2.47: "There are two forms that are more excellent than all others. Among solid forms there is the globe or sphere—for so we may translate the Greek *sphaera*. And among plane forms there is the circle or orbit—the Greek is *kyklos*. These two forms alone possess total uniformity in all their parts, and every point on the extremity or circumference is equally distant from the center. And there is nothing that can be better fitted or more compact than that."

120 For the Stoic argument as to why the cosmos is destructible or perishable given the fact that it is generated, see Diogenes Laertius *Lives* 7.141.

121 The contention that God or the gods lack nothing is evident from Homer (late eighth century BC) to the fourth century AD Basil of Caesarea (or someone who wrote *Letter* 366 in his name), who surmised, "God seems to be self-control because he desires nothing but has everything in himself"—that is, he lacks nothing, where desire is an indication or form of lacking.

122 One may protest that the cosmos contains many things that are not perfect. The Stoics would simply reply that such an observation is a matter of faulty judgment. Considering the elements out of which the cosmos is generated, it is "the best that could be produced." "Now the management of the cosmos contains nothing that may possibly be faulted. Given the natural elements, the best that could be produced from them has been produced. Let someone, therefore, show that the cosmos could have been better. But no one will ever show this. And anyone who wishes to improve some part of the cosmos will either make it worse or will be asking for something impossible given the nature of things" (Cicero, *On the Nature of the Gods* 2.86-87).

123 More specifically, it is the view of the Stoic Arius Didymus.

124 Keep in mind that aside from "principle," *archē* also means "beginning," "origin," or "cause." Consequently, "two principles" also means two beginnings, origins, or causes.

125 Diogenes Laertius, *Lives* 7.134. As are the two principles, so is everything in the cosmos corporeal or body (think body-stuff)—everything but for place, the void, time, and "things said" or "sayables."

126 For "*The elements*," see Diogenes Laertius *Lives*, 7.56, 136-137.

127 Compare Diogenes Laertius' statement that the passive principle "matter is that from which anything whatever is produced." He further reports that "the

four elements together constitute substance without quality, that is, matter" (*Lives* 7.137).

[128] For "*The passive principle—substance or matter,*" see Diogenes Laertius, *Lives* 7.134, 137, 150.

[129] Diogenes Laertius elsewhere describes body as something that is extended in three ways—length, width, and height. See *Lives* 7.135.

[130] Johannes Stobaeus reports the Stoic view that for a thing to exist means that it shares in substance: "Zeno says that whatever has a share in substance exists"(*Anthology* 2.5). Recall that substance is matter, as matter is "the substance of all things."

[131] For "*The active principle—God, reason, mind,*" see Diogenes Laertius, *Lives* 7.134-135, 137-138, 147; Eusebius, *Preparation for the Gospel* 15.15; Cicero, *Academica* 1.39; Hippolytus, *Refutation of All Heresies* 1.18; Aetius 1.6; Sextus Empiricus, *Outlines of Pyrrhonism* 3.218; Cleanthes, *Hymn to Zeus* 2 and 21. Note that "God" (*theos*) here refers to the one God, the one active principle—and so the capital G, though it could just as well be rendered with the lower case. As for reason (Reason) and mind (Mind) in reference to God, they are given with a lower case, though they could have also been given with capital letters.

[132] Aside from Eusebius, *Preparation for the Gospel* 15.15, see Diogenes Laertius, *Lives* 7.148, "Zeno says that the substance of God is the whole cosmos and the heaven," and 7.137, "The term cosmos has three meanings. One meaning refers to God himself."

[133] It may be helpful to imagine the fire in a bronzesmith's workshop morphing into any number of crafted objects—a shield, a spear, greaves, cups, a plow, a bracelet—as the fire (the active principle) becomes one with the bronze (the passive principle).

[134] God may pervade even putrid things, but that does not mean that God is putridness, not to mention other things that are counted, at least in some ways, bad.

[135] The full text reads "perfect or intelligent in happiness" (see Diogenes Laertius, *Lives* 7.147). Some excise "intelligent" or "intellectual" (*noeros*—of or related to the intellect or mind, *nous*) as a later gloss (see Brad Inwood and Lloyd P. Gerson, *The Stoics Reader*, 55). If retained, the "intelligent" happiness would refer to the fact that God's happiness has to do with the intellect or mind; therefore, it is a rational rather than a merely emotional or passion-based happiness.

[136] For "*The production or generation of the cosmos,*" see Diogenes Laertius, *Lives* 7.136-137, 142; Cicero, *On the Nature of the Gods* 2.57, 152.

[137] At this point we must admit that however much the outline of Stoic cosmology is clear from the sources we have, the details are, at times, less clear than we would like them to be.

[138] "In the beginning (*archē*)" may also be given as "In the origin." Regardless, note the roundabout reference to the active principle (*archē*), the primordial state in which the two principles alone exist.

[139] And as good Stoics, if such we wish to be, we don't have to pretend to have actual or complete knowledge here. Again, the details are not as clear as we'd like.

[140] Since the Stoic language is not always consistent in discussing the active and passive principles in the production of the cosmos, it is impossible to describe their view with consistency using their own language. At times they speak as though God, the active principle, acts upon and transforms God. At others, it is clearly God producing from matter, the passive principle. The production of the cosmos is somewhat like a dance in which the two partners are so close that they can almost be spoken of interchangeably. Where there is one, there is the other. So if God transforms God, what is really meant is that the active principle transforms the passive principle.

[141] For "*The arrangement of the cosmos and the things therein,*" see Diogenes Laertius, *Lives* 7.137, 155; Cicero, *On the Nature of the Gods* 2.33-34 (for the hierarchy of nature), 42-43, 78, 84, 87, and Cicero, *On Ends* 3.62, 67; Eusebius, *Preparation of the Gospel* 15.15.

[142] Regarding the celestial circles, Diogenes Laertius adds, "First, there is the arctic circle, which is always visible. Second is the summer tropic. Third comes the circle of the equinox. Fourth, the winter tropic. Fifth, the antarctic, which is invisible to us" (*Lives* 7.155)

[143] Recall that the gods, as produced from God the active principle, can take on human form, whereas God the first principle does not since God is formless.

[144] Aside from Eusebius, see also Sextus Empiricus, *Against the Physicists* 1.131: "The Stoics declare that humans have a certain just relation and interaction with one another and with the gods."

[145] For "*The management of the cosmos and the things therein,*" see Diogenes Laertius, *Lives* 7.61, 74, 138; Cicero, *On the Nature of the Gods* 2.75.

[146] Aside from Diogenes Laertius, see also Cicero, *On the Nature of the Gods* 2.58, where "the cosmos itself" is termed "a craftsman"; it is "that which cares and looks out for the benefit and timeliness of everything." See also Hippolytus, who states the Stoic position that God's "providential care pervade[s] everything" (*Refutation of All Heresies* 1.18).

[147] For "*Against Epicureanism,*" see Diogenes Laertius, *Lives* 10.97, 113, 123, 139 (covering Epicurus); Cicero, *On the Nature of the Gods* 2.59, 115. To read more about Epicurus and Epicureanism, see the Cave's *The Best of Epicurus: The Life, Writings & Teachings of Epicurus the Greek Philosopher*.

[148] It is because of the difference between the Stoic and Epicurean positions regarding the gods and the management—or not—of the cosmos that we much later hear the Roman emperor Marcus Aurelius repeatedly sound the refrains of "providence or chance" and "order or atoms" and "purpose or no purpose" in his Stoic-inspired meditations, *To Himself*. That is, there is either order and purpose thanks to providence or atoms move by chance with no purpose.

[149] For "*Arguments for divine providence and intelligent design,*" see Cicero, *On the Nature of the Gods* 2.78, 87, 93, 120. The argument in simple terms: If a thing demonstrates rational arrangement, then there is a rational arranger behind it.

The cosmos is such a thing. Therefore, there is a rational arranger behind the cosmos.

[150] This argument from Cicero is likely the source of the well-known argument having to do with monkeys and Shakespeare—that no matter how long one gives a roomful of monkeys to monkey around with typewriters, they will never type out even a single, coherent line from Shakespeare; so it is that this cosmos—with its intricate machinery (if we may call it such) from the stars and planets to DNA—cannot be the result of chance. For other examples of intelligent purpose or design, see *On the Nature of the Gods* 2.88 ff.

[151] For *"The purpose of divine providence,"* see Cicero, *On the Nature of the Gods* 2.37, 58, 81, 127, 133, 166; Eusebius, *Preparation for the Gospel* 15.15.

[152] Diogenes Laertius, *Lives* 7.149. For the following discussion of fate, human freedom, and human responsibility, see Diogenes Laertius, *Lives* 7.149; Cicero, *On Fate* 43; Hippolytus, *Refutation of All Heresies* 1.18.

What does it mean that all things are fated? And what does it mean for human beings in terms of freedom and responsibility?

First, a few definitions of fate. "Fate is defined as an ongoing string of things responsible for existing things." Fate, then, is the cause of things, one thing after and related to another. More importantly, though, "Fate is the rational principle by which the cosmos produces." So fate is not blind; it is the "string of things" marked by reason.

We may wonder, if everything is *rationally* fated, then are we humans free? And are we responsible for anything we do? Should we be praised or punished for anything? The Stoic reply is yes. We are free to make good or beneficial use of our human nature in response to various external events and internal impulses. Not only are we free to do so but we are responsible for making such a beneficial use. Failure to do so will result in various negatives—pain, suffering—that do not have to occur.

To understand, let's take a look at the case of Zeno of Citium and his slave. The report is that "Zeno was once chastising a slave for stealing. When the latter said that he was fated to steal, Zeno replied, 'Yes, and you are also fated to receive a beating.'" Was the slave, absolutely speaking, "fated to receive a beating"? No. The Stoics would say that he was only contingently fated to receive a beating. Since he stole, and since he was caught stealing, and since punishment usually follows upon getting caught, then, yes, he was "fated to receive a beating."

But what if the slave had behaved otherwise? What if he had responded to the impulse to steal (presumably the desire to possess something valuable, pleasant, or beneficial) in line with human nature or reason? That is, what if he had responded rationally rather than impulsively? If he had, then the outcome—the fate—would have been very different.

As we've already learned, the Stoics believe that we humans naturally—by nature—act thanks to reason. That is, we are (fully) human only insofar as we act in line with reason. When we behave rationally, from and in line with reason, we behave as human beings. That stated, we are nevertheless moved by impulse. But this is merely our animal nature, the Stoics believe—something we share with animals. Consequently, just as animals are moved to behave in certain ways thanks to impulse or instinct (to eat and drink; to have sex; to possess valuable, pleasant, and beneficial things; to be in community; to defend possessions, territory, and community; and like things), so too are we humans moved to act in similar ways.

The big difference is reason. As the Stoics put it, "For those beings we call rational [that is, human beings], *the rational life* correctly became *the natural life* when reason was given to them by means of a more perfect rule. Reason was added to shape impulse as a skilled craftsman." Accordingly, unlike animals who will, if they can, move and act in line with impulse, we humans can rationally respond to impulse by either giving in to it or refusing to give in. A wolf, for instance, will, driven by the impulse to eat, steal a farmer's chicken. A hungry human, by contrast, will, in response to reason, refuse to take the property of another (this without getting into whether it is okay to take something for the sake of hunger). A male buffalo will, driven by the impulse to reproduce, fight for and mate with any and every female buffalo that is in heat. A male human will, in response to reason and even though he wishes to have sex with many females, restrain himself in order to have sex with the right female at the right time and place (to cite Aristotle).

So what's the difference? What is fated and what is not? The simple answer: "All things happen by fate." Yes all—but not really all. This is true because even though humans *as* humans are fated to possess reason, they are not fated to use reason *well* to "shape impulse as a skilled craftsman." So there is this kind of shadowy realm of response, of choice, one that the early Stoics do not exactly—at least in sources we possess—expound at length, that involves making good use of human nature (reason) to respond well (rationally in line with virtue) to our animal nature (impulse), to assent or refuse to assent to impulse.

Using the analogy of an inanimate object, a roller, Chrysippus explains the two (rational nature and impulse) in terms of principal (or primary) and proximate (or secondary) causes. "In the same way, therefore, . . . as a man who has pushed a roller forward has given it a beginning of motion but has not given it its circular motion, so a presentation, when it occurs, will indeed impress or stamp itself and, as it were, seal its likeness or image on the rational soul, but assent will be in our power. It is as we declared in the instance of the roller: though given an external push [the proximate cause], as for the rest—its capacity to roll—the roller will move by its own power and nature [the principal cause]." Presentations or impulses (proximate causes)—say of a piece of chocolate cake or someone cutting us off in traffic or bad news—will inevitably occur. But, thanks to our rational nature (the principal cause), it is in our power to respond in one way or another to the impulse.

Impulses are inevitable but insufficient causes (for human beings). We humans necessarily and unavoidably experience a whole range of impulses all the time. Someone cuts us off in traffic. A colleague offers us a moist piece of chocolate cake. The Wi-Fi connection goes out. A classmate presents us with the key to the exam. We meet an attractive person other than the one we are committed to. A relative dies. Our host asks if we want another drink. We're told we have cancer. And so on. Things like this, and to one degree or another, happen every day. But they are, according to the Stoic understanding, only proximate or secondary causes. Even though they happen and may in some secondary sense *cause* us to respond or behave in a certain manner, they do not have the power to force us into any kind of behavior.

What is more important is the principal or primary cause, our rational human nature or reason. Whereas impulse is an inevitable but insufficient secondary cause, reason is, it seems, *not* inevitable insofar as we may or may not make use of reason. Nevertheless, if we make good use of reason, if we properly assent or refuse to assent to an impulse according to reason, then it is a sufficient cause. Said another way, reason empowers us to behave as humans and thus flourish as humans.

So as human beings, we are free since we possess reason, and reason gives us choice. Accordingly, we are responsible—or we are held responsible. The big question, then, whenever we are faced with inevitable impulses—ones that are often contrary to reason—is how we will respond. Will we respond like animals, always giving in to impulse if we can (that is, if we are in the position to)? Or will we only do so when it is right to do so, when it is good?

[153] For *"The destruction of the cosmos in the great conflagration,"* see Cicero, *On the Nature of the Gods* 2.118; Diogenes Laertius, *Lives* 7.134; Eusebius, *Preparation for the Gospel* 15.18.

[154] For *"The end or goal (telos) of life,"* see Diogenes Laertius, *Lives* 7.7, 10-11, 28, 88; Epictetus, *Discourses* 3.24.2.

[155] For *"The addition and role of impulse (hormē),"* see Cicero, *On the Nature of the Gods* 2.82-83, 128; Diogenes Laertius, *Lives* 10.85-86, 129, 137; Cicero, *On Ends* 3.16, 17, 62-63.

[156] Some Stoics held that a plant's or tree's *hēgemonikon* or leading part was located in the roots. See Cicero: "As for trees and plants that spring up from the earth, people suspect that the leading part is in their roots" (*On the Nature of the Gods* 2.29).

[157] Though the four examples do not literally appear in the text, they, or something very much like them, are clearly what the Stoics have in mind. We know this given the parameters of the first desires "for healthy things" that appear "immediately upon birth." They are the desires that any baby has.

[158] See *Hierocles the Stoic: "Elements of Ethics," Fragments, and Excerpts,* trans. David Konstan, 91.

[159] For *"The addition and role of reason,"* see Diogenes Laertius, *Lives* 7.86. Although the Stoics counted the gods and other divine beings rational, the section refers to humans alone. Other animals—giraffes, apes, mice, and dogs, for instance—were not judged rational (contrary to what many believe today).

[160] For *"Virtue and vice,"* see Diogenes Laertius, *Lives* 8, 29, 89-91, 94, 120, 126-127; Cicero, *On Ends* 3.34, 48; Johannes Stobaeus, *Anthology* 2.5. For a list of primary and secondary or subordinate virtues and vices, see "The Virtues & Vices" in "Other Matters of Interest Related to the Early Stoics." To learn more about what the ancient Greeks thought and said about *aretē*, see the Cave's *Aretē: Excellence or Virtue*.

[161] This in contrast to Epicurus who declares, "We choose the virtues for the sake of pleasure and not on their own account, even as we take medicine for the sake of health" (Diogenes Laertius, *Lives* 10.138), or "While it is hard enough for a wrongdoer [the man who commits vice] to avoid getting caught, it is impossible for him to maintain confidence that he will remain uncaught" (*Vatican Sayings* 7). To understand Epicurus' position in greater detail, read the Cave's *The Best of Epicurus: The Life, Writings & Teachings of Epicurus the Greek Philosopher*.

[162] Cleanthes wrote a book, now lost, *On the Notion That Virtue Is the Same for Men and Women* (see Diogenes Laertius, *Lives* 7.125). Much later, the Stoic Musonius Rufus also explored the sameness of the virtues for men and women. In his lectures, he declares that "a desire for virtue and an affinity for it belong by nature not only to men but also to women." Further, he observes that "it is obvious that there is not one type of virtue for a man and another for a woman." He goes on to suggest that "daughters should get the same education as sons." See *Musonius Rufus: Lectures and Sayings*, trans. Cynthia King, ed. William B. Irvine (CreateSpace, 2011), 28, 31. For the mutual involvement of the virtues, see Johannes Stobaeus, *Anthology* 2.5 and Diogenes Laertius, *Lives* 7.125-126. Finally, in the *Lives* we learn that Chrysippus and other Stoics taught that "the man who has one virtue has them all inasmuch as the virtues have common principles" (7.125).

[163] For *"Duty or what is fitting,"* see Diogenes Laertius, *Lives* 7.88, 107-108.

[164] For *"The good, the bad, and the indifferent,"* see Diogenes Laertius, *Lives* 7.94, 102. For a chart of the good, the bad, and the indifferent, see "The Good, the Bad & the Indifferent" in "Other Matters Related to the Early Stoics."

[165] The Stoic Diogenes defines the good as "that which is by nature perfect." See Cicero, *On Ends* 3.33.

[166] For *"The turning or perversion of the rational soul,"* see Diogenes Laertius, *Lives* 7.89, 110, 115, 125; Marcus Aurelius, *Meditations* or *To Himself* 3.2.

[167] Of course the point may be debated. What looks like an imperfection in the form of perishability or destruction, may simply reveal sustainability, in that a new cosmos always comes from the old.

[168] Such a teaching, of course, flies in the face of what many of our contemporaries believe. For them, the natural equals whatever we happen to desire. Thus, to follow our desires or passions is natural—or, to put it into Stoic terms, to follow our impulses is natural. In response to the question why we contemporaries behave as we do, we respond, "It's just my nature or it's just my character." The Stoics would respond (echoing a much later Spaniard), "No, it's your lack of character"—which is to say, we lack a proper formation in virtue.

[169] For "*The passions (bad and good)*," see Johannes Stobaeus, *Anthology* 2.10; Diogenes Laertius, *Lives* 7.110-111. For more on the passions, see "The Passions" in "Other Matters of Interest Related to the Early Stoics."

[170] For "*The right judgment imperative*," see Diogenes Laertius, *Lives* 7.118.

[171] Such as the natural impulse toward self-defense (which may lead to irrational anger or wrath) or the acquisition of property (which may lead to irrational envy or jealousy).

[172] For "*Stoic happiness*," see Diogenes Laertius, *Lives* 7.89, 127; Cicero, *Academica* 1.35. For more on Stoic and other ancient Greek views on happiness, see the Cave's forthcoming *Happiness: What the Ancient Greeks Thought and Said about Happiness*.

[173] For wise men being happy, see Cicero, *On Ends* 3.26. "We may assume" only because, as pointed out in the next section, "The Stoics usually did not make a practice of identifying wise human beings." See also Sextus Empiricus, *Against the Physicists* 1.133.

[174] Recognizing the wisdom of Socrates and Zeno, the late Stoic teacher Epictetus advises, "Whenever you are about to meet with someone, particularly if he is one of those who are judged 'outstanding,' ask yourself, 'What would Socrates or Zeno do in this situation?' In doing so, rather than being at a loss, you'll know the best thing to do with whatever happens" (*Handbook* 33.12). To benefit more from the *Handbook* of Epictetus, pick up the Cave's forthcoming *The Handbook of Epictetus: Pocket Edition*.

[175] Diogenes Laertius, *Lives* 7.117. That is, he is without the "bad" passions rather than the "good."

[176] Cicero, *On Ends* 3.26.

THE GENERAL PARTS & PROPER ORDER
OF STOIC PHILOSOPHY OR PHILOSOPHICAL DISCOURSE

IN BRIEF: *After Sextus Empiricus' brief mention of the Stoic divisions of philosophy, Diogenes Laertius summarizes Stoic philosophy in terms of its three general parts—logic, natural philosophy or physics, and ethics. He further explains how various Stoics presented each part, whether together or separately, and in what order. Next, Plutarch reports Chrysippus' thinking regarding the proper order of study—that one should begin with logic, proceed to ethics, and finish with physics, including a study of the gods. He explains, however, that in practice Chrysippus began and ended with physics, particularly with the gods and certain features of the cosmos.*

Sextus Empiricus, *Outlines of Pyrrhonism* 2.13

THE STOICS AND several others say that there are three divisions of philosophy, namely, logic, natural philosophy or physics, and ethics. And they begin their teaching with logic.

Diogenes Laertius, *Lives* 7.38-41, 160-161

I have decided to give a general account of Stoic teachings in the life of Zeno because he was the founder of the school. I have already given a list of his many writings, in which he has spoken like none of the other Stoics.[1] His teachings, in general, are as follows. In accord with my usual practice, I have provided a summary statement.

[39] The Stoics declare that philosophical discourse has three parts. One part, physics, has to do with natural philosophy. Another has to do with ethics. A last concerns itself with logic.

Zeno of Citium was the first to make this division in his *On Philosophical Discourse*. Chrysippus did the same in the first book of his

On Philosophical Discourse and the first book of his *Natural Philosophy*, as did Apollodorus and Syllus in the first part of their works introducing Stoic doctrines, and Eudromus in his *Ethical Elements*, and Diogenes the Babylonian and Posidonius.[2]

Apollodorus called these parts "topics," whereas Chrysippus and Eudromus called them "specific subdivisions." Others designated them "generic divisions."

[40] The Stoics say that philosophy is like an animal. Logic corresponds to the bones and sinews, ethics to the fleshy parts, and physics to the soul. Yet again, they compare philosophy to an egg, calling logic the shell, ethics the white, and physics the yolk. Or they liken it to a fertile, all-productive field. Logic is the fence that goes around the field, ethics is the crop, and physics is the soil or the fruit tree. Or they liken it to a well-walled city managed in accord with reason.

Some Stoics declare that no single part of philosophy is independent of any other part; rather, they are all united and mixed together. It was not usual to teach the parts separately.

Other Stoics, however, begin with logic, move on to physics in the second place, and in the third finish with ethics. Among those who present philosophy in this manner are Zeno in his *On Philosophical Discourse*, Chrysippus, Archedemus, and Eudromus.

[41] Then again, Diogenes Ptolemais begins with ethics, whereas ethics is second for Apollodorus. Yet again, Panaetius and Posidonius begin with physics—as reported by Phanias, the student of Posidonius, in the first book of his *Lectures of Posidonius*.

Cleanthes says there are six parts: dialectic, rhetoric, ethics, politics, physics, and theology. Even so, others declare that these are not parts of philosophical discourse but of philosophy itself—as does Zeno of Tarsus. . . .

[160] Ariston[3] wished to discard both logic and physics, saying that physics was beyond our reach and logic does not concern us. All that matters to us is ethics. [161] He said that dialectical arguments are like spiders' webs. Though they seem to display some artistic skill and workmanship, they are nevertheless useless.

Plutarch, *On Stoic Self-Contradictions* 1035a-d

Chrysippus thought that young students should first learn logic, then ethics, and after these two parts, physics. He likewise thought that they should study the gods last of all.

Now since these things have been often said by him, it will be enough to set down what is found in the fourth book of Chrysippus' *On Lives*. Here it is word for word:

> First, then, it seems to me, according as it has been rightly said by the ancients, that there are three kinds of philosophical speculations—those having to do with logic, ethics, and physics or natural philosophy. It follows that, of these, those having to do with logic should be placed first, those with ethics second, and those with physics third. And of physics, discourse concerning the gods should be last. It is for this reason that the traditions about this are called 'mystic rites of initiation.'

But the one Chrysippus says should come last, the discourse concerning the gods, he usually puts first before every ethical question. He does not say anything about ends or justice or good and evil or marriage or the education of children or law or citizenship without first adding a word about Zeus, Fate, providence, and about the cosmos being held together by one power, and about its unity and finitude—just as those who propose decrees to the assembly of citizens first mention Good Fortune.

And no one can be persuaded to believe any of this without a deep study of natural philosophy. Hear what Chrysippus says about this in the third book of *On Gods*:

> Regarding justice, one can discover no other beginning or any other generation except for that which is from Zeus and common nature. For if we are going to say anything about good and evil, then from these must every such thing have its beginning.

Again, in his *Theses about Physics*, he says, "One cannot in any other way or more properly come to the discussion of good and evil or the virtues or happiness than from common nature and the administration of the cosmos." . . .

According to Chrysippus, therefore, the study of physics or natural philosophy is both before and after the study of ethics.

NOTES

[1] For Diogenes Laertius' "life of Zeno" as well as the "list of his many writings," see Four of Part 2.

[2] Unless otherwise noted, sources mentioned by Diogenes Laertius and other authors were Stoics. To learn more about the most significant of these, see "The Cast of Significant Stoics" in "Other Matters of Interest Related to the Early Stoics" toward the back of this book.

[3] Ariston was counted as one of the "heterodox Stoics." See Seven of Part 2, "Other Early Stoics."

PART 1

STOIC LOGIC, PHYSICS & ETHICS
IN DIOGENES LAERTIUS' *LIVES*

STOIC LOGIC
IN DIOGENES' *LIVES*

IN BRIEF: *Diogenes Laertius covers "the logical part of philosophy," including rhetoric, dialectic, the canons or criteria, and definitions. He begins with rhetoric before moving on to dialectic, which has to do with "things signified" and "utterance." Dialectic expounds subjects by means of question and answer; it is "the science of true statements, false statements, or neither." Next in his treatment are presentations, which come from existing, real things and agree with them. Presentations may be directly apprehended, sense-based, rational, or skill-based, or they may be none of these. Differing from presentations are phantasms—apparitions in the intellect such as those that may appear in sleep. We apprehend different things by sensation and reason. Conceptions come in various ways—by direct experience, resemblance, analogy, transposition, combination, opposition, nature, and deprivation. The criterion of truth is related to the direct apprehension of a presentation. Next is "utterance," under which Diogenes discusses speech, dialectic, letters, and things spoken, including the five parts of speech and the virtues and vices of discourse. Definition is related to matters such as genus, species, division, and verbal ambiguity. Returning to dialectic, there are various kinds of proposition. Diogenes reviews the Stoic understanding of arguments, of syllogisms and the like. The significance of the logical part is that the wise man will be skilled in argumentation in order to understand the nature of things so that he will be able to act and be well.*

S OME STOICS DIVIDE the logical part of philosophy into two sciences—rhetoric and dialectic. Some would add the subdivision of definitions and another part having to do with canons and criteria. Others dispense with the part about definitions.

[42] Stoics accept the part that deals with canons and criteria as a means of discovering the truth. They use it to explain the different kinds of presentations[1] that we have. Similarly, they accept the part about definitions as a means of recognizing the truth, inasmuch as real things are objects that are grasped by means of conceptions.

By rhetoric they understand the science of speaking well on matters set out in detailed narrative speeches or expository speeches.

By dialectic they understand the science of correctly discussing subjects by means of question and answer. Another definition of dialectic is the science of true statements, false statements, or neither.

Rhetoric itself, they say, has three parts—the deliberative part, the judicial or forensic part, and the part concerned with panegyric or encomiastic. [43] According to them, rhetoric may be divided into invention of arguments, their expression in words, their arrangement, and their delivery. A rhetorical speech may be divided into an introduction, a narrative, replies to opponents, and the conclusion.

They hold that dialectic is divided into the topics regarding the things signified and the utterance. The topic regarding the things signified is divided into the topic about presentations and the topic about things said to which presentations give rise. Included in the topic about things said are propositions and complete expressions and predicates and similar terms, whether active or passive, and genera and species, as well as arguments and modes and syllogisms and fallacies or sophisms, whether due to the utterance or the subject matter. [44] The latter include both false and true and negative arguments, the Sorites paradox and the like, whether defective, insoluble, or conclusive, and the fallacies known as "the Veiled," "the Nobody," and "the Mowers."

The second part that belongs to dialectic mentioned above is that of the utterance itself. Written utterance and the parts of discourse are included in this part. There is a discussion of errors in syntax and in single words, poetic diction, verbal ambiguities, euphony and music, and, according to some writers, chapters on terms, divisions, and style.

[45] Stoics hold that the study of syllogisms is very useful. Such a study shows us what is demonstrative or what offers proof. This contributes a good deal to the correction of judgments or opinions. Their arrangement and retention in memory give a scientific character to our comprehension of things.

An argument is in itself a whole that contains premises and a conclusion. A syllogism is an inferential argument composed of these parts. Demonstration is an argument that infers something that is less clearly grasped by means of things that are better grasped.

A presentation is an impression on the soul. The name is borrowed from the impress made by the seal ring upon the wax.

[46] There are two kinds of presentation. One directly apprehends real things; the other does not. The former, which they take to be the criterion or the test of reality, is that which proceeds from real things. It comes into being from an existing thing, being sealed and impressed on the soul by the existing thing itself. The latter, or non-apprehending kind of presentation, is that which does not proceed from any existing thing—or, if it does, it fails to agree with the existing thing itself. It is neither distinct nor clearly imprinted.

They hold that dialectic itself is necessary and a virtue, and that it encompasses the other kinds of virtues.

Deliberateness or freedom from rashness is the knowledge of when one should assent to something or not.

Discretion or levelheadedness is a strong rational stance relative to what merely seems to be so as not to be taken in by it.

[47] Irrefutability is strength in arguments so that one is not drawn over by the argument to the opposite side.

Earnestness or absence of frivolity is the habit of referring presentations to right reason.

Knowledge itself, they say, is either a firm and direct apprehension or a habit that is, in the reception of presentations, unchangeable by argument.

Without the study of dialectic, the wise man cannot guard himself in argument so that, as in a wrestling match, he will never be thrown. This is because the study of dialectic enables him to distinguish between truth and falsehood, and to judge well between what is plausible and what is ambiguously expressed.[2] And without the study of dialectic, the wise man cannot methodically ask questions and give answers.

[48] Overhastiness in judgment affects the actual course of events, so that those who are untrained in presentations fall into disorder and a lack of purpose. There is no other way that a wise man may show himself to be sharp, ready-witted, and generally skillful in argumentation. It belongs to the same man to converse well and to argue well, and to discuss properly those subjects that are proposed to him, and to answer readily whatever questions are put to him. All these qualities belong to the man skillful in dialectics.

Such is, summarily stated, the substance of the Stoics' logical teaching.

In order to give it in detail, as well, let me now cite as much of it as comes within the scope of their introductory handbook. I will quote verbatim what Diocles of Magnesia says in his *Summary of Philosophers*.[3] These are his words:

[49] The Stoics have chosen to address first the doctrine of presentation and sensation, inasmuch as the criterion by which the truth of things is tested is a kind of presentation. Moreover, the account of assent and that of direct apprehension and that of intelligence, which precedes all the rest, cannot be given apart from presentation. This is so because the presentation comes first, then the intellect, which is capable of expressing itself, puts into the form of a word that which it receives from the presentation.

[50] There is a difference between a presentation and a phantasm—which is to say a vision or phantom appearance. A phantasm is an apparition in the intellect, the kind that may occur in sleep. A presentation is an impression on the soul. As Chrysippus states in the second book of his treatise *On the Soul*, it is an alteration. For, he says, we should not take "impression" in the literal sense of the impress of a seal since it is impossible to suppose that a number of such impressions will occur in one and the same spot at one and the same time. The presentation meant is that which comes from an existing or real thing, agrees with it, and has been stamped and

impressed and sealed on the soul in a way that would not be the case if it came from a non-existing or unreal thing.

[51] According to the Stoics, some presentations are sense-based and others are not. Sense-based presentations are received by means of one or more of the senses or sense organs. Presentations that are not sense-based are those received through the intellect itself, as in the case with incorporeal things and all the other presentations that are received by reason. Of sense-based presentations, some are from existing or real things and come to be by yielding and assent. But there are also presentations that are reflection-appearances—they come to be as if from existing or real things.

Presentations may further be classified as rational or non-rational. The former are those of rational animals; the latter are those of non-rational animals. Rational presentations are thoughts, whereas those that are non-rational do not have a name.

Again, some presentations are skill-based, while others are not skill-based. A statue, anyway, is viewed differently by a trained and skilled craftsman in sculpting, for instance, than it is by one who is not trained and skilled.

[52] The Stoics apply the term sense-perception or sensation to the following: one, the breath or current passing from the leading part of the soul to the senses; two, direct apprehension by means of the senses; three, the equipment of the sense organs—though for some, these may be disabled. Moreover, the operation or activity of the sense organs is itself also called sensation.

According to the Stoics, it is by sensation that we apprehend black and white, and rough and smooth, whereas it is by reason that we apprehend the conclusions of demonstrations—such as the existence of the gods, as well as their foreknowledge.

Regarding conceptions, some come to be by direct experience, some by resemblance, some by analogy, some by transposition, some by combination, and some by opposition. [53] Sense objects are thought about by means of direct experience. We think about things related to those things near at hand by means of resemblance—as when we think of Socrates from a statue of Socrates. We think about things by means of analogy in terms of increasing the size of the thing, as with the giant Tityus and the Cyclops, and in terms of decreasing its size, as with the pygmy. In this way, the center of the earth is thought about analogously in terms of smaller spheres. An example of transposition is when we think about a man having eyes on his chest. We think about things such as a centaur, a half-man and half-horse creature, by means of combination. And things such as death by means of opposition. Moreover, by means of a kind of transition, we think about some things such as place and the meaning of words. Some conceptions such as justice and goodness come by means of nature. And some by means of deprivation, such as the man without hands.

This, then, is what they teach about presentation, sensation, and intelligence or understanding.

[54] The Stoics declare that the criterion of truth is a presentation that is directly apprehensible or graspable, that is, that which comes from an existing or real thing—this according to Chrysippus in the twelfth book of his *Natural Philosophy*, as well as according to Antipater and Apollodorus in their works. Boethus, on the other hand, admits a plurality of criteria—namely, mind, sensation, appetite, and knowledge. But Chrysippus differs in the first book of his treatise *On Reason*, where he declares that sensation and preconception are the only criteria. A preconception is a natural conception of universals or general concepts. Yet again, some others of the older Stoics make right reason the criterion, as does Posidonius in the treatise *On the Criterion*.

[55] In their theory of dialectic, most Stoics begin with the topic of the sound of the voice or utterance. Now utterance is a percussion of the air or the proper object of the sense of hearing, as Diogenes the Babylonian declares in his handbook *On Utterance*. While the sound of the voice or cry of an animal is just a percussion of air brought about by natural impulse, human utterance is articulate and, as Diogenes asserts, emitted by the intellect, which reaches maturity by the age of fourteen.

Furthermore, according to the Stoics, the sound of the voice or utterance is something corporeal, as Archedemus declares in his treatise *On Utterance*, as do Diogenes and Antipater, and Chrysippus in the second book of his *Natural Philosophy*. [56] For everything that produces an effect is a body. And the sound of the voice or utterance, as it proceeds from those who utter it to those who hear it, does produce an effect.

Speech, as Diogenes says, is the sound of the voice or utterance that contains letters. Take, for example, "Day." A statement is the sound of the voice or utterance that is emitted by the intellect and signifies something, such as, "It is day." Dialect is a variety of speech that is stamped on one part of the Greek world as distinct from another, or on the Greeks as distinct from other people groups. Or, yet again, dialect means a form of speech peculiar to some particular region, which is to say it has a certain linguistic quality. For example, the word for "sea" in Attic Greek is *thalatta* and not *thalassa*; and in Ionic Greek, day is *hēmerē* and not *hēmera*.

The twenty-four letters are the elements of speech. The term "letter," however, has three meanings—the element, the character of the element, and the name, as with "Alpha." [57] Seven of the letters are vowels: *a, e, ē, i, o, u, ō*. Six are mutes: *b, g, d, k, p, t*.[4]

There is a difference between the utterance or sound of the voice and speech for the following reason: while the sound of the voice may include mere noise, speech is always articulate. And speech differs from a statement because the latter always signifies something, whereas a spoken word, such as *"blituri,"* may be unintelligible. Such is not possible for a statement. And to frame a statement is different from mere utterance. For while vocal sounds are uttered, things stated are real things, that is, they are "things said."

There are five parts of speech. Diogenes says this in his treatise *On Utterance*—as does Chrysippus. They are the proper name, the common noun, the verb, the conjunction, and the article. In his work *On Speech and Saying Things*, Antipater adds what he calls the "middle position" or the participle.[5]

58 *Diogenes Laertius discusses the five parts of speech with examples.*

[59] There are five virtues of discourse: purity (that is, good Greek), clarity, conciseness, suitability, and elaboration. Good Greek is

correct style, faultless in point of grammar and free from any random form of expression. Clarity is a style that presents the thought in a way that is easily understood. Conciseness is a style that employs no more words than are necessary for communicating the subject at hand. Suitability is found in a style that is appropriate or related to a subject. Elaboration is the avoidance of common expression.

Among the vices of discourse, barbarism is the violation of the usage of those Greeks of good reputation. Solecism is when discourse is incongruously constructed.

[60] In his treatise *On Style*, Posidonius defines a poetical phrase as one that is metrical and rhythmical, avoiding all resemblance of prose. An example of such a rhythmical phrase is: "O greatest earth, O pure sky of Zeus." If such poetic phraseology is significant, and if it includes a portrayal or representation of human and divine things, then it is poetry.

As Antipater declares in the first book of his *On Definitions*, a definition is an expressed statement in accord with a precise analysis or reduction. According to Chrysippus in his book of the same name, a definition is an account of what is distinct. Delineation is a statement that brings one to a knowledge of the subject in outline. Or it may be called a definition that embodies the force of the definition itself in a simpler form.

Genus or general kind is the comprehension or inclusion in one thing of a number of inseparable objects of thought—for example, "animal," for this term includes all specific animals.

[61] A notion or thought-object is a phantasm in the intellect that is neither something real nor any quality; rather, it is an apparent thing and an apparent quality. For example, a mental image of a horse may come to be even though there is no horse present.

Species or specific kind is that which is included under genus, as when "human" is included under "animal." The most general kind is the general kind that does not have a genus, for example, being itself. The most specific kind is the specific kind that does not have a species, as with "Socrates."

Division is the partition of a genus into its proximate species. For example, of animals, some are rational and some are non-rational.

Contrary division separates the genus into species by means of the opposite, as with negation. For example, of things that are, some are good and some are not good. Subdivision is division applied to a previous division. For example, following upon "of things that are, some are good and some are not good," we say, "of things that are not good, some are bad and some are indifferent, that is, neither good nor bad."

[62] Partition is an arrangement or organization of a general kind into topics—as Crinis says. For example, of good things, some are goods of the soul and some are goods of the body.

Verbal ambiguity arises when speech properly, rightfully, and in accord with customary usage denotes two or more different things so that at one and the same time we may understand the word in several distinct senses. Take, for example, "*aulētris peptōke*." The same verbal expression may mean something such as, "A courtyard wall has fallen three times," or something such as, "The flute girl has fallen."

Posidonius says that dialectic is the knowledge of truth and falsehood and that which is neither true nor false. Chrysippus declares that dialectic has to do with things that signify and things that are signified.

Such, then, is what the Stoics have to say in their theory of utterance or the sound of the voice.

[63] Under the topic related to real things and things signified, they include an account of things said. This account includes those things said that are complete in themselves, as well as propositions and syllogisms. It also includes incomplete expressions consisting of both active and passive predicates.

63-76 Diogenes Laertius goes on to give a full account of the Stoic teaching regarding "things said"—predicates, propositions (general and specific kinds), syllogisms, questions, and inquiries, among other things said (imperatives, addresses, and oaths). These various definitions prepare the discussion for its turn to argumentation and the different kinds of arguments.

[76] As the followers of Crinis declare, an argument consists of

something taken as true (a major premise), an additional assumption (a minor premise), and a conclusion. For example, this: "If it is day, it is light. It is day. Therefore, it is light." In this case, the sentence, "If it is day, it is light," is the major premise. The minor premise is, "It is day." And the conclusion is, "Therefore, it is light."

A mode of a proposition is, as it were, the form of an argument. For instance, "If the first, then the second. But the first. Therefore, the second."

[77] An argument mode is a combination of both the argument and the mode. For example, "If Plato is alive, Plato breathes. But the first. Therefore, the second." The argument mode was introduced so that, when dealing with long complex, arguments, we would not have to repeat a long minor premise in order to state the conclusion. Rather, we would be able to arrive at the conclusion as concisely as possible. "But the first. Therefore, the second."

Of arguments, some are endless or inconclusive, and some are conclusive. Inconclusive arguments are such that the opposite of the conclusion does not conflict with the combination of the premises. For example, "If it is day, it is light. But it is day. Therefore, Dion walks."

[78] Of conclusive arguments, some are denoted by the common name of the whole genus, "conclusive." But others are "syllogistic." Syllogistic arguments are arguments that do not admit of, or they are reducible to arguments that do not admit of, immediate proof in relation to one or more of the premises. For example, "If Dion walks, then Dion is in motion. Dion is walking. Therefore, Dion is in motion."

Those arguments that are specifically conclusive are those that draw conclusions without the use of a syllogism. For example, "It is false that it is day and it is night. It is day. Therefore, it is not night."

Non-syllogistic arguments are those that plausibly resemble syllogistic arguments, but they do not conclude or make the inference. For example, "If Dion is a horse, he is an animal. But Dion is not a horse. Therefore, Dion is not an animal."

[79] Further, of arguments, some are true and some are false. True arguments draw their conclusions by means of true premises.

For example, "If virtue is beneficial, then vice is harmful. But virtue is beneficial. Therefore, vice is harmful." False arguments have something false in at least one of the premises. Or a false argument is an inconclusive argument, as with the following example: "If it is day, it is light. It is day. Therefore, Dion is alive."

There are also possible and impossible arguments, and necessary and non-necessary arguments.

Further, there are some arguments that are indemonstrable because they do not need demonstration. They are employed in the construction of every argument.

79-81 Diogenes Laertius presents the five kinds of indemonstrable arguments.

[81] According to the Stoics, a truth follows from a truth. For example, "It is light" follows from "It is day." And a falsehood follows from a falsehood. "It is dark" follows from "It is night" —if, that is, the latter is false. And a truth follows from a falsehood. For example, "The earth exists" follows from "The earth flies." However, a falsehood does not follow from a truth, for "The earth flies" does not follow from "The earth exists."

[82] There are also certain insoluble arguments: the Veiled Men, the Disguised, the Sorites, the Horned Men, and the Nobodies. The Veiled is as follows: . . .[6] "It cannot be that if two is few, three is not so likewise, nor that if two or three are few, four is not so likewise. And so on up to ten. But two is few. Therefore, so also is ten." . . . The Nobody argument is an argument whose major premise consists of an indefinite and a definite clause, followed by a minor premise and a conclusion. For example, "If someone is here, that one is not in Rhodes. Someone is here. Therefore, there is not someone [or "there is nobody"] in Rhodes."

[83] Such, then, is the logic of the Stoics by which they seek to establish their point that the one skilled in logical argument is the only wise man. For all things, they say, are perceived by means of logical study, including whatever belongs to the topic of natural philosophy or physics and again whatever belongs to ethics. For if

the rational and logical man must say something about the correct use of terms, how could he fail to appoint the customary terms for actions? Moreover, of the two kinds of habit that relate to its virtue, one considers the nature of each existent thing, and the other asks what it is called. So much for their logic.

NOTES

[1] See the "Introduction" for what the Stoics meant by "presentation." For a simple definition, see Diogenes Laertius, *Lives* 7.45: "A presentation is an impression on the soul."

[2] Plausible (*pithanos*) could also be given as "persuasive" or "probable."

[3] Diocles of Magnesia (first century BC) was an ancient historian and writer of biography and summaries. He concentrated on the views, sayings, and lives of the earliest philosophers.

[4] Using the Greek alphabet, the vowels are α, ε, η, ι, ο, υ, ω, and the mutes are β, γ, δ, κ, π, τ.

[5] The participle is a part of speech that is, as it were, in between a verb and a noun, having characteristics of both. Thus, it is *in the middle* or in the "middle position."

[6] There are several lacunae or gaps in the text in this paragraph. The example that follows, "It cannot be that if two is few, three is not so likewise . . ." serves to explain the Sorites (from *sōros*, the Greek for "quantity" or "heap"). Examples for the Veiled Men (where one simultaneously knows and does not know his father or brother because they are veiled or masked), the Horned Men (where one ends up actually having horns simply because he has not lost them), and the Disguised are missing. For a list of similar "insoluble arguments" or "dialectical arguments" by the Megarian Eubulides of Miletus (fourth century BC), see Diogenes Laertius, *Lives* 2.108.

STOIC NATURAL PHILOSOPHY OR PHYSICS
IN DIOGENES' *LIVES*

IN BRIEF: *Diogenes Laertius explains that the Stoics discuss natural philosophy under general and specific topics, answering questions having to do with the basic nature of the cosmos, the things within it, and causes. As for the cosmos, there are two principles: reason, which is active, and matter, which is passive. Reason is also called God, mind, fate, and Zeus—and as God, many other names, including Athena, Hera, Hephaestus, Poseidon, and Demeter. The cosmos is from God —by means of a process of God "adapting matter to himself" — so that all comes from and returns to God. In this way, the cosmos has a beginning and an end; it is generated and perishes. The elements (fire, air, water, earth) arise from the two principles. From the elements, everything else comes to be. Since mind (or reason or God) pervades matter, the cosmos is living and rational. God manages the cosmos through providence. The cosmos itself is a finite, corporeal unity surrounded by the infinite, incorporeal void. Diogenes also discusses the early Stoic view of time, nature, fate, the various heavenly bodies (sun, moon, stars, planets), the seasons and winds, daemons and heroes, various meteorological phenomena (rainbows, comets, meteors, rain, hail, lightning and thunder), earthquakes, human sensation (seeing and hearing), sleep, and sexual reproduction.*

THE STOICS DIVIDE physics, or their account of nature, into the following topics: bodies, principles, elements, the gods, limits, place, and what is empty or void.

The former is a specific division.

There are three topics in the general division. One has to do with the cosmos. Another is about the elements. And the third is an investigation or account of causes.

The Stoics say that the topic having to do with the cosmos is divided into two parts. The mathematicians have a share in one part of its investigations insofar as they seek to answer questions relating to the fixed stars and the planets—for example, whether the sun is or is not as large as it appears to be; and the same about the moon; and the question regarding their revolutions; and other inquiries of the same kind. But there is another investigation or field of cosmological inquiry that belongs to the natural philosophers alone. [133] This part of the investigation includes such questions as what the substance of the cosmos is. And whether the sun and the stars consist of matter and form. And whether the cosmos had a beginning or no beginning. And whether it is living or not living. And whether it is destructible (perishable) or indestructible (imperishable). And whether it is managed by providence—and the rest.

The part having to do with the investigation or account of causes also has two parts. Medical inquiry has a share in one part of its investigations insofar as it involves investigation of the leading part of the soul and what happens in the soul, as well as originating seeds and the like. But the other part is also claimed by the mathematicians—for example, how we see; what is responsible for the presentation of a reflected image in a mirror; what is the origin of clouds, thunder, rainbows, halos, comets, and the like.

[134] The Stoics hold that there are two principles of the whole cosmos—the active and the passive. The passive principle is substance without quality, that is, matter. The active principle is the reason within the passive principle, which is to say, God. This God is everlasting and the maker of each thing throughout the whole. Zeno of Citium includes this teaching in his *On Substance*; Cleanthes in his work *On Atoms*; Chrysippus in the first book of his *Natural Philosophy*, toward the end; Archedemus in his treatise *On Elements*; and Posidonius in the second book of his *Physical Exposition*.

The Stoics say that there is a difference between principles and elements. The former are without beginning and are indestructible, whereas the elements are destroyed in the great conflagration. Moreover, the principles are corporeal[1] and without form, while the elements have form.

[135] As Apollodorus declares in his *Natural Philosophy*, body is that which is extended in three dimensions—length, width, and height. This is also called "solid body." Surface is the limit or extremity of a body, or it is that which has length and width alone without height. In the third book of his *Celestial Phenomena*, Posidonius maintains that surface exists not only in our thought but also in reality. A line is the limit or extremity of a surface, or it is length without width, or it is that which has length alone. A point is the limit or extremity of a line, the smallest possible mark or dot.

God and mind and fate and Zeus are one thing. God is also called by many other names.

[136] In the beginning, God was by himself. He turned all substance into water by means of air—for just as in animal generation the seed is surrounded by fluid, so in cosmic generation the generative principle of the cosmos remains in the fluid and makes the matter of the cosmos serviceable to God for the next stage of generation. And so God first produced the four elements, fire, water, air, and earth. They are discussed by Zeno in his treatise *On the Whole*, by Chrysippus in the first book of his *Natural Philosophy*, and by Archedemus in a work *On Elements*.

An element is that from which particular things first come to be at their birth and into which they are finally resolved. [137] The four elements together constitute substance without quality, that is, matter. Fire is the hot element, and water is the moist; air is the cold, earth the dry—though this last quality is also found in the air.

Fire is the highest element. It is also called aether and is first generated in the sphere of the fixed stars. Next comes the sphere of the planets. Next to that is the air. Next is the water. And the lowest of all is the earth, which is at the center of all things.

The term cosmos has three meanings. One meaning refers to God himself, the being whose distinct quality is derived from the whole of substance. God is indestructible or imperishable and without beginning or generation. He is the maker of the orderly arrangement of the cosmos. At certain periods of time, he absorbs into himself the whole of substance and once again produces it from himself. [138] They say that another meaning of the term cosmos refers to the orderly arrangement of the stars—the arrangement in itself.[2] The third meaning refers to the combination of both.

Again, the cosmos is defined as the separate quality of the whole of substance. Or, in the words of Posidonius in his elementary treatise on *Celestial Phenomena*, it is a system made up of heaven and earth and the natures in them. Or, again, it is a system constituted by gods and men and all things produced for their sake. Heaven is the extreme circumference or ring in which everything divine is found.

The cosmos is managed by mind and providence inasmuch as mind pervades every part of it just as the soul pervades every part of us—this according to what Chrysippus says in the fifth book of his treatise *On Providence*, and Posidonius in the third book of his work *On the Gods*. That said, there is a difference of degree. In some parts there is more of mind, in others less—[139] for mind spreads through some parts as a permanent state or condition, as is the case with bones and sinews. But it spreads through other parts as mind itself, as is the case with the leading part of the soul. In this way, then, the whole cosmos is a living and rational animal, having aether as its leading part—this according to Antipater of Tyre in the eighth book of his treatise *On the Cosmos*. Chrysippus, in the first book of his work *On Providence*, and Posidonius in his book *On the Gods*, say that heaven is the leading part of the cosmos, and Cleanthes says that it is the sun. Nevertheless, in the same work, Chrysippus gives a somewhat different account—namely, that the leading part is the purer part of the aether, the same which they say is the first God that is spread in a sensible manner through those things in the air, and through every animal and plant, and also through the earth itself as a permanent state or condition.

[140] They say that the cosmos is one and finite, having a spherical form. This spherical form is the most suitable for motion—this according to what Posidonius says in the fifth book of his *Discourse on Nature* and the followers of Antipater in their works *On the Cosmos*.

Spread around the outside of the cosmos is the infinite emptiness or void, which is incorporeal. The incorporeal void is that which is not occupied by bodies, even though it can be so occupied.

There is no emptiness or void within the cosmos. Rather, the cosmos is fully united. This necessarily follows from the sympathy and agreement or joined tension of heavenly things in relation to earthly things. . . .

[141] Again, time is also incorporeal. It is the measure of the interval of the movement of the cosmos. Past time and future time are infinite, whereas present time is finite.

The Stoics hold that the cosmos is destructible or perishable inasmuch as it is generated. This is based on the analogy of those things that are understood by the senses. If a thing has parts that are perishable, then that thing as a whole is perishable. But the parts of the cosmos are perishable since they transform into one another. Therefore, the cosmos is perishable. Moreover, if something is capable of transformation into an inferior state, then it is perishable. The cosmos is capable of such a transformation since it can be dried up and yet again transformed into water.

[142] The cosmos comes into being when its substance is changed from fire into moisture by means of air. And then the denser part of the moisture condenses into earth, and the finer part is turned into air. And this process of rarefaction goes on more and more until it generates fire. Then plants and animals and the other general kinds of things come from the mixture of these elements.

Zeno discusses the generation and the destruction of the cosmos in his treatise *On the Whole*, Chrysippus in the first book of his *Natural Philosophy*, Posidonius in the first book of his work *On the Cosmos*, as does Cleanthes, as well as Antipater in the tenth book of his *On the Cosmos*. But Panaetius declared that the cosmos is indestructible or imperishable.

Chrysippus, in the first book of his treatise *On Providence*, and Apollodorus in his *Natural Philosophy*, and Posidonius as well, say that the cosmos is a living being or animal and rational and ensouled and intelligent. [143] It is a living being in the sense that it is a substance that is alive and endowed with sensation. For a living being is better than a non-living being or non-animal. But nothing is better than the cosmos. Therefore, the cosmos is a living being. Moreover, it is ensouled as is clear from the fact that each of our souls is a fragment of it. But Boethus says that the cosmos is not a living being.

The unity of the cosmos is maintained by Zeno in his treatise *On the Whole,* by Chrysippus and by Apollodorus in their works *Natural Philosophy,* and by Posidonius in the first book of his *Physical Discourse.*

As Apollodorus says, the all or the totality of things means, in one sense, the cosmos. In another sense it means the system composed of the cosmos and the external void. So then, the cosmos is finite, and the void is infinite.

[144] Of the stars, some are fixed and carried around with the whole heaven or sky. But the wandering stars or planets have their own unique motions.

The sun travels in an oblique path through the zodiac. Similarly, the moon travels in a spiral path. The sun is pure fire—this according to what Posidonius says in the seventh book of his *Celestial Phenomena.* And it is larger than the earth, as the same author says in the sixth book of his *Discourse on Nature.* Moreover, according to this same author and his school, the sun is spherical in shape like the cosmos itself. That it is fire is proved by its producing all the effects of fire. That it is larger than the earth is shown by the fact that all the earth is illuminated by it—as is the sky or the heaven. Also, the fact that the earth casts a conical shadow proves that the sun is greater than it. And it is because of its great size that the sun is seen from every part of the earth.

[145] The moon, however, is of a more earthly composition since it is nearer to the earth.

Moreover, they say that these fiery bodies and other stars are nourished. The sun gains nourishment from the great sea, the sun being an intelligent ignited mass. The moon gains nourishment from drinkable waters, with an admixture of air, as close as it is to the earth—as Posidonius says in the sixth book of his *Natural Philosophy.* The others gain nourishment from the earth.

They hold that the stars and the immovable earth are spherical in shape. And that the moon does not shine by its own light but by the borrowed light of the sun when it shines on the moon.

An eclipse of the sun takes place when the moon passes in front of it on the side that is toward us—as Zeno shows with a diagram in his treatise *On the Whole*. [146] For the moon is seen approaching at conjunctions and occluding it, and then again receding from it. One can best observe this when they are reflected in a basin of water.

The moon is eclipsed when it falls into the shadow of the earth. For this reason, an eclipse happens only at the full moon—and not always then, even though it is diametrically opposite to the sun every month. This is so because when its motions are obliquely toward the sun, it does not find itself in the same place as the sun, being either a little more to the north or a little more to the south. When, however, the moon's motion in latitude has brought it into the sun's path through the zodiac, and the moon, therefore, is diametrically opposite to the sun, there is an eclipse. Now the moon is in latitude right on the zodiac when it is in the constellations of Cancer, Scorpio, Aries, and Taurus—according to Posidonius and his followers.

[147] Moving on, God is an immortal living being, rational, perfect in happiness,[3] accepting nothing evil into himself, taking providential care of the cosmos and of the things in the cosmos. To be sure, though, God's form is not human. But he is the maker of the whole cosmos, and he is, as it were, the father of all things, both in general and in that part of him that pervades everything, that which is called many names according to its various powers.[4]

The Stoics call God *Dia* (Through or By-Means-Of) since all things are through him or by means of him. They call him *Zēna* insofar as he is the cause of *zēn* (living or life), or insofar as he pervades all *zēn* (living or life).[5] The name *Athena* is given since the leading part of God extends to the aether. And *Hera* since he extends to the air. And *Hephaestus* since he spreads to the skillful fire. And *Poseidon* since he extends to the moist sea. And *Demeter* since he extends to the earth. Similarly, men have given God his other familiar names by focusing on one or another of his unique attributes.

[148] Zeno says that the substance of God is the whole cosmos and the heaven or sky. The same is said by Chrysippus in the first book of *On the Gods*, and by Posidonius in the first book of *On the*

Gods. And Antipater, in the seventh book of his work *On the Cosmos*, says that the substance of God is similar to air. But Boethus, in his work *On Nature*, speaks of the sphere of the fixed stars as the substance of God.

The Stoics sometimes use the term "nature" to mean that which holds the world together. Sometimes nature means that which causes terrestrial things to spring up. Nature is a permanent state or condition moving from itself, producing and holding together all things that arise out of it at determined times and in accord with the generative principles, and effecting results homogenous with their sources. [149] Nature, they hold, aims at both the advantageous and at pleasure, as is clear from the creative activities of human beings.

In his treatise *On Fate*, Chrysippus declares that all things happen by fate. Posidonius says the same in the second book of his *On Fate*, as does Zeno, and Boethius in the first book of his *On Fate*. Fate is defined as an ongoing string of things responsible for existing things. Or fate is the rational principle by which the cosmos produces.

Moreover, they say that all divination and prophecy are real if providence is also real. And they show that it is an art or skill based on the evidence of certain results — as Zeno says, and Chrysippus in the second book of his *On Divination*, as well as Athenodorus, and Posidonius in the second book of his *Discourse on Nature* and in the fifth book of his *On Divination*. But Panaetius denies that divination has any real existence.

[150] They say that the substance of all existing things is primary matter — as Chrysippus says in the first book of his *Natural Philosophy*, as well as Zeno. Matter is that from which anything whatever is produced. It is called both "substance" and "matter" in reference to the whole cosmos and in reference to apportioned things or parts. That in reference to the whole neither increases nor diminishes, while that in reference to the various parts both increases and diminishes. According to the Stoics, substance is a body that is finite — this according to what Antipater says in the second book of his *On Substance*, and Apollodorus in his *Natural Philosophy*. Matter is passive, which is to say that it can be acted on, as the same author says. For if it were unchangeable, the things that are produced

would never have been produced from it. Thus, there is the further teaching that matter is indefinitely divisible. Chrysippus says that the division itself is infinite but not indefinitely—for there is nothing infinitely small to which the division can extend. But the division goes on incessantly.

[151] According to Chrysippus in the third book of his *Natural Philosophy*, their explanation of the mixture of two things is that they permeate each other through and through in such a way that the particles of one thing do not merely enclose those of another, nor are they merely juxtaposed. Therefore, if a little drop of wine is thrown into the sea, it will be equally diffused over the whole sea for a while before being destroyed altogether and blended with the sea.

The Stoics also hold that there are daemons who sympathize with human beings and watch over human affairs. Heroes are the souls of excellent men who have left behind their bodies.[6]

Of the changes that go on in the air, they describe winter as the cooling of the air above the earth due to the sun's departure to a greater distance from the earth. [152] Spring is the right temperature of the air that follows from the sun's approach to us. Summer is the heating of the air above the earth when it travels to the north. And fall is the sun falling away from us.

As for the winds, they are streams of air, variously named according to the locations from which they blow. And the cause of their production is the sun through the evaporation of the clouds.

The rainbow is explained as the reflection of the sun's rays from watery clouds. Or, as Posidonius says in his *Meteorology*, a rainbow is an image of a segment of the sun or moon in a cloud suffused with dew, which is hollow and visible without intermission. As if in a mirror, the image shows itself in the form of a circular arch.

Comets and bearded stars and meteors are fires that arise when dense air is carried up to the region of aether. [153] A shooting star is the sudden kindling of a mass of fire in rapid motion through the air, which leaves a trail behind it, presenting an appearance of length.

Rain is the transformation of cloud into water, when moisture drawn up by the sun from the earth or the sea has been partially evaporated. If this is cooled down, it is called hoarfrost. Hail is frozen cloud, crumbled by a wind. Snow is moist matter from a frozen cloud, as Posidonius says in the eighth book of his *Discourse on Nature*.

Lightning is a kindling of clouds from being rubbed together or being torn by wind, as Zeno says in his treatise *On the Whole*. Thunder is the noise these clouds make when they rub against one another or burst. [154] The term thunderbolt is used when the fire is violently kindled and hurled to the ground with great force as the clouds grind against one another or are torn by the wind. Others say that it is a compression of fiery air descending with great force.

A typhoon is a great and violent thunderstorm like a whirlwind, or it is a whirlwind of smoke from a burst cloud. A hurricane is a cloud separated by the force of fire and wind.

They say that earthquakes happen when the wind finds its way into, or it is imprisoned within, the hollow parts of the earth—this according to what Posidonius says in the eighth book of his *Discourse on Nature*. Some earthquakes are a shaking of the earth; some are an opening; some are a lateral shifting; some are vertical shifts.

[155] They believe that the parts of the cosmos are arranged in the following manner. The earth is in the middle, located in the center. Next comes water, which is shaped like a sphere all around, concentric with the earth so that the earth is within the water. After the water comes a spherical layer of air. There are five celestial circles. First, there is the arctic circle, which is always visible. Second is the summer tropic. Third comes the circle of the equinox. Fourth, the winter tropic. Fifth, the antarctic, which is invisible to us. The celestial circles are called parallel because they do not incline toward one another. Nevertheless, they are described around the same center. The zodiac is an oblique circle since it crosses the parallel circles.

[156] And there are five terrestrial zones. First, there is the northern zone, which is beyond the arctic circle. It is uninhabitable because of the cold. The second is a temperate zone. A third, called the hot zone, is uninhabitable because of scorching heat. The fourth is also a temperate zone—but opposite the second. The fifth southern zone is uninhabitable because of cold.

The Stoics hold that nature is a skillful fire, proceeding on the road to production as a fiery and artistic breath.

And the soul is a nature capable of sensation. And they regard it as the breath of life that is congenital with us. For this reason, they say that it is a body and that it remains after death. Nevertheless, it is perishable, even though the soul of the whole cosmos is imperishable—that of which the individual souls of animals are parts. [157] Zeno of Citium and Antipater, in their treatises *On the Soul*, and Posidonius, say that the soul is a warm breath. For by this we are alive and we breathe, and by it we are set in motion. Cleanthes holds that every soul persists until the great conflagration—that is, the great reversion and conversion of all things into fire. But Chrysippus says that only the souls of the wise do so.

Of the soul, the Stoics say there are eight parts: the five senses, the generative seeds or principles in us, our power of speech or the vocal part, and the rational part.

They hold that we see when the light between the visual organ and the object stretches in the form of a cone—this according to what Chrysippus says in the second book of his *Natural Philosophy*, as well as Apollodorus. The apex of the cone in the air is at the eye. The base is at the object seen. Therefore, the thing seen is reported to us by the medium of the air stretching out toward it, as if by a stick.

[158] We hear when the air between the sonant body and the organ of hearing suffers concussion, a vibration that spreads spherically and then forms waves and strikes upon the ears, just as the water in a reservoir forms wavy circles when a stone is thrown into it.

They say that sleep is caused by the slackening of the tension in our senses, which affects the leading part of the soul.

They believe that variations of the vital breath are responsible for the passions.

They say that seed or sperm is that which is capable of generating offspring like the parent. And that the human seed, which is emitted by a human parent in a moist vehicle, is mingled with parts of the soul, blended in the same ratio in which they are present in the parent. [159] In the second book of his *Natural Philosophy*, Chrysippus declares it to be in substance identical with vital breath, as is clear from seeds that are cast into the earth, which, if they are kept until they are old, they do not germinate, plainly because their power has evaporated. Sphaerus and his followers also hold that the seed is derived from the whole body. Anyway, every part of the body can be reproduced from it. They say that the female seed is sterile since it is, as Sphaerus says, without tension, scanty, and watery.

And the leading part is the soul's most dominant part, in which presentations and impulses arise, and from which rational speech comes.[7] It is in the heart.

[160] Such, then, are the Stoic teachings about nature.

NOTES

[1] Other manuscripts read "incorporeal."

[2] The basic meaning of *kosmos* (cosmos) is "order."

[3] The full text reads "perfect or intelligent in happiness" (see Diogenes Laertius, *Lives* 7.147). Some excise "intelligent" or "intellectual" (*noeros*—of or related to the intellect or mind, *nous*) as a later gloss (see Brad Inwood and Lloyd P. Gerson, *The Stoics Reader*, 55). If retained, the "intelligent" happiness would refer to the fact that God's happiness has to do with the intellect or mind; therefore, it is a rational rather than a merely emotional or passion-based happiness.

[4] "Father of all things" echoes a traditional Greek descriptive for Zeus, that Zeus, or God, is "the father of gods and men"—an epithet that goes back at least to Homer (late eight century BC).

[5] *Dia* and *Zēna* are both grammatical forms of the name "Zeus."

[6] On the nature and role of the demon or daemon (*daimōn*) and the hero (*hērōs*) in Greek history and literature, see Walter Burkert, *Greek Religion*, trans. John Raffan (Cambridge: Harvard University Press, 1985), 179-181, 328, 331-332 (for daemons) and 203-208 (for heroes).

[7] The "leading part" (*hēgemonikon*) of the soul is 'reason' or 'the reasoning power.' See Aetius 4.21 in Twelve of Part 4.

STOIC ETHICS
IN DIOGENES' *LIVES*

IN BRIEF: *Diogenes Laertius begins with a summary of the Stoic teaching about "impulse," which makes animals naturally pursue what is suitable. For humans, reason is added and exists for the skillful shaping of impulse. Next, he discusses the end or goal of human life, which is to live in harmony with nature in accord with reason and virtue. The virtuous life is the happy life. He goes on to present the Stoic teaching about the nature and types of virtue, including the primary virtues. He does the same for vice. A discussion of good things, bad things, and "things indifferent" follows, the latter being neither good nor bad. Good things are advantageous, beautiful, choice-worthy, and the like. Bad things are not. Some good things are related to the soul; some are externals. Some are ends; some are means to ends. Some are simple; some mixed. Virtue is an example of a good thing; vice of a bad thing; health and wealth of things indifferent. Still, of things indifferent, some are preferred and some are rejected or not preferred based on "value." Health and wealth are "things preferred," whereas disease and poverty are "things rejected." Next, Diogenes discusses duty or what is fitting before moving on to the eight parts of the soul and the soul's passions or emotions, including a discussion of the four bad passions (grief, fear, desire, pleasure) and the three good passions (joy, caution, willing). The chapter finishes with a description of the wise man, what he is and does.*

THE STOICS DIVIDE the ethical part of philosophy into the following topics: on impulse, on good things and bad things, on passions, on virtue, on the end or goal of life, on primary value and actions, on duties or what is fitting, and on exhortations or what encourages and on what discourages or hinders or prevents. This is how Chrysippus, Archedemus, Zeno of Tarsus, Apollodorus,

Diogenes, Antipater, Posidonius, and their followers divide the ethical part of philosophy. Zeno of Citium and Cleanthes, as might be expected from the original thinkers, treated the subject somewhat less elaborately. Nevertheless, along with ethics, they did subdivide both logic and physics.

[85] The Stoics say that an animal's first impulse is to self-preservation since nature endears the animal to itself from the beginning, as Chrysippus affirms in the first part of his work *On the Goal of Life*. There he says that the dearest thing to every animal is its own constitution and the awareness of this. For it is not natural for any animal to be alienated from itself—or even to be brought into such a state so that it is indifferent to itself, being neither alienated from nor friendly to itself. We must assert that nature has made the animal so that it is near and dear to itself. As such, it pushes away all that is harmful and pulls near all that is suitable and fitting.

The Stoics declare false the assertion—made by some—that the first urge or impulse of animals is directed toward pleasure. [86] By contrast they say that pleasure, if it is anything at all, is a byproduct that never comes until nature by itself has sought and taken those things suitable to the animal's constitution—a byproduct that is comparable to animals that have a cheerful expression and plants that are luxuriant or in full bloom.

The Stoics declare that nature originally made no difference between plants and animals. Nature regulates the life of plants without the use of impulse and sensation, just as certain plant-like processes go on in us. But for animals, impulse was added to this general rule of nature later on. Impulse makes animals pursue what is suitable. Nature's rule for animals is to follow the direction of impulse. Lastly, for those beings we call rational, the rational life correctly became the natural life when reason was given to them by means of a more perfect rule. Reason was added to shape impulse as a skilled craftsman.

[87] In his treatise *On the Nature of Man*, Zeno, for the reason given a moment ago, was the first to say that the end or goal of life is to live in agreement with nature, which is the same as living in accord with virtue since nature leads us toward virtue.[1] Cleanthes

says the same in his treatise *On Pleasure*, as do Posidonius and Hecaton in their works *On the Goal of Life*. Again, living in accord with
virtue is equivalent to living in accord with the experience of nature
as it actually happens—just as Chrysippus says in the first book of
his *On the Goal of Life*. For our individual natures are portions of the
whole of nature, which is to say the whole cosmos.

[88] This is why the goal of life is to live in conformity with nature—that is, with our own nature as well as with the nature of the
whole cosmos. Accordingly, one holds back from every action forbidden by the law common to all things—that is to say, the right
reason that pervades all things and is the same as Zeus, who leads
the administration of every existing thing. This very thing is the virtue of the happy man and the good flow of life, when all actions
promote the harmony of the divine power dwelling in each man
with the will of the administrator of the whole cosmos.

So then, Diogenes specifically declares that the goal of life is to
act with sound reason in the selection of those things that follow
nature. And Archedemus says that the goal is to live while carrying
out every duty, that is, whatever is appropriate.

[89] By the nature with which our life should conform, Chrysippus understands both common or universal nature and, more particularly, human nature. But Cleanthes takes the common or
universal nature alone as that with which we should conform, without adding the particular human portion of nature.

Virtue is a harmonious disposition, choiceworthy for its own
sake—not from fear or hope or any external motive. Happiness consists in virtue, which is the state of the soul that tends to make the
whole of life harmonious. And when a rational being is turned aside
or perverted, this is due to the persuasiveness of external pursuits or
sometimes to the influence of acquaintances, since the starting-points
offered by nature are incapable of turning aside or perversion.

[90] Virtue is in one sense the perfection of anything in general,
say of a statue. Virtue may be non-intellectual, such as health, or
intellectual, such as practical wisdom. Hecaton declares in the first
book of his *On the Virtues* that some virtues are knowledge and the-
ory-based—those that have a structure of theoretical principles,

such as practical wisdom and justice. Others are non-intellectual—
those that are regarded as coextensive and parallel with the former,
such as health and strength. For health follows and is coextensive
with the intellectual virtue of moderation just as strength is a result
of the building of an arch. [91] The latter are called non-intellectual
because they do not require the mind's assent. They come about
and occur even in base men—for example, health and courage.

In the first book of his treatise on *Ethics*, Posidonius declares that
the proof that virtue really exists is the fact that Socrates, Diogenes,
and Antisthenes, as well as their followers,[2] made moral progress.
And vice exists as the opposite of virtue.

In the first book of his work *On the Goal of Life*, Chrysippus says
that virtue can be taught. Cleanthes and Posidonius—in the *Exhortations*—and Hecaton declare the same. That virtue can be taught is
clear from the case of base men becoming good.

[92] Panaetius says that there are two kinds of virtue, theoretical
and practical virtue. Others say there are three kinds—logical, natural, and ethical. That said, the school of Posidonius recognizes four
kinds of virtue. And Cleanthes, Chrysippus, Antipater, and their
followers count more than four. As for Apollophanes, he talks
about one virtue alone, practical wisdom.

Among the virtues, some are primary, and some are subordinate
to these. The following are the primary virtues: practical wisdom,
courage, justice, and moderation. Specific virtues are magnanimity,
self-control, patient endurance, ready-mindedness, and good counsel.

Stoics define practical wisdom as the knowledge of good and
bad things, and what is neither. And courage is the knowledge of
what is choiceworthy and what one must be wary of and avoid, and
what is neither. [93] And justice . . .[3]

They define magnanimity as the knowledge or habit that makes
one superior to whatever commonly happens to both base and excellent men. Self-control is an unbeatable disposition relative to
those things that are in accord with right reason or a habit that is
never conquered by pleasure. Patient endurance is the knowledge
or habit that suggests what we must—and what we must not—
abide by and endure, and what is neither. Ready-mindedness is a

habit that discovers the appropriate thing to be done at any moment. Good counsel is the knowledge by which we see what to do and how to do it if we are to act in a useful and profitable manner.

Similarly, among the vices, some are primary, and some are subordinate. Folly, cowardice, injustice, and immoderation are primary, and lack of self-control, slow-mindedness, and bad counsel are subordinate. The vices are ignorance of those things of which the virtues are the knowledge.

[94] Generally speaking, good is that from which there is some advantage or benefit. More specifically, it is either what is the same as or not different from what is useful or beneficial or advantageous. Therefore, it follows that virtue itself, and whatever participates in virtue, is spoken of as good in three ways: one, as the source from which the benefit results; two, as that according to which the benefit results—for example, the action done according to virtue; and three, as that by the agency of which the benefit results—for example, the excellent man who participates in virtue.

"The fulfillment or perfection of a rational being *as* a rational being following nature" is another particular definition the Stoics give for the good. Virtue is such a perfection since acts done according to virtue and excellent men are participants in virtue, as are its accompanying byproducts, joy and merriment and like things.

[95] So it is with bad things. They are either vices such as folly, cowardice, injustice, and like things, or they are things that participate in vice, such as acts done in accord with vice and base men, as well as its accompanying byproducts, despair and anxiety and like things.

Again, of good things, some are related to the soul and some to external things, while some are neither related to the soul nor to externals. The goods related to the soul are the virtues and acts done according to virtue. External goods are things such as having an excellent homeland and an excellent friend and the happiness that comes from these. To be excellent and happy in oneself is the sort of good thing that is neither external nor related to the soul.

[96] Conversely, of bad things, some are related to the soul—the vices and actions done according to them. And some are external

things such as a foolish homeland and a foolish friend and the un-happiness of these. To be base and unhappy in oneself is the sort of bad thing that is neither external nor related to the soul.

Further, of good things, some have the nature of ends, some have the nature of means, while some are both ends and means. Accordingly, a friend and the benefits that come from him are the means to good things, whereas courage and highmindedness and freedom and merriment and freedom from pain and every act done according to virtue have the nature of ends.

[97] The virtues are goods that have both the nature of ends and means. Inasmuch as they produce happiness, they are means to good things. On the other hand, inasmuch as they are the fulfillment of happiness, being a portion of happiness itself, they are ends.

Similarly, of bad things, some have the nature of ends, some have the nature of means, while some are both. Your enemy and the harm that comes to you from him are means. Consternation and dejection and slavery and melancholy and depression and extreme grief and every act done according to vice have the nature of ends.

Vices have the nature of both ends and means. Whenever they produce unhappiness, they are means. But whenever they serve to make unhappiness complete, being a portion of unhappiness itself, they are ends.

[98] Again, of the goods related to the soul, some are habits, and some are dispositions, and some are neither habits nor dispositions. The virtues are dispositions, whereas practices are habits. Activities or operations are neither habits nor dispositions.

Generally speaking, there are some mixed goods such as the blessing of children and a good old age. But knowledge is a simple good. Moreover, some goods are permanent, such as the virtues, whereas others are not, such as joy and walking.

Every good is advantageous and binding and profitable and use-ful and serviceable and beautiful and beneficial and choiceworthy and just. [99] A good is advantageous because it brings about things that benefit us by their occurrence. It is binding because it causes unity where unity is required. It is profitable inasmuch as it repays all the care that is expended on it so that the return yields a balance of benefit. It is useful because it secures the use of a benefit. It is serviceable because the utility it provides is praiseworthy. It is beautiful because the good is symmetrical with its own use. It is beneficial because it benefits by means of its essential nature. It is choiceworthy because it is such that to choose it is reasonable. It is just because it is in harmony with the law, and it is the means by which partnerships and communities are produced.

[100] The Stoics say that the perfect good is beautiful or noble because it has in full all the factors required by nature or because it is perfectly symmetrical.

Of the beautiful or noble they say that there are four specific kinds—that which is just, courageous, ordered, and knowledgeable. For it is by means of these that one accomplishes beautiful or noble deeds. Analogously, of the ugly or base there are four specific kinds—that which is unjust, cowardly, disorderly, and foolish.[4]

The beautiful or noble uniquely means that good which renders those who possess it praiseworthy. Or it is a good worthy of praise. In another sense, it signifies that which is well-adapted for its own function. Otherwise, it is that which adorns, as when we say that the wise man alone is good and beautiful or noble.

[101] And the Stoics say that the only beautiful or noble thing is a good thing—this according to Hecaton in the third book of his treatise *On Goods*, and Chrysippus in his work *On the Beautiful*. But this is virtue and whatever participates in virtue, which is the same as saying that all that is good is beautiful or noble, or that the term "good" is equivalent to the term "beautiful" or "noble,"—which amounts to the same thing. For when it is good, it is beautiful or noble. But it is beautiful or noble. Therefore, it is good.

They hold that all good things are equal and that every good thing is choiceworthy in the highest degree and admits of no lowering or heightening of intensity.

Of existing things, the Stoics declare that some are good, some are bad, and some are neither. [102] Good things are the virtues, including practical wisdom, justice, courage, moderation, and the rest. Bad things are the opposite—folly, injustice, and the rest. Things that are neither are those things that neither benefit nor harm—things such as life, health, pleasure, beauty, strength, wealth, good reputation, and noble birth, as well as their opposites, death, disease, pain, ugliness, weakness, poverty, bad reputation, low birth, and the like—this according to Hecaton in the seventh book of his *On the Goal of Life*, and Apollodorus in his *Ethics*, and Chrysippus. These things[5] are not good things, but they are "things indifferent"—specifically, they are "things preferred."

[103] For just as being hot, rather than being cold, is the unique property a hot thing, so too is being beneficial, rather than being harmful, the unique property of a good thing. But wealth and health do no more benefit than harm; therefore, neither wealth nor health is a good thing. Moreover, they say that what can be used well and badly is not a good thing. But wealth and health can be used well and badly; therefore, neither wealth nor health is a good thing. Nevertheless, Posidonius maintains that these are also good things. Otherwise, Hecaton, in the ninth book of his treatise *On Goods*, and Chrysippus, in his work *On Pleasure*, declare that pleasure is not a good thing. They say this because some pleasures are shameful, and nothing shameful is a good thing. [104] To benefit is to move or to restrain oneself or something in accord with virtue. To harm is to move or to restrain oneself or something in accord with vice.

The Stoics say that the term "indifferent" has two meanings. For one, it denotes those things that contribute neither to happiness nor to unhappiness—things such as wealth, reputation, health, strength, and like things. It is possible to be happy apart from these things. It is the particular way that we employ these things that makes for happiness or unhappiness. Otherwise, something is indifferent if it neither excites impulse nor disgust for a thing—as with the fact that the number of hairs on your head is odd or even or whether you point or hold back your finger. By contrast, it was not in this latter sense that the former things mentioned above were called indifferent since those things do actually excite inclination or disgust for those things. [105] That is why of those things having to do with the first kind of indifference, some are chosen, and some are not chosen, whereas of the other things having to do with the second kind, there is an equal reason for choosing or avoiding them.

Regarding indifferent things, they say that some are preferred and some are not preferred—that is, they are rejected. Those things that have value are preferred, while those that do not have value are rejected.

They define value, firstly, as a contribution to a harmonious life. In this sense, every good has value. Secondly, value is some intermediary power or advantage that contributes toward living life in accord with nature. In other words, it is the assistance that wealth and health may offer in living life in accord with nature. Thirdly, value is the price set by an appraiser, as determined by his experience with the facts, as when an appraiser says that wheat is worth so much barley with a mule thrown in to make up the difference.

[106] So then, preferred things are those that have value. For example, among things of the soul, there are natural ability, skill, moral progress, and like things. Among bodily things, there are life, health, bodily strength, vigor, wholeness, beauty, and so on. Among external things, there are wealth, reputation, noble birth, and like things.

As for those things that are rejected, among things of the soul there are a lack of natural ability, a lack of skill, and like things. Among bodily things, there are death, disease, weakness, lethargy, disability, ugliness, and like things. Among external things, there are poverty, bad reputation, low birth, and like things.

Those things that are in neither category are neither preferred nor rejected.

[107] Yet again, of things preferred, some are preferred for their own sake, some for the sake of something else, and others are preferred both for their own sake and for the sake of something else. Those preferred for their own sake include natural ability, moral progress, and like things. Those preferred for the sake of something else include wealth, noble birth, and like things. Those preferred both for their own sake and for the sake of something else include strength, senses that work well, and wholeness.

Things are preferred for their own sake because they are in accord with nature. Things are preferred for the sake of something else because they produce more than a little of what is required or

useful. The same may be said to hold true for those things rejected—only the opposite.

Moving on, the Stoics say that duty—what is fitting or appropriate—is that which, when done, may be supported by a reasonable
account—for example, whatever is in conformity with living life.
This is something that applies both to plant and animal life. For one
may perceive, even with these, that which is fitting or appropriate.

[108] Zeno was the first to use the word *kathēkon* for "what is
fitting" or "what is appropriate." Etymologically, it is derived from
kata tinas hēkein, that is, "belonging to something or someone." It is
a fitting action or activity in relation to nature's arrangements.

Of actions done in relation to impulse, some are fitting, some are
not fitting, and some are neither fitting nor are they not fitting.
Those acts that are fitting are the ones that reason within us seizes
upon and chooses to do, such as honoring one's parents, brothers,
sisters, and homeland, and adapting oneself to and spending time
with one's friends. Those acts that are not fitting are the ones that
reason within us does not choose, such as neglecting one's parents,
ignoring one's brothers and sisters, failing to be agreeable and
available to one's friends, despising one's homeland, and like
things. [109] Those acts that are neither fitting nor not fitting are the
ones that reason neither chooses to do nor forbids, such as picking
up a twig, holding a writing utensil or a scraper, and like things.

Again, some things are fitting activities or duties regardless of
the circumstances, while others depend on the circumstances.
Those fitting activities that do not depend on the circumstances include taking care of one's health and one's sense organs and the
like. Those that depend on circumstances include, for example,
maiming oneself and sacrificing or giving away one's property.[6]
The same holds analogously for those acts that are not fitting.

Once again, of those acts that are fitting, some are always fitting
and some are not always fitting. It is always fitting to live in accord
with virtue. But asking and answering questions and walking
around and the like are not always fitting or appropriate. The same
explanation goes for acts that are not fitting. [110] There is also a
certain kind of fitting activity among intermediate activities. For

example, obedience is fitting for boys when they are with those in charge of them.

Moving on, the Stoics say the soul has eight parts. There are the five sense faculties, the vocal part, the intellectual part, which is the intellect itself, and the productive part.

From falsehood or error there arises a distortion or perversion, which extends throughout the intellect. And from this distortion grow many passions or emotions, which are responsible for much confusion and instability.[7]

According to Zeno, a passion or an emotion is itself a motion or an excessive impulse of the soul that is contrary to reason and nature.

According to Hecaton in the second book of his work *On the Passions*, and Zeno in his own treatise *On the Passions*, there are four major kinds of passions: grief, fear, desire, and pleasure.[8]

[111] The Stoics think that the passions are decisions or judgements—this according to what Chrysippus says in *On the Passions*. Avarice, for example, is the assumption that money is noble. It is similar with drunkenness and immoderation and the other passions.

Grief or pain is a contraction of the soul contrary to reason. Specific kinds of grief are pity, envy, jealousy, rivalry, heaviness, annoyance, distress, anguish, and confusion. Pity is the pain felt at undeserved suffering. Envy is the pain felt when one sees the goods of other people. Jealousy is the pain felt when someone has something that one desires. Rivalry is the pain felt when someone possesses what one has. [112] Heaviness is a pain that weighs us down. Annoyance is a pain that confines us and gives us a sense of a lack of room. Distress is a pain brought on by anxious rumination that lasts and increases. Anguish is a difficult pain. Confusion is an irrational pain of the mind that wears one out and prevents one from viewing the situation as a whole.

Fear is the expectation of something bad or unfortunate. The following come under fear: terror, shame, hesitation, consternation, panic, and mental agony. Terror is a fear that produces fright. Shame is the fear of a bad reputation. Hesitation is the fear that one will have to act. Consternation is fear due to a presentation of some unusual occurrence. [113] Panic is fear after a rush of sound. Mental agony is fear of some uncertain event.

Desire or longing is an appetite that is contrary to reason. The following are arranged under desire: want or lacking, hatred, love of strife, anger, erotic love or desire, wrath, and spiritedness. The state of want or lacking is the failure of desire, when desire does not reach its object but is nevertheless attracted to it in vain, stretching out to it. Hatred is the growing and lasting desire for things to go badly for someone. Love of strife is desire connected with partisanship or a philosophical school. Anger is the desire for revenge against the one who appears to have done one an undeserved injury. Erotic love or desire is a desire that is not present in excellent men. It is the effort to win affection due to the visible presence of beauty. [114] Wrath is a longstanding and vengeful anger, ever-waiting for its chance to act, as is illustrated by the lines, "Even if he swallows down his anger for one day, he will nevertheless hold on to his wrath for the future, until it is satisfied."[9] Spiritedness is the first stirring of anger.

Pleasure is an elation that is contrary to reason that arises from getting and amassing what seems to be choiceworthy. The following are arranged under pleasure: enchantment, joy in the misfortune of others, delight, and relaxation. Enchantment is pleasure that charms the ear, casting a spell over it, as it were. Joy in the misfortune of others is the pleasure that comes when bad things happen to other people. Delight is, as it were, a turning of the soul. It is a certain stimulus for the soul toward loosening or letting go. And relaxation is the breaking down of virtue.

[115] Moreover, just as we say that there are certain bodily illnesses or infirmities, for example, gout and arthritic disorders, so also are there soul illnesses, such as love of reputation and love of pleasure, and similar things. By illness or infirmity is meant a disease accompanied by weakness. By disease is meant an excessive notion about something that seems choiceworthy. And just as there is a tendency toward certain maladies in the body, such as the buildup of mucus and diarrhea, so with the soul there is a tendency to enviousness, pitifulness, quarrelsomeness, and similar things.

[116] The Stoics say that there are three good passions: joy, caution, and willing. Joy, the opposite of pleasure, is sensible elation, that is,

elation backed by good reason. Caution, that is, discretion or circumspection, is the opposite of fear. It is avoidance backed by good reason, or the reasonable turning of one's course. Even though the wise man will never fear anything, he will nevertheless act with caution. And they say that willing is the opposite of desire insofar as willing is reasonable appetite, that is, appetite backed by good reason.

And so, just as there are certain passions that fall under the primary passions, so also are there certain good passions that fall under the primary good passions. Under willing they arrange goodwill, kindliness, being welcoming, and brotherly love. Under caution there are respect or modesty and religious purity. Under joy there are gladness, merriment, and cheerfulness.

[117] They say that the wise man is without passion because he has no such propensities. They add that, in another sense, the same term "without passion" is applied to the base man in that he is unyielding and relentless. Furthermore, the wise man is not puffed up with pride since the esteem of others and a bad reputation are equal to him. That said, he is not the only one who is not puffed up with pride. There is also the base man who behaves randomly, without any purpose. They also say that every excellent man is austere since he does not busy himself with pleasure nor does he tolerate the pleasure-seeking activities of others. They apply the term austere or harsh to others in the sense that one says that wine is harsh when it is used as a medicine rather than for drinking.

[118] Wise men are genuinely earnest for and attentive to their own improvement, employing a manner of life that hides the base away while making what good there is in things appear. And they are not fake or phony. Rather, they have stripped themselves of all affectation in both voice and appearance. And they refrain from meddling in politics, declining to do anything except for what is fitting. And they will drink wine, but they will not get drunk. Nor will they go crazy. To be sure, strange presentations will occur at times, those that are due to melancholy or delirium—not according to the principle of what is choiceworthy but contrary to nature. Nor will the wise man feel grief because grief is an irrational contraction of the soul as Apollodorus declares in his *Ethics*.

[119] Wise men are godly or divine, for they have something like a God within them. But the base man is godless. The term "godless" has two senses: one is opposite of the meaning of "godly." The other disregards the divine. The latter sense does not apply to every base man.

Wise men are also religious. They are experienced with the laws and customs having to do with the gods—and piety is the knowledge of how to serve the gods. Furthermore, they will sacrifice to the gods and keep themselves pure since they will avoid all acts that are a failure before the gods. And the gods admire them since they are holy and just relative to the divine.

Only wise men are priests since they have examined matters having to do with sacrifices, temple construction, purifications, and other things having to do with the gods.

[120] The Stoics also hold that the wise man will honor and do homage to his parents and brothers and sisters in the second place after the gods. They further declare that parental affection for children is natural for the wise but not for the base.

The Stoics hold that all failures or sins[10] are equal—this according to what Chrysippus says in the fourth book of his *Ethical Inquiries*, as well as Persaeus and Zeno. For if one truth is not more true than another truth, then neither is one falsehood more false than another falsehood. In the same way, one deception is not more deceptive than another deception, nor is one failure or sin more of a failure or more sinful than another failure or sin. For the man who is one hundred stadia from Canopus and the man who is only one stadium away are equally not in Canopus.[11] In this way, the man who commits the greater and the one who commits the smaller sin are equally behaving incorrectly. [121] Nevertheless, Heraclides of Tarsus, the follower of Antipater of Tarsus, and Athenodorus both assert that failures or sins are not equal.

The Stoics say that the wise man will participate in politics if nothing prevents him—so declares Chrysippus in the first book of his work *On Various Types of Life*. He will do this to restrain vice and promote virtue.

And he will marry, as Zeno says in his *Republic*. And he will have children.

Moreover, they say that the wise man will never form mere opinions—that is, he will never assent to anything that is false.

They say that the wise man will live like a Cynic since Cynicism is the shortest road to virtue, as Apollodorus says in his *Ethics*.[12]

Depending on the circumstances, the wise man will eat human flesh.

The wise man alone is free, and base men are slaves—for freedom is independent action, whereas slavery is the loss of independent action. [122] That said, there is another form of slavery that consists in submission, and a third which consists in both possession by and submission to another. Being a despot or master is the opposite—and this is also base.

Wise men are not only free, but they are also kings. This is so since kingship is a kind of absolute freedom that no one but the wise can maintain. That is what Chrysippus says in his treatise vindicating Zeno's use of terminology. For he says that the ruler should know about good and bad things, and that no base man understands these things. Similarly, they alone are fit to be magistrates, judges, or orators, whereas among the base there is not one who is qualified in this way.

Furthermore, the wise are without fault or sin and are not liable to sin or error. [123] And they are harmless since they do not harm others or themselves. At the same time, they are not full of pity and make no allowance for anyone. They never relax the penalties fixed by the laws since indulgence and pity and even equitable consideration are the signs of a weak soul that substitutes kindness for chastisement. Nor do they suppose that such punishments are too severe.

Again, they say that the wise man is never astonished by any of the things that appear extraordinary—things such as Charon's caverns and tidal currents and hot springs and fiery eruptions.

Neither will the wise and excellent man live in solitude since he is naturally made for a community and action.

Indeed, the wise man will submit to training or exercise in order to build up his body's power to endure.

[124] The Stoics say that the wise man will offer prayers and ask for good things from the gods—this according to what Posidonius

says in the first book of his treatise *On What is Fitting,* and Hecaton in his third book *On Paradoxes.*

They say that friendship only exists between excellent men because of their similarity. And by friendship they mean the common use of all that has to do with life, where we treat our friends as ourselves. They say that a friend is choiceworthy for his own sake and that it is a good thing to have many friends. But among the base, there is no such thing as friendship. And so, no base man has a friend.

They also hold that the foolish are all mad. They are not wise. Rather, the source of all they do is their madness, which is the same as their folly.

[125] The wise man does everything well in the same way that we say Ismenias plays everything well on the flute. Moreover, everything belongs to the wise. For the law, they say, has given them complete authority over everything. It is true that certain things are said to belong to the base, just as that which has been dishonestly acquired may be said, in one sense, to belong to the state, and in another sense to those who are using it.

The Stoics hold that the virtues involve one another. The man who has one virtue has them all inasmuch as the virtues have common principles—this according to what Chrysippus declares in the first book of his work *On Virtues,* and Apollodorus in his *Natural Philosophy According to the Early Stoics,* and Hecaton in the third book of his treatise *On Virtues.* [126] For he who is virtuous is able to perceive and practice what is to be done. And what is to be done is choiceworthy. And what is to be done is also what is to be endured and what one must stay with. And it is what is justly assigned. Consequently, if one does some things by choice, and some with endurance, and some by means of just assignment, and some by staying power, then he is wise and courageous and just and moderate.

Each of the virtues has a particular subject with which it is concerned. For example, courage is concerned with things that must be endured. Practical wisdom with what is to be done, and what is not to be done, and what is neither. Similarly, each of the other virtues has to do with their own proper things.

Good counsel and understanding follow upon practical wisdom. And good order or discipline and propriety or decorum follow upon moderation. And equality and fair-mindedness upon justice. And unshakeable determination and vigor upon courage.

[127] The Stoic belief is that there is no middle ground between virtue and vice, whereas the Peripatetics say that there is the middle ground of moral progress. The Stoics declare that just as a stick must be either straight or crooked, so a man must either be just or unjust. Neither are there degrees of justice and injustice. The same is the case for the other virtues.

Moreover, while Chrysippus holds that virtue can be lost, Cleanthes maintains that it cannot be lost. Chrysippus says that it can be lost through drunkenness and melancholy. Cleanthes says it cannot be lost because of the certainty of our perceptions.

Virtue is choiceworthy in itself and for its own sake. We are, anyway, ashamed when we do things badly. It is as though we know that the beautiful or noble alone is good.

Moreover, virtue is sufficient in itself for happiness—this according to what Zeno says, as well as Chrysippus in the first book of his treatise *On Virtues*, and Hecaton in the second book of his treatise *On Goods*. [128] "For," Zeno says, "if magnanimity is sufficient for making one superior to all things, and if magnanimity is a part of virtue, then virtue is sufficient for happiness, looking down on those things that seem troublesome." Both Panaetius and Posidonius, however, deny that virtue is sufficient for happiness. Rather, they say that health is necessary as well as some means of living and strength. And, in their view, virtue is exercised in everything—as Cleanthes and his followers declare. For virtue can never be lost since the excellent man is always utilizing a soul that is in perfect condition.

They say that justice exists by nature and not by convention, just as the law and right reason do—this according to what Chrysippus says in his work *On the Beautiful*.[13]

[129] The Stoics do not believe that disagreement among the philosophers is any reason for abandoning the study of philosophy since given this point one would forsake life altogether—this according to what Posidonius says in his *Exhortations*.

Chrysippus declares that the ordinary or general Greek education is useful.

Again, it is the Stoic belief that there is no justice between us human beings and other animals because they are so unlike us—this according to what Chrysippus says in the first book of his treatise *On Justice*, and Posidonius in the first book of his *On What is Fitting*.

Moreover, the Stoics say that the wise man will be in love with young men who, by their countenance, show a natural endowment for virtue—this according to what Zeno says in his *Republic*, Chrysippus in book one of his work *On Modes of Life*, and Apollodorus in his *Ethics*.

[130] Erotic love or desire is the effort to win affection due to the visible presence of beauty. It is not about sex, but friendship. Anyway, even though Thrasonides had the one he loved in his power, he did not touch her because she hated him. So then, as Chrysippus says in his treatise *On Love*, erotic love or desire is for affectionate friendship. And it is not sent by the gods. And beauty they describe as the bloom or flower of virtue.

Of the three kinds of life—the speculative or contemplative, the practical or active, and the logical or rational—they declare that we should choose the third life. For the rational animal was designedly brought into being by nature for contemplation and action.

The Stoics declare that the wise man will make his own exit from life for good reason—for the sake of his homeland or his friends or if he is experiencing unyielding pain or multiple disabilities or incurable disease.

[131] It is also their belief that there should be a community of wives among the wise with a free choice of partners, as Zeno says in his *Republic*, and Chrysippus in his treatise *On Government*—as well as Diogenes the Cynic and Plato.[14] Under these circumstances, we will equally feel paternal affection for all the resulting children. Moreover, the jealousies arising from adultery will be removed.

They hold that the best form of government is a mixture of democracy and monarchy and aristocracy.

Such, then, are the things they say in their ethical teachings—with much more as well, along with suitable explanations and proofs. Nevertheless, may these be enough for a general statement of them in summary and elementary form.

Notes

¹ Virtue (*aretē*), in the broadest sense, means excellence. In *Lives* 7.90, Diogenes Laertius explains that "virtue is in one sense the perfection of anything in general." To learn more about what the ancient Greeks thought and said about *aretē*, see the Cave's *Aretē: Excellence or Virtue*.

² Antisthenes of Athens and Diogenes of Sinope and "their followers" were Cynic philosophers. To learn more about the ancient Cynics and Cynicism, that which inspired the early Stoics and Stoicism, see the Cave's *The Best of the Cynics: The Lives, Writings & Teachings of the Ancient Cynics*.

³ There is a lacuna or gap here in the text. Johannes Stobaeus reports that Zeno defined justice as "knowledge of the distribution of valuable things to each man" (*Anthology* 2.5). See Thirteen of Part 4.

⁴ Note that the one word *kalos*, a multivalent word, is behind "beautiful or noble." Similarly, *aischros* is behind "ugly or base."

⁵ Diogenes Laertius means the first part of the list, "life, health, pleasure, beauty, strength, wealth, good reputation, and noble birth."

⁶ "Maiming oneself" may sound like an odd example. But there are several instances from ancient history in which a man dutifully mains himself — to infiltrate a city, for example. See Herodotus, *Histories* 3.153-160.

⁷ One word (*pathos*) is behind "passion or emotion" or "passions or emotions." Both are sometimes given in order to offer a broader range of meaning. Otherwise, where you see "passion" or "passions" alone, understand that the words "emotion" or "emotions" are implied.

⁸ For a chart of the passions, including Greek terms used for each, see "The Passions" in "Other Matters of Interest Related to the Early Stoics." Grief may also be given as "pain," as in "pain of the mind." According to Cicero's logic (see *Tusculan Disputations* 4.11 below in Ten of Part 3), grief or pain is paired with pleasure, which Cicero prefers to call "delight," in that each is the experience of a present (imagined) evil or good, whereas fear and desire is the experience of fearing or desiring a future (imagined) evil or good.

⁹ See Homer, *Iliad* 1.81-82.

¹⁰ The one word *hamartēma* is behind "failure or sin."

¹¹ The stadium (*stadion*) or stade is about 600 feet.

¹² To read the late Stoic Epictetus' discourse (3.22) on the true nature of the Cynic way of life, see Fourteen of the Cave's *The Best of the Cynics: The Lives, Writings & Teachings of the Ancient Cynics*.

¹³ The Stoic position is in contrast to that of Epicurus, who said, "There is no such thing as justice in itself. Rather, justice is an agreement neither to harm

nor be harmed that is made when men gather together from time to time in various places." See Epicurus, *Principal Teachings* 33, which may be found in the Cave's *The Best of Epicurus: The Life, Writings & Teachings of Epicurus the Greek Philosopher*.

[14] See Diogenes Laertius, *Lives* 6.72, where he reports that "Diogenes [the Cynic] argued that women should be held in common. . . . For this reason, he also held that sons should be held in common." The passage may be found in Five of the Cave's *The Best of the Cynics: The Lives, Writings & Teachings of the Ancient Cynics*. As for Plato (or Socrates), see the *Republic*, 5.449 ff.

PART 2

The Lives & Sayings of the Early Stoics
in Diogenes Laertius' *Lives*

FOUR

ZENO OF CITIUM
IN DIOGENES' *LIVES*

IN BRIEF PART 1: *Diogenes Laertius begins with Zeno's parents, place of birth, and physical description. Next, he narrates how Zeno came to read ancient literature, study and practice philosophy with the Cynic philosopher Crates of Thebes, and later on with other philosophers (Stilpon, Xenocrates, Polemon, among others). He then moves on to Zeno's lectures, the founding of the Stoic school, and a list of his writings. The first part finishes with a brief sketch of Zeno's students, including his "most notable" students Persaeus of Citium, Ariston of Chios, Herillus of Carthage, Dionysius of Heraclea, Cleanthes of Assos, and Sphaerus of Bosporus, as well as a few other students.*

PART 1: EARLY LIFE, EDUCATION, SCHOOL & WRITINGS[1]

ZENO, THE SON of Mnaseas, or the son of Demeas, was a citizen of Citium in Cyprus, a Greek city that had received Phoenician settlers.

In his book *On Lives*, Timotheus of Athens says that Zeno had a slightly bent neck. And Apollonius of Tyre says that he was lean, fairly tall, and dark-skinned—hence, someone called him an Egyptian vine branch, according to what Chrysippus says in the first book of his *Proverbs*. He had fat, flabby, and weak legs. For this reason, Persaeus, in his *Convivial Reminiscences*, says that he declined most invitations to dinner. They say that he was fond of eating green figs and of basking in the sun. . . .

[12] Antigonus of Carystus[2] tells us that Zeno himself never denied that he was a citizen of Citium. For when he was one of those who contributed to the restoration of the baths, and his name was

inscribed upon the pillar as "Zeno the Philosopher," he requested that the words "of Citium" should be added.

Zeno's Turn to Literature & Philosophy

[2] As stated before, Zeno was a student of Crates. Next they say he attended the lectures of Stilpon and Xenocrates for ten years, as Timocrates says in his *Dion*, as well as Polemon.[3]

Hecaton, and Apollonius of Tyre in his first book *On Zeno*, state that Zeno consulted the oracle to know what he should do in order to live the best life. The god's reply was that Zeno would live the best life if he made contact with the dead. Perceiving what this meant, he studied the works of the ancients.

Zeno came across Crates in this way. Zeno was shipwrecked on a voyage from Phoenicia to Piraeus with a cargo of purple dye. He went up to and entered into Athens and sat down in a bookseller's shop. He was then thirty years old. As he went on reading the second book of Xenophon's *Memorabilia*, he was so delighted that he inquired where he could find such men—that is, men like Socrates.

[3] Crates passed by right then, just at the right time. The bookseller pointed to him and said, "Follow that man."

From that day on, Zeno became Crates' student. And though he was in other ways very energetic in his approach to philosophy, he was nevertheless too full of shame for Cynic shamelessness.[4] Therefore, Crates, desiring to cure the defect in him, gave him an earthen pot full of lentil soup to carry through the Ceramicus. When Crates saw that Zeno was ashamed and tried to hide the pot of soup, he broke the pot with a blow of his staff. As Zeno fled with the lentil soup flowing down his legs, Crates said, "Why do you flee, my little Phoenician? You have suffered nothing terrible!"

[4] For a time, then, Zeno listened to and followed Crates. . . . But in the end, he left Crates, and he followed the men mentioned above for twenty years.

Consequently, he is reported to have said, "I made a prosperous voyage when I shipwrecked." Others say that he made this remark in reference to his time with Crates. [5] A different version of the story is that he was staying in Athens when he heard that his ship was wrecked, and so he said, "Fortune does well in driving us to philosophy." Still, some say that he disposed of his cargo in Athens before turning his attention to philosophy. . . .

[15] Zeno's inclination was toward searching and inquiry. He was precise in everything. . . .

[16] Zeno used to dispute very carefully with Philo the dialectician and studied with him. For this reason, Zeno, who was the younger man, admired Philo no less than his teacher Diodorus. . . .

[31] In his work *Men of the Same Name*, Demetrius of Magnesia[5] says that his father, Mnaseas, often went to Athens as a merchant and carried back many books about Socrates for Zeno while he was yet a boy. [32] As a result, Zeno had been well-trained in his homeland. And so he came to Athens and encountered Crates.

Zeno's Lectures & School

[5] Zeno used to arrange his arguments and deliver his lectures while walking back and forth in the painted colonnade or *stoa*, which is also called the colonnade of Peisianax, even though it received its name "painted" because of the painting of Polygnotus. He walked this way back and forth because he wanted to keep the spot free from people standing around. It was the same spot where 1,400 citizens had been put to death in the time of the Thirty Tyrants.

Here, then, people came out to listen to Zeno. For this reason, they were called Stoics, after the painted stoa. And his followers were at the same time given the same name, those who had formerly been known as Zenonians—this according to what Epicurus says in his letters. And yet, according to Eratosthenes[6] in his eighth book *On the Old Comedy*, the poets who spent all their time in the colonnade were first called Stoics. And they made the name still more famous.

Zeno's Writings

[4] Aside from his *Republic*, Zeno wrote the following works: *On Life According to Nature*; *On Impulse* or *On Human Nature*; *On the*

Passions; On Duties or *On What is Fitting; On Law; On Greek Education; On Vision; On the Whole Cosmos; On Signs; Pythagorean Questions; Universals; On Varieties of Style; Homeric Problems*—in five
books; *On the Reading of Poetry.*

These are also by him: *Art* or *Skill;* also, *Solutions;* also, *Refuta-
tions*—in two books; *Recollections of Crates; Ethics.*

This is a list of his writings.

Zeno's Students

[36] Of the many students of Zeno, the following are the most notable. There is Persaeus of Citium, the son of Demetrius. Some say he
was Zeno's friend, but others say that he was a household slave,
one of those sent by Antigonus to Zeno to act as his scribe. He had
taken care of Antigonus' son Halcyoneus. And once, when Antigonus wanted to test Persaeus, he caused some false news to be
brought to him that his estate had been ravaged by the enemy. And
when Persaeus appeared sad to hear this, Antigonus said, "Do you
see that wealth is not a matter of indifference?"

The following works are by Persaeus: *On Kingship; The Spartan
Constitution; On Marriage; On Impiety; Thyestes; On Desire* or *On Love;
Exhortations; Studies; Anecdotes and Sayings*—in four books; *Memora-
bilia;* a seven book reply to Plato's *Laws.*

[37] Another notable student is Ariston of Chios, Miltiades' son,
who introduced the teaching of "the indifferent."

Herillus of Carthage said that knowledge is the goal of life.

Then there is Dionysius, who changed the goal to pleasure. He
did this because of the severity of his ophthalmia. He no longer had
the nerve to call physical suffering something indifferent. He was
from Heraclea.

There are also Sphaerus of Bosporus and Cleanthes of Assos, the
son of Phanias. Cleanthes was Zeno's successor in the school. Zeno
used to compare him to hard waxen tablets that are difficult to write
on but retain the characters written on them. Sphaerus also became
Cleanthes' student after Zeno's death. We will say something about
him in the *Life of Cleanthes.*

[38] Moreover, according to Hippobotus,[7] the following were students of Zeno: Philonides of Thebes, Callipus of Corinth, Posidonius of Alexandria, Athenodorus of Soli, and Zeno of Sidon.

IN BRIEF PART 2: *Diogenes Laertius presents a string of stories about Zeno. In them we discover what Zeno was like — that he was concise, frugal, content with little, austere, capable of endurance, self-controlled, accommodating though somewhat touchy, observant, clever, eager to learn, high-minded, earnest, moralistic, straightforward, and, we might say, dry witted. Though some of them do not, many of the stories imply or explicitly include a moral point — that, for instance, it is useful to share and listen; that it is beneficial to be silent, wise, and open to good advice rather than being too proud or conceited; that being prepared, impartial, appropriate, dutiful, patient, and manly are good qualities to have.*

PART 2: ANECDOTES & SAYINGS[8]

Zeno made a hollow lid for an oil flask and used to carry money around in it so that there might be a provision ready at hand for the necessities of his teacher Crates.

[13] They say that he had more than a thousand talents when he came to Greece, and that he lent out the money secured with the cargo of a ship.

Zeno used to eat small loaves of bread with honey and drink a small amount of fragrant wine. He rarely employed young male servants. In fact, once or twice he had a young girl wait on him so that he would not appear to be a misogynist.

He shared the same house with Persaeus. And when the latter brought in a little flute player to him, he immediately led the girl straight back to Persaeus.

They say that Zeno was very accommodating — so much so that king Antigonus often broke in on him with a noisy party. Once, he took him along with other revelers to the harp player Aristocles. Nevertheless, in a little while Zeno escaped them.

[14] They say that he disliked being brought too near to people. Accordingly, he would take the end seat of a couch to avoid at least one

half of such an annoyance. Neither would he walk around with more than two or three people. And he would occasionally ask bystanders for a few copper coins so that, for fear of being asked to give, they would stop mobbing him—this according to what Cleanthes says in his work *On Bronze*. When several people stood around him in the colonnade, he pointed to the wooden railing, which surrounded the altar at the top, and said, "This was once open to all. But because it was found to be a hindrance, it was railed off. So then, if you will take yourselves out of the way, you will be much less annoying to us." . . .

[16] Zeno himself was sour with a frowning face. He was very frugal, too, practicing at times a stinginess unworthy of a Greek on the pretext of good stewardship.

If he reproved anyone, he would do it concisely and without an effusion of words—doing so, as it were, at as distance. I mean, for example, what he said to the pretty boy who embellished his face to show it off. [17] When he was slowly making his way across a gutter, Zeno said, "He looks askance at the mud with good reason, for he cannot see his face in it."

When a certain Cynic man declared that he had no oil in his oil-flask and asked Zeno for some, he refused to give him any. However, as the man went away, Zeno urged him to consider which of the two was the more shameless.

Zeno was very much in love with Chremonides. Once, when he and Cleanthes were both sitting by him, Zeno rose up. Astonished by this, Cleanthes said, "I hear from good physicians that the best medicine for inflammation is quiet and rest."

There were once two men reclining next to each other over cups of wine. The one who was sitting next to Zeno kicked the other man. So Zeno himself kicked the man with his knee. When the man turned around, Zeno asked, "How do you think your neighbor liked what you did to him?"

[18] To a lover of boys, Zeno said, "Just as teachers lose their mind by spending all their time with boys, so it is with people like you."

He used to say that refined and precise words were like coins struck by Alexander: they were beautiful in appearance and well-rounded like the coins but no better because of this. As for the opposite kind of words, he would compare them to the Attic tetradrachm, which, though struck carelessly and awkwardly, nevertheless outweighed the elaborate speech.

When his student Ariston discoursed at length in an uninspired manner, sometimes in a headstrong and overly confident manner, Zeno said, "Your father must have been drunk when he begot you." Therefore, he would call him a babbler since he himself was very concise in his speech.

[19] There was a glutton who was so greedy that he left nothing for his table companions. When a large fish was served, Zeno took it up as if he were going to eat the whole thing. When the other man looked at him, he said, "What do you suppose those who live with you feel every day if you can't, just once, put up with my gluttony?"

Once a youth was asking him questions with a curiosity unsuited to his age. Consequently, Zeno led the youth to a mirror, urged him to look into it, and asked him whether such questions appeared suitable to the face he saw there.

A man said that he did not in general agree with Antisthenes. So Zeno produced Antisthenes' essay on Sophocles and asked him if he thought it was at all noble. The man said he didn't know. "Then are you not ashamed," he said, "to pick out and mention anything wrong said by Antisthenes, while you suppress the good things without giving them any thought?"

[20] When someone said that he thought the petty speeches of the philosophers seemed small, Zeno said, "You're right. To be sure, the very syllables should be short, if possible."

Speaking about Polemon, someone said that his lecture was different from the topic he had announced. Frowning, Zeno said, "At what price would have you been content with what was offered?"

Zeno said that we should be earnest when conversing, and, like actors, we should have a loud voice and great strength. Nevertheless, we should not open the mouth too wide. That is what a senseless chatterbox does.

He used to say that there was no need for those who spoke well to leave those listening space to look around them as good workmen do who want to have their work seen. On the contrary, those who are listening should be so absorbed in the speaking itself as to have no time even to take notes.

[21] Once, when a young man was talking a lot, Zeno said, "Your ears have slipped down and merged with your tongue."

To the handsome youth who said that it seemed to him that a wise man would not fall in love, Zeno replied, "In that case, there will be no one more miserable than you handsome fellows."

About philosophers, Zeno used to say that most were unwise about many things, and ignorant about small and chance things.

And he used to cite the sayings of Caphisius, who, when one of his students was attempting to blow the flute with great gusto, gave the student a slap and told him that to play well does not depend on volume, though playing loudly may follow upon playing well.

And to a youth who was arguing in too bold a manner, he said, "I would rather not tell you, young man, what I am thinking."

[22] A Rhodian man, who was handsome and wealthy, but nothing more, insisted on joining his class. But so unwelcome was the student that Zeno first of all made him sit on benches that were dusty so that his cloak would be covered with dust. Then he consigned him to the place where the beggars sat so that he would have to rub shoulders with their rags. Finally, the young man went away. Zeno declared that nothing was more unbecoming than vanity, particularly in the young.

Zeno used to say that it was not the words and expressions that we ought to remember, but we should engage our mind in arranging to our advantage what we hear, instead of, as it were, tasting a well-cooked dish or a well-dressed meal.

He said that the young should behave with perfect propriety in the way they walk and carry themselves and dress. Accordingly, he used to quote the lines of Euripides about Capaneus: "Though he was happy in riches, he had no more pride than a poor man."[9]

[23] Zeno would say that if we want to master the sciences, there is nothing as fatal as supposition or self-conceit. Further, there is nothing we lack as much as time.

To the question, "Who is a friend?" Zeno's answer was, "Another self."

They say that Zeno was once chastising a slave for stealing. When the latter said that he was fated to steal, Zeno replied, "Yes, and you were also fated to receive a beating."

Zeno called beauty the bloom of moderation. According to others, he said that moderation was the bloom of beauty.

Once, when he saw the slave of one of his acquaintances marked with the signs of a beating, Zeno said, "I see the imprints of your anger."

To a man who was drenched with perfume, he said, "Who is this that smells like a woman?"

When Diogenes Metathemenus asked him why he was the only student he did not correct, Zeno said, "Because I do not trust you."

To a young man who was talking nonsense, Zeno said, "The reason why we have two ears and only one mouth is so that we may listen more and talk less."

[24] Zeno was once reclining in silence at a drinking party. When he was asked the reason, he told his critic to carry word to the king that there was one present who knew how to hold his tongue. Now those who inquired of him were ambassadors of Ptolemy. They wanted to know what message they should take back from him to the king.

When Zeno was asked how he felt when people abused him, he replied, "As an ambassador feels when he is sent away without an answer."

Apollonius of Tyre tells us how, when Crates grabbed Zeno by the cloak to drag him from Stilpon, Zeno said, "The right way to seize a philosopher, Crates, is by the ears. So then persuade me and drag me off by them. But if you use violence, my body will be with you, but my mind will be with Stilpon."

[25] According to Hippobotus, Zeno spent time with Diodorus, studying dialectic with him. And when he was already making progress, he would enter Polemon's school because of his freedom from vanity. Consequently, Polemon reportedly said to him, "I'm not unaware, Zeno, that you slip in through the garden door and steal my teachings, clothing them as a Phoenician."[10]

A dialectician once showed Zeno seven logical forms concerned with the sophism known as "The Reaper," and Zeno asked him how much he wanted for them. When he was told a hundred drach-mas, Zeno promptly paid two hundred. That's how far he would go to satisfy his love of learning.

They say that Zeno was the first one to use the term "duty" [*kathēkon*] and that he wrote a treatise on the topic.

It is also said that he altered Hesiod's lines in this way: "Best of all is that man who is won over by good advice. And noble too is that one who thinks about everything himself."[11] [26] The reason he gave for this alteration was this: the man who is capable of giving a proper hearing to what is said and profiting by it is superior to him who understands everything by himself. This is so because the one has understanding alone, whereas in obeying good advice, the other has added doing or acting to his understanding.

When Zeno was asked why he relaxed at a drinking party even though he was usually so austere, he said, "Lupin beans are also bitter. But when they are soaked, they become sweet." In the second book of his *Anecdotes and Sayings*, Hecaton says that Zeno freely indulged at such gatherings.

Zeno would say that it is better to trip with the feet than with the tongue.

He would say that getting well happens little by little but that well-being is nevertheless no small thing. (Others attribute this to Socrates.)

[27] Zeno was most capable of endurance and very frugal. His food required no fire, and his threadbare cloak was thin, so that it was said of him: "Neither the cold of winter, nor the endless rain, nor the flame of the sun, nor dread disease, nor the passion urged at a festival of the people conquers him. But unwearied and unyielding, he clings to his studies day and night."

Moreover, the comic poets, without intending it, praise him by means of their jokes. In this way, Philemon declares in his drama the *Philosophers*, "A loaf of bread with fig relish and water besides— this man adopts a new philosophy, teaching hunger, and yet he gets students." Others attribute these lines to Poseidippus.

By this time, he had almost become a proverb. Anyway, "More self-controlled than the philosopher Zeno" used to be said about him. Poseidippus includes it in his *Men Transported*: "So that for ten days he was more self-controlled than Zeno."

IN BRIEF PART 3: *The final part begins with criticism. Diogenes Laertius mentions various "charges" against Zeno and his teachings. Next is a description of Zeno's interaction with Antigonus, the king of Macedonia. Zeno did not allow Antigonus' admiration for and attention to him to change him for the worse. Finally, Diogenes presents various versions of Zeno's death, as well as his burial and the honors he received from Athens and his homeland.*

PART 3: CRITICISMS, KING ANTIGONUS, DEATH, BURIAL & HONORS[12]

Criticisms of Zeno

There are some—among them Cassius the skeptic and his followers—who make many charges against Zeno.

Their first charge is that in the beginning of his *Republic* Zeno declares that ordinary education is useless.

The second charge is that he calls all men who are not excellent "adversaries" and "enemies" and "slaves" and "strangers to one another"—parents to their children, brothers to brothers, and family to family. [33] Yet again, in the *Republic* he presents excellent men as the only true citizens, as well as friends and family members and free men. Accordingly, in the view of the Stoics, parents and children are adversaries since they are not wise.

And in the *Republic*, Zeno gives as his opinion that there should be a community of wives. And at line 200, he prohibits the construction of temples, lawcourts, and gymnasia in cities. As for currency, he writes that he does not think that it is necessary to introduce it either for purposes of exchange or for traveling abroad. Additionally, he calls on men and women to wear the same clothing and to leave no part uncovered.

[34] In his treatise *On the State*, Chrysippus affirms that the *Republic* is Zeno's work.

In the beginning of his writing *The Art of Love*, Zeno discusses love matters. Furthermore, in the *Studies* he writes about similar things.

So much for the charges made by Cassius, as well as by the orator Isidorus of Pergamum.

Isidorus also declares that the worthless sayings made by the Stoics were cut out of their books by Athenodorus the Stoic, the curator of the library at Pergamum. Later on, when Athenodorus was detected and threatened, they were replaced. So much regarding the passages in his writings that were rejected as spurious.

Zeno's Interaction with King Antigonus of Macedonia [13]

[6] Antigonus also favored Zeno. Whenever he came to Athens, he listened to him lecture, and he often invited the philosopher to visit him. But Zeno declined his offer, sending one of his friends, Persaeus, the son of Demetrius and a native of Citium, who flourished in the 130th Olympiad. Zeno was already an old man by this time. According to what Apollonius of Tyre says in his work *On Zeno*, the letter of Antigonus was as follows:

> [7] King Antigonus to Zeno the philosopher, greeting.
>
> I consider myself superior to you in glory and wealth. But in reason and education, and in the perfect happiness you have attained, I acknowledge that I am far behind you. Therefore, I have decided to ask you to visit me, being persuaded that you will not refuse the request.
>
> By all means, then, do your best to meet with me, understanding that you will not only be instructing me but all the Macedonians together. For he who teaches the Macedonian ruler and guides him along the path of virtue will also be training his subjects to be good men. For as the ruler is, so, for the most part, we may expect the subjects to become.

And Zeno wrote back to him as follows:

> [8] Zeno to King Antigonus, greeting.
>
> I welcome your love of learning inasmuch as you hold to the truth that stretches out toward advantage and not to that popular kind of instruction that tends only to the corruption of morals. If anyone has longed for philosophy, turning away from well-known pleasure that renders effeminate

the souls of some of the young, it is clear that he is inclined to nobility of life not only by nature but by deliberate choice. If any man with a nature such as yours receives a reasonable amount of training, in terms of un-grudging instruction, he will easily reach perfect virtue.

[9] As for me, I am unable to join you due to old age and subsequent bodily weakness—I am eighty years old.

But I send to you certain men who have studied with me, men whose mental powers are not inferior to mine, while their bodily strength is far greater. If you join with these men, you will lack nothing that is necessary for perfect happiness.

So he sent Persaeus and Philonides the Theban. Epicurus mentions them both as living with Antigonus in his letter to his brother Aristobulus. . . .

[14] When Demochares, the son of Laches, greeted him and told him that he only had to speak or write for anything he wanted to Antigonus, who would be sure to grant all his requests, Zeno, after hearing this, would have nothing more to do with him.

[15] After Zeno's death, Antigonus is reported to have said, "What a spectacle I have lost!" For this reason he employed Thraso as his ambassador to ask the Athenians to bury Zeno in the Ceramicus. And when queried why he admired him, he said, "Because the many and great gifts I gave him never filled him with conceit nor yet did they cause him to appear lowly." . . .

Zeno's Death

[28] Zeno surpassed everyone in self-control and dignity—also, by god, in bliss—for he was ninety-eight when he died, free from sickness, and healthy to the end.

Persaeus, however, in his ethical lectures, declares that he died at the age of seventy-two, having come to Athens at the age of twenty-two. But Apollonius says that he presided over the school for fifty-eight years.

The manner of his death was as follows. As he was leaving the school, he tripped and fell, breaking a toe. Striking the ground with his fist, he quoted the line from the *Niobe*, "I come, why are you crying aloud to me?" And he died straightaway by holding his breath. . . .

[31] We have ourselves spoken of the manner of Zeno's death in the *Pammetros*, our collection of poems in all meters: "The story goes that Zeno of Citium, after enduring many hardships by reason of old age, was set free—some say by stopping to take food, whereas others say that once when he had tripped, he beat with his hand upon the earth and cried, 'I come of my own accord—why then call me?'" For there are some who hold this to have been the manner of his death.

So much, then, concerning his death.

Honors for Zeno & His Place of Burial

[6] The people of Athens honored Zeno very much, as was shown when they entrusted him with the keys of the city walls, and when they honored him with a golden crown and a bronze statue. This honor was also given him by the citizens of his hometown, who considered his statue a credit to their city. And the men of Citium living in Sidon also claimed him as their own. . . .

[9] It has also seemed good to me to add on the decree that the Athenians passed concerning him. [10] It reads as follows:

In the archonship of Arrhenides, in the fifth prytany of the tribe Acamantis, on the twenty-first day of Maemacterion, at the twenty-third plenary assembly of the prytany, one of the presidents, Hippo, the son of Cratistoteles, of the deme Xypetaeon, and his co-presidents put the question to the vote. Thraso, the son of Thraso, of the deme Anacaea, moved:

Whereas Zeno of Citium, the son of Mnaseas, has for many years been devoted to philosophy in the city and has continued to be a good man in all other respects, exhorting to virtue and moderation those of the youth who come to him to be taught, directing them to what is most excellent, offering to all in his own manner of living a pattern for imitation in perfect conformity with his teaching, [11] it has seemed good to the people— and may it so happen—to bestow praise on Zeno of Citium, the son of

Mnaseas, and to crown him with a golden crown according to the law for his virtue and moderation, and to build for him a tomb in the Ceramicus out of public funds. And that for the making of the crown and the building of the tomb, the people shall now elect five men from the Athenian population, and the recorder shall inscribe this decree on two stone pillars, and he shall be given the power to set up one in the Academy and the other in the Lyceum. And that the magistrate presiding over the administration shall apportion the expense incurred on the pillars so that all may know that the Athenian people honor good men both during their life and after their death.

[12] For the making of the crown and the building, Thraso of the deme Anacaea, Philocles of Piraeus, Phaedrus of Anaphlystus, Medon of Acharnae, Micythus of Sypalettus, and Dion of Paeania have been elected.

Such are the terms of the decree. . . .

[29] The Athenians buried Zeno in the Ceramicus and honored him in the decrees already cited above, bearing additional witness to his virtue.

Here is the epitaph composed for him by Antipater of Sidon: "Here lies great Zeno, dear to Citium, who scaled high Olympus, though he piled not Pelion on Ossa nor toiled at the labors of Heracles, but his path was a path to the stars—the way of moderation alone."

[30] Here too is another by Zenodotus the Stoic, Diogenes' student: "You, O Zeno, made self-sufficiency your rule, letting go of empty riches. With gravity of deportment—venerable, revered— you discovered a manly doctrine. And with foresight you contended by means of a deliberate plan, the mother of fearless liberty. And even if your fatherland was Phoenicia, what need is there for ill-will? Didn't Cadmus come from there, the place from which Greece has writing and papyrus?"

And Athenaeus the epigrammatist speaks of all the Stoics in common as follows: "You who are acquainted with the words of the Stoic Porch, you have committed to your divine books the best of teachings, that virtue of the soul is the only good. Her decrees alone protect the lives of men and cities. But those other men who declare that the goal of life is the enjoyment of the flesh are ruined by one of the Muses, the daughters of Memory."[14]

NOTES

[1] For Part 1, see Diogenes Laertius, *Lives* 7.1, 12, 2-5, 15-16, 31-32, 36-38.

[2] Antigonus of Carystus was a writer and bronzeworker who lived in Athens and Pergamum during the third century BC.

[3] Crates of Thebes (c. 365-c. 285 BC) is known for his radical conversion to Cynicism. He was Diogenes of Sinope's student and his eventual successor as leader of the Cynics. Stilpon (Stilpo) of Megara (fourth century BC), head of the Megarian school, focused on ethics. Xenocrates of Chalcedon (fourth century BC) was the student of Plato and the third head of the Academy. Polemon (Polemo) of Athens (fourth to third century BC) was the fourth head of the Academy.

[4] For the Cynics and Cynic shamelessness (*anaideia*), see the Cave's *The Best of the Cynics: The Lives, Writings & Teachings of the Ancient Cynics*.

[5] Demetrius of Magnesia was a first century BC biographer.

[6] The third century BC director of the library at Alexandria, Eratosthenes of Cyrene, carried out research in many areas of study. He is most famous for measuring the circumference of the earth.

[7] Hippobotus was a late third to early second century BC historian of philosophy.

[8] For Part 2, see Diogenes Laertius, *Lives* 7.12-14, 16-27.

[9] See Euripides, *Suppliant Women* 861-863.

[10] "A Phoenician" because Citium, Zeno's hometown, was, as Diogenes Laertius puts it, "a Greek city that had received Phoenician settlers" (7.1). Others thought Zeno's "fatherland" was Phoenician (see Zenodotus the Stoic in *Lives* 7.30).

[11] The original lines from Hesiod's *Works and Days* 293-295 read, "Best of all is that man who thinks about everything himself. And noble too is that one who is won over by good advice." To read it in context, see the Cave's *The Best of Hesiod's Theogony & Works and Days*.

[12] For Part 3, see Diogenes Laertius, *Lives* 7.32-34, 6-12, 14-15, 28, 31, 29-30.

[13] Antigonus (called Gonatas) was the king of Macedonia from c. 277-239 BC. His interest in the life of the intellect was manifest in the form of having philosophers, poets, and historians visit him at his court in Pella. He is reported to have declared that "kingship is honorable service" —an ancient precursor, perhaps, of today's "servant leadership."

[14] Athenaeus the epigrammatist is referring either to the Cyrenaics, founded by Aristippus of Cyrene (c. 435-356 BC), or the Epicureans, founded by Epicurus (341-270 BC). As for the Muse, he likely means Euterpe. For Epicurus, see the Cave's *The Best of Epicurus: The Life, Writings & Teachings of Epicurus the Greek Philosopher*.

CLEANTHES OF ASSOS
IN DIOGENES' *LIVES*

IN BRIEF: *Diogenes Laertius relates how Cleanthes became Zeno's student. He offers a number of anecdotes, describing, among other stories and sayings, how Cleanthes' poverty drove him to hard work, which he embraced with gusto, earning him the nickname, "a second Heracles." He was teased by many, bearing it with patience. And though he had "no natural aptitude" for much of philosophy, he became Zeno's successor in the Stoic school. Cleanthes valued Zeno, hard work, self-reproach, simplicity, silence, the practice of philosophy, epic poetry, and writing.*

CLEANTHES, THE SON of Phanias, was from Assos. This man, says Antisthenes in his *Successions of Philosophers*, was at first a boxer. According to what some say, he arrived in Athens with just four drachmas. And approaching Zeno, he intensely studied philosophy, sticking with those same teachings from that time on.

Cleanthes was renowned for his love of hard work. In fact, he was spurred on to work for a living thanks to his poverty. So it was that by night he used to draw water for gardens, and by day he exercised himself in arguments—hence the nickname "Phreantlēs" or "The-One-Who-Draws-from-a-Well" was given him.

It is said that he was brought into court to answer the inquiry how so sturdy and well-conditioned a man as he was supported himself. He was acquitted when he introduced as his witnesses the gardener in whose garden he drew water [169] and the woman who sold the barley meal he used to crush. The Areopagites were satisfied and voted him a donation of ten minas, which Zeno forbade him to accept. We are also told that Antigonus made him a present of three thousand drachmas.

Once, when Cleanthes was conducting some youths to a public spectacle, the wind blew his cloak aside and disclosed the fact that he wore no undershirt.[1] Seeing this, the Athenians applauded him—as Demetrius of Magnesia[2] declares in his work on *Men of the Same Name*. This bit, then, also increased the admiration felt for him.

There is another story that when Antigonus was attending his lectures, he asked Cleanthes why he drew water. In reply, Cleanthes said to him, "Is drawing water all I do? What?—do I not dig?—and do I not water the garden?—or undertake any other labor for the love of philosophy?"

Zeno used to exercise Cleanthes in this manner of working and told him to bring him an obol from his wages. [170] One day he brought his distinguished acquaintance a collection of small coins and said, "If he wished, Cleanthes could even support a second Cleanthes, whereas there are those who possess the means to keep themselves yet seek to live at the expense of others even though they have plenty of time to spare from their study of philosophy." For this reason Cleanthes was called a second Heracles.

Cleanthes was hard-working, but he had no natural aptitude for natural philosophy and was extraordinarily slow. Because of this, Timon describes him this way: "Who is this docile man inspecting the ranks of men, the one who sits with things, simmering, a lover of epic poetry, from Assos, cautious?"

Whenever his fellow students teased him, Cleanthes rose up to it. And when he heard them calling him "the ass," he accepted it, telling them that he alone was strong enough to carry Zeno's load.

[171] Once, when he was reproached for being a coward, he replied, "That is why I so rarely miss the mark."

Again, when extolling his own manner of life above that of the wealthy, he used to say that, while they were playing at ball, he was at work digging hard and barren ground.

Cleanthes would often rebuke himself. When Ariston heard him doing this, he said, "Who are you rebuking?" And laughing, Cleanthes said, "A gray old man with no sense."

To someone who declared that Arcesilaus did not do what he should, Cleanthes reply was, "Stop—and don't say this. For if he tears down what is to be done with his speech, he at least sets it up by his deeds." And Arcesilaus said, "I'm not open to flattery." "Very true," Cleanthes said to him, "but I flatter you by saying that your speaking is different from your doing."

[172] When someone asked what advice he should give his son, Cleanthes said, "That of the *Electra*—'Silent, silent, may your step be slight.'"[3]

When a Lacedaemonian declared that hard work was good, he was delighted and said, "You come from a noble family, dear child."

According to Hecaton in his *Anecdotes and Sayings*, when a good looking boy declared, "If when a man strikes his belly he is '*belly-striking*,' then when he strikes his thighs he is '*thigh-striking*," Cleanthes said, "Indeed, boy, but you are separating your thighs. Analogous acts do not always indicate analogous sounds."

Once, in conversation with a youth, he put the question, "Do you see?" When the youth nodded, he said, "Why, then, don't I see that you see?"

[173] When he was present in the theater and the poet Sositheus said about him, "Cleanthes urges men on by his folly," he remained unmoved, having the same expression and manner. Those in the audience were so astonished that they applauded him and drove Sositheus off the stage. Later, when the poet apologized for the insult, Cleanthes accepted the apology, saying that it would be absurd for him to be upset by any chance slander when Dionysus and Heracles were ridiculed by the poets without getting angry.

Cleanthes used to say that the Peripatetics[4] were in the same condition as lyres—although they sound beautiful, they do not hear themselves.

They say that when Cleanthes asserted that according to Zeno a man's character could be grasped from his looks, certain witty young men brought before him a catamite, who was nevertheless strong and tough looking from working in the field, and requested that he give an account of his character. Cleanthes was puzzled and ordered the man to go away. But then, just as he was leaving, the man sneezed. "I have it," Cleanthes said. "He is effeminate."

[174] To the solitary man who talked to himself, he remarked, "You are not talking to a base man."

When someone reproached him for his old age, he said, "As for me, I also wish to depart. But whenever I consider that I am healthy in every way and that I can still write and publish, I wait."

We are told that since he lacked the few coins it cost to purchase paper, Cleanthes wrote down Zeno's sayings on oyster shells and the shoulder blades of oxen.

Such he was. And even though Zeno had many other remarkable students, Cleanthes was the sort of man that he was able to succeed him in leading the Stoic school.

Cleanthes has left some very fine writings, which are as follows: *On Time; On the Natural Philosophy of Zeno*—in two books; *Interpretations of Heraclitus*—in four books; *On Sensation; On Art; To Democritus; To Aristarchus; To Herillus; On Impulse*—in two books; [175] *Ancient History; On Gods; On Giants; On the Bridal Song; On the Poet; On Duty*—in three books; *On Good Counsel; On Gratitude; An Exhortation; On Virtues; On a Good Disposition; On Gorgippus; On Envy; On Desire* or *On Love; On Freedom; The Art of Love; On Honor; On Reputation* or *On Glory; The Statesman; On Counsel; On Laws; On Giving Judgment; On Leadership; On Reason*—in three books; *On the Goal of Human Life; On Beautiful Things; On Actions; On Knowledge; On Kingship; On Friendship; On the Drinking Party; On the Notion that Virtue Is the Same for Men and Women; On the Wise Man Employing Sophisms; On Anecdotes and Sayings; Lectures*—in two books; *On Pleasure; On Private Interests; On Difficulties; On Dialectic; On Style in Speaking or Writing; On Predicates*. These, then, are his books.

[176] Cleanthes' end was as follows. He had severe inflammation of the gums, and by the advice of his doctors he abstained from food for two days. As it happened, this treatment worked, so his doctors gave him permission to resume his usual diet. To this, however, he would not consent. Rather, declaring that he had already gone too far down the road, he went on fasting for the remainder of his life until he died.

According to some, he died at the same age as Zeno. He had lived and studied with Zeno for nineteen years.

My lighter verse about him goes like this: "I praise Cleanthes, but I praise even more Hades, who could not bear to see him old, so at last he gave him rest among the dead, the one who had drawn so much water while alive."

NOTES

[1] One would typically wear a *chitōn* (a tunic or undergarment—clothing worn next to the skin) beneath a *himation* (an outer garment or cloak). When the wind blew, it was discovered that Cleanthes was *achitōn*, "without a tunic or undershirt."

[2] Demetrius of Magnesia was a first century BC biographer.

[3] See Euripides, *Electra* 140.

[4] The school of philosophy founded by Aristotle.

CHRYSIPPUS OF SOLI
IN DIOGENES' *LIVES*

IN BRIEF: *Diogenes Laertius begins with Chrysippus' turn to philosophy. Though he studied with Cleanthes and possibly Zeno (and later at the Academy), he differed from them in his own teaching. His focus was on dialectic. Diogenes goes on at length about how much Chrysippus wrote, his writings and style, and whether his writing was successful or not. He describes his appearance (slight in body) before offering a number of anecdotes that give some idea of what he was like and what was important to him. He was independent, self-confident, and haughty late in life. Diogenes next gives examples of the kinds of arguments Chrysippus would employ, and of the "shameful" topics he would discuss. After reporting several accounts of his death, Diogenes finishes with a very long listing of Chrysippus' many writings.*

CHRYSIPPUS, THE SON of Apollonius, came either from Soli or from Tarsus, as Alexander relates in his *Successions*. He was Cleanthes' student. Before this he used to train for the long course in running. Then he studied with Zeno—or Cleanthes, as Diocles and most people say.[1] While Cleanthes was still living, he left him, becoming a successful philosopher.

Chrysippus was naturally suited to philosophy. His mind was sharp relative to all its parts—so much so that he differed from Zeno on most points, and from Cleanthes as well. He often used to say to Cleanthes that he only needed to be taught the doctrine— that he would discover the proofs for himself. Nevertheless, whenever he criticized Cleanthes, he would repent, so that he constantly uttered these lines: "In other things I am a blessed man, except for my interaction with Cleanthes. In this I am not happy."[2]

[180] Chrysippus became so well-known for dialectic that most people supposed that the gods would adopt his system if dialectic ever existed among them.

Chrysippus had an abundance of written material, but in style he was not successful. In hard work and industry, he surpassed everyone, as is clear from the list of his writings, for there are more than 705 of them. He increased their number by repeatedly arguing on the same subject, setting down anything that occurred to him, making many corrections, and citing numerous authorities—so much so that in one of his treatises he copied out nearly the whole of Euripides' *Medea*. And so when someone picked up the book and was asked what he was reading, he replied, "The *Medea* of Chrysippus."

[181] In his *Collection of Doctrines*, Apollodorus of Athens, wishing to show that what Epicurus wrote with force and originality unaided by quotations was far greater in amount than the books of Chrysippus, says, to quote his exact words, "If one were to strip the books of Chrysippus of all extraneous quotations, his pages would be left bare." So much for Apollodorus.

According to Diocles, the old woman who sat beside Chrysippus used to say that he wrote 500 lines per day.

Hecaton says that Chrysippus took up the study of philosophy because the property that he had inherited from his father had been taken for the king's treasury.

[182] Chrysippus was slight in his body, as is clear from the statue of him in the Ceramicus—the one that is mostly hidden by a statue of a horseman nearby. And this is why Carneades called him Horse-hidden (*Krupsippos*).[3]

Once when somebody reproached him for not going with the multitude to hear Ariston, Chrysippus said, "If I had followed the multitude, I would not have studied philosophy."

When some dialectician got up and attacked Cleanthes, proposing sophistical fallacies to him, Chrysippus called out to him, saying, "Stop distracting the old man from important matters; rather, offer that to those of us who are young."

Someone was steadily conversing with Chrysippus in private, asking a question. Then, when the man saw a crowd approaching, he became more contentious, and Chrysippus said, "Alas, my brother! Your eye is troubled. You were sane, but now you're growing mad."

[183] Chrysippus used to behave quietly at wine parties. That said, he was unsteady on his legs, a fact that caused one slave woman to say, "As for Chrysippus, his legs alone get drunk."

He was so self-confident that when someone asked, "To whom should I entrust my son ?" he replied, "To me, for if I thought that there was anyone better, I would have studied philosophy with him." So it was that people used to say of him, "He alone understands; others flit like shadows." And, "If there had been no Chrysippus, there would have been no Stoic Porch."

In his eighth book, Sotion tells us that Chrysippus finally joined Arcesilaus and Lacydes and studied philosophy with them in the Academy. [184] This is why he sometimes argued against and sometimes for ordinary experience, and why he used the Academy's method when discussing magnitudes and numbers.

Hermippus says that his students once summoned Chrysippus to a sacrifice when he was conducting his school in the Odeon. It was then that he drank sweet wine unmixed with water, and he was seized with dizziness and left the world of men five days later during the 143rd Olympiad, having lived for seventy-three years—this as Apollodorus says in his *Chronology*.

I have toyed with the matter in the following: "Chrysippus lost his head after greedily gulping down Bacchus. He spared neither the Stoic Porch nor his homeland nor his own life but went to the house of Hades."

[185] Others say that his end was caused by a violent fit of laughter. For after an ass had eaten up his figs, he told an old woman to give it unmixed wine to wash them down, and so he died from excessive laughter.

Chrysippus appears to have become a very haughty man. Anyway, he dedicated none of his writings to the kings.

And one old woman was enough for him—so says Demetrius in *Men of the Same Name*.

When Ptolemy wrote a letter to Cleanthes asking him to come to him or send someone else, Sphaerus went while Chrysippus declined. Instead, he sent for his sister's sons, Aristocreon and Philocrates, and he trained them.

Demetrius, the one mentioned before, is also the one who reported that Chrysippus was the first who ventured to hold an outdoor school in the Lyceum. . . .

[186] Chrysippus used to make the following kinds of arguments. "He who speaks about the mysteries to the uninitiated is impious. But the initiating priest speaks about the mysteries to the uninitiated; therefore, the initiating priest is impious."

Another is: "That which is not in the city is not in the house. But a well is not in the city; therefore, there is no well in the house."

Another is: "There is a certain head, but you do not have that head. There is a certain head that you do not have; therefore, you do not have a head."

[187] Another is: "If someone is in Megara, he is not in Athens. But there is a man in Megara; therefore, there is not a man in Athens."

And again: "If you say something, it passes out of your mouth. But you say 'wagon'; therefore, a wagon passes out of your mouth."

Also: "If you have not lost something, then you have it. But you did not lose horns; therefore, you have horns." Others, however, say this one is from Eubulides.

187-188 *Diogenes Laertius mentions various criticisms of Chrysippus, including what he says about the gods (that what he says "is better suited to prostitutes than the gods"), as well as incest ("that a man may be sexually joined with mothers and daughters and sons") and cannibalism (that we should "eat those who have died").*

[188] In the second book of *On Life and Earning a Living*, while considering how a wise man should earn a living, Chrysippus says,

> [189] And yet why should he earn a living? After all, if it is for the sake of life, life is a thing indifferent. And if for pleasure, it is also indifferent. And if it is for virtue, it is sufficient in itself for happiness. The ways by which one may earn a living are also laughable. Take, for example, the way of being supported by a king—you will then have to entreat and give

way to him. And by friends—friends will then be products sold for gain. And by means of wisdom—wisdom will then be available for hire.

And these are the charges brought against earning a living in these ways.

Since the reputation of his books stands so high, I have decided to make a separate catalogue of them, arranged according to the class of subject treated. They are as follows:[4] . . . Those books on topics related to logic about various matters. . . . Those books on topics related to logic about words or phrases and the speech consisting of them. . . . Those books on topics related to logic about arguments and modes. . . . Those books on moral or ethical theory—on the classification of moral or ethical concepts. . . . Those books on ethical topics concerned with the common view and the arts and excellences arising therefrom. . . . Those books on ethical topics concerned with good and bad things.

NOTES

[1] Scholars judge it unlikely that Chrysippus met Zeno, let alone studied with him, since Zeno died in 263 BC when Chrysippus was yet in his mid teens. Chrysippus did not come to Athens until around 260 when he was nineteen or twenty. Diocles of Magnesia (first century BC) was an ancient historian and writer of biography and summaries. He concentrated on the views, sayings, and lives of the earliest philosophers.

[2] See Euripides, *Orestes* 540-541.

[3] *Krupsippos*, the Academic Carneades' nickname for Chrysippus, is from *kruptos* (hidden) or *kruptō* (to hide) and *hippos* (horse). It is a play on Chrysippus' name, "Golden-horse" or "Gold-horse" (Chrysippos), which is from *chryseos* (golden) or *chrysos* (gold) and *hippos* (horse).

[4] The following content comes from Diogenes Laertius, *Lives* 7.189-202. Of the many, many books named by Diogenes Laertius (that, if included, would run on for another five or six pages), example titles include: *Logical Theses; On Propositions; On Imperatives; On Predicates; On the Arrangement of Sentences; The Art of Logic and of Modes; On the Rules for Syllogisms; Introduction to Fallacies; On the "Nobody" Puzzle; Outline of Ethical Theory; Definitions of the Good; On Proverbs; On Direct Apprehension; On the Kinds of Virtues; Proofs that Pleasure is Not the Goal of Human Life.*

OTHER EARLY STOICS
IN DIOGENES' *LIVES*

IN BRIEF: *Diogenes Laertius discusses the teachings and writings of the three heterodox Stoics, who differed from other Stoics in one way or another—Ariston, Herillus, and Dionysius. Next, Diogenes reports the fact that Sphaerus of Bosporus was Zeno's student, before relating two anecdotes having to do with Sphaerus and Ptolemy Philopator, the ruler of Egypt. He finishes by listing Sphaerus' writings.*

SOME OF THE Stoics differed from the rest. They are the following. Ariston of Chios, the Bald, who was nicknamed "the Siren," declared that the goal of life was to live in a state of indifference to everything between virtue and vice. He did not recognize variation among things indifferent but treated them all alike. Accordingly, he said that the wise man is like a good actor, who, if called on to take the part of a Thersites or of an Agamemnon, will impersonate them in a suitable manner.[1]

Ariston wished to discard both logic and physics, saying that physics was beyond our reach and logic does not concern us. All that matters to us is ethics. [161] He said that dialectical arguments are like spiders' webs. Though they seem to display some artistic skill and workmanship, they are nevertheless useless.

Ariston did not introduce a plurality of virtues as Zeno did. Nor did he agree that virtue is one thing called by many names as the Megarians asserted. Rather, he treated virtue in accord with the category of relative modes. Teaching this sort of philosophy and lecturing in the Cynosarges, he became influential enough to be called the founder of a school. Accordingly, Miltiades and Diphilus were called Aristonians. He was a persuasive speaker and pleased the crowd. So it was that Timon said about him, "And one who, from Ariston's wily kind, traced his descent."

[162] Diocles of Magnesia² says that Ariston changed his views after meeting Polemon while Zeno was suffering from a protracted illness.

The Stoic teaching to which Ariston attached most importance was the wise man's refusal to hold mere opinions. Persaeus was contending against this teaching when he induced one of a pair of twins to deposit a certain sum with Ariston and later got the other to reclaim it. Ariston was reduced to perplexity by this and thus utterly refuted.

Ariston criticized Arcesilaus. And one day when he saw a monstrous bull that had a womb, he said, "Alas! Here is an argument for Arcesilaus against the evidence of the senses."

[163] When some Academic alleged that he had no certainty of anything, Ariston said, "Do you not even see your neighbor sitting by you?" When the other answered that he could not, Ariston said, "Who could have blinded you? Who robbed you of luminous eyesight?"

The books attributed to him are the following: *Exhortations*—in two books; *On Zeno's Teachings*; *Dialogues*; *Lectures*—in six books; *Dissertations on Philosophy*—in seven books; *Dissertations on Love Matters*; *Notes on Empty Opinions*; *Notes*—in twenty-five books; *Memorabilia*—in three books; *Anecdotes and Sayings*—in eleven books; *Against the Rhetoricians*; *Against the Answers of Alexinus*; *Against the Dialecticians*—in three books; *Letters* addressed to Cleanthes—in four books.

Panaetius and Sosicrates say that the letters alone are genuine. They attribute the rest to Ariston the Peripatetic.

[164] The story goes that since Ariston was bald, his head burned under the sun, and so he died.

I have composed the following playful poem for him in limping iambics: "Why, O Ariston, did you let the sun roast the top of your head? Well then, seeking more warmth than you should have, you've discovered cold Hades against your will."

[165] Herillus of Carthage said that knowledge is the goal of life—that is, the goal is always to live by referring everything in life to knowledge rather than being misled by ignorance. He said that knowledge is the habit of not falling away from reason in the reception of presentations.

Herillus once said that there is no one goal of life. Rather, it shifts according to the circumstances and events, just as the same bronze may become a statue either of Alexander or Socrates. Moreover, Herillus said that the chief goal of life and the goal that serves as a means of achieving the chief goal are different. Even the unwise man may aim at the latter, whereas the wise man alone seeks the former. Herillus said that everything between virtue and vice is indifferent.

His writings, even though they do not occupy much space, are full of vigor. They contain some replies addressed to Zeno.

[166] They say that many loved Herillus when he was a boy. Since Zeno wished to drive them away, he compelled Herillus to have his head shaved, and this turned them away from him.

The following are his books: *On Training*; *On the Passions*; *On Assumption*; *The Legislator*; *The Skill of Midwifery*; *The Challenger*; *The Teacher*; *The Reviser*; *The Controller*; *Hermes*; *Medea*; *Dialogues*; *Ethical Theories*.

Dionysius [of Heraclea]—the one who changed his position— said that the goal of life is pleasure. This was thanks to the circumstance of his suffering from ophthalmia. The suffering was so painful that he hesitated to say that physical suffering is indifferent.

Dionysius was the son of Theophantus and a citizen of Heraclea. According to what Diocles says, he was at first the student of Heraclides, his fellow citizen. Then he moved on to Alexinus, and finally to Zeno.

[167] Dionysius was at first fond of literature and attempted to make all kinds of poetry. Then he attached himself to Aratus, striving to imitate him. When he left Zeno, he turned to the Cyrenaics[3] and frequented brothels and openly enjoyed himself. And after living eighty years, he died by starving himself to death.

The following books are attributed to him: *On Apathy*—in two books; *On Training*—in two books; *On Pleasure*—in four books; *On Wealth and Favors and Revenge*; *On the Usefulness of Men*; *On Good Luck*; *On Ancient Kings*; *On Praised Things*; *On Non-Greek Customs*.

These three, then, are the heterodox Stoics.

[177] As mentioned before,[4] among those who were the students of Zeno, there was also Sphaerus of Bosporus.

After making sufficient progress in his studies and dialectic, he went to Alexandria to be with Ptolemy Philopator. One day there was a discussion about whether the wise man would hold a mere opinion. Sphaerus declared that he would not hold a mere opinion. Wishing to test him, the king ordered some wax pomegranates to be set out. When Sphaerus was deceived in this manner, the king called out that he had given his assent to a false presentation. But Sphaerus was ready with a sage reply. "I assented not to the proposition that they are actually pomegranates, but that it is reasonable to judge them so. There is a difference between assent based on direct apprehension and that founded on good reason."

When Mnesistratus accused Sphaerus of denying that Ptolemy was a king, his reply was, "Being such as he is, Ptolemy is indeed a king."

[178] Sphaerus wrote the following books: *On the Cosmos*—in two books; *On Elements*; *On Seed*; *On Fortune*; *On the Smallest Things*; *Against Atoms and Images*; *On Sense Organs*; *On Heraclitus*—in five lectures; *On the Arrangement of Ethics*; *On Duty*; *On Impulse*; *On the Passions*—in two books; *On Kingship*; *On the Laconian (Spartan) Constitution*; *On Lycurgus and Socrates*—in three books; *On Law*; *On Divination*; *Dialogues on Things Related to Love or Desire*; *On the Eretrian Philosophers*; *On Things That Are Similar*; *On Definitions or Terms*; *On Habits*; *On Contradictions*—in three books; *On Reason*; *On Wealth*; *On Reputation* or *On Glory*; *On Death*; *On the Art of Dialectics*—in two books; *On Predicates*; *On Ambiguities*; Letters.

NOTES

[1] Thersites and Agamemnon both appear in Homer's *Iliad*. Thersites is a common soldier; Agamemnon is the leader of the Achaeans.

[2] Diocles of Magnesia (first century BC) was an ancient historian and writer of biography and summaries. He concentrated on the views, sayings, and lives of the earliest philosophers.

[3] Founded by Aristippus of Cyrene (c. 435-356 BC), Cyrenaicism was an ancient Greek philosophy that promoted pleasure as the chief goal of life.

[4] For the prior passage ("As mentioned before . . ."), see 7.37. It reads, "Sphaerus also became Cleanthes' student after Zeno's death."

INTERLUDE
A HYMN & PRAYER

of Cleanthes of Assos

HYMN TO ZEUS
RULER OF THE COSMOS

IN BRIEF: *Cleanthes of Assos hymns Zeus, who rules the cosmos, guiding it according to universal law by means of the universal rational principle. Though bad men flee it, a noble life is fostered by obeying this law. Zeus orders all, the noble with the ignoble. Cleanthes prays that all may know Zeus' purpose and so honor him.*

M OST GLORIOUS OF immortals, you of many names, all-powerful and everlasting Zeus, the origin and leader of nature, guiding all things with law—greetings!
For it is right that all mortals should speak to you.
For we are your offspring, having received your voice-image, we alone of all mortals who live and move on earth.
And so I will hymn you and always sing of your strength.
The whole cosmos, wheeling around the earth, obeys you, wherever you take it, readily ruled by you.
Such is the servant you carry in your unconquered hands, the two-edged, fiery, ever-living thunderbolt.
For under its blows the whole of nature shudders.
By it you direct the universal rational principle that moves through all things, mixing with the greater and lesser lights.
By it you have become so great, highest king over all and forever.
Nor does any work upon earth take place apart from you, god, nor in the divine aethereal vault of heaven, nor in the sea—none but what is done by bad men in their own folly.

But you put a stop to what is excessive and set up what is suitable, ordering what is disordered; for you what is unpleasant is pleasant.

In this manner you have joined together all noble things with things ignoble, so that there is one everlasting rational principle in all things.

This is what wicked mortals flee from and leave alone—ill-fated ones, those always yearning for the property of good men.

They neither see the universal law of God, nor do they hear it.

If they wisely obeyed it, they would have a noble life.

But unrefined, these same ones rush off, going one way or another—some bearing miserable, strife-ridden zeal for a glorious reputation, some turning toward immoderate gain, and others toward relaxation and the pleasures of the body.

Pressing on, the very opposite of these things happens.

But Zeus, giver of all, shrouded in dark clouds, ruler of the thunderbolt, deliver human beings from mournful ignorance, scatter it from their souls.

And grant that they may encounter the purpose you rely on to guide all things with justice, so that being so honored, we may in turn favor you with honor, hymning your works from beginning to end as is fitting for mortals, considering there is no greater honor-prize, neither for mortals nor for gods, than to hymn rightly and always the universal law.

PRAYER TO ZEUS & DESTINY
THE IMPERATIVE TO FOLLOW

IN BRIEF: *With the following prayer of Cleanthes, the late Stoic Epictetus indicates the powers—Zeus and Destiny—that guide everything in the cosmos, and the necessity and good of following these.*

Upon every occasion, we should have the following at hand:

Lead me, O Zeus, and you, O Destiny,
to whatever station you have assigned me.
I will follow without hesitation.
And if I am not willing to follow
because I have become a bad man,
even so, I will follow.*

---

*For 52 more entries from Epictetus' *Handbook* (*Enchiridion*), see the Cave's forthcoming *The Handbook of Epictetus: Pocket Edition.*

PART 3

STOIC LOGIC, PHYSICS & ETHICS
IN CICERO'S WORKS

from

- *On the Nature of the Gods*
- *On the Ends of Good and Evil (On Ends)*
- *Tusculan Disputations*
- *Academica*
- *On Fate*

EIGHT

STOIC LOGIC
IN CICERO'S WORKS

IN BRIEF: *In the first selection from* On the Nature of the Gods, *Balbus the Stoic praises the divine gifts of the mind and speech. In the second from* On Ends, *Marcus Cato observes that the Stoics call dialectic a virtue. In the third set of selections from Book 1 of the* Academica, *Varro explains a few elements of Stoic logic or epistemology having to do with sensation (including presentations). In the final set of selections from Book 2 of the* Academica, *Lucullus offers Zeno's definition of a presentation, and Cicero presents the Stoic position on the wise man, as well as Zeno's hand illustration showing the movement from assent to knowledge.*[1]

Cicero, *On the Nature of the Gods* 2.147-148

Balbus the Stoic extols "the soul and mind of man" — the intellectual powers that enable us to understand things, which are the result of divine care. He then expresses amazement at the "power to speak," which helps us learn and teach — a power that exhorts, persuades, consoles, checks, and soothes. Speech joins us together in the justice of law and civil society.[2]

L OOKING NOW AT the soul and mind of man, — his reason, deliberation, and practical judgment, — one who cannot discern that these owe their achievements to divine care must himself, it appears to me, be lacking these very things.

I wish you would furnish me with your eloquence, Cotta, while I'm on the topic. How would you speak about it? First, you would discuss the great extent of our intelligence or understanding. How we collect our ideas. How we join conclusions to premises. How we establish principles, draw consequences, define things separately, and judge them with clarity. From this we understand the strength and nature of knowledge, which is the best thing even in God.

How truly great are those powers that you Academics[3] deny and destroy—the perception and comprehension of external things by means of our senses and rational soul. [148] It is by collecting and comparing these perceptions that we establish the arts that are necessary for the support and pleasures of life.

Then take speech, the queen of the arts as you customarily call it. What a brilliant and divine power it is, the power to speak! First, it enables us to learn things we do not know and to teach things we do know to others. Second, it is the means by which we exhort and persuade one another. By it we console the afflicted; we decrease the terrors of the terrified; we check strong feelings; we extinguish the flames of desire and anger. Finally, it is this power that has joined us together in justice, law, and civil society. It is this that has separated us from an inhuman and beastly life.

Cicero, *On Ends* 3.72

Marcus Cato explains that the Stoics call dialectic a virtue since it preserves truth and avoids falsehood.[4]

[72] To the virtues we have discussed, the Stoics add dialectic . . . , for which they use the term "virtue." Dialectic offers a method that guards us against giving assent to any falsehood or ever being tricked by deceptive probability. And it enables us to maintain and to defend the truths that we have learned about good and bad things. They hold that without the art of dialectic any man may be tricked and led away from what is true or actual toward what is false or deceptive. If, therefore, thoughtlessness and ignorance are in all matters faulty and full of misfortune, then the art that removes them is correctly termed "virtue."

Cicero, *Academica* 1.40-42
(with a summary of the surrounding text given in italics)

In the first passage taken from Book 1 of the Academica, *Marcus*

Terentius Varro reviews Zeno of Citium's epistemology, including Zeno's notion that sensation consists of the joining of an external impulse or influence (a presentation) with the internal, voluntary assent of the rational soul. He further discusses which presentations are trustworthy (those that are "graspable"), as well as what knowledge, opinion, and "credible" things are. He finishes with an examination of what sensation is and why the senses are trustworthy.[5]

1-39 Cicero sets the stage by describing his encounter with Varro at his villa at Cumae. Cicero's friend Atticus is also present.

After some initial discussion, Cicero asks Varro to give what may be called a brief history of philosophy from Socrates on. Agreeing to the task, Varro begins with Socrates, describing the way he "called philosophy away from hidden things concealed by nature herself" and led it "to common or ordinary human life." He expounds the Socratic method of discussion—that Socrates would "confirm nothing" as certain; rather, he would "expose the fallacies of others." His "conversations were spent in praising virtue and in encouraging a fondness or zeal for virtue." But then, Varro explains, there was a shift toward dogmatism with Plato as well as with the Academic and Peripatetic schools that followed him—a shift that produced "an art of philosophy" and a "clearly defined plan of instruction."

Varro goes through each of the three parts of philosophy "received from Plato"—ethics, physics, and logic. In doing so, he expounds the teachings of Antiochus (of the so-called Old Academy) regarding each. As for ethics, the major points have to do with the goods of the body and mind, as well as external goods; that "happiness exists in virtue alone"; that there is the need to follow a plan of life in accord with nature. As for physics or natural philosophy, the chief ideas are that there are two principles of nature, one active and one passive; that there are primary elements (fire, air, water, earth, and Aristotle's added fifth element) and the things derived from them; that there is matter on the one hand, and quality or force, on the other, "the soul of the world," variously called God, providence, necessity, or Fortune. Finally, Varro details logic or "the third part of philosophy, identified with reason and the examination or discussion of things," including the nature of knowledge and the fact that it is the mind and not the senses that is "the judge of things," among other points.

Having covered the "primary system left behind by Plato," Varro
moves on to present the changes that have been made by one philosopher
or another, including those of Aristotle, Theophrastus, and the Stoic Zeno
of Citium. The latter, Varro reports, was "very subtle in discussing
things." Importantly, he reformed the way philosophy was taught. He goes
on to expound Zeno's improved teaching "as it used to be explained by
[the Academic] Antiochus." After discussing Zeno's views on ethics and
physics (for these, see Nine for physics and Ten for ethics), he turns to
Zeno's logic, here classified as "the third part of philosophy."

[40] As for logic, the third part of philosophy, Zeno the Stoic made
many changes. First, he said some new things about sensation itself.
He proposed that sensation is a joining or combination of a kind of
impulse or influence or impact presented from outside the individual sensing. In Greek, he called this a *phantasia* or "presentation"; in
Latin, we may use the term *visum* (an appearance). . . .

To these presentations received by the senses, Zeno joined the
assent of the rational soul, which he located within us and declared
a voluntary act.

[41] Zeno judged that not all presentations are trustworthy, but
only those that have an exposition or disclosure proper to themselves of the things presented.

And when a trustworthy presentation is perceived as such by
its own intrinsic nature, he terms it "graspable."[6] . . . But after it
has been accepted and approved, he terms it a "grasp," resembling things that are grasped by the hand. . . . That itself which is
grasped by sensation he calls a "sensation." And if it is grasped in
such a way that it cannot be torn away by reason or an argument,
he calls it "knowledge." If it is otherwise, he calls it "ignorance."
Ignorance is the source of opinion or conjecture, which is weak
and shares attributes with what is false and what is unexamined.
[42] And between knowledge and ignorance, he puts that grasp
about which I have spoken. And he counts it neither correct nor
incorrect, but declares it to be only "credible" or "believable."

From this, Zeno had confidence in the senses. He did so because,
as I said above, he held that a grasp made by the senses was both

true and faithful. This was so not because it grasped every aspect of a thing, but because it let go of nothing that was capable of being grasped, and because nature had given, as it were, in this grasp made by the senses, a "measuring rod" or "standard" of knowledge and a first principle of nature itself. From these grasps made by the senses, conceptions of things were thereafter impressed upon the rational soul—from which not only first principles but certain broader ways toward the end of rational discovery were devised. On the other hand, Zeno eliminated things such as error, thought-lessness, ignorance, opinion, and distrust—in a word, everything foreign to firm and steady assent—from virtue and wisdom.

43-46 In the remainder of Book 1 of the Academica, *Cicero responds to Varro's request to explain the "innovations of Arcesilaus" and the founding of the so-called New Academy. Aside from Cicero's judgment in agreement with Antiochus that "the Stoic theory should be considered a modification of the Old Academy rather than a new system of instruction," there is nothing more said of the Stoics or Stoicism.*

Cicero, *Academica* 2.18, 66, 76-77, 126, 143-145
(with a summary of the surrounding text given in italics)

In the following set of selections taken from Book 2 of the Academica, *Lucullus briefly gives Zeno's definition of a presentation. Next, Cicero makes several points. One is that the wise man neither errs when it comes to being deceived, nor does he form opinions. Still, there is the recognition that different Stoics held different views on these matters. The last selection presents Zeno's illustration involving a hand (from open to clinched) representing the nature of what happens in the process of knowing, from the initial presentation, to assent, to grasping or comprehension, to knowledge.*

1-17 After lauding "the great capacity and natural talents of Lucius Lucullus" and his devotion to literature and philosophy (despite the "many who have no love whatsoever for Greek literature, and the even greater number who have no love for philosophy"), and after briefly discussing the positions as well as the critics of "the Academic system," Cicero turns to report the conversation he had with Catulus, Hortensius, and Lucullus at Hortensius' villa at Bauli.

Catulus asks Lucullus to tell them about "the teachings you heard from Antiochus" (the man who turned away from Arcesilaus' skepticism, returning to an earlier Academic position he claimed was that of the Old Academy). While tracing the lineage of the New Academy (including Arcesilaus and Carneades), Lucullus offers Zeno of Citium's definition of a "presentation" (phantasia or visum) in the context of discussing Philo of Larissa, Antiochus' teacher.

[18] A "presentation" . . . was, as Zeno defined it, an appearance impressed and formed from the thing from which it originated, with a constitution or nature that it could not have if it originated from a thing that was not the one it actually did originate from. And we affirm that Zeno's definition is right. For how can anything be grasped or comprehended so that one is assured that the thing is clearly understood and known if it has a constitution or nature that could belong to it even if it were false?

19-65 Further, Lucullus declares that the verdicts of the senses are "clear and certain." He goes on to prove "our ability to perceive and grasp many things," arguing that ethical practice and the wisdom it is based on demand as much. Sensation or perception is necessary for wisdom to begin its own work. He likewise defends reason as the initiator of research that aims at discovery—and not in vain.

Lucullus combats several Academic positions that he judges fallacious, including the contention that true presentations are not trustworthy simply because false ones may masquerade as true ones (as with mistaking one twin for another or in dreams or the strange visions of a madman).

Once finished with presenting "the case against the Academy," Lucullus falls silent, and Cicero, upon the request of Catulus, begins to speak, explaining the fact that he often holds mere opinions. By contrast, he says, the wise man does not.

[66] In the view of Arcesilaus,[7] in agreement with Zeno, the greatest strength of a wise man is when he guards against being captivated

by a presentation, making sure that he is not deceived—for nothing is more disconnected from the notion we have of the dignity of a wise man than error, fickleness, or thoughtlessness.

67-75 Cicero goes on to contend that, given the high stakes of assent and possible error, the wise man will withhold his assent (the Academic position). "The habit of assenting seems dangerous—like a slippery slope," he says. "The wise man should not commit himself to such a precipitous slope." He next implies that Antiochus of Ascalon departed from the Academic school with less than stellar motives having to do with a desire for attention. He follows this line of ad hominem argument with the contention (disputed by Lucullus) that earlier philosophers—including Anaxagoras, Democritus, Empedocles, Parmenides, Xenophanes, Socrates, and Plato—held that nothing could be known. After mentioning these "authorities," he offers the following imaginary dialogue between Arcesilaus and Zeno of Citium.

[76] Arcesilaus did not engage with Zeno in order to disparage him. Instead, as can be discerned in what follows, he truly wanted to discover the truth. . . .

[77] It is possible, he thought, for a man to hold no opinions. As for the wise man, it is not only possible—that he hold no opinions—but necessary. For Arcesilaus, this view was both true and respectable and proper for a wise man.

We may imagine that Arcesilaus asked Zeno what would happen if, one, a wise man was unable to perceive anything, and, two, whether he was unable—as a wise man—to form an opinion.

Zeno, I believe, replied that the wise man's reason for not forming an opinion was that he would be able to perceive something.

"What, then, is this thing?"

"A presentation"—I trust this was his answer.

"Tell me, then, what is the nature of a presentation?"

He defined it this way: "A presentation is that which is impressed and sealed and formed from a real thing—just as the thing is."

There followed another question: "Yet what if a true presentation is the same kind as a false presentation?"

Here Zeno was sharp enough to see that he would not be able to perceive a presentation if, even though it came from a real, existing thing, it was the same kind as that which came from an unreal, non-existing thing.

Arcesilaus agreed that the addition to the definition was correct, for it is impossible to perceive a false presentation. It is also not possible to perceive a true presentation if it is just like a false presentation.

78-126 Cicero uses the latter part of the imaginary dialogue to make his major point: that "If we do away with opinion and perception, it certainly follows that we must withhold every act of assent. Therefore, if I demonstrate that nothing can be perceived, you must concede that the wise man will never assent."

Toward the end of making this point, Cicero argues that, first, and against Lucullus' arguments to the contrary, the senses are uncertain and "give false evidence." We mistake one person for another and can mistake things such as one statue or seal print with another identical one. The point is also demonstrated with the phenomena of hallucinations arising while asleep—in dreams—or when insane or full of wine.

Second, nor can reason in the form of dialectic distinguish "or judge between truth and falsehood." Cicero demonstrates this with two seemingly irrefutable fallacies, both "inventions of Chrysippus" the Stoic. They are "the Sorites," which addresses the problem of relative qualities or quantities (such as rich or poor, many or few, great or small), and "the Liar," in which the one speaking the truth is lying.

Next, Cicero explains that Academics such as Carneades and the Carthaginian Clitomachus held that "the wise man will take advantage of whatever apparently probable presentation he encounters." The point is that certainty based on perception or understanding is not necessary for acting or living life; rather, probability is enough. Therefore, even though "the wise man withholds assent," he nevertheless "follows the lead of probability." Not only is this the case, but probability is also sufficient for things such as forming memories and various sciences and arts.[8] The suspension of assent is possible and compatible with action. The Academics, Cicero declares, do not "get rid of truth altogether." Rather, they acknowledge that some things are true and some false. The point is that neither are perceivable precisely as such; they are only apparent.

Then there is this issue: if one is forced to choose a dogmatic teacher or school to follow, or those who put forward dogmatic answers, how can it be done if they disagree as they do with one another? They do so regarding the natural world (for example, its eternity or not; its cause; its center; its elements; the human body and mind). Members of the same school even dispute one another—as the Stoics do.

[126] Will the Stoics be permitted to debate among themselves while no one is permitted to debate with them? Zeno and many of the other Stoics see the aether as the highest god, furnished with a mind by which everything in the cosmos is governed. By contrast Cleanthes, . . . , who was a student of Zeno, holds that the sun is lord and master of the world. Therefore, the disagreement of the wise forces us to be ignorant of our own lord inasmuch as we do not know whether we are the servants of the sun or of the aether.

127-142 *Cicero praises natural philosophy, declaring that "the consideration and contemplation of nature affords a kind of natural nourishment for the rational soul." Our minds are elevated, he says, when we engage in such activity. But Academics will study nature without assenting.*

Continuing the argument, Cicero points out that the dogmatic schools, such as the Stoic school, disagree about ethics—namely, regarding good and evil, that is, the highest good or goods to achieve and those evils to avoid. "What about the fact," he asks, "that the arguments made on either side seem to me both discerning and equally valid?" The same holds regarding the virtues and the passions or emotions or feelings. The Stoics, for instance, hold that the wise man will not be moved by emotions, whereas the Academics teach that "the feelings or emotions . . . were furnished by nature to our souls for useful purposes—fear, for instance, to motivate caution," and so on.

Finally, Cicero comes "to the third part of philosophy," logic. The question is, What is the criterion of truth?—if, indeed, there is such. Once again, the dogmatic schools, including the Stoics, disagree.

[143] What controversy there is!—even on a matter that is part of the basics taught by the dialecticians, the proper way to judge the truth or falsehood of a hypothetical judgment such as, "If it is day,

it is light." Diodorus approves one view. Philo another. Chrysippus yet another. Then, how many points of difference there are between Chrysippus and his teacher Cleanthes? . . .

[144] Both Zeno and Antiochus deny that you know anything. "What do you mean by that?" you will say. "For we hold that even an unwise man grasps many things."

[145] But you deny that anyone except a wise man *knows* anything. And Zeno used to demonstrate the point—that only the wise man has knowledge—with a gesture.

Before another man, he would show his hand with the fingers outstretched and say, "A presentation is like this." Next, he would draw in his fingers a little and say, "An assent is like this." Then, he would press his fingers closely together and make a fist, and say, "A grasp or comprehension is like this." And by this analogy, he introduced the name *katalēpsis* (grasp or comprehension), which was not used before. But then he would move his left hand to that fist in order to squeeze it tightly and with might. And he would say, "Such is knowledge," and that no one but a wise man was the master of knowledge.

But who is a wise man—now or in the past? The Stoics themselves do not usually give an answer to this question. Accordingly, Catalus, you do not now *know* that the light of day is shining, nor do you, Hortensius, *know* that we are at your villa.

146-148 *Cicero returns to the idea that the arts are established on "what is sufficient." He suggests that they can further explore "the great differences of opinion" among the various schools on another occasion. Lucullus agrees to this proposition. Then Catulus and Hortensius briefly share their views on the whole matter—the former says that the wise man will hold opinions but know that he is doing so, while the latter simply laughs and says, "Away with it!" indicating his move to withhold assent.*

NOTES

[1] Note that aside from the initial "In Brief" summary of the content of the selections of this chapter, you will also find a summary prior to each selection.

[2] For the context of *On the Nature of the Gods* 2.147-148, as well as further selections from the same text, see Nine ("Stoic Natural Philosophy in Cicero's Works").

[3] "You Academics" includes Cotta—Gaius Aurelius Cotta (124-73 BC), who was an orator and statesman. In *On the Nature of the Gods*, Cicero makes Cotta the proponent of the Academic point of view, which, by his time, was one with skepticism. The Academy was founded by Plato in the first half of the fourth century BC. For about 200 years, from the 260s BC on, the Academy (variously called the Middle or New Academy) and its Academics identified Platonism with skepticism. These Academics proposed the impossibility of knowledge and thus the need to suspend judgment. This long phase of skepticism ended with Antiochus of Ascalon (c. 130-68 BC), who returned the Academy to a more dogmatic Platonism, one which held that knowledge was actually possible.

[4] Marcus Porcius Cato (95-46 BC) was a Roman statesman and convinced Stoic. For the context of *On Ends* 3.72, as well as further selections from the same text, see Ten ("Stoic Ethics in Cicero's Works").

[5] Marcus Terentius Varro (116-27 BC) was a Roman scholar and prolific writer, who studied philosophy in Athens with Antiochus of Ascalon.

What is extant of the *Academica* (or *Academics*)—our Book 1 and Book 2—is actually the remains of two editions of the work published by Cicero, the latter edition meant to be a revision of the former. Our Book 1, with Varro and Cicero as the chief interlocutors, corresponds to the first part or book (of four books) of the second edition (sometimes called the *Academica Posteriora*). Our Book 2, with Lucullus and Cicero as the main speakers, though it also includes Catalus and Hortensius, corresponds to the second part or book (of two books) of the first edition (sometimes called the *Academica Priora* and called by Cicero *Lucullus* after his partner in dialogue). Together, our Books 1 and 2 preserve about three-quarters of Cicero's total work.

[6] Note that any form of "grasp" (*comprehensio*, from *comprehendō*, to seize, grasp, apprehend), may also be read as "apprehension" ("to apprehend") or "comprehension" ("to comprehend") and their corresponding forms. The corresponding Greek is *katalēpsis*, from *katalambanō*, to seize upon, lay hold of; to seize or grasp with the mind, apprehend, comprehend.

[7] Arcesilaus (or Arcesilas) was the founder of what Cicero in *Academica* 1.46 terms the New Academy (though Diogenes Laertius in *Lives* 1.14, and Sextus Empiricus in *Outlines of Pyrrhonism* 1.220, call it the Middle Academy), which introduced Pyrrho's skepticism into Plato's Academy in the middle of the third century BC. The basic idea of this skepticism was that knowledge was not possible; therefore, the wise man would withhold assent. Generally speaking, Arcesilaus and Zeno of Citium did not agree since the latter was a dogmatist (positively proposing certain knowledge about many things), whereas the former was not.

[8] Cicero states that we Academics "do not take away the light of day, but, whereas you [followers of Antiochus and the Stoics] speak of things as being

'perceived' and 'grasped' or 'comprehended,' we say the same things 'appear' as long as they are probable."

NINE

STOIC NATURAL PHILOSOPHY OR PHYSICS
IN CICERO'S WORKS

IN BRIEF: *After Cicero offers a few points regarding the Stoic view of the soul (in the* Tusculan Disputations*), he (through Marcus Cato in* On Ends*) gives the Stoic reasons for honoring natural philosophy as a virtue—that a grasp of natural philosophy is necessary to live in accord with nature and thus virtuously. Next (as Varro in the* Academica*), Cicero summarizes Zeno's thinking about the four elements, including the role of fire and how only bodies or corporeal substances can act on things or be acted on. Then (from* On Fate*) he explores various views of fate and causation, including that of the Stoic Chrysippus. Finally, Cicero (as the Stoic Balbus in* On the Nature of the Gods*) presents the Stoic teaching about the gods, covering the existence of the gods, their nature, their providential government of the cosmos, and their care for human beings, both generally and specifically. Along the way, he considers points related to the Stoic view of the nature of things, including the nature of the whole cosmos; the four basic elements; the stars, planets, sun, moon, and earth; the orders of being (plant, animal, human, divine); the wonders of nature indicating intelligent design; the periodic regeneration of the world from fire; how everything is made for the gods and humans; the excellent structure of the human body; human reason; and sexual reproduction.*

Cicero, *Tusculan Disputations* 1.19, 77

Cicero reports the Stoic view that the soul is fire and long-lasting.

ZENO THE STOIC understands the soul to be fire. . . . [77] The Stoics bestow on our souls a generous term of life. . . . They nevertheless affirm that, even though our souls will remain alive for a long time, they will not last forever.

Cicero, *On Ends* 3.72-73

Through the voice of Marcus Cato,[1] Cicero offers the Stoic view that nat-ural philosophy is a virtue insofar as it helps one understand and live in accord with nature.

[72] To the virtues we have discussed, the Stoics add . . . natural philosophy, for which they use the term "virtue" . . .

[73] The honor [of terming it virtue] is bestowed on natural phi-losophy with good reason since he who is to live in accord with nature must base himself on the management and order of the en-tire cosmos. Moreover, no man can truly make judgments regard-ing good and bad things unless he knows about the whole plan of nature, and also about the life of the gods, and the answer to the question whether human nature is or is not in harmony with the whole—that is, with the cosmos. And without natural philosophy, no one can consider the meaning of the ancient maxims of the wise—a meaning that is quite significant—that command us to "submit to the right moment" and "follow God" and "know your-self" and to take "nothing in excess." Also, this knowledge alone is able to convey the power of nature to cultivate justice and maintain friendship and the other kinds of love. Nor can we truly understand piety toward the gods nor the amount of gratitude we owe them without an explanation of nature.

Cicero, *Academica* 1.39

Through the voice of Marcus Terentius Varro,[2] Cicero summarizes two points in Zeno of Citium's natural philosophy: one, that there are only four natural elements, and that of the four, fire produces all things, including sensation and the mind; two, that incorporeal substances are "incapable of acting on anything." Therefore, he says, the reverse is implied: only bodies or corporeal substances can act on things or be acted on.[3]

[39] Zeno's views regarding the natural elements were as follows. First, regarding the four primary elements of nature, he did not add

the fifth element,[4] which those who came before supposed to be the cause of sensation and the mind. In fact, he decided that fire itself was the natural element that produced everything, including the mind and sensation.

Zeno also differed from those who came before in thinking that an incorporeal substance—such as Xenocrates and also those who came before had declared the rational soul to be—was incapable of acting on anything, whereas anything capable of acting on anything or being acted on by anything in any manner could not be incorporeal.

Cicero, *On Fate* 39–43

Cicero explores various views of fate and causation, including that of the Stoic Chrysippus, that things, including human beings, are fated, and yet they also move from within themselves, by means of their own power and nature.

[39] My own view is that Chrysippus—as an honorary judge, so to speak—wished to find a middle course between the two views held by the old philosophers. On the one hand, there was the view of those who judged that everything happens by fate—a fate that moves things forward by the force of necessity. This was the view of Democritus, Heraclitus, Empedocles, and Aristotle. On the other hand, there were those who understood the movements of the rational soul to be voluntary and not at all set in motion by fate. . . .

[40] Let us, if you like, look at the nature of this teaching relative to the topic of assents. . . .

Those old philosophers who thought that everything happens by fate declared that an assent is caused by force and necessity.

By contrast, those who disagreed with them liberated assents from fate. They further denied that necessity could be separated from an assent if fate applied to an assent.

They argued in the following manner: "If everything happens by fate, then everything happens by means of an antecedent cause. And if desire or appetite is caused in such a way, then likewise those things that follow upon desire. Therefore, assents are likewise caused. But if the cause of desire is not located within us, then, in fact, desire itself is not in our power. And if this is so, then those things that are caused by desire are not located within us. Therefore, neither assents nor actions are in our power. We may conclude from this that we are not being just when we praise or blame someone or hand out rewards or punishments."

But since this is an invalid conclusion, they suppose that they may conclude with probability on their side that not everything that happens, happens by fate.

[41] By contrast, Chrysippus—since he both rejected necessity and decided that nothing happens without preceding causes—distinguishes between different kinds of causation in order both to escape from necessity and to maintain fate. "Some causes," he says, "are perfect and principal; others are auxiliary and proximate. Therefore, when we Stoics say that everything happens by fate by means of antecedent causes, we want you to understand auxiliary and proximate causes rather than perfect and principal causes."

Accordingly, he counters the argument I made a moment ago by saying that, "If everything happens by fate, it *does* in fact follow that everything happens by means of antecedent causes—not by principal and perfect causes, however, but by auxiliary and proximate causes. And yet if these causes themselves are not in our power, it does not follow that desire is in fact not in our power. But if, on the other hand, we declared that everything happens by means of perfect and principal causes, then it would follow that desire would not be in our power since those causes would not be in our power."

[42] Therefore, the conclusion of the argument will be strong against those who introduce fate in such a way that they connect it to necessity. But it will have no strength against those who do not assert perfect and principal causes as antecedent causes. For the latter suppose that they can easily explain the meaning of the statement that assents happen by means of prior causes. For even though an assent cannot occur unless aroused by a presentation, nevertheless, the presentation supplies a proximate and not a principal cause.

This point is explained, as Chrysippus would have it, by the account we stated a moment ago. The point is not that an assent can happen with no external force having stimulated it—for it is necessary for an assent to be aroused by a presentation. Rather, he goes back to his roller and spinning top, which cannot begin to move unless they are pushed. When this has happened, however, he thinks they continue to move by their own nature, the roller rolling and the top spinning.

[43] "In the same way, therefore," says Chrysippus, "as a man who has pushed a roller forward has given it a beginning of motion but has not given it its circular motion, so a presentation, when it occurs, will indeed impress or stamp itself and, as it were, seal its likeness or image on the rational soul, but assent will be in our power. It is as we declared in the instance of the roller: though given an external push, as for the rest—its capacity to roll—the roller will move by its own power and nature. If something were caused without an antecedent cause, then it would be false that everything happens by fate. But if it is probable that all things happen by means of an antecedent cause, then what will prevent one from acknowledging that everything happens by fate?—if, that is, we understand the distinction and difference that exists between the causes."

Cicero, *On the Nature of the Gods* 2.3-168
(with a summary of the surrounding text given in italics)

Cicero presents the Stoic teaching regarding the gods in the voice of Quintus Lucilius Balbus, who discusses the topic under four headings. First, the existence of the gods is demonstrated by the observation of the heavens, the consensus of humankind, recorded epiphanies, and divination. Balbus also includes arguments for their existence from Chrysippus and Zeno, as well as from natural philosophy. Second, the divine nature is explained along with true religion (as opposed to superstition). Third, the providential government of the cosmos is established and explored from the nature of the divine itself and of the cosmos. Finally, the providential care of the gods for human beings, both generally and for specific humans, is shown. Along the way, Balbus discusses many points related to the Stoic view of the nature of things, including the nature of the whole cosmos (involving, among other points, its divinity and rationality); the four basic elements;

the stars, planets, sun, moon, and earth; the orders of being, including plants, animals, and humans; the wonders of nature indicating intelligent design; the periodic regeneration of the cosmos from fire; how everything is made for the gods and humans; how animals and plants exist for humans; the excellent structure of the human body; human reason; and sexual reproduction.

[3] Quintus Lucilius Balbus[5] said, "I submit to your desire to hear me speak, Cotta, and I will be as brief as I am able. . . .

"Generally speaking, the members of our Stoic school divide the inquiry regarding the immortal gods into four parts. First, they show that the gods exist. Next, they address their nature. Third, they explain how the gods manage or govern the cosmos. Finally, they discuss how they care for human beings and human-related things. In this discussion, however, let's address the first two points. As for the third and fourth, I think it is better to put them off to another time since they are much more involved." . . .

Cotta calls on Balbus to address all the points.

[4] "The first point, that the gods exist," Lucilius Balbus said, "does not even seem to need a persuasive speech. After all, when we look up to the sky and contemplate the celestial bodies, what can possibly be so clear and so evident as the conclusion that there must be some power or divinity of superior intelligence by which these things are ruled? If it were not so, then why does everyone approve the words of Ennius, when he says, 'Behold this shining brilliance on high, which all men call upon as Jove'? Yes, and not only when we call upon him as Jove but as the lord of the cosmos, ruling all things with the nod of his head. According to the same Ennius, Jove is 'the father of gods and men.' He's the God who is always present and very powerful. If a man doubts this, I can by no means understand why the same man should not also be capable of doubting the existence of the sun. [5] I mean how is the latter more evident than the former? Nothing but the presence in our minds of a known and grasped concept of God can account for the stability and permanence of our belief in him—a belief that is confirmed by the passage of time and grows more deeply rooted with

each generation and through the ages of mankind." *By contrast, he says, fictitious beliefs dwindle with time. . . .*

[6] "So it is that, among our own people and others, the veneration of the gods and the inviolability of religious feeling and moral obligation grow stronger and improve each day. Nor does this happen randomly or by chance. Rather, it is because the gods often reveal their power in person. Take the Latin War, for example. At the battle of Lake Regillus—the one between the dictator Aulus Postumius and Octavius Mamilius of Tusculum—the gods Castor and Pollux were seen fighting on horseback at the front of our army."

Balbus offers other examples. . . .

[7] "Then there is the evident reality of prophecies about future things and the presentiments we have of them. These prove that future things are manifest or made known or foretold or predicted to men." *. . . Balbus alludes to examples from the Greeks. Then, he says,* "Should we not let examples from our own people prove the power of the gods?"

7-11 Balbus presents examples from Rome's history showing this divine power—examples of those who failed to pay attention to, and even mocked, various signs of the gods, and thus experienced unfortunate ends, and those who esteemed the gods and their communications.

[12] "The authority of the augur is great. Is not the art of the haruspex divine? Is not one who witnesses" *the successful prediction of the augur and the haruspex,* "not to mention numerous similar phenomena, forced to acknowledge that the gods exist? If there are those who interpret or explain the direction of certain beings, then it follows that those beings themselves must exist. But there are those who interpret or explain the direction of the gods; therefore; we must acknowledge that the gods exist.

"It may possibly be said, however, that predicted things do not always happen as predicted. Sure. And sick people do not always get well. But that doesn't prove there is no art of medicine. Signs of future things are shown by the gods. If some men are off in interpreting or explaining these signs, it is not the nature of the gods that is the problem but the conclusions drawn by the men.

"As has been said, every man of every people agree about the most important point—that in the minds of everyone, there is an innate and, as it were, engraved notion that the gods exist.

[13] "As for the nature of the gods, there are various views—but no one denies their existence. Our own Cleanthes said that four things cause notions of the gods to form in the minds of men. The first he offered is the cause I mentioned a moment ago, the one about our foreknowledge of future things.

"Another is the great number of benefits we get from our temperate climate and the fruitfulness of the earth and the more than ample supply of other benefits.

[14] "The third is the fear in our minds inspired by lightning, storms, rain, snow, hail, floods, plagues, earthquakes that are often accompanied by loud noises, stone showers, rain-like drops of blood, landslides and chasms suddenly opening in the earth, monstrous births of men and animals, meteors in the sky, and blazing stars called 'comets' by the Greeks and 'long-haired stars' by us." *Balbus offers recent examples. . . .* "When they were shaken with fear by these phenomena, humans came to believe in the existence of some celestial and divine power.

[15] "The fourth and strongest cause is the uniform motion and consistent revolution of the celestial bodies, as well as the variation, benefit, beauty, and order of the sun, moon, and all the stars. Just seeing these things is enough to show us they are not the products of chance. Accordingly, when someone comes into a house or a gymnasium or a public assembly, and he sees that everything is happening in a rational and disciplined way, it is not possible for him to conclude that the order and discipline is happening without a cause. No, he understands that there is someone who rules and someone who obeys. How much more, then, when he sees the enormous paths of motion and huge cycles of change among the celestial bodies, the ordered movement of a great many things that has never failed through the endless time of the infinite past, must he conclude that these vast movements of nature are governed by some mind?

[16] "Even though Chrysippus' intellect is very sharp, he nevertheless expresses himself in such a way that his teaching seems to

come from nature itself than his own discovery. 'If indeed,' he says, 'there is something among natural things that the mind of a human being—its reason, strength, and power—is not able to cause or produce, then that which causes or produces it must be better than a human being. But a human being is not able to produce the perpetual order of the celestial bodies and everything therein; therefore, that which produces it is better than a human being. But what, among beings we can identify, is better than God? Indeed, if the gods do not exist, then what is there among natural things that is better than a human being? Reason exists in him alone—and nothing is more excellent than reason. But it is an act of foolish arrogance to think that there is nothing better in the whole cosmos than a human being; therefore, there is something better. It follows that God actually exists.'

[17] "And truly, if you see a large and beautiful house, you cannot be led to think—even if you do not see the master builder or the head of the household—that it was constructed by mice and weasels. Will you not, then, be judged a simple moron if you think all this— the majestic splendor of the cosmos, the great variety and beauty of celestial things, and the massive power and size of the sea and the earth—is home to you alone and not the immortal gods? . . .

[18] "And from the ingenuity of human beings themselves we are able to detect the existence of another mind in the cosmos that is even more clever and divine. Otherwise, as Socrates says in Xenophon,[6] where did humans 'lay hold of' the mind we possess? If anyone asks about the source of the fluid and warmth in our bodies, and the solid earthlike stuff in our guts, and, finally, the breath of life within us, we declare that it is apparent we have taken the one from the earth, the other from water and fire, and the last from the air we breathe. But where did we find and how did we obtain that which surpasses all the rest? By this I mean our reason—or, if many words are okay, our mind, our ability to plan, our ability to think, our practical judgment. Will the cosmos furnish everything else but this one thing that is the best? But there is certainly nothing among all things that is better than the cosmos—nothing that is more excellent, nothing that is more beautiful. Not only does nothing better

exist, but we cannot even think of anything better. And if there is nothing better than reason and wisdom, then we must concede that these exist in that which is the best.

[19] "What, then? Who is not summoned to accept what I have been saying regarding the harmony, agreement, and interconnection of everything in the cosmos? In what other way would it be possible for the earth to bloom with fruit and flowers at one time and then be desolate with the opposite at another? Or how would it be possible for us to know that the transformation of so many things around us points to the approach and retreat of the sun at the summer and winter solstices? Or that the rise and fall of the tides in the sea and straits are driven by the rising and setting of the moon? Or that the different courses of the stars are preserved by the one revolution of the entire sky? These things—considering the harmony of every part of the cosmos—most definitely could not occur as they do without a single divine and continuous spirit holding and connecting them together.

[20] "When these points are investigated in a free and flowing manner, as I propose to do, they easily avoid the tricks of the Academics. But when discussed in a brief and subtle way, as Zeno used to do, they are more exposed to attacks. . . .

"The thoughts we freely expand are compressed by Zeno in this way: [21] 'That which employs the faculty of reason is better than that which does not employ the faculty of reason. But nothing is better than the cosmos; therefore, the cosmos employs the faculty of reason.'

"A similar argument can be used to show that the cosmos is wise, happy, and eternal—since to possess all of them is better than lacking them, and so nothing is better than the cosmos. The cosmos is shown to be God by means of this argument.

"Zeno put the same point this way: [22] 'Nothing that lacks sensation or perception has a part that is able to sense or perceive things. But the cosmos has parts that are able to sense or perceive things; therefore, the cosmos does not lack sensation or perception.' He goes on to press the argument more closely. 'Nothing,' he says, 'without a living soul and reason is able to generate from itself something that is living and rational. But the cosmos is able to generate something that has a living soul and reason; therefore; the cosmos is living and rational.' . . .

[23] "Even though I said that the existence of the gods is evident to everyone, and that it did not require a long speech to prove, I now nevertheless want to demonstrate their existence by means of arguments taken from natural philosophy—that is, from the nature of things.

"It is a fact that all things capable of nourishment and growth contain in themselves the power of heat without which they could neither nourish themselves nor grow. For everything with a hot and fiery nature is stimulated and directed by its own motion. But that which is nourished and grows employs a fixed and uniform motion. Sensation and life remain in us as long as this motion remains in us. But we die, our lives extinguished, as soon as the heat cools to nothing.

[24] "Using arguments like these, Cleanthes shows how great the power of heat is in every living body. He observes that there is no food so heavy that it cannot be digested in a single night and day. And even what remains of this process of digestion,—the remnants that nature rejects—, even these contain heat. And the veins and arteries in a body always throb with fiery motion. . . . Every living thing, therefore, whether an animal or a plant produced by the earth, lives thanks to the heat contained within the animal or plant. From this fact, one should understand that the very nature of heat has within itself the power of life that pervades the whole cosmos.

[25] "The point will be easier to understand with a more detailed explanation of every form this fiery power takes in permeating everything.

"As I was saying, all parts of the cosmos—though I will only address the most important—are supported and sustained by heat. This can be perceived, first of all, in the nature of earthly things. For example, we see that fire is produced by striking or rubbing stones together. And just after digging, we see 'the warm earth steaming.' And warm water is drawn from ever-flowing springs—something that happens most of all in wintertime. Why at this time? A great quantity of heat is contained in the hollows of the earth. During winter, the earth is more compact, and thus it squeezes the heat found within the earth. [26] I would need to speak for a long time with many arguments in order to show that all the seeds conceived by the earth, and all the plants generated from her and held fixed by their roots in her, both spring up and grow from the warm composition of the earth.

"That water is also mixed with heat is shown, first, by the fluidity of water—that water is a liquid. Water would neither be frozen by cold nor solidified into snow and hoarfrost unless it could also become fluid when melted and liquified by mixing heat with it. This is why liquid is frozen and hardened by northern and other cold winds, and, in turn, it softens and melts again with heat. We observe that the sea also, when agitated by the wind, grows warm. From this we can easily see that heat is stored in this great body of liquid. For we cannot imagine that this heat is somehow external or foreign to the sea, but that it is stirred up from the lowest depths of the sea by means of agitation just as our own bodies grow warm again by means of motion and exercise.

"And the air itself, even though by nature it is the coldest element, is by no means devoid of heat. [27] Indeed, there is a great quantity of heat mixed with the air. Air itself is generated by the respiration of water since air is, as we believe, a kind of vaporized water, and this respiration or vaporization appears thanks to the heat contained in water. We can detect something like this when fire causes water to boil.

"There remains a fourth part of the cosmos. This part by nature is fiery hot in itself so that it shares with every other nature a healthful and life-giving heat. [28] From this fact, that every part of the cosmos is sustained by heat, we may conclude that the cosmos itself has been preserved for a very long time by a similar phenomenon. More than this, we should understand that the power and cause of generation and production in the cosmos belong to this hot and fiery heat that is united with every nature. It is responsible for the birth and growth of every living thing, whether an animal or a plant whose roots are held by the earth.

[29] "There is, therefore, a nature that holds the whole cosmos together and maintains it, a nature that most certainly possesses sensation and reason. I say this because the cosmos is neither an isolated nor a simple thing, but it is an interconnected nature of many things with other things, and any such nature must have within it some leading part. So it is that the mind rules in human beings. And there is something like the mind in lower animals that is the origin of their desire for things. As for trees and plants that spring up from the earth, people suspect that the leading part is in their roots.

"My term 'leading part'⁷ is a stand-in for what the Greeks call *hēgemonikon*. There cannot be and should not be anything superior to it in any kind of thing. It follows, then, that the thing which contains the leading part of the whole of nature must be the best of all things and the most worthy of power and rule over all things.

[30] "We observe that the parts of the cosmos—and there is nothing in the whole cosmos that is not part of the totality of things—contain sensation and reason. We may conclude, then, that the part which contains the leading part of the cosmos necessarily contains sensation and reason—and these more intensely and in greater abundance. It follows that the cosmos is wise, and that the nature which joins all things together must be superior in the perfection of its reason. The cosmos, therefore, is a divine being, a god, and every cosmic force is bound by the divine nature.

"We may further observe that the heat of the cosmos is purer and clearer and livelier, and thus it is far more likely to stimulate sensation than our own heat by which the things we come to know are retained and alive to us. [31] Since human beings and animals are kept alive and in motion and they feel and experience things thanks to this heat, it is absurd to say that the cosmos is without sensation, considering that the same heat holds it together, a heat that is full and free and pure, a heat that thoroughly penetrates a thing and moves faster than anything—particularly since this cosmic heat is neither stirred up by another thing nor driven on by some external push, but it is moved spontaneously from within and by itself. For can anything be more powerful or effectual than the cosmos, that which drives and moves its own heat by which it is held together?

[32] "Let us listen to Plato, one who is like a god among philosophers. He says there are two kinds of motion—one from within and one from without. The one that moves spontaneously from itself is more divine than the one that is driven on by the push of another. He locates this motion—that which moves spontaneously from itself—in the soul alone. The soul, he thinks, is the principal source of motion. For this reason, since all motion arises from the cosmic heat, and since this heat moves spontaneously from itself and is not driven on by another, it necessarily follows that this heat is soul. This proves that the cosmos is ensouled—that is, it is a living or animated being.

"And from this we are able to gather that intelligence belongs to the cosmos since the cosmos as a whole is better than any single nature within the cosmos. For even as we ourselves are greater than any single part of our body, so the whole cosmos is necessarily greater than any part of the cosmos. If this is the case, it follows that the cosmos is wise. If this does not follow, then a human being, who is part of the cosmos, is necessarily greater than the whole cosmos since humans are rational.

[33] "Let's advance, if we want to, from the lowest natures, which are imperfect, to the highest natures, which are perfect. If we do, we will inevitably reach the nature of the gods.

"First, we observe that nature sustains things that spring up from the earth. For these, nature grants nothing more than the ability to nourish themselves and to grow.

[34] "To animals she gives sensation and motion, together with a kind of appetite or desire that draws them toward health-giving things and withdraws them from destructive things.

"She gives even more than this to human beings. For them, she added reason, by which the appetites or desires of the soul are controlled—sometimes giving them free rein and sometimes holding them back.

"The fourth and loftiest stage belongs to those beings that are naturally good and wise. From the very beginning, these beings are born with right and consistent reason, which is superior to human reason. This stage belongs to a divine being, to the cosmos, in which perfect and complete reason necessarily exists.

[35] "There is, in anything that is organized or arranged, some final perfection. This we cannot deny. We see this, for instance, with the growth of a vine or a cow. Unless some power hinders it, nature follows its own path until it comes to its final goal. We see this as well with painting and building things and the other arts. Each one has its own ideal of perfection it is working toward. This movement toward completion and thus perfection is necessarily true for the whole of nature—but even more so. And even though individual things may encounter many external impediments to their progress toward perfection, nothing is able to impede the progress of the whole of nature because the whole itself embraces and contains every natural thing. That is why there is necessarily this fourth and highest stage, which no power can touch. [36] This is the stage on which universal nature stands. Since the whole is like this—it is superior to all things and nothing can impede it—the cosmos is necessarily perceptive or intelligent and wise, even.

"What is more ignorant than to declare that the all-inclusive nature is *not* the best? Or if one admits its superiority, to go on to declare, first, that it is *not* a living being, then to say it is *not* rational and *not* a master of deliberation, and finally, to say it is *not* wise?

"In what other way can it be the best? If it is similar to plants or even animals, then there is no reason to judge it 'the best' versus 'the worst.' And if it shares in reason but was not wise from the very beginning, then the condition of the cosmos would be lower than that of the general human condition. For a human being can become wise. But the cosmos—assuming it has been unwise through the eternity of past time—will never attain wisdom in time to come. And so it will be inferior to a human being. But this is absurd! Therefore, the cosmos has been wise from the very beginning, and thus divine.

[37] "Truly, there is nothing else, except for the cosmos, that lacks nothing, nothing else that is equipped in every way, perfect and full in terms of its measure and parts.

"Chrysippus cleverly made the point this way: just as the shield cover was produced for the sake of the shield and the scabbard for the sake of the sword, so was everything else produced for the sake of some other thing—everything except for the cosmos. So it was that the grain and fruits produced by the earth were created for the sake of animals, and animals for the sake of human beings. The horse, for example, was made for the sake of riding, and the ox for plowing, and the dog for hunting and guarding.

"Man himself, however, is born to contemplate and imitate the cosmos. And though he is by no means perfect, he is a small part of that which is perfect. [38] By contrast, the cosmos is entirely perfect—this is so because it includes everything since that which exists is contained within it. How, then, can it lack that which is best? But there is nothing better than mind and reason. The cosmos, therefore, cannot lack these things.

"With the help of analogies, Chrysippus makes a strong case that everything complete and fully grown is better than something incomplete and just born. So it is that a horse is better than a foal, a dog is better than a puppy, and a man is better than a boy. Similarly, the very best thing in the whole cosmos must be something complete and perfect. [39] But there is nothing in the cosmos better than excellence or virtue. Virtue, therefore, is an essential attribute of the cosmos since nothing is more complete than the cosmos. Again, even though human nature is, indeed, not perfect, virtue may nevertheless be realized completely in a human being. How much easier it is, then, in the cosmos! There is, therefore, virtue in it. It is wise, therefore, and so for this reason a divine being.

"Now that we have perceived the divinity of the cosmos, we must also attribute the same divinity to the stars, which are born from the quickest and purest part of the aether without the admixture of any other nature or element. The stars are hot and translucent throughout. So it is right to declare them living beings endowed with sensation and intelligence.

[40] "Cleanthes thinks that we may establish that the stars consist entirely of fire thanks to the testimony of the senses—those of touch and sight. For the heat and brightness of the sun is far more

obvious than any fire. First, it shines far and wide through the boundless cosmos. And the touch of its light is so powerful that it not only warms but often burns. It could do neither if it were not made of fire. 'Therefore,' Cleanthes goes on, 'since the sun is made of fire and is nourished by the moisture or vapors from the ocean' — since a fire is unable to persist without something feeding it—'it must be similar either to the fire we ordinarily use for cooking or warming ourselves or that which is contained in the bodies of living things. [41] But our fire, the one required everyday, consumes and destroys everything. . . . By contrast, the body's warmth brings life and health. It preserves, nourishes, grows, and sustains all things, imparting sensation to everything.' Therefore, he says there can be no doubt about which of these fires the sun is like since the sun causes everything to flourish and ripen or mature according to its own kind. Since the fire of the sun is like the fire that is in the bodies of living beings, the sun itself must also be a living being. So too must the other stars be living beings since they come to be in this heavenly heat, which we call the aether or sky.

[42] "Since, therefore, some living beings are born on the earth, and others in the water, and others in the air, it is absurd—Aristotle notes—to think that no living being is born in that part which is most adapted for the production of living beings. But the stars occupy the aethereal place. And since this element is the most rarefied, and it is always in vigorous motion, it follows that the living being born therein is the sharpest in sensation and the quickest in speed. Accordingly, since the stars come into being in the aether, it is reasonable to conclude that sensation and intelligence belong to them. Thus, we should count them among the gods."

Balbus compares the greater intelligence of people who inhabit certain regions of earth with the location of the stars and their superior intelligence. . . .

[43] . . . "The invariable order and regular motion of the stars clearly manifest their sensation and intelligence. For it is impossible for anything to move rationally and with measure without an intended plan or design, which contains nothing thoughtless or unpredictable or accidental. Now the order and eternal regularity of the stars signify neither a natural inclination, since the order and

regularity are completely rational, nor chance, since chance loves variety and spurns regularity. It follows, therefore, that the stars move by their own free will and their own understanding and divinity."

[44] *Aristotle's view, he observes, "that the motion of all living bodies is due" either to natural, forced, or voluntary motion, supports the point.* "Anyone who sees this conclusion would—if he denied the existence of the gods—show not only ignorance but impiety. Nor, in fact, is there a great difference between denying their existence and taking away their management of the cosmos and other activity. In my mind, whatever is wholly inactive is practically non-existent.[8] Therefore, it is clear the gods exist—so clear that I can hardly judge the one who denies it to be of sound mind.

[45] "It remains for us to consider the qualities of the divine nature. In this, nothing is a greater challenge than to lead the mind away from the direct experience of the eyes. This difficulty has led both the uneducated multitude and the philosophers who resemble the uneducated to be unable to consider the immortal gods without thinking of them in terms of the human form. . . . That said, assuming we have the definite notion in our souls that God is, first, a living being, and then that there is nothing else in the whole of nature that is more excellent than God, I see nothing that is more consistent with this notion than to recognize that this cosmos, which is the most excellent of all being, is itself a living being and God.

[46] "Let Epicurus joke about this notion if he wants to." *He's not even a good joker. . . .* "Let him say it is impossible to understand God as revolving and round." *Still, even* "he holds that gods exist since there must be some mode of outstanding and excellent being." *Such is the cosmos,* "a living being that possesses sensation, reason, and mind." *Thus,* "the cosmos is God." . . .

[47] *Moving on, it is not the cone, cylinder, or pyramid, as Velleius' school thinks, that is the most beautiful form.* "There are two forms that are more excellent than all others. Among solid forms there is the globe or sphere—for so we may translate the Greek *sphaera*. And among plane forms there is the circle or orbit—the Greek is *kyklos*. These two forms alone possess total uniformity in all their parts, and

every point on the extremity or circumference is equally distant from the center. And there is nothing that can be better fitted or more compact than that. . . ."

Of course the Epicureans, who believe in countless cosmoses, and that the cosmos can be any form, do not know this. . . .

[49] ". . . There are two kinds of stars. Some journey from east to west in unchanging stages never varying at all from their usual course. The others complete a double revolution with an equally constant regularity. Both demonstrate the rotation of the cosmos and the circular revolution of the stars—something that is only possible with a spherical form. There is the sun, the first among the stars." *Balbus describes the sun's celestial motion and influence on earth, including day and night, summer and winter.*

[50] "And there is the moon." *Balbus similarly discusses the moon.*

[51] "Most admirable is the motion of the five stars that are falsely called 'wandering stars' or 'planets.' I say this because a thing cannot 'wander' if it forever preserves constant and established motions, going forward and turning backward, and so on.

52-53 *The mathematicians debate the length of "what they call the great year, which is completed when the sun, moon, and five planets, having all finished their courses, have returned to the same positions relative to one another." Balbus gives the Latin and Greek name of the five planets, as well as their relative distance from the earth, their path and length of course. They are Saturn (Phaenōn, the shining star), Jupiter (Phaethōn, the blazing star), Mars (Pyroeis, the fiery star), Mercury (Stilbōn, the gleaming star), and Venus (Phōsphoros, the light-bearing star—Lucifer when it precedes the sun but Hesperos when it follows).*

[54] "I cannot understand this regularity of the stars, this harmony of motion through time in all eternity—and this despite various courses—without mind, reason, and purpose. And if we see these attributes in the stars, we must count them in with the number of gods. The so-called 'non-wandering' or fixed stars also reveal the same rational mind and practical wisdom or purpose. Their motion occurs daily in a regular and constant manner." *And this, Balbus*

explains, is not because the aether "holds the stars and causes them to re-volve by its own force." . . . [55] "The ongoing and unbroken courses of these stars, as admirable and as beyond belief as they are in their regularity, plainly reveal a divine power and mind in them. So it is that anyone who is unable to perceive that they possess a divine power is unable to understand anything at all.

[56] "I conclude, then, that there is nothing in the sky above that is chance-based or accidental or random or without purpose. By contrast, everything is a matter of order, truth, reason, and regular-ity. Whatever lacks these latter qualities, whatever is deceptive, false, and full of error, is situated in that realm between the moon, which is the lowest of all the heavenly bodies, and the earth, and upon the surface of the earth herself. From this conclusion, then, I suppose that a man who has no share in mind or reason judges that the admirable order and incredible regularity of the stars, from which the preservation and prosperity of all things originate, is lacking in mind or reason.

[57] "Therefore, I will not at all go wrong in this discussion—or so I believe—if I follow the lead of Zeno, who is himself the guide of those searching for the truth. Zeno defines nature this way: 'Nature,' he says, 'is a craftsmanlike or skillful fire that proceeds methodically to the work of production or generation.' He proposes that the most significant attribute of art or craft-making is to create and produce things—to bring things into being. Whatever we accomplish with our hands in our own works of art or craftsmanship, nature accom-plishes far more skillfully—nature, as I said, the 'craftsmanlike fire' that is the teacher of everyone else who practices an art. According to this line of argument, the whole of nature is craftsmanlike since it follows a specific way and adheres to a definite method.

[58] "The reality of the cosmos itself, which encompasses and contains all things in its own embrace, is not only 'craftsmanlike' or 'skillful,' but, as Zeno puts it very simply, the cosmos is an artist or craftsman, that which cares and looks out for the benefit and time-liness of everything. And as the other natures are born and grow from their own seeds, and they are limited by the same, so the na-ture of the cosmos possesses every voluntary motion, every effort

and strong inclination—what the Greeks call *hormai*. And the cosmos employs these with suitable actions in the same way we act when moved by our minds and senses. Since this is what the mind of the cosmos is like, we may for this reason correctly term it 'practical wisdom' or 'providence'—for *pronoia* is the term in Greek. And this providence is chiefly directed toward and occupied with, first, making sure the cosmos is the best constructed so that it will last, and, after that, making sure it lacks nothing—most importantly that it contains uncommon beauty and every adornment.

[59] "So far I have said something about the cosmos as a whole, and I have also said something about the stars. From this, it is now apparent that there is a multitude of active gods.

"Yet even though they are active, they do not have to pursue their endeavors by means of difficult and troublesome toil. For they are not composed of veins, nerves, and bones. And their food and drink do not negatively affect the composition of their bodies. Nor are their bodies such that they have to fear falls or blows or the dangers of disease. Thanks to these things, Epicurus invented his shadowy, do-nothing gods. [60] By contrast, the gods are gifted with an utterly beautiful form and located in the purest region of the sky and carry themselves along in their measured course in such a way that they seem to preserve and support everything in accord with one another.

"In addition to the sidereal divinities, the natures of many other gods have been identified and named by the wisest men of Greece and by our ancestors from the great benefits they offer—and this not without reason. For they judged that whatever confers great utility on human beings must arise from divine goodness. And so the name of the god was given from the gift or production of the god." *Examples include Ceres and Liber relative to grain and wine. . . .* [61] "In other cases, a significant power is named a god. Take, for example, Faith and Mind," *with their shrines in Rome. . . .* "There is the temple of Virtue restored as the temple of Honor by Marcus Marcellus but established many years before." *There are other temples to Wealth, Safety, Concord, Liberty, Victory, all which* "imply divine governance," *as well as Desire, Pleasure, and Venus Lubentina,* "things vicious and unnatural." . . .

[62] "It has also been a general custom to deify with fame and gratitude those men who have conferred the most excellent of benefits on mankind. So it is that we have Hercules, Castor and Pollux, Aesculapius, Liber," *the son of Semele*, . . . "and Romulus. These benefactors are properly honored as gods since they are the best of men and immortal, their souls contentedly lasting forever.

[63] "Take another idea—this from reason and natural philosophy. It has given rise to a great multitude of gods, who, clothed in human form, have furnished the poets with stories and have filled human life with every superstition. This topic was handled by Zeno, and was later explained with even more words by Cleanthes and Chrysippus. For instance, there was the ancient belief in Greece that the god Caelus was castrated by his son Saturn, and that Saturn himself was imprisoned by his son Jupiter.[9]

[64] "Now these impious stories actually contain something rational and sophisticated from natural philosophy. In the aforementioned belief, the idea was that the highest celestial nature—that which is aethereal and fiery and generates all things—is without the body part that requires sexual union with another in order to produce offspring."[10]

64-69 Balbus goes on to describe a more rational rather than fabulous relationship between Saturn and Jupiter (how Time—or Saturn—both devours all and yet is limited to specific periods by Jupiter) before offering similar explanations for all the other major gods—for Jupiter (Zeus), Juno (Hera), Neptune (Poseidon), Dis (Ploutos), Proserpina (Persephone), Ceres (Demeter), Minerva (Athena), Janus, Vesta (Hestia), the Penates (household gods), Apollo, Diana (Artemis), and Venus (Aphrodite).

[70] "Do you not see, therefore, how these imaginary and made-up gods have been drawn from the reasonable and useful discoveries of natural philosophy? Thus, we have false beliefs and confusing errors and superstitions that are no better than old wives' tales. From these stories we come to know what form the gods take and how old they are, what they wear, and how they decorate themselves. We know their family genealogies, marriages, and relationships. And

everything is reduced to the image of human weakness so that they too experience soul disturbance—lust, melancholy, irascibility." *These gods even take part in wars, such as in Homer and that between the Titans and the Giants. . . .*

"These stories and beliefs are totally stupid—full of shallow nonsense. [71] Still, even though we reject and scorn these stories, we may nevertheless grasp that a god pervades the substance of every nature—Ceres pervades the earth, Neptune pervades the sea, and so on, other gods pervading the rest. And it is our duty to worship and care for the gods under the names that custom has given them, whatever they are and whatever their qualities. But the best, purest, and holiest way to care for the gods, the way of profound piety, is to worship them always with our whole minds and true words. For both philosophers and our ancestors distinguished between true religion and superstition." [72] *Balbus explains the difference between superstition and religion in terms of etymology.*

"It seems to me that I have said enough to demonstrate the existence of the gods and what sort of beings they are.

[73] "I next have to show that the cosmos is managed by the providence of the gods. This is a vast topic" —*one that is debated by the Academics, Balbus observes, and misunderstood by the Epicureans. . . .*

[74] "The term 'providence' itself is shorthand or an abbreviated term. Look at it this way. When someone says, 'The Athenian city-state is ruled by the council,' the words 'of the Areopagus' are left unspoken. So it is when we say, 'The cosmos is managed by providence.' We don't say, 'of the gods,' but this is what we mean. The fully spoken statement, then, complete in itself is, 'The cosmos is managed by the providence of the gods.' . . .

[75] "I declare, therefore, that the cosmos and every part of the cosmos was formed from the beginning by the gods and is managed by the providence of the gods through all time.

This topic is a discussion that our school usually divides into three parts. Led on by rational reflection, the first part shows that the gods exist. If this is granted, it must be conceded that the cosmos is managed by the council of the gods—by their wise deliberation. The second part shows that everything is subject to a perceptive nature that sustains everything most beautifully. Given this point, it follows that the cosmos was generated from living first principles. The third topic is derived from our admiration for things in the sky and upon the earth."

76-77 Balbus details the first part of the argument—that the gods exist, are superior to all things, are intelligent, and that they govern the cosmos by their providence.

[78] "From the fact that the gods do actually exist, . . . it necessarily follows that they are living beings. And not only are they living beings, but they are also rational beings, joined together as citizens, we might say, in a community of friendship. As such, they rule over the one cosmos as a shared city-state.

[79] "It follows that the gods possess the very same kind of reason as human beings, and the same truth and law that enjoin what is right and shun what is wrong. From this we understand that humans attain practical wisdom and judgment from the gods. And from this we grasp why it was the custom of our ancestors to publicly recognize and honor Understanding, Faith, Virtue, and Concord as gods. How, then, can we deny that these exist among the gods when we worship their venerable and sacred images? And if understanding, faith, virtue, and concord belong to humankind, then from where—if not from the gods above—did these things come to us upon the earth? Furthermore, since we possess the ability to plan, and we possess reason and practical wisdom, then the gods necessarily have these to the greatest possible degree. They do not merely possess them, but the gods employ them relative to the greatest and the best things. [80] But nothing is greater nor better than the cosmos. It follows, therefore, that the cosmos is managed by the deliberation and providence of the gods. Finally, since we have satisfactorily demonstrated the divinity of those beings whose extraordinary power and bright form we see—I mean the sun, the moon, the wandering stars or planets, the fixed stars, the sky, and the cosmos itself with its many other powers that are of great service and benefit to humankind—we must conclude that everything is ruled by divine understanding and practical wisdom.

"That's enough for the first part of my demonstration. [81] I next have to show that all things are subject to and dependent upon nature, by which they are produced and sustained in the most excellent manner. But first I must briefly explain what nature itself is so that we may easily understand what I want to show.

"Some judge that nature is a non-rational power or force that causes necessary motions in corporeal things.

"Others think that it is a force that participates in reason and order, advancing methodically, so to speak, manifesting the cause that produces each thing and what follows—an expertise that neither artist nor craftsman nor workman is able to imitate. Such is the power of a seed, they say, that, even though its size is small, if it falls into a receptive nature that binds with it, and if it obtains therein the kind of sustenance that is able to nourish and cause it to grow, then it fashions and produces things according to its own kind—some nourished by means of their own roots, while some are able to move, and to feel and think, and to desire and strive for things, and to give birth to offspring similar to themselves.

[82] "For others, the term 'nature' means everything in the cosmos. For example, there is Epicurus, who divides the nature of all existing things into bodies, the void or emptiness, and their attributes.

"By contrast, when we Stoics say that the cosmos exists in accord with and is managed by nature, we do not mean it in the manner of Epicurus, as if the cosmos is like a lump of earth or a piece of rock or anything else that does not have its own natural property of coherence. Instead, the cosmos is like a tree or an animal, in which nothing is accidental or arbitrary. Order is manifest, as well as something resembling art or craftsmanship.

[83] "But if the art of nature supports plants that are rooted to the earth, giving them life and causing them to thrive, then surely the art of nature supports the earth herself by the same power. When the earth is impregnated with seeds, she gives birth to all things in abundance, nourishing their roots in her embrace, fostering their growth. She, in turn, is nourished by natural elements that are above and external to her. Moreover, her own exhalations

nourish the air and the aether and everything that is above. Therefore, if nature supports the earth and causes her to thrive, then the
same conclusion applies to the rest of the cosmos. For a plant's roots
cling to the earth. By contrast, animals are sustained by breathing
air. And air itself sees with us and hears with us and speaks with
us—for none of these functions can be performed without air. Air
also moves with us, for wherever we go or move, it seems to give
place and withdraw before us.

[84] "Whatever is at the cosmos' center, which is its lowest part,
and whatever moves from the center to that which is above, and
whatever revolves in circles around the center—these together produce the self-coherent, single nature of the cosmos.

"There are four kinds of bodies. The nature of the cosmos continues on thanks to the change of these four—for water rises up
from earth, air from water, and aether from air. Then again, things
are reversed as air comes from aether, water comes from air, and
earth, the lowest natural element, comes from water. So it is that the
parts of the cosmos are held together by the ongoing passage up
and down, and side to side, of these four bodies by which all things
are composed. [85] And this same cosmos, equipped as it is, must
either be everlasting or at least very long lasting, continuing in existence long into the future—practically forever.

"Whatever the case, it follows that nature manages the cosmos.
Consider the navigation of a fleet of ships or the marshalling of an
army or,—to return to those things managed by nature,—the generation of a vine or a tree, or even the generation of the limbs of an animal
in terms of their shape and symmetry. Compared with the cosmos
itself, which one of these manifests the expertise of nature in the production of things? Therefore, either nothing is directed by a sentient
nature, or we must admit that the cosmos is ruled by such a nature.

[86] "Think about it. The cosmos contains within itself every nature along with the seeds of every nature. How, then, is it possible
that the cosmos itself is not managed by nature? Take a parallel example. If someone declares that a man's teeth and beard exist by
nature but that the man himself to whom these belong does not exist by nature, then that one would fail to grasp that things which

produce something from themselves possess more perfect natures than those things that are produced from them. But the cosmos is the author, the creator, the father, so to speak, of everything managed by nature. It brings up everything, nourishes everything. So it is that the cosmos embraces and sustains everything as a body does its own limbs and parts. But if the parts of the cosmos are managed by nature, it follows that the cosmos itself is managed by nature.

"Now the management of the cosmos contains nothing that may possibly be faulted. Given the natural elements, the best that could be produced from them has been produced. [87] Let someone, therefore, show that the cosmos could have been better. But no one will ever show this. And anyone who wishes to improve some part of the cosmos will either make it worse or will be asking for something impossible given the nature of things.

"But if the parts of the cosmos are arranged so that they could neither be more useful nor more beautiful in appearance, then let us see whether this arrangement is a matter of chance or whether, on the contrary, the parts of the cosmos are arranged in a way that they could not possibly have been if they were not ruled by an intelligent and divine providence. If, then, the works of nature are better than the works of art, and if the arts produce nothing without reason, then nature also participates in reason.

"When you look at a statue or a painting, you see at once the presence of art. Likewise, when you see a ship sailing along some course, you do not doubt that it is moved along by reason and art. Or when you observe a sundial or a water clock, you grasp that it declares the hour of the day by means of an art and not by means of chance. How, then, does it make sense to suppose that the cosmos, which includes these very works of art and the craftsmen who made them and everything else, has no share in deliberation or reason?

[88] "Or picture this. A traveler carries into Scythia or into Britain the sphere recently produced by our friend Posidonius—the one that at each revolution reproduces the same motions of the sun, the moon, and the five planets that take place in the heavens each day and night. Would even one barbarian doubt that this sphere was the accomplishment of a rational being? Even so, those

thinkers, including Epicurus, raise doubts about the cosmos itself, from which all things rise and have their being. They question whether the cosmos itself is produced by chance or by some necessity or by a rational and divine mind. In their judgment, Archimedes' achievement in making an imitation of the revolution of the spheres is greater than nature's actual work in producing the spheres themselves—even though the perfection of the original is far more clever and skillful than the copy."

89-90 Balbus gives the example of the shepherd who, in Accius' Medea, *has never seen a ship before. Even though he is at first astonished by the sight of the Argonaut's ship, the Argo, he begins to understand, upon seeing its "young sailors," that the ship is not "some lifeless thing devoid of sensation," but, he suspects, it is piloted by these same men.*

[90] "Similarly, if the philosophers were confused by the cosmos when first studying it, they should have later on,—upon discerning its definite and uniform motions, and judging how everything is regulated by an immutable and constant succession,—inferred the existence of some being that not only dwells in this celestial and divine house, but one who is also the master, director, and architect, so to speak, of this spectacular building.

"As it is, it seems they do not even suspect the marvels observed in the sky and upon the earth."

91-92 Balbus specifies these marvels—the earth, air, and aether, including the many fires (the sun and other stars) that arise from the aether, and how these fires benefit the earth rather than being harmed by them.

[93] "Must I not, at this point, express amazement that there are any men who persuade themselves that certain solid bodies they call atoms, which are carried along by the force of their own weight, produce, by the chance encounter of these bodies, this very well furnished and most beautiful cosmos?

"It seems that anyone who thinks that such a chance production is possible will also believe that, if we shake up and toss onto the ground a vast number of the letters of the alphabet—all twenty-one, varied in form and composed of gold or whatever nature—, then it would be possible to produce the continuous text of the *Annals* of Ennius, all ready for us to read. As for me, I doubt whether chance would be able to produce even a single verse![11]

[94] "How, then, can our Epicurean friends or anyone else assert that the cosmos is brought about by means of the random and chance collisions of tiny bodies that have neither color nor any other quality (what the Greeks call *poiotēs*) nor sensation? Or countless worlds or cosmoses, for that matter, popping into existence at any time, some being born and some dying?

"If collisions of atoms are able to produce the cosmos, why can they not produce a colonnade or a temple or a house or a city? Relative to the cosmos, these are simple works and far easier to produce.

"Certainly such men speak thoughtlessly about the cosmos. It seems to me that they have never looked up and seen this marvelous and splendid sky. [95] To the point, Aristotle brilliantly says,

Imagine beings who have always dwelled beneath the earth in comfortable, well-lit dwellings, furnished with statues and pictures, and done up with every abundant thing enjoyed by those judged to be happy. Further, imagine that, even though they have never gone up above the surface of the earth, they have learned about the existence of certain gods and divine powers by listening to a variety of news reports. Now, what would happen if, at some point, the jaws of the earth open wide and they are able to go out into our dwelling places upon the surface of the earth? They would suddenly see the earth and the sea and the sky above. And they would know the magnitude of the clouds and feel the strength of the winds, and they would observe the sun, understanding not only its great size and beauty but also its influence and generative power in producing the day by pouring out its light into the whole sky. Then, when night darkens the earth, they would see the whole sky spangled and adorned with stars, and the varied light of the moon, now waxing and now waning, and the rising and setting of all these heavenly bodies, their courses immutable through all eternity. Surely, upon seeing these things, these beings would believe the gods exist and judge these great works to be the production of the gods.[12]

[96] "That's, anyway, how Aristotle saw things. For our part, let's consider a darkness similar to that which was caused by the eruption of the fires of Mount Etna, the darkness that for two days covered the area surrounding the volcano and made it so that no human being could recognize any other human being. When the sun shone again on the third day, they felt as though they had come to life again. Now suppose that we humans were enveloped in the same kind of darkness—but from the beginning of time. What would happen if we suddenly beheld the light of the sun? Or if we saw the spectacle of the sky above? As it stands, their daily recurrence habituates our eyes and souls to their sight, and so we neither wonder at nor inquire into the reason for these things since we always see them." . . .

97-114 *Balbus goes on, arguing that surely the wonders of the cosmos disclose a "rational design or purpose," the order of which reveals a wisdom that transcends our own human wisdom. He describes the wonders of the earth, first, with all its vegetation, rivers, animals, and human beings. Then he advances to the sea and the air and the aether, with the sun, moon, planets, and stars. He quotes poetry to illustrate the ordered array of the constellations that "clearly manifests the skill of a divine artist."*

[115] "Is it possible for any sensible person to observe all the stars, arranged as they are, and the vast sky, so splendidly ornate, and yet to regard them as being produced from bodies randomly falling here and there and quickly moving back and forth? Or could have any other nature devoid of mind and reason produced these effects, which not only demand reason to bring them into existence, but it is impossible to understand what kind of things they are without the most advanced reasonings and calculations.

"Not only are the stars remarkable, but there is nothing more so than the stability and coherence of the cosmos. Indeed, it is impossible to imagine any cosmos better adapted to endure than this one.

For all its parts everywhere equally strive for and advance toward its center point. Moreover, bodies joined one to another remain so as though they are somehow fastened together by means of a bond encompassing them. Nature itself produces these bonds throughout the whole cosmos, preparing everything by means of judgment and reason, and drawing and directing everything back toward the center.

[116] "Therefore, if the cosmos is spherical, and thus all its parts everywhere are held together by and with one another in equilibrium, the same is necessarily true for the earth. All its parts are inclined to the center. . . . Consequently, there is nothing that is able to break the earth apart and so destroy the massive pressure that results from its weight and mass. For the same reason, the sea, even though it is higher than the earth, nevertheless strives for the center point of the earth so that it is massed with the earth into a sphere, uniform everywhere, never flooding or overflowing its limits. [117] The air, which touches the sea, is carried upward because of its lightness. Nevertheless, it spreads itself over every part of the sea. And even though it touches the sea, as has been said, it is naturally carried upward toward the sky, whose thinness and heat mingle with it in due proportion to supply living beings with the breath of life and health. This happens when the air itself is embraced by the highest part of the sky, termed 'aethereal,' which unites with the outer portion of the air, while retaining its own rarefied heat that has not yet been condensed due to an association with air.

"The stars revolve in their courses in the aether. . . . [118] They have a fiery nature, nourished by the vapors that rise from the earth, sea, and other bodies of water, having been summoned by the sun from the fields it warms and out of the waters. And when nourished and restored by these vapors, the stars and the whole aether let them flow again before drawing them up once more from the same source. This happens in such a way that nothing of the vapor is lost but for a very small amount that is consumed by the fire of the stars and the flame of the aether. Consequently, or so those of our Stoic school believe—though some say that Panaetius doubted the teaching—there will finally occur a conflagration of the whole cosmos. Why? Because all the moisture will have been con-sumed. Therefore, it will neither be able to nourish the earth, nor will the air go up since it cannot rise after the water is gone. In this way, nothing will remain but fire. Yet since this fire is a living being and God, it may once again initiate the regeneration of the cosmos, and therefore the same splendid order will appear."

119 *Balbus details the harmonious cooperation of the planets toward the conservation of the cosmos.*

[120] "Let's move, now, from celestial matters until we come to those things that exist upon the earth. Which of these fail to mani-fest rational design or purpose of an intelligent nature?

"Take, first, the plants that rise up from the earth. Their stems are sustained by their roots, which draw from the earth a nourish-ing moisture contained by the roots. As for trees, their trunks are covered with a rind or bark that defends each tree from the cold and heat. Then there are the vines that cling to their posts with ten-drils that are like hands, elevating themselves as if they were ani-mated." *If cabbages are planted nearby, they shun them. . . .*

[121] "Next, consider what a great variety there is of animals." *Balbus marvels at each kind of animal's ability to preserve itself, and notes their differences in terms of protection from the elements, armor, food, and internal organs.*

[122] "Nature has also given to each animal both sensation and appetite. The latter stirs in them the impulse to hunt for and take food that is natural to them. The former helps them distinguish between destructive and healthy things." *Balbus explains that animals approach and appropriate their food variously.*

[123] "Some animals were given a kind of artifice or cunning. For instance, . . . the mussel, or *pina* as it is called in Greek, is a large shell-fish that enters into a sort of partnership with a very small shrimp to get food. When little fish swim within the reach of the mussel's open shells, the shrimp signals the mussel with a bite, and so the mussel snaps shut its shells. So it is that two dissimilar animals seek their food together. [124] The partnership leaves us to wonder whether

they associate by some agreement or they are joined together by nature from the beginning.

"Those aquatic animals that are born on land are also a cause of wonder. I refer to crocodiles, for example, and river tortoises, and certain snakes. Though born out of the water, they nevertheless seek water as soon as they are able to move.

"Take another example. We often put duck eggs under hens. Accordingly, the ducklings are hatched from beneath these hens, and they are nourished and reared by them as though the hens were their mothers. Yet when a duck sees water, its natural home, it leaves its hen mother and even shuns her when she chases after it. Such is the instinctual guard of self-preservation that nature has implanted in animals!" *Balbus goes on to depict the remarkable eating habits of the "bird called the spoonbill," the sea-frog, and the "kind of natural war" that exists between the kite and the crow. . . .*

[125] "Another remarkable fact—cited by Aristotle, the source of most of these examples—is that cranes fly in the form of a triangle when traveling across the sea to warmer places. And with the tip of the triangle, they push aside the air in front of them. Their wings serve as oars to facilitate their flight, while the base of the crane-formed triangle is pushed along by the wind when the wind is, so to speak, astern. Those birds flying behind other birds rest their necks and heads on the ones in front of them. And the leader, since he has no one to lean on and is thus unable to rest—goes to the rear of the formation so that he is also able to rest. Meanwhile, an already-rested bird takes his place. In this way, they preserve themselves by taking turns during the whole journey."

[126] *Other stories also illustrate the precautions animals take for their security. . . .* "Let me mention another remarkable fact—something that was only recently, within the past few generations, discovered by the cleverness of physicians. Dogs cure their bellies by vomiting and ibises in Egypt do so by purging." *Other animals have similar means of defense against various dangers.*

[127] ". . . In order to secure the ongoing splendor of the cosmos, the gods in their providence have taken great care to perpetuate the different kinds of animals and trees and every other plant rooted to

the earth. The latter all have within themselves the seed from which the many are produced from the one. In plants, the seed is enclosed in the innermost part of the fruit that is scattered from each plant. In addition to renewing the earth, filling it with each kind of plant, these same seeds provide humans with an abundance of food.

[128] "Moving on to animals, we see the same reason at work to secure the perpetual preservation of their kind. First, we observe that some are male and some female. Nature uses this design to cause an ongoing succession of each animal. Then the parts of their bodies are perfectly adapted to one another for the act of procreation and the goal of conceiving offspring. Even more, there is the extraordinary longing, in both males and females, to join their bodies together. Later, when the seed is fixed in place, it seizes and carries every bit of available nourishment to itself. And so a living animal is formed within the womb. Now, when this living animal has dropped from the womb and emerged into the world, nearly all the nourishment taken by the mother begins to turn into milk—if, that is, it is a mammal. And the little animal, born just a moment ago, is led by nature without any instruction to seek the teats of its mother's breasts in order to satisfy itself with their abundance.

"We may understand that none of these things happens by chance and that all are the work of nature's providential care and skill when we see that nature has given many teats to animals who produce many young, such as pigs and dogs, while animals who give birth to a few have only a few teats.

[129] "And look at how much love animals show in rearing and protecting the offspring they have produced. They do so up to the point when the young are finally able to defend themselves." *This is true for many animals but not, Balbus acknowledges, for all such as fish, turtles, and crocodiles.* . . .

[130] "Human skill and diligence also contribute to the preservation and maintenance of animals and plants produced by the earth—for there are many animals that are now domesticated, and many plants, that could not survive without human care.

"There are also great opportunities for the cultivation of abundance by human beings. . . . Egypt, for example, is irrigated by the

Nile, whose waters cover the land throughout the summer, flooding it, but then, when the river recedes, it leaves fields soft and covered with mud for planting. Mesopotamia is made fruitful by the Euphrates, which, as it were, carries into the land new fields every year. The Indus, which is the largest river of all rivers, not only fertilizes and softens the fields, but it actually sows them with seed — for people say that it carries down with it a great quantity of seeds that resemble grain. . . .

[131] "How great is the benevolence of nature in producing such an abundance and variety of pleasing food, doing so throughout the year so that we are always delighted by a bounty of new things. Then there is the gift of the Etesian winds.[13] How suitable they are and how useful! And this not only for humankind but also for the different kinds of domesticated animals and for every plant that rises from the earth. Their blowing moderates the excessive heat of summer and adds speed and precision to our seagoing journeys." . . . [132] *Balbus mentions other benefits of nature having to do with various resources and cycles.*

[133] "At this point, someone will ask: for whose sake was so great a cosmic system fashioned? Was it for senseless trees and plants that are sustained by nature? This answer, doubtlessly, doesn't match the facts. What about animals, then? It is no more likely that the gods labored so much for the sake of speechless animals that understand nothing. For whom, then, should we declare the cosmos was made? It is clear that it was made for those living beings that employ reason—that is, for the gods and for humans, who surpass all things in excellence since reason is the best thing of all. So it makes sense to believe that the cosmos and everything within the cosmos was fashioned for the sake of the gods and human beings. As for humans, we will readily understand how the immortal gods care for us if we take a look at the whole structure of the human body, surveying every form and perfection of human nature."

134-139 *Balbus illustrates how the hand of providence may be seen in the structure and nature of human beings—for instance, in the mouth, teeth, lungs, stomach, liver, bowels, veins, heart, bones, and nerves. These all "testify to an extraordinary degree of skillful and divine labor."*

[140] "We could add many other examples regarding the diligent and skillful providence of nature that would help us understand the valuable things the gods have given to humans. Nature, for instance, has raised us humans up from the ground to stand straight and tall so that we are able to take a closer look at the sky above and come to a knowledge of the gods. For we humans not only live upon and cultivate the earth, but we observe things high above in the sky. There is no other kind of living being that applies itself to this spectacle.

"Next, the senses, which are the interpreters and messengers of things, are placed in the head, as in a tower. They are wonderfully made and situated for their proper uses. As our lookouts, the eyes occupy the highest place, from where they see the most and so perform their function. [141] And the ears are rightly set in a high part of the body since their job is to perceive sound, which is naturally carried upward. The nostrils are also rightly set up high since odor floats upward. But more. Since they have a great deal to do with judging food and drink, they have with good reason been set nearby the mouth. Taste, which is responsible for distinguishing the quality of whatever we eat, is stationed in that part of the mouth most exposed to food and drink. As for touch, it is evenly spread all over the body so that we are able to feel every contact and the approach of excessively cold or warm weather. And finally, just as house builders turn drainage pipes away from the eyes and noses of those who own the house, — for otherwise the flow within would necessarily be offensive, — so has nature similarly removed the body's drainage parts from its senses." . . .

142-144 *Balbus continues his discussion of the senses.*

[145] "Human vision is excellent relative to the visual arts such as painting, engraving, and sculpting since we spot subtle differences in bodily motion and gesture. The eyes are able to judge well, so to speak, the appropriate color and form of a work, as well as its

beauty and arrangement. More than these things, however, the eyes can perceive the difference between the virtues and the vices. For instance, they can tell whether a man is calm or angry, joyful or sad, full of energy or sluggish, daring or fearful."

[146] . . . "The nostrils, the sense of taste, and the sense of touch, at least in some areas, are great judges. Unfortunately, the arts we humans have invented to seize and delight the senses are more in number than I prefer." . . .

147-149 *Balbus next discusses "the soul and mind of man,—his reason, deliberation, and practical judgment."*[14] *Given the position of the tongue and other points, the "mechanism of speech" also "displays nature's skill."*

[150] "And consider the hands, those helpful assistants that nature has given to human beings so that we may engage in the many arts. The flexibility of the finger joints facilitates the opening and closing of the fingers so that we may easily perform each motion. Accordingly, the hand is formed for painting, modeling, and engraving, or for plucking the strings of a lyre or fingering the holes of a flute. In addition to these arts that give delight, there are those that satisfy certain needs—I mean the cultivation of fields and the building of houses, as well as the weaving and stitching of clothes, and making things with bronze and iron. From these points, we see that it was by applying the hand of the craftsman or artist to the understanding of the rational soul and the perception of the senses that we have buildings and clothing, cities, walls, houses, and temples.

[151] "Moreover, it is our work—that is, work done by human hands—that acquires for us a variety and abundance of food." *This happens by means of farming, taming animals, collecting metals, cutting wood, navigating the sea, and irrigating fields.* . . . [152] "It is by means of our hands that we strive to produce another nature, as it were, out of things found in nature.

[153] "And what about human reason? Has it not ventured into the sky? For truly, we are the only animal that knows the courses of the stars in their rising and setting. We humans know the length of each day, each month, and each year. And we know about

eclipses of the sun and the moon and can predict when they will occur in the future as well as how long they will last. Moreover, in gazing upon the stars, the rational soul comes to the knowledge of the gods. This knowledge is the source of piety, which is connected to justice and the other virtues. From these, emerge a happy life, one that resembles the life of the gods in everything but immortality—which, by the way, contributes nothing to living well.

"I think that the disclosure of these points has been sufficient to show how human nature surpasses that of all living beings. We should accordingly understand that none of these things—whether the form and arrangement of the body's parts or the strength of the mind and intellect—can possibly have been produced by chance.

[154] "In conclusion, I will demonstrate that everything in the cosmos that we humans use and benefit from has been produced and provided for our sake.

"First, the cosmos itself was produced for the sake of the gods and human beings. And the things therein that were provided for our sake were invented for our use and enjoyment. For the cosmos is, as it were, the common dwelling place of the gods and humans, the city that belongs to both. I say this because they alone benefit from reason; they alone live by justice and law. Therefore, just as Athens and Sparta must have been settled and built for the sake of the inhabitants of Athens and of Sparta, and everything within those cities belongs by right to the people therein, so everything within the cosmos belongs to the gods and human beings.

[155] "Further, even though the revolutions of the sun and the moon and the rest of the stars contribute to the coherence of the cosmos, they are nevertheless a spectacle made for humans to behold. It is impossible to grow tired of looking at them! For there is no more beautiful spectacle, nor is there one that is superior in terms of reason and skill. And by measuring their courses, we know the fullness of the seasons, their variety and changes. And if these things are observed by humans alone, then we may conclude that they were produced for the sake of humans.

[156] "And what about the earth? Does it produce a variety of fruit and grain in abundance for the sake of wild animals or for

human beings? As for grapevines and olive trees, animals have no use for their plentiful and pleasing fruits. Not even domesticated animals know how to plant or care for crops, or the right time to gather them in, or how to store their bounty in storehouses. Yet humans diligently practice these things.

[157] "Therefore, just as we declare that lyres and flutes are made for the sake of those who are able to use them, so must we acknowledge that fruit, grain, and the rest have been provided for those who make use of them. And even if these things are stolen or carried off by some animal, we will not say that they were designed for the sake of animals. After all, humans do not store grain for the sake of mice and ants but for their spouses and children and those in their household. . . .

[158] "Moreover, we see that animals were actually made for human beings. For example, what purpose do sheep have unless they are used for their wool, which, when dressed and woven, clothe us humans? . . . And consider dogs, how they are faithful and affectionate to their masters but weary of strangers, and how they are brilliant at finding game thanks to their noses, and, consequently, they are eager to chase it. These facts indicate that dogs were made for the advantage of human beings." [159] *The same kind of argument applies to oxen, mules, and asses. Each has been made to serve humans.*

[160] "As for the pig, it exists for no other purpose than to be food. Chrysippus declares that a pig's life is given to it as a kind of salt to keep it from rotting. And since this domesticated animal is given to be human food, nature has made it very prolific. And what should I say about the multitude of fish and birds that are agreeable to eat? These give us so much pleasure that sometimes it is tempting to see a kind of Epicurean providence rather than our own Stoic conception of providence." *And some birds, Balbus goes on, serve as omens. . . .*

[161] *Animals offer exercise to us when we hunt them. We also train and use them, and some animals provide medicines. . . .*

"Now imagine the whole earth and all the seas as if they were set out before your eyes. You will see vast and fruitful plains, densely forested mountains, flock-filled pastures, and winds moving with extraordinary speed across the sea. [162] And look not only upon the surface of the earth but also within its darkest recesses where there are many beneficial things that are discovered and used by human beings alone."

162-163 *Advancing, Balbus considers how the art of divination in knowing future events is perhaps the strongest proof of divine providence regarding human matters. We see this relative to the inspection of sacrificial victims, oracles, prophecies, dreams, and portents.*

[164] "The immortal gods not only care and provide for the whole of humankind but also for individual human beings. To see this, we may focus on gradually smaller and smaller groups, moving from the universal to the individual. . . .

"The gods care for all human beings everywhere, in every land extending from the sunrise to the sunset. . . . [165] But if they care for those who dwell in this land that is like a huge island, which we call 'the circle of the earth,' then they also care for those who occupy this land's parts—Europe, Asia, and Africa. Therefore, they value the parts of these parts—for example, Rome, Athens, Sparta, and Rhodes. And they value individual humans from each of these cities." *Balbus offers the examples of individuals from Roman history to demonstrate the point, and claims the same for Greece. . . .*

[166] "This is why the poets, and Homer in particular, join certain gods to their leading heroes as companions during critical and trying moments of danger—such heroes as Ulysses,[15] Diomedes, Agamemnon, or Achilles. Moreover, the frequent presence of these gods . . . reveals that they care both for the cities of men and for individual men therein." . . . *This is also revealed by the "foreknowledge of future events" offered to men, whether they are awake or asleep. And even though this is true for all men, it is particularly true for "great" men, who always experience some form of "divine inspiration." But, it may be asked, what if such men experience some "accident" or "misfortune"?*

[167] "We may not conclude that a god begrudges or is indifferent to the man who experiences some accident or misfortune—as when his crops or vineyards are harmed by a storm or when an accident has carried off one of the comforts of life. The gods care about important

things, after all, not unimportant things. As for great men, they always prosper in everything—if, that is, our own Stoic philosophers and Socrates, the leading man of philosophy, have adequately spoken about the abundance that is produced by virtue.

[168] "These are the things that have come into my mind regarding the nature of the gods."

The conversation concludes with Balbus explaining to Cotta, who is a member of the Academic school that argues both sides of any issue, how "wicked and impious" it is to argue in support of atheism.

NOTES

[1] Marcus Porcius Cato (95-46 BC) was a Roman statesman and convinced Stoic. For the context of *On Ends* 3.72-73, as well as further selections from the same text, see Ten ("Stoic Ethics in Cicero's Works").

[2] Marcus Terentius Varro (116-27 BC) was a Roman scholar and prolific writer, who studied philosophy in Athens with Antiochus of Ascalon.

[3] Acting on includes causing, effecting, and so on.

[4] The four are fire, air, water, and earth. As for the fifth element, see *Academica* 1.26 where Varro reports that "Aristotle said that there existed a certain fifth kind of element, in a class by itself and unlike the four . . . , which was the source of the stars and of thinking minds."

[5] We first encounter Quintus Lucilius Balbus in Book 1 of *On the Nature of the Gods*. Cicero explains that he had "a very detailed and careful discussion regarding the immortal gods" with a number of men. The participants were Gaius Cotta (an Academic or skeptic), Gaius Velleius (an Epicurean), and Quintus Lucilius Balbus (a Stoic), "who had progressed greatly in Stoic philosophy—so much so that he was comparable to the most excellent Stoics among the Greeks" (1.15). Apart from Cicero's dialogue, Balbus is otherwise unknown.

[6] See Xenophon, *Memorabilia* 1.4.8.

[7] The Latin term is *principatus*.

[8] The point is directed against Epicurus, who argued that the gods, even though they do exist, have nothing to do with the management of the cosmos.

[9] Caelus, here, is the same as the Greek god Ouranos (Uranus), whose name means "Sky." Saturn is the equivalent of the Greek god Kronos (Cronus). Jupiter is Zeus. For the Greek story (*mythos*) of these gods, see Hesiod's *Theogony* 137-210; 617-720 in the Cave's *The Best of Hesiod's Theogony & Works and Days*.

[10] The "highest celestial nature" refers to Caelus (see 2.63) who lost his penis or generative member thanks to Saturn.

[11] Composed by Quintus Ennius (239-169 BC), the *Annals* (*Annales*) was an epic poem about the early history of the Roman people. The point is likely the

source of the well-known argument having to do with monkeys and Shake-speare—that no matter how long one gives a roomful of monkeys to monkey around with typewriters, they will never type out even a single, coherent line from Shakespeare; so it is that this cosmos—with its intricate machinery (if we may call it such) from the stars and planets to DNA—cannot be the result of chance.

[12] The passage comes from Aristotle's lost dialogue, *On Philosophy*.

[13] The Etesian winds are north-western winds that prevail during the summer in the eastern parts of the Mediterranean Sea.

[14] For the full discussion found in 2.147-148, see Eight, "Stoic Logic in Cicero's Works."

[15] Ulysses is the Latin form of the Greek Odysseus.

TEN

STOIC ETHICS
IN CICERO'S WORKS

IN BRIEF: *First, in a handful of selections from the* Academica, *Cicero, through Varro and in his own voice, presents the ethical doctrine of the Stoics. Virtue alone is good and sufficient for happiness. Other things are neither good nor bad. Still, some of these, being in accord with nature, should be chosen as valuable and thus preferable. The wise man is free from disturbing passions. Next, the Stoic Balbus, in* On the Nature of the Gods, *relates how our eyes "recognize the virtues and vices" in others and contemplate the heavens and so help us arrive "at a knowledge of the gods" from which various virtues arise. In the following selection, the Stoic Marcus Cato, in* On Ends, *expounds the Stoic system of ethics, explaining, among other things, how humans can advance from the natural impulse toward self-preservation to a rational understanding of the good life, which is one of virtue, of moral goodness. Finally, Cicero goes through the Stoic classification of passions in a passage from the* Tusculan Disputations.

Cicero, *Academica* 1.35-39

In the voice of Varro, Cicero summarizes the ethical doctrines of Zeno of Citium, including the notion that virtue alone is good and sufficient for happiness. Other things are neither good nor bad. Still, of these, some are in accord with nature and should thus be chosen. Finally, rather than merely restraining them, the wise man wishes to be free from all passions that arise as a result of voluntary opinion and judgment.

ZENO never restricted virtue as Theophrastus had done.[1] By contrast, he declared that everything having to do with the happy life belonged to virtue alone. He counted nothing else with the good, calling virtue, 'the noble' or "the morally good,' which is a certain simple, exceptional, and single good.[2]

[36] "Otherwise, things are neither good nor bad. Still, some of them are in accord with nature, he said, while others are contrary to nature. Among these, he counted others 'interposed' and 'intermediate.' Zeno taught that things in accord with nature were to be chosen and appraised as having a certain value. And things contrary to nature were not to be chosen since they have no value. And things that are neither he left among the 'intermediate.' He declared that nothing at all is moved or motivated by these.

[37] "As for things to be chosen, some were to be appraised as having more value, and others, less. He called that which is more valuable, 'preferred,' and that which is less valuable, 'rejected.' . . .

[38] "Whereas others who came before him asserted that not every virtue is found in reason, but that certain virtues are perfected either by nature or by habit, Zeno assigned all the virtues to reason. . . . He argued that not merely the exercise of virtue, as they held, but the mere state of virtue is in itself a remarkable thing—even though no one possesses virtue without continuously exercising it.

"Again, whereas others did not eradicate from human beings those disturbing passions that affect the soul,—saying that suffering and desire and fear and delight are natural, but instead they restrained and confined them,—Zeno held that the wise man wishes to be free from all these disorders.[3]

[39] "And whereas those who came before said that these passions are natural and non-rational, and they located desire and reason in different parts of the soul, Zeno did not agree with these views. For he thought that these passions are voluntary and experienced thanks to opinion and judgment. The mother of all these passions, he believed, is a kind of immoderation and excess."

Cicero, *Academica* 2.130

Ariston demonstrates that virtue is the only good and vice is the only evil.

[130] "Ariston, who was Zeno's student, demonstrated what Zeno

had proved with words—that nothing is good except virtue, and that nothing is evil except for that which is contrary to virtue."

Cicero, *Academica* 2.134-135

Next, we learn that, for Zeno, virtue is sufficient for happiness. The wise man is not affected by the passions—desire, delight, fear, or suffering pain.

[134] "Behold an even greater disagreement: Zeno thinks that the happy life is found in virtue alone. And what about Antiochus?⁴ 'I grant,' he says, 'that the happy life is found in virtue alone—but not the happiest.' Zeno was a god who insisted that virtue lacks nothing. By contrast, Antiochus is a little man who argues that many things besides virtue are dear to human beings—some even necessary." . . .

[135] "Zeno and the Stoics agree . . . that the wise man's soul is neither moved by desire nor by delight. . . . And that the wise man is never afraid and never suffers pain. This is a hard teaching. But for Zeno, it is a necessary teaching since nothing besides the noble or morally good is counted among the good."

Cicero, *Academica* 2.138-140

In this selection, Cicero reviews Chrysippus' thinking about the goal of human life, whether it is a moral good, or pleasure, or both together. For Chrysippus, it is the noble or that which is morally good.

[138] "Chrysippus often testifies that there are only three views that can be defended regarding the goal of life. He disregards most, reducing their significance. He says the goal is either that which is noble or morally good, or it is pleasure, or it is both together. . . .

[139] "But the truth itself and right reason appears, saying, 'What are you doing? When that which is honorable or morally good naturally disregards pleasure, will you join them together as though joining a human being with a wild animal?'

[140] "There remains, therefore, one battle to fight—one, so far as I can tell, that Chrysippus fought without much exertion. It is the

battle between pleasure and the noble or morally good. After all, many things are ruined if one pursues pleasure. Most of all, fellowship among men, affection, friendship, justice, and the rest of the virtues are ruined since they exist without any expectation of a reward or payment such as pleasure. For virtue urged on to duty by pleasure as a reward is not virtue but a kind of deceptive image and false show of virtue."

Cicero, *On Ends* 3.1-76[5]
(*with a summary of the surrounding text given in italics*)

In conversation with Cicero, Marcus Cato[6] offers to "expound the whole system of Zeno and the Stoics." He begins with the impulse toward self-preservation that humans naturally have. Pleasure, by contrast, is not one of the "primary objects of natural impulse." Further, "that which is in itself in accord with nature" is "deserving of choice" and thus "valuable." An "appropriate act," therefore, is one in accord with nature. The goal is to build fixed habits by means of conditioning choice with appropriate actions. Ultimately, however, the goal is to rationalize such choice and behavior, to understand "the order and . . . the harmony that governs conduct," and to realize this as "the highest good of a human being, the thing that is praiseworthy and desirable for its own sake." Moral goodness, then, is activity in conformity with nature, specifically "the order and . . . the harmony that governs conduct." To say it another way, "the final aim is to live in agreement and harmony with nature." This is the life of virtue. From "primary natural instincts," then, humans move to wisdom. It is the wise who are always happy. In addition to these central points, Cato discusses others, including the fact that moral baseness is the only evil; the Stoic teaching regarding things preferred and things not; the virtues; the origin of human communities in "parental affection for their children"; and friendship.

1-6 Having dealt with Epicureanism or "pleasure"[7] in the first two books of On Ends *(the conclusion: "Let us send pleasure away; . . . we have driven pleasure away"), Cicero advances to explore further the final and ultimate good. "The question," he says, "is this: What is the highest good?"[8] He explains how he has to employ "new terms [in Latin] to convey new [Greek] ideas [to Romans]." Such a coinage of terms is itself nothing new, he avers. "Of all the philosophers" —where he notes in passing that "philosophy is the art of life" —"the Stoics have been the greatest innovators in this respect, and Zeno their founder was actually an inventor of new terms rather than a discoverer of new ideas." Cicero then moves on to the conversation and its circumstances.*

[7] "I [Cicero] was down at my place at Tusculum. I wanted to consult some books from the library of the young Lucullus, so I went to his villa, as I was in the habit of doing, to help myself to the ones I needed. On my arrival, I found Marcus Cato seated in the library. I had not known he was there. He was surrounded by many books on Stoicism—for he possessed, as you are aware, an insatiable appetite for reading and could never get enough of it." . . .

8-9 Cicero greets Marcus Cato, explaining that he came to the countryside due to the beginning of the games in Rome. They briefly discuss Lucullus (for whom Cato has charge) and his education and studies that "will render him better equipped when he comes to the business of life." Cato then asks Cicero why he has come "when you have so large a library of your own." Cicero clarifies—"for some notes and writings of Aristotle," he says.

[10] "How I wish," Marcus said, "that you had been inclined to the Stoics! You of all men might have been expected to count virtue as the only good."

"Perhaps *you* might rather have been expected," I answered, "to refrain from adopting a new terminology for things when in substance you think as I do. We are united in our account of things; it is our language that battles."

"Indeed," he said, "our language does not agree in the least. Once pronounce anything to be desirable, once reckon anything a good other than the noble or morally good, and you have extinguished the very light of virtue,—that is, moral goodness itself—, and you have overthrown virtue entirely."

[11] "That all sounds great, Cato," I said, "but are you aware that you share your glorious talk with Pyrrho [the skeptic] and with

Ariston, who make all things equal? So I want to know what you think about them."

"You ask what I think?" he said. "My view is that those good, brave, just, and moderate men—those we learn about from history or we ourselves have seen in public life—accomplished many praiseworthy things by following nature itself rather than receiving any instruction. Those men were better educated by nature than they could possibly have been by philosophy had they accepted any other system of philosophy than the one that counts moral goodness the only good and moral baseness the only evil. Other ways of philosophy—those which count things good or evil that have nothing to do with virtue—do not merely fail to help us in becoming better men, but they corrupt our natural character. Either this point must be firmly held, that moral goodness is the only good, or there is no way to prove that virtue produces a happy life. And if that is true, then I do not know why we exert ourselves to study philosophy. For if it is possible for the wise man to be wretched, then I would not much value this virtue that is so celebrated and talked about."

12-15 Cicero again contends that Cato's views are the same as any "follower of Pyrrho or Ariston." Cato disagrees. The Stoics choose among things "in accord with nature," he says, whereas the others make everything equal, thereby leaving no means of judgment and so "destroying virtue itself." But to explain thoroughly, he will give a full account of Stoicism. "Since we are at leisure, I will expound the whole system of Zeno and the Stoics." Cicero gladly agrees to the proposal. After a brief discussion regarding the use of Latin words in place of the original Greek, Cato commences his account.

[16] "It is the view of those whose system I accept," he said, "that a living being feels an attachment to itself from the very moment it is born—which, by the way, is the right place to start. From this moment on, it feels an impulse to preserve itself and to feel affection for its own constitution and for those things that tend to preserve that constitution. By contrast, it feels an aversion for destruction and for those things that appear to bring destruction.

"In order to show the accuracy of this account, the Stoics point out that infants, even before they have experienced pleasure or pain, desire healthy things and reject the opposite. But this would not happen unless they prized their own constitution and feared destruction. Even then it would be impossible for them to desire at all unless they possessed self-consciousness wherein they felt affection for themselves. From this we may understand that the first impulse to action arises from this prizing of self—this self-love or self-affection. This leads to the conclusion that it is love of self that supplies the primary impulse to action.

[17] "But pleasure, according to most Stoics, is not to be placed among the primary objects of natural impulse. And I very strongly agree with them—for many shameful things will occur if we think that nature has placed pleasure among the first objects of desire.

"But the fact of our affection for the objects first adopted at nature's prompting seems to require no other proof than this—that there is no one who, given the choice, would not prefer to have all the parts of his body sound and whole rather than maimed or distorted even though equally serviceable.

"Again, acts of cognition,—those which we may term 'comprehensions' or 'perceptions,' or, if these words are distasteful or obscure, then we can fall back on the Greek *katalēpseis* or 'direct apprehensions,'—these acts we consider suitable to be adopted for their own sake because they possess an element that, so to speak, embraces and contains the truth. This can be seen in the case of children who take pleasure, we may observe, in finding something out for themselves by the use of reason, even though they gain nothing by it.

[18] "We also hold that the sciences[9] are things that should be chosen for their own sake—partly because there is in them something worthy of choice, partly because they consist of acts of cognition and contain an element of fact established by methodical reasoning. The mental assent to what is false, the Stoics believe, is more repugnant than all the other things that are contrary to nature." . . .

19 *As an aside, Cato comments on the "bald style" of his discourse so far*

given the topic. Cicero responds that "any clear statement of an important
topic possesses excellence of style."

[20] "To proceed then," Cato said, "since we have been digressing
from the primary impulses of nature. And with these impulses the
later stages must be in harmony.

"The next step is the following fundamental classification. It is
that which is in itself in accord with nature, or which produces
something else that is so, and which, therefore, is deserving of
choice since it possesses a certain amount of positive value—*axia*,
in Greek, as the Stoics call it. They call this 'valuable'—for so I suppose we may translate it. On the other hand, that which is the contrary of the former they term 'valueless.'

"The initial principle being thus established—that things in accord with nature are 'things to be taken' for their own sake, and
their opposites similarly are 'things to be rejected,'—the first 'duty'
or 'appropriate act' (for so I render the Greek *kathēkon*) is to preserve
oneself in one's natural constitution. The next is to retain those
things that are in accord with nature and to repel those that are the
contrary. Then, when this principle of choice and rejection has been
discovered, there follows choice conditioned by appropriate action.
And these continue on, a fixed habit. And finally choice is fully ra-
tionalized and in harmony with nature. It is at this final stage that
the good—properly so-called—first emerges and comes to be understood in its true nature.

[21] "A human being's first attraction is toward the things that
are in accord with nature. But as soon as he has understanding—
or, rather, as soon as he becomes capable of a 'notion,' which is
called *ennoia* or 'concept' by the Stoics—and has discerned the order
and, so to speak, the harmony that governs conduct, he consequently values this harmony far more highly than all the things for
which he originally felt an affection. And by exercise of intelligence
and reason he infers the conclusion that 'herein resides the highest
good of a human being, the thing that is praiseworthy and desirable
for its own sake.' This thing consists in what the Stoics term *homo-
logia*, which we will call 'conformity' or 'agreement'—if the term is

acceptable to you. In this resides that good which is the end to which all else is a means—moral conduct and moral goodness itself. It alone is counted as a good. And although it is a later development, it is nevertheless the sole thing that is desirable for its own efficacy and value, whereas none of the primary objects of nature is desirable for its own sake.

[22] "But since those actions that I have termed 'duties' or 'appropriate acts' are based on the primary natural objects, it follows that the former are means to the latter. So it may correctly be said that all appropriate acts are means to the end of attaining the primary needs of nature. Yet it must not be inferred that their attainment is the ultimate good, inasmuch as moral action is not one of the primary natural attractions, but is an outgrowth of these, a later development, as I have said. At the same time, moral action is in accord with nature and stimulates our desire far more strongly than all the objects that attracted us earlier.

"At this point a word of caution is necessary. It will be an error to infer that this view implies *two* ultimate goods. For even though a man resolves to aim accurately with a spear or arrow at some target, we say that his ultimate end, corresponding to the ultimate good, would be to do all he could to aim straight. The man in this illustration would have to do everything to aim straight, and yet, even though he did everything to achieve his purpose, his 'ultimate end,' so to speak, would be what corresponded to what we call the highest good in the conduct of life, whereas the actual hitting of the target would be, as we say, 'to be chosen' but not 'to be desired.'

[23] "Again, as all 'appropriate acts' are based on the primary impulses of nature, it follows that wisdom itself is also based on them. Nevertheless, even as one man who is introduced to another often values this new man more highly than he does the man who gave him the introduction, so in like manner it is by no means surprising that, even though we are first entrusted to wisdom by the initial instincts of nature, later on wisdom itself becomes dearer to us than the instincts from which we came to her. And just as our limbs are so fashioned that it is clear that they were given to us with a view to a certain mode of life, so the appetite or

grasping impulse of the soul—which is called *hormē* in Greek—
was obviously designed not for any kind of life one may choose
but for a particular mode of life. And the same is true regarding
reason and perfected reason.

[24] "For just as an actor or dancer has assigned to him not any
but a particular part or dance, so life has to be led in a certain kind of
fixed way—not in any way we like. This fixed way we speak of as
conformable and suitable. In fact we do not consider wisdom to be
like piloting a ship or medicine; rather, it is like the arts of acting and
dancing just mentioned. Its end, being the actual exercise of the art,
is contained within the art itself and is not something extraneous to
it. At the same time there is another point that marks a dissimilarity
between wisdom and these arts as well. In the latter, a movement
perfectly executed nevertheless does not involve all the various motions that together constitute the subject matter of the art. By contrast,
in the sphere of conduct, what we may call, if you approve, 'right
actions' or 'rightly performed actions' (in Stoic terms, *katorthōmata*),
contain all the factors of virtue. For wisdom alone is entirely self-con-
tained. But this is not the case with the other arts.

[25] "It is erroneous, however, to place the end of medicine or of
navigation exactly on a par with the end of wisdom. For wisdom
includes also magnanimity and justice and a sense of superiority to
everything that happens to a man, but this is not the case with the
other arts. Again, even the very virtues I have just mentioned cannot be attained by anyone unless he has realized that all things are
indifferent and indistinguishable except for those that are morally
good and morally base.

[26] "We may now observe how strikingly the principles I have established support the following corollaries. Inasmuch as the final
good—and you have doubtlessly observed that I have all along been
giving the Greek term *telos* either as final or ultimate or highest good,
and for final or ultimate good we may also give end or goal—inasmuch, then, as the final good is to live in agreement and harmony with
nature, it necessarily follows that all wise men at all times enjoy a
happy, perfect, and fortunate life, free from all hindrance, interference,
or want. The essential principle—not merely of the school of

philosophy I am discussing but also of our life and fortunes—is that we should judge moral goodness to be the only good. . . .

[29] "Once again, could it be denied that it is impossible for there ever to exist a man of steadfast, firm, and lofty mind—such a one as we call a brave man—unless it be established that pain or suffering is not an evil? For just as it is impossible for one who counts death as an evil not to fear death, so in no case can a man disregard and despise a thing that he judges to be evil. If this is admitted, we adopt as our premise that the great and brave soul looks down on and disregards whatever may possibly happen to a man. The conclusion follows that nothing is evil that is not base. More: the lofty, excellent, magnanimous, and truly brave man, who judges all human vicissitudes beneath him,—I mean, the character we desire to produce, our ideal man,—must unquestionably have faith in himself and in his own character both past and future. He must think well of himself, holding that no ill can befall the wise man. From this we understand that moral goodness alone is good, and that to live honorably, that is virtuously, is to live happily. . . .

[31] "We conclude, then, that the highest good consists in applying to the conduct of life a knowledge of the working of natural causes, choosing what is in accord with nature and rejecting what is contrary to it. In other words, the highest good is to live in harmony and in agreement with nature.

[32] "But in the other arts, when we speak of an 'artistic' or 'skillful' performance, this quality must be considered as being in a sense subsequent to and a result of the action. It is what the Stoics term *epigennēmatikon* (a result or consequence). By contrast, in conduct, when we speak of an act as 'wise,' the term is appropriately applied from the very beginning of the act. For every action that the wise man initiates must necessarily be complete straightaway in all its parts. This is so since the thing desirable, as we term it, consists in his activity. To explain, both the performance of and the results that come upon the following acts are morally sinful—when we betray our country or use violence against our parents or rob a temple. By contrast, the passions of fear, grief, and desire are moral faults from the very beginning, even if one does not act based upon the passion

or there are no consequences. Similarly, actions arising from virtue are to be judged right from their very beginning and not in their successful completion.

[33] "Again, the term 'good,' which has been employed so frequently in this discourse, is also explained by definition. The Stoic definitions do indeed differ from one another in a very small way, but they all point in the same direction. Personally, I agree with Diogenes in defining the good as that which is by nature complete. He was led by this also to pronounce the 'beneficial'—let us translate the Greek *ōphelēma* in this way—to be a motion or state in accord with that which is by nature complete.

"Now notions of things are produced in the soul when something has become known either by experience or combination of ideas or analogy or logical inference. The mind ascends by inference from those things in accord with nature until finally it arrives at the notion of good. [34] At the same time goodness is absolute and is not a matter of degree. The good is recognized and pronounced to be good from its own inherent properties and not by comparison with other things. Just as honey, though extremely sweet, is yet perceived to be sweet by its own unique kind of flavor and not by being compared with something else, so this good that we are discussing is indeed superlatively valuable, yet its value depends on its unique kind and not on quantity. . . . The value of virtue is therefore unique and distinct; it depends on its kind and not on degree.

[35] "Moreover, the passions of the soul render the life of the unwise wretched and harsh. By the way, the Greeks call the passions *pathē*.[10] I could have translated this term literally and called them 'diseases.' But the word 'disease' would not work in every instance. For example, no one speaks of pity or anger as a disease; rather, the Greeks term these *pathos*. Let us, then, accept the term 'passion' (*perturbatio*), the very sound of which seems to denote something vicious. These passions are not excited by any natural influence. The list of the passions is divided into four kinds, with many subdivisions.

"The four passions are grief, fear, desire, and the one the Stoics commonly call by the name *hēdonē* (pleasure), the one related both to the body and the soul, which I prefer to call 'delight,' meaning the sensuous elation of the soul when in a state of exaltation.[11] These passions, I say, are not excited by any natural influence; rather, they are all mere beliefs and fickle judgments. Therefore, the wise man will always be free from them.

[36] "The view that all moral goodness is intrinsically desirable is one that we hold in common with many other systems of philosophy. Aside from three schools that shut out virtue from the highest good altogether, all the remaining philosophers are committed to this view, and most of all the Stoics with whom we are now concerned, and who hold that nothing else but moral goodness is to be counted as a good at all. But this position is one that is extremely simple and easy to defend. For who is there that possesses an avarice so consuming and appetites so unbridled, that, even though he is willing to commit any crime to achieve his end, and even though he is absolutely sure of impunity, yet he would not a hundred times rather attain the same object by innocent than by guilty means? . . .

[38] "On the other hand, what man of honorable family and good upbringing and education is not shocked by moral baseness as such, even when it is not calculated to do him personally any harm? Who can view without disgust a person whom he believes to be dissolute and an evildoer? Who does not hate the base, the empty, the frivolous, the worthless? Moreover, if we decide that baseness is not a thing to be avoided for its own sake, what arguments can be given against men who want to indulge in every sort of disgraceful activity when alone and under cover of darkness, unless they are deterred by the essential and intrinsic repulsiveness of what is base? Endless reasons could be given in support of this view, but they are not necessary. For nothing is less open to doubt than that what is morally good is to be desired for its own sake, and, similarly, what is morally base is to be avoided for its own sake.

[39] "Again, the principle already discussed, that moral goodness is the sole good, involves the corollary that it is of more value than those neutral things which it procures. On the other hand, when we say that folly, cowardice, injustice, and immoderation are to be avoided because of the consequences they entail, this statement must

not be so construed as to appear inconsistent with the principle already set down, that moral baseness alone is evil. This is so because the consequences referred to are not a matter of bodily harm but of the base conduct to which vices give rise—and I prefer the term *vitium* or 'vice' to 'badness' as a translation of what the Greeks call *kakia*." . . .

40-41 Cicero agrees to Cato's use of the Latin term "vitium" for vice, saying, "It seems to me that you are teaching philosophy to speak Latin and thus naturalizing her as a Roman citizen." Resuming his description of Stoicism, Cato points out that the disagreement between the Peripatetic school and the Stoics is substantial rather than merely verbal. This is true regarding both good and bad things.

[42] "The Stoic account that considers pain no evil clearly proves that the wise man retains his happiness amid the worst torments. The mere fact that men endure the same pain more easily when they voluntarily undergo it for the sake of their country than when they suffer it for some lesser cause shows that the intensity of the pain depends on the belief or expectation of the sufferer and not on its own intrinsic nature. . . .

[43] *And as for bodily or external goods,* . . . "The Peripatetics hold that the happy life includes bodily advantages or conveniences. We Stoics deny this altogether. We hold that even a multitude of those goods—those we call 'actual goods'—does not make for a happier or more desirable or valuable life. Even less, therefore, is the happy life made by the accumulation of bodily advantages or conveniences.

[44] "Clearly if wisdom as well as bodily strength and health are both desirable, a combination of the two would be more desirable than wisdom alone. But even if both are counted valuable, it does not follow that wisdom *plus* bodily strength and health is worth more than wisdom by itself separately. We judge bodily strength and health to be deserving of a certain value, but we do not count it a good. At the same time we rate no value so highly as to count it above virtue. This is not the view of the Peripatetics, who are bound to say that an action that is both morally good and not attended by

pain is more desirable than the same action if accompanied by pain. We see things differently." . . .

[45] *To illustrate the point,* "The light of an oil lamp is rendered insignificant as it disappears in the light of the sun. A drop of honey is lost in the vastness of the Aegean sea. An additional few coins is nothing amid the wealth of Croesus[12] — as is a single step in the journey from here to India. Similarly, if we accept the Stoic definition of the end of goods, — that is, the ultimate end of goods —, it follows that all the value you set on all these bodily things must necessarily be overwhelmed and rendered insignificant by the splendor and excellence of virtue. And just as opportuneness is not increased by prolongation in time — since things we call opportune have attained their proper measure — so right conduct, as well as suitable conduct, and lastly the good itself . . . are not capable of increase or addition.[13] [46] For these things that I speak of, such as opportuneness mentioned before, are not made greater by prolongation. For this reason, the Stoics do not judge the happy life to be any more attractive or desirable if it is long lasting compared to if it is short. . . .

[48] "So it would be consistent with the principles already stated that on the theory of those who judge the end of goods — that which we call the extreme or ultimate good — to be capable of degree, they should also hold that one man can be wiser than another, and similarly that one can commit a more sinful or more righteous action than another. But this is a position that is not available for us to take — those of us who do not think that the end of goods can vary in degree. For just as a drowning man who is so close to the surface of the water that at any moment he might come up into the air is no more able to breathe than if he were actually at the bottom already, and just as a puppy on the point of opening its eyes is no less blind than one just born, similarly a man that has made some progress toward the state of virtue is no less in misery than the one who has made no progress at all.

"I am aware that all this seems paradoxical. But as our previous conclusions are undoubtedly true and well established, and as these are the logical inferences from them, the truth of these inferences also cannot be called into question. Yet even though the Stoics deny that either virtues or vices can be increased in degree, they nevertheless believe that each of them can be in a sense expanded and widened in scope. . . .

[50] "After conclusively proving that moral goodness alone is good and moral baseness alone is evil, the Stoics go on to affirm that among those things that are of no importance for happiness or misery, there is nevertheless an element of difference making some of them of positive and others of negative value, and others neutral.

[51] "Among things valuable—for example, health, unimpaired senses, freedom from pain, fame, wealth, and the like—they say that some present us with adequate grounds for preferring them to other things, while others do not. Similarly, among those things that are of negative value, some present us with adequate grounds for rejecting them—things such as pain, disease, loss of the senses, poverty, disgrace, and the like. Others do not.

"In Zeno's terminology, there consequently arose the distinction between *proēgmena* (things preferred) and *apoproēgmena* (things not preferred). Zeno, in using the well-supplied Greek language, still employed novel words coined for the occasion—a license not permitted to us who must use the poor vocabulary of Latin, even though you are fond of saying that Latin is actually better supplied than Greek.

"To make it easier to understand the meaning of this term *proēgmena*, it will not be out of place to explain the method that Zeno followed in coining it. [52] He remarks that in a royal court, no one speaks of the king himself as 'promoted' to honor (for that is the meaning of *proēgmenon*), but the term is applied to those holding some office of state whose rank most nearly approaches—though it is second to—the royal supremacy. Similarly, in the conduct of life, the title *proēgmenon*—that is, 'promoted,'—is given not to those things that are in the first rank but to those that hold the second place. . . .

[53] "Since we declare that everything that is good occupies the first rank, it follows that this which we term 'preferred' or 'superior' is neither good nor evil. We accordingly define it as being indifferent but having a moderate value." . . .

54 *Cato further discusses and illustrates the point.*

[55] "Next comes the division of goods into three kinds. First, there are those that belong to the ultimate end. . . . Secondly, there are those that are productive of the end. . . . Thirdly, there are those that are both. The only instances of goods that belong to the ultimate end are morally good actions. The only instance of a productive good is a friend. As for the last, the Stoics say that wisdom belongs both to and produces the end. Since it is an appropriate activity, it belongs; since it causes and produces morally good actions, it is productive.

[56] "The things we call 'preferred' are sometimes preferred for their own sake, sometimes because they produce a certain result, and sometimes for both reasons. We prefer certain facial expressions or bodily postures or sensations . . . for what they are in themselves. We prefer other things because they produce a certain result. Take money, for example. As for other things, such as unimpaired senses and good health, we prefer them for both reasons.

[57] "About 'good reputation' (that term being a better translation of the Stoic expression *eudoxia* in this context than 'glory'), Chrysippus and Diogenes used to declare that it is, apart from any practical value it may possess, not worth stretching out a finger for. And I strongly agree with them. On the other hand, their successors, finding themselves unable to resist the attacks of Carneades, declared that good reputation, as I have called it, is preferred and desirable for its own sake, and that a man of good upbringing and liberal education will desire to be well-regarded by his parents and relatives, and by good men also—and that for its own sake and not for any practical advantage. And they argue that just as we desire the welfare of our children for their own sake—even the welfare of those that may be born after we are dead—, so a man should be mindful of his reputation even after death, for itself and apart from any advantage. . . .

[62] "The Stoics hold that it is important to understand that nature creates in parents a love and affection for their children. This love and affection is the source to which we trace the origin of the association of humankind in communities. The point is clear from the configuration of the body and its members, which are enough by themselves to reveal that nature's scheme includes the

procreation of offspring. Still, it would not be consistent to hold that nature wills offspring to be born and yet makes no provision for that offspring, when born, to be loved and cherished. We can perceive nature's influence relative to these points even in the activity of the lower animals. Observing the labor they spend on bearing and rearing their young, we seem to be listening to the voice of nature itself. Accordingly, as it is manifest that it is natural for us to shrink from pain, so it is apparent that we are driven by nature itself to love those whom we have begotten.

[63] "From this impulse arises the sense of mutual attraction that unites human beings—something that is also directed by nature." *Cato mentions other animals, some "born for themselves alone," others such as the ant and bee that "do certain actions for the sake of others."* . . . "With human beings, this bond of mutual aid represents an even greater or closer connection. It follows that we are by nature equipped to form marital unions, assemblies, and cities or states.

[64] "The Stoics hold that the cosmos is governed by divine will. It is both a city and a state of which both men and gods are members—and each one of us is a part of this cosmos. From this, it naturally follows that we should prefer the common advantage more than our own. For just as the laws set the safety of all above the safety of individuals, so a good, wise, and law-abiding man, conscious of his duty to the state, has regard for the advantage of all more than his own advantage or that of any single individual. The man who betrays his country does not deserve greater censure than the man who betrays the common advantage or security for the sake of his own advantage or security. This explains why praise is owed to one who dies for the republic since it is fitting for us to love our own fatherland more than ourselves. And as we feel it inhuman and wicked for men to declare . . . that they do not care if, when they themselves are dead, the conflagration of the whole earth follows, it is certainly true that we are bound to have regard for the good of posterity for its own sake.

[65] "This is the feeling that has given rise to the practice of making a will and appointing guardians for one's children when one is dying. And the fact that no one would care to pass his life alone in a

desert—even though supplied with never-ending, abundant pleasures—readily shows that we are born for marriage, society, and for a natural partnership with our fellow men. Moreover, nature moves us with the desire to benefit as many people as we can, particularly by handing on information and the principles of wisdom.

[66] "Consequently, it would be hard to discover anyone who would not hand on to another any knowledge that he may himself possess—so strong is our propensity not only to learn but also to teach. And just as bulls have a natural instinct to fight with all their strength and force in defending their calves against lions, so men of exceptional gifts and capacity for service,—those like Hercules and Liber in the legends,—feel a natural impulse to be the protectors of mankind. Also, when we confer upon Jove the titles of Most Good and Most Great, of Savior, Lord of Guests, and Supporter, what we wish to convey is that he watches over the safety of humankind. But how inconsistent it would be for us to expect the immortal gods to love and value us when we ourselves despise and neglect one another! Therefore, just as we actually use our limbs before we have learned what they were given to us for, so we are united and allied by nature in the common society of the state. If this were not the case, there would be no place either for justice or benevolence.

[67] "But just as the Stoics hold that man is united with man by the bonds of justice, so they consider that no justice exists between human beings and animals. Chrysippus said it well when he said that all other things were created for the sake of men and gods. . . . So men can make use of animals for their own purposes without injustice. And the nature of man, he said, is such that, as it were, a code of law exists between the individual and humankind. He who upholds this law will be counted just. He who departs from it will be counted unjust. . . .

[68] "Again, since we see that man is designed by nature to safeguard and protect his fellow men, it follows from this natural disposition that the wise man should desire to support and manage the republic. He also desires to live in accord with nature by joining with a wife in order to have children by her—for even the passion of love, when it is pure, is not judged inconsistent with a wise man. . . ."

69 After briefly addressing "the principles and habits of the Cynics" and whether they are "appropriate for the wise man," Cato discusses "benefits and injuries" and "advantages and disadvantages" relative to the community.

[70] "The Stoics recommend the cultivation of friendship, classing it among 'things beneficial.' In friendship, some profess that the wise man will hold his friends' interests as dear as his own while others say that a man's own interests must necessarily be dearer to him. At the same time, the latter admit that to enrich oneself by another's loss is an action repugnant to that justice toward which we seem to possess a natural propensity. But the school I am discussing emphatically rejects the view that we adopt or approve either justice or friendship for the sake of their utility. For if we did, the same claims of utility would be able to undermine and overthrow them. In fact, the very existence of both justice and friendship will be impossible if they are not desired for their own sake.

[71] "Justice, moreover, properly so-called, exists by nature. And it is foreign to the nature of the wise man not only to wrong but even to hurt anyone. Nor again is it right to enter into a partnership in wrongdoing with one's friends or benefactors. And the Stoics most vehemently and truly maintain that it is not possible to separate fairness from usefulness, and that whatever is fair and just is also honorable, and conversely, whatever is honorable will also be just and fair. . . .

[74] "I have let myself be carried beyond the requirements of the plan that I set before me. The truth is that I have been led on by the admirable structure of the Stoic system and the extraordinary sequence of its topics. By the immortal gods, are you not amazed?" . . .

75-76 Cato closes with one last portrayal of the consistent nature of the wise man—the one who is a true king and master, rich, beautiful, and free. He is "the slave of no appetite." Cato's final question: [76] "If, then, it is true that all the good and none but the good are happy, what possession is greater than philosophy, or what is more divine than virtue?"

. . .

Cicero, *On Fate* 28-30

Cicero presents the so-called "Lazy Argument" and Chrysippus' response to it having to do with "co-fated" events.

[28] "Nor will we be hindered by what is called the 'Lazy Argument' . . . since if we gave in to it, we would be led in life to do nothing at all. The argument proceeds in the following manner:

"'If it is fated for you to recover from this disease, you will recover whether you turn to a physician for help or you do not turn to a physician for help. [29] Likewise, if it is fated for you *not* to recover from this disease, you will not recover whether you turn to a physician for help or you do not turn to a physician for help. One or the other is fated. Therefore, it does you no good to turn to a physician for help.'

"This kind of argumentation is correctly termed 'lazy' and 'motionless' since the same argument will do away with every action or motion in life.

"It is even possible to change the form of the argument by not including the term 'fate' and yet to keep the same meaning. So, in this way, if the declaration, 'You will recover from that sickness' has been true from eternity, then 'you will recover whether you turn to a physician for help or you do not turn to a physician for help.' And similarly if the declaration, 'You will recover from that sickness' has been false from eternity, then 'you will not recover whether you turn to a physician for help or you do not turn to a physician for help.' And so on.

[30] "Chrysippus refutes the 'Lazy Argument.' For, he says, some things are simple and some are conjoined. A simple thing is, 'Socrates will die on *that* day.' With this example, whether Socrates does or does not do something, the day of his death has been determined. But if it is fated that 'Laius will beget Oedipus,' it will not be possible to add, 'whether Laius joins with a woman or does not join with a woman.' For in fact the two events are joined together by fate. Chrysippus terms such events 'co-fated' since, in the example, it is fated that Laius will sleep with his wife and that Oedipus

will be produced from her. Similarly, if someone said, 'Milo will wrestle in the Olympic games,' and somebody responded, 'Therefore, he will wrestle whether he has an opponent or he does not have an opponent,' the respondent would be wrong. For in fact 'Milo will wrestle' is a conjoined statement since there can be no wrestling without an opponent.

"Therefore, all fallacious arguments are refuted in the same way. 'You will recover whether you turn to a physician for help or you do not turn to a physician for help' is a fallacious argument insofar as turning to a physician for help is fated just as long as recovering is fated. As I said, Chrysippus terms these conjoined events 'co-fated.'"

Cicero, *Tusculan Disputations* [14] 4.9, 11-16, 22-23

As "M.," Cicero presents the Stoic view of the four passions—delight, desire, grief, and fear—and the various subdivisions that come under these.

[9] M.[15] "Since, in discussing the passions of the soul, Chrysippus and the Stoics have devoted considerable space to subdividing and defining them, the part of their discourse on the topic where they claim to cure the soul and prevent it from being disturbed is actually very short. . . .

[11] "In describing these passions, let us employ the definitions and subdivisions of the Stoics who, it seems to me, show the greatest intelligence in handling the examination of the passions. Accordingly, the following is Zeno's definition of passion, which in Greek he terms *pathos*. Passion is an agitation of the soul that has turned away from right reason and is contrary to nature.[16] Some Stoics offer a briefer definition. For them, passion is a longing that is too intense—one that significantly differs from the harmony of nature.

"The Stoics hold that there are divisions of passion originating in two kinds of imagined good and two kinds of imagined evil, so that there are four in all. Desire and delight originate in what is good—delight in a present good and desire for a future good. Fear and grief, they judge, originate in what is evil—fear relative to a future evil and grief relative to a present evil. Events whose coming is feared also cause grief by their presence.

[12] "By contrast, delight and desire rest upon a belief in a prospective good—this since desire excited by temptation is hurried on to the apparent good, and delight reveals itself in joyful transport at having finally secured something desired. For by nature all men pursue what seems to be good and shun the opposite. For this reason, as soon as the semblance of any apparent good presents itself, nature itself prompts men to secure it. When this happens in a resolute and wise manner, the Stoics use the Greek term *boulēsis* for this kind of desire. We will call it 'willing'[17]—something they think is found in the wise man alone. They define it in this way: willing is a rational desire for anything. That said, where willing is opposed to reason and is too violently excited, it is desire or unbridled longing—something that is found in all fools.

[13] "When we are satisfied that we possess some good, this comes about in two ways. When the soul possesses this satisfaction rationally and in a tranquil and resolute manner, then the Stoics call it 'joy.' By contrast, when the soul is in a transport of meaningless extravagance, then the satisfaction can be termed exuberant or excessive delight. This they define as the irrational elation of the soul. And since we naturally desire good in the same manner as we naturally turn away from evil, such a turning away, when rational, is called 'circumspection' or 'caution.' This is only found in the wise man. But when it is irrational and associated with a base terror that shivers, as it were, it is called fear. Therefore, fear is caution that has turned away from reason.

[14] "The wise man, however, is not subject to the influence of any evil.

"Fools are subject to grief and feel its influence in the face of an imagined evil. And their souls are downcast and shrunken in their noncompliance with reason. And so the first definition of grief is that it is a shrinking of the soul in opposition to reason.

"In conclusion, there are four disturbing passions and three resolute passions.[18] This is so since there is no resolute passion in opposition to grief.

"The Stoics think that every passion is due to judgment and be-lief. Consequently, they define each passion more precisely so that we may realize not only how faulty each is but also to what extent each is under our control. Grief, then, is a newly formed belief rel-ative to present evil. The person who experiences passion judges it right to feel a sinking and shrinking of the soul. Delight is a newly formed belief relative to a present good, where the one experienc-ing it judges it is right to feel carried away. Fear is a belief about impending evil that seems unbearable. Desire is a belief about a po-tential good. The one experiencing it thinks it is advantageous to possess it at once and on the spot.

[15] "The Stoics do not think that the passions alone depend on the judgments and beliefs from which the passions come, as I have said, but that the results of the passions also depend on them. So it is that grief results in some sting as though the sting of pain, fear in a kind of withdrawal and flight of the soul, delight in lavish hilarity, and desire in unbridled longing.

"As for the 'opinion' or 'act of belief' that we have included in all previous definitions, they hold this to be a weak 'assent' or a weak 'act of assent.'

[16] "Numerous subdivisions of the same kind are brought un-der the head of the separate or single passions.[19] For example, under grief come envy, . . . rivalry, disparagement, pity, heaviness, mourning, sadness, anguish, woe, lamenting, apprehension, dis-tress, annoyance, despair, and anything of the same kind. Under fear come hesitation, shame, terror, timidity, dread, faintness, be-wilderment, and awe. Under pleasure[20] come malevolence (taking delight in another's misfortune), enjoyment, ostentation, and the like. Under desire come anger, rage, hatred, enmity, discord, want or lacking, ardent longing, and the rest of this kind. . . .

[22] "They say that the source of all disorders is immoderation, which is a rebellion against the mind and right reason that turns from the rule of reason so that the soul's appetites cannot be con-trolled or limited by any measure. Therefore, just as moderation quiets the appetites and causes them to submit to right reason, and maintains the well-considered judgments of the mind, so its enemy

immoderation excites, confuses, and agitates the whole condition of the soul. Therefore, grief and fear arise—and every other passion.

[23] "Just as bodily disease and sickness begin when the blood is in a bad state or there is an overflow of phlegm or bile, so the disturbing effect of distorted beliefs, one warring against another, robs the soul of health and disturbs it with disease."

NOTES

[1] Theophrastus was Aristotle's student and successor as leader of the Peripatetic school. Varro earlier explains that "Theophrastus . . . in a way broke even more vehemently with the authority of the old teaching—for he stripped virtue of her beauty and rendered her weak by denying that the happy life is only possible with virtue alone" (see *Academica* 1.33).

[2] The same teaching, that "'the noble' or 'the morally good' is the only good," is mentioned again in *Academica* 2.71. In both cases, the Latin term *honestum* or *honestus* could also be given as "that which is distinguished" or "the eminent" or "that which is fine" or "that which is beautiful" or even "that which has integrity"—the idea being that virtue is that which elevates a person, making him or her noble, outstanding, whole. Such a person is the truly fine or beautiful person. The term (*honestum* or *honestus*) is equivalent to *to kalon* or *kalos* in Greek.

[3] The list of the four terms used for the passions here is slightly different from the list we will encounter in a moment in *On Ends*. Though similar in meaning, the biggest difference is "suffering" (from *condolēscō*) instead of "grief" (*aegritūdō*). Otherwise, "desire" or "to desire" here is *concupīscō* instead of *libido*, and "fear" or "to fear" is *extimēscō* instead of *formīdō* or *metus*. For the other terms, see endnote 11 below.

[4] Antiochus of Ascalon (c. 130-68 BC) was an Academic philosopher with whom Cicero studied for a time.

[5] The translation that follows is a modified version of H. Rackham's translation of *De Finibus Bonorum et Malorum* or *On the Ends of Good Things and Bad Things* (1914).

[6] Marcus Porcius Cato (95-46 BC) was a Roman statesman and convinced Stoic.

[7] For Cicero's treatment of Epicureanism in the voice of L. Manlius Torquatus, see Eighteen, "Epicureanism in Cicero's *On the Ends of Good Things and Bad Things*" in the Cave's *The Best of Epicurus: The Life, Writings & Teachings of Epicurus the Greek Philosopher*. The Latin word for pleasure in the text is *voluptas*. In Book 2 of Cicero's *On Ends*, M. Cato states, "I mean the same by 'pleasure' [*voluptas*] as Epicurus does by [the Greek] *hēdonē*. One often has some trouble discovering a Latin word that is the precise equivalent of a Greek word. In this case, however, no search was necessary. No instance can be found of a Latin

word that more exactly conveys the same meaning as the corresponding Greek word than does the word *voluptas*. Every person in the world who knows Latin attaches to this word two ideas—that of gladness of mind, and that of a delightful excitation of agreeable feeling in the body" (2.13).

[8] The Latin for "highest good" is *summum bonum*. Elsewhere, he gives it as "the final [*extremum*] and ultimate [*ultimum*] good" (*On Ends* 1.29).

[9] "Science" here is *ars*, which ranges in meaning from "art" or "practical skill" to "knowledge" or "general principles" (a general understanding of things). Elsewhere, we give *ars* as art or skill.

[10] *Pathē* (singular) is the Greek that appears in Cicero's text. It is any passive state— what happens to a person. Others give *pathos* (singular) (passion, emotion) in place of *pathē*. Rather than *pathē*, Cicero gives *pathos* a few lines later and in *Tusculan Disputations* 4.11.

[11] The Latin terms Cicero uses are the following: grief is *aegritūdō* (grief, sorrow, care—relative to the mind); fear is *formīdō* (fearfulness, fear, terror, dread, awe) or *metus* (fear, dread, apprehension, anxiety); desire is *libido* (desire, lust, longing, pleasure); and, what Cicero ends up terming 'delight,' is *laetitia* (joy, exultation, rejoicing, gladness, pleasure, delight). For other slightly different terms, see endnote 3 above.

[12] Croesus was the fabulously wealthy king of Lydia (ruled c. 560-546 BC).

[13] After "opportuneness," Cicero parenthetically adds, "For let us translate the Greek *eukairia* in this way," and after "right conduct," he explains, "Thus I translate *katorthōsis* since *katorthōma* is a single right action."

[14] The translation that follows is a modified version of J.E. King's translation of *Tusculanae Disputationes* (1927).

[15] Cicero labels the two interlocutors of the *Tusculan Disputations* as "A." and "M." What or who these abbreviations stand for is not known. The M., for instance, has been thought either to refer to "Marcus,"—part of Cicero's own name (*praenomen*) (Marcus Tullius Cicero),—or to stand for the Latin *magister* (instructor or teacher).

[16] The Latin term for "passion" here is *perturbatio*, which can also signify emotion, disorder, confusion, disturbance, disquiet. Zeno's definition of passion given in *Tusculan Disputations* 4.47 is virtually the same.

[17] Or wish or wishing.

[18] Compare these passions, both "disturbing" and "resolute," to Diogenes Laertius account in *Lives* 7.111-116.

[19] For a similar list of sub-passions, see Diogenes Laertius, *Lives* 7.111.

[20] Cicero gives "pleasure" (*voluptas*) here rather than the expected "delight."

PART 4

STOIC LOGIC, PHYSICS & ETHICS
IN OTHER ANCIENT AUTHORS

from

Sextus Empiricus
Hippolytus of Rome
Aetius
Plutarch
Origen
Augustine of Hippo
Eusebius of Caesarea
Nemesios of Emesa
Johannes Stobaeus
Alexander of Aphrodisias
Clement of Alexandria

ELEVEN

STOIC LOGIC
IN OTHER ANCIENT AUTHORS

IN BRIEF: *After a Stoic definition of dialectic (Sextus), Hippolytus notes their emphasis on syllogisms and definitions. Aetius discusses the Stoic notion of the leading part of the soul and how it is filled up with conceptions and preconceptions, as well as explaining distinctions made between presentations, things presented, phantastics, and phantasms. Next, Plutarch relates Chrysippus' position on the proper use of reason or argumentation. Sextus explores the Stoic view on "the truth" and "the true" as well as the criterion of truth. Finally, Origen and Augustine of Hippo note that the Stoics base knowledge on the corporeal senses.*

Sextus Empiricus, *Against the Ethicists* 1.187

THE STOICS DECLARE that dialectic is the knowledge of things that are true, and things that are false, and things that are neither true nor false.

Hippolytus, *Refutation of All Heresies* 1.18

Hippolytus notes the Stoic emphasis on the syllogism and definitions.

By developing the art of the syllogism, the Stoics expanded philosophy. They further included almost everything under definitions. Both Chrysippus and Zeno agree on this point.

Aetius 4.11 (Pseudo-Plutarch 900b-c)[1]

Aetius describes the nature of the leading part of the soul, how it is like a sheet of writing paper, and how it is filled up with preconceptions and concepts as one gains experience or an acquaintance with things.

The Stoics say that when a human being is born, the leading part of the soul is like a sheet of paper that is easy to write on. It is on this that he inscribes each one of his concepts. The first manner of inscribing something on it is by means of the senses. When, for example, one senses something white, one has a memory of it after the thing departs. And when there occur many memories of a similar kind, then one is said to have "an acquaintance with"[2]—for "an acquaintance with" is a multitude of memories of a similar kind.

Some of these concepts come into being naturally according to the aforementioned way—and this without the art of teaching. Others, however, come into being through our instruction and care. These latter ones alone are called "concepts" or "conceptions," whereas the others are called "preconceptions."

But reason, by which we humans are called "rational," is said to be filled up with preconceptions in the first seven years.

Aetius 4.21 (Pseudo-Plutarch 903a-c)

Aetius compares the seven parts of the soul (sight, smell, hearing, taste, touch, seed, and voice) that grow from the leading part of the soul to the arms of an octopus. The leading part itself is located in the head. It is responsible for presentations, assents, sensations, and impulses.

The Stoics say that the highest part of the soul is the leading part, which produces presentations[3] and assents and sensations and impulses. And they call this "reason" or "the reasoning power."

Seven parts of the soul grow from the leading part, stretching out into the body, just as arms grow from an octopus. Of these seven parts, five are assigned to the senses of sight, smell, hearing, taste, and touch. Of these five, sight is a breath extending from the leading part to the eyes. Hearing is a breath extending from the leading part to the ears. Smell is a breath extending from the leading part to the nose. Taste is a breath extending from the leading part to the tongue. And touch is a breath extending from the leading part to the surface of the body relative to the perceptive touching of contacted things. Of the rest, one is called "seed," which is itself a breath extending from the leading part to the testicles. The other, mentioned as "the vocal" by Zeno, which they also call "voice" or "utterance," is a breath extending from the leading part to the throat and tongue and related organs.

As it is in the cosmos, so the leading part itself is situated in our head, which is round.[4]

Aetius 4.12 (Pseudo-Plutarch 900d-900f)

Aetius explains the distinctions Chrysippus makes between presentations, things presented, phantastics, and phantasms.

Chrysippus says that these four—the presentation, the thing presented, the phantastic, and the phantasm (which is to say a vision or phantom appearance)—are different from one another.

A presentation, then, is a modification that occurs in the soul. In itself it makes plain what made it. For example, when by vision we see something white, there is a condition that occurs in the soul by means of vision. Thanks to this condition we have, we say that there is something white that moves us. It is the same with touch and smell. . . .

The thing presented is that which makes the presentation. For example, the white thing and the cold thing and everything that has the power to move the soul—this is the thing presented.

The phantastic is a hollow attraction, a condition in the soul that occurs thanks to no presented thing—as with those who fight with shadows and lay their hands on nothing at all. For a presented thing is behind a presentation, but nothing is behind the phantastic.

A phantasm is that to which we are drawn in a hollow attraction. This is what happens with melancholic and frenzied or mad men.[5]

Plutarch, *On Stoic Self-Contradictions* 1037b

Plutarch recounts Chrysippus' position on the use of reason or argumentation, that they should only be used for discovering truth.

In his book *On the Use of Reason or Argumentation*, Chrysippus says that we should no more use the power of reason or argumentation than we should the power of weapons for things that are not fitting. He adds this: "For reason or argumentation should be employed in the discovery of truths and for relating them together—not for the contrary, though many do it."

Sextus Empiricus, *Outlines of Pyrrhonism* 3.242

Sextus Empiricus criticizes the Stoic "notion of the apprehending presentation" as involving circular reasoning. In doing so, he reveals what the Stoics believe about apprehending presentations.

[242] The way of the Stoics, in presenting the concept of the apprehending presentation, is logically unsound. For in stating, on the one hand, that an apprehending presentation is that which is derived from a real object, and, on the other hand, that a real object is that which is capable of giving rise to an apprehending presentation, they fall into a circular argument.

Sextus Empiricus, *Against the Logicians* 1.38-42, 151-152, 227-231; 2.11-12[6] (*with a summary of the surrounding text given in italics*)

Sextus Empiricus explores the Stoic view regarding "the truth" and "the true" and the Stoic understanding of the criterion of truth.

Book 1

1-37 After looking at how various schools have answered the question of whether philosophy has one or more parts, Sextus Empiricus accepts "the view of those who divide philosophy into physics, ethics, and logic" as "more satisfactory." He then turns to logic and, more specifically, the criterion of truth. The question is, Does such a criterion exist? Before answering, we must make a further division, he says, that between a criterion of knowing how to act and one knowing the true and the false, for instance, what exists and what does not. In this work, Sextus is concerned with the latter sense. Consequently, he turns to "the truth" or "truth."

[38] It is thought by some, and particularly by the Stoics, that "the truth" or "truth" differs from "the true" or "true" in three ways—in substance, in composition, and in power.

According to the Stoics, "the truth" and "the true" differ in substance insofar as "the truth" is corporeal whereas "the true" is incorporeal. And naturally so, they say. For "the true" is a proposition. And a proposition is "a thing said" or "expression." And "a thing said" is incorporeal. Whereas "the truth" is corporeal insofar as it seems to be "knowledge that declares all true things." [39] And all knowledge is a "particular state or condition of the leading part," just as the fist is thought to be a particular state or condition of the hand. And, according to the Stoics, the leading part is corporeal. Therefore, "the truth" is also corporeal in kind.

[40] They differ in composition inasmuch as "the true" is thought of as something uniform and simple in nature—such as, for example, "It is day," and, "I am conversing,"—whereas "the truth," as consisting of knowledge, is thought of as composite or systematic as a collection of several things. [41] So, just as "the people" is one thing and "the citizen" is another—"the people" being a collection composed of many citizens, whereas "the citizen" is the one thing—so, by the same reasoning, "the truth" is distinguished from "the true"—"the truth" corresponding to "the people" on the one hand and "the true" to "the citizen" on the other because the former is composite or systematic, whereas the latter is simple. . . .

[42] They differ in power since "the true" is not entirely dependent on knowledge—for in fact the base man and the infant and the frenzied or madman say something true at times, but they do not possess knowledge of something true. By contrast, "the truth" is viewed as something that involves knowledge. Consequently, the one who possesses "the truth" is the wise man since he has knowledge of true things. . . .

43-150 *Regarding the criterion of truth, some philosophers have rejected and some have retained a criterion. The latter vary according to whether they retain a criterion relative to rational discourse or to non-rational self-evident facts or to both. Sextus offers examples of those thinkers who reject a criterion of truth as well as those who retain one, whether presentation, sensation, reason, or otherwise, and what is meant by each. It is in this context that he discusses the Stoic criterion or criteria.*

[151] The Stoics declare that there are three criteria: knowledge, opinion, and placed midway between these, direct apprehension. Of these, knowledge is a firm and certain direct apprehension unalterable by argument. Opinion is weak and false assent. And direct apprehension, the one between these other two, is a presentation that is directly apprehensible. [152] And, according to them, a presentation that is directly apprehensible is one that is true and is such that it cannot become false.

And they say that, of these three, knowledge exists in wise men alone, opinion in thoughtless men alone, whereas direct apprehension is common to both. And direct apprehension is set up as the criterion of truth. . . .

153-226 Sextus next presents Arcesilaus' and Carneades' (both skeptic Academics) arguments regarding the criterion of truth. Carneades rejects a general criterion of truth but accepts one "for the conduct of life and for the attainment of happiness" based on probability. Sextus next "deals with the Cyrenaic position," that of the Cyrenaic school of philosophy.[7] Following them, he moves on to those who "declare the senses to be the criterion of truth"—including certain physicians and the Epicureans. After these, he explores the Peripatetic position before looking at the Stoics.

[227] The Stoics declare that the criterion of truth is a presentation that is directly apprehensible. We will know what this is after we have first learned what—according to them—a presentation is and what its particular differences are.

[228] According to the Stoics, then, a presentation is an impression on the soul. But about this point, they promptly began to disagree. For whereas Cleanthes understood "impression" as a thing that is both

pressed in and standing out, similar to the impression made in wax by signet rings, [229] Chrysippus judged this position absurd. For in the first place, he says, when the intellect has presentations at one and the same time of a triangular object and a quadrangular object, the same body[8] must necessarily hold different forms at the same time and thus become triangular and quadrangular or even circular—which is by its very nature absurd. Furthermore, when many presentations occur in us simultaneously, the soul will be impressed with many formations—which is worse than the first problem.

[230] Chrysippus himself believed that the term "impression" was used by Zeno in the sense of "alteration" so that the definition of the word is this: "a presentation is an alteration of the soul." It is no longer absurd that, when many presentations coexist in us at one and the same time, the same body receives many alterations. [231] It is just like the air when many people simultaneously speak; it receives numerous and different blows and has many alterations. So will the leading part experience something analogous to this when it receives a variety of presentations."

232-446 *After further addressing the Stoic position, Sextus moves on to other topics having to do with the criterion, including "the criterion 'by whom,' or agent, which is to say the human being," again exploring the positions of the various philosophers and schools.*

Book 2

1-10 *Sextus begins the second book of* Against the Logicians *by summarizing the first: "We have now reviewed the difficulties that are usually stated by the skeptics in order to do away with the criterion of truth." Now, he says, he will turn to the topic of the true itself, about which there is so much disagreement that the skeptic position of "suspended judgment" is best. Regarding those who have looked into the matter, "some say that there is not, and others that there is, something true. And of the latter, some have said that only intelligibles are true, others that only sensibles, and others that both sensibles and intelligibles alike are true." Sextus gives examples of each before moving on to another matter.*

[11] There was another controversy among the dogmatists about the true. In this one some placed the true and the false in the thing signified, others in the utterance, and others in the motion of the intellect.

The chief proponents of the first opinion were the Stoics, who said that three things are linked together: the thing signified, the thing that signifies, and the existing thing or object. [12] Of these, the thing that signifies is the utterance—for example, "Dion." And the thing signified is the real thing or object indicated by the utterance that we take hold of when it is in our intellect. By contrast, even though non-Greeks hear the utterance, they do not understand it. And the existing thing or object is the external real object, such as Dion himself.

Of these three, two are corporeal, the utterance and the existing thing or object, and one is incorporeal, namely the real thing or object signified and also said or sayable, the very thing that is true or false.

13-481 *In the remainder of Book 2, unnecessary to our purpose here, even though the Stoics are frequently mentioned, Sextus continues to probe the topic of the true, including, among other points, a discussion of self-evident and unclear things; of signs that "seem to make something evident" or that "indicate an unclear thing"; of various kinds and modes of argumentation; of the corporeality or incorporeality of things said (a point, he observes, the Stoics dwell on); of proof, what it is and whether it exists (on this, he comments on the Stoic elaboration of "the modes of proof"); and of logical theory or the art of argumentation (including that of the Stoics).*

Origen, *Against Celsus* 7.37

Origen states that Stoic knowledge is based on the senses.

The Stoics reject all intellectual substances. They hold that all that we apprehend is apprehended through the senses, and that all knowledge comes through the senses.

Augustine of Hippo, *City of God* 8.7

Augustine of Hippo points out that the Stoics base all their knowledge on corporeal senses rather than basing some on the incorporeal mind (which, of course, the Stoics do not accept).

As for the teaching regarding what they call logic, that is, rational philosophy, we should not compare the Platonists with those who fix the bodily senses as the judge of truth and thought that all we learn should be measured by their untrustworthy and fallacious standards. Such were the Epicureans and everyone from that school. Such also were the Stoics, who attributed to the bodily senses that expertise in disputation, which they so ardently love.

The Stoics called this disputation dialectic, asserting that it was from the bodily senses that the mind conceives notions, called by them *ennoiai* or "concepts" — that is, those things which they expound by definition. From this they develop the whole system of their learning and teaching, and all the connections therein.

I often wonder relative to this how the Stoics can say that no one but the wise is beautiful. For by what bodily sense have they perceived that beauty? By what fleshly eyes have they seen wisdom's form and splendor?

NOTES

[1] Aetius was the late first century AD author of a now-lost work that compared the views of Greek philosophers on natural philosophy. Falsely attributed to Plutarch (hence, "Pseudo-Plutarch"), it is known as *Placita Philosophorum* (*Opinions of the Philosophers* or *On the Doctrines of the Philosophers*).

[2] The Greek term (*empeiria* or *empeiros*) means that one is experienced with a thing and thus comes to be acquainted with it. For example, in sensing milk and summer clouds and cotton, one comes to be acquainted with white things.

[3] Others give *phantasia* as "imagination" (for example, Goodwin, 1874); in this case, it may also be given as "the power by which an object is presented to the mind."

[4] The implication is that the sun, the leading part, is situated in the cosmos, which is round or spherical, just as the *hēgemonikon* (the leading part of the soul) is situated in the head, which is round.

[5] Aetius goes on to explain with two examples. One comes from Euripides' *Orestes* (255-256) when Orestes sees a vision of "maidens with bloodshot eyes and snaky hair." The other is from Homer's *Odyssey* (20.350-357), when the seer Theoclymenus sees a great number of phantom-forms waiting to go down to Hades.

⁶ Or, alternatively, *Against the Mathematicians* 7. 38-42, 151-152, 227-231; 8.11-12. An alternative title for *Against the Mathematicians* as a whole is *Against the Professors* (*Pros Mathēmatikous*). Scholars believe that the eleven books that form *Against the Mathematicians* originally consisted of two parts or works. The first work, books 1-6, was *Pros Mathēmatikous* (*Against the Professors*); it was written against various academic disciplines (six of the seven liberal arts): grammar, rhetoric, geometry, arithmetic, astrology, and music. The second work, books 7-11, was *Pros Dogmatikous* (*Against the Dogmatists*). Of the latter work that covered the three parts of philosophy (logic, physics, and ethics), books 7-8 covered logic, 9-10 physics, and 11 ethics.

⁷ Founded by Aristippus of Cyrene (c. 435-356 BC), Cyrenaicism was an ancient Greek philosophy that promoted pleasure as the chief goal of life.

⁸ That is, the physical or corporeal intellect or mind.

TWELVE

STOIC NATURAL PHILOSOPHY OR PHYSICS
IN OTHER ANCIENT AUTHORS

IN BRIEF: *Eusebius begins by providing summary points about the cosmos as a whole, the care of God for humans, and the origin and nature of the soul. Next, Hippolytus reports Stoic views regarding God, fate, and the conflagration of the cosmos. Aetius covers the basic principles (God and matter), the nature of God, and how the notion of God was deduced from the ordered beauty of the cosmos. Plutarch relates the nature of the Stoic's four primary elements, Chrysippus' position asserting the potential equality of gods and humans in terms of happiness and virtue, and the Stoic view of the development of the cosmos. Along with Johannes Stobaeus, he explores the Stoic view of time. Nemesios relates the Stoic idea of tensional motion. Origen reports Stoic thinking on the cause of a thing's motion. Alexander of Aphrodisias offers their position on the breath or spirit that pervades all, and on fate, and Chrysippus' theory of mixture. Finally, Sextus Empiricus explores the Stoic arguments for the existence of God or gods, as well as their notions of cause, and various intangible or incorporeal things.*

Eusebius of Caesarea, *Preparation for the Gospel* 15.15, 18, 20

Eusebius reports the teachings of Stoicism given by the first century BC Stoic Arius Didymus. Included are points about the cosmos as a whole, the beneficent care of God for humans, and the origin and nature of the soul.

THE STOICS CALL the whole cosmos with all its parts God. They furthermore say that God alone is one, finite, living, eternal, and divine. All bodies are contained in God, and in him there is no void. . . .

They say that the cosmos is eternal, but its orderly arrangement is produced and subject to change at infinite periods, both in the past and in the future. . . . The term "cosmos" also means the system consisting of heaven and the air and earth and sea and the natures contained in these. Again, the term "cosmos" means the dwelling place of the gods and men and of all things made for their sake. . . .

There is a community that exists between the gods and men since they participate in reason, which is the law of nature. . . .

We must suppose that the God who manages the whole takes into consideration humankind, being beneficent, kind, and friendly to humans, as well as being just and possessing all virtues. Indeed, it is for this reason that the cosmos is also called "Zeus" since he is the cause of our life. And insofar as from eternity he manages all things unchangeably by connected reason, he is also called fate. . . .

Cleanthes thinks the sun is the leading power of the cosmos since it is the greatest of the heavenly bodies and contributes most to the management of the whole by making the day and the year and the other seasons. Some Stoic philosophers, however, think the earth is the ruling power of the cosmos. But Chrysippus thinks it is the aether, which is the clearest and purest as the most mobile of all things, carrying around the whole course of the cosmos. . . .

[18] The oldest members of the Stoic school hold that all things are changed into aether when at certain very long periods all things are resolved into an aethereal fire. . . . This is the great destruction of the cosmos that takes place after long periods . . . the doctrine of the dissolution of the cosmos into fire, which they call "conflagration." . . . For it is held by the Stoic philosophers that the universal substance changes into fire, as into a seed. And coming back again, from this seed it completes its organization such as it was before. And this is the doctrine that was accepted by the first and oldest leaders of the school—Zeno, Cleanthes, and Chrysippus. But they say that Zeno [of Tarsus], who was the student and successor of Chrysippus, had doubts regarding the conflagration of the cosmos. . . .

[20] Zeno says that the seed man emits is breath combined with moisture, a portion and fragment of the soul, and a blending of the parents' seed, and a concrete mixture of the various parts of the soul. For this seed, having the same laws as the cosmos, when emitted into the womb, is caught up by another breath and made a portion of the

female's soul and grows into a unity with it. And being stirred and kindled there, it grows in secret, continually receiving additions to the moisture and increasing itself. . . .

Regarding the soul, Cleanthes, in presenting the teachings of Zeno for comparison with other natural philosophers, says that Zeno calls the soul an exhalation with sensation. . . . So, then, like Heraclitus, Zeno represents the soul as an exhalation. And he says that it is sensitive for the reason that the leading part is capable of being impressed through the senses by real and substantial objects and receiving their impressions. . . .

They say that the soul is generated and perishable. But it does not perish immediately when freed from the body but abides for some time by itself—the soul of the good until the resolution of all things into fire, but the soul of the foolish merely for certain periods of time. . . . The souls of the foolish and of irrational animals perish together with their bodies.

Such are the doctrines of the Stoic philosophy collected out of the *Epitomes* of Arius Didymus.

Hippolytus, *Refutation of All Heresies* 1.18

Hippolytus reports Stoic views regarding God, the "originating principle of all things," fate, and the conflagration or purification of the cosmos.

The Stoics suppose that God is the one originating principle of all things. He is a body of the utmost refinement. His providential care pervades everything.

These thinkers are certain about the existence of fate everywhere. Accordingly, they employ the following kinds of illustration. Suppose a dog is attached to a wagon. If, in fact, he is disposed to follow along, he is both drawn along and follows voluntarily, making an exercise of free power in combination with necessity, that is, fate. But if he is not disposed in this way to follow, he will wholly be coerced to do so. The same, of course, holds true in the case of human beings. For even though they may not be willing to follow, they will wholly be coerced to engage in what has been decreed. . . .

The Stoics accept the teaching that there will be a conflagration or purification of the cosmos. Some say this conflagration will happen to the whole cosmos; others say it will only happen to a portion.

Aetius 1.3 (Pseudo-Plutarch 878b-c)

Aetius reports Zeno's view on the two principles of the cosmos.

Zeno of Citium, the son of Mnaseas, says the [two] principles are God and matter, the one being responsible for acting, whereas the other is acted upon—including the four elements.

Aetius 1.6 (Pseudo-Plutarch 879c-880d)

After offering the Stoic definition of the substance of God—"an intelligent and fiery breath," Aetius explains how the Stoics came to their notion of God from the ordered beauty of the cosmos, including the regular movement of the stars in the sky that serve as regulators of everything else.

The Stoics define the substance of God this way: it is an intelligent and fiery breath that has no shape but changes into whatever it wishes, becoming like all things. They first obtained the concept of this God from the beauty of the things that appeared to them. For beautiful things do not come into being without a plan and by chance but only by the art and skill of someone working at it. But the cosmos is beautiful as is clear from its shape and its color and its magnitude and also from the diverse stars around the cosmos. And the cosmos is spherical, the first of all shapes. . . .

It is from [*the stars and the heavenly constellations*] that we grasp the concept of God—for the sun and the moon and the rest of the stars go beneath the earth and always rise up bearing the same colors and sizes and in the same places and at the same times.

Therefore, those who by tradition delivered to us the reverence for and worship of the gods did so in three ways: first, from nature; second, from stories and myths; and third, from the testimony of custom and laws. The philosophers taught the way according to nature, the poets according to myth, and the constitution of each city according to custom and laws.

The whole teaching of the Stoics is divided into seven kinds. The first is based on those things that appear high in the sky. It is from the appearance of the stars that we have a concept of God, when we see that they are responsible for the great celestial harmony, and by their rising and setting they order both days and nights, winter and summer, and—of those things on the earth—animals that produce offspring and plants that bear fruit. For this reason they thought the sky was a father who began these things and that the earth was a mother. Of these, the one is father since the outflow of rain functions as seed whereas the other is mother since she receives the seed and produces offspring. And seeing that the stars are always moving and make it possible for us to see things, they addressed the sun and the moon as gods.

Plutarch, *On Common Conceptions (Against the Stoics) 1076a-b*

Chrysippus asserts similarity between the gods and human beings in terms of happiness and virtue.

According to Chrysippus, the gods do not differ from human beings in terms of happiness and virtue. . . . The Stoics say that if a human is not missing anything of virtue, then he will not be lacking anything of happiness.

Plutarch, *On Common Conceptions (Against the Stoics) 1085c-d*

Plutarch identifies some of the qualities of what the Stoics identify as the primary elements—fire, air, earth, and water.

The Stoics call the four bodies—earth and water, air and fire—primary elements. . . . They make part of them simple and pure, and part of them compounded and mixed. For they teach that earth and water are neither themselves cohesive nor make others so, but that they preserve their unity by sharing a breath-like and fiery force. Air and fire, however, preserve there own tension through their elasticity and, mixed with the other two, give them tension and permanence and substantiality.

Nemesios, *On the Nature of Man* 2

Nemesios relates the Stoic idea of tensional motion.

There are those like the Stoics who say that there is a tensional motion in bodies that moves simultaneously inward and outward. The outward movement gives rise to quantities and qualities, while the inward movement produces unity and essence.[1]

Johannes Stobaeus, *Eclogues* 1.104, 106

Johannes Stobaeus presents Zeno's and Chrysippus' notions of time.

[1.104] Zeno said that time is the interval of movement that holds the measure and standard of swiftness and slowness. . . . [1.106] Chrysippus defined time as the interval of movement that sometimes is also called the measure of swiftness and slowness, or the interval proper to the movement of the cosmos. And it is in time that everything moves and exists. It seems that time is to be taken in two senses, just like the earth and the sea and the void, namely in the sense of the whole and its parts. In the same way as the void is all-infinite everywhere, so time is all-infinite in both directions, indeed, past and future are both infinite. And he states most clearly that no time is entirely present. For the division of continua goes on infinitely, and by this distinction time, too, is infinitely divisible. Therefore, no time is strictly present, but it is defined only loosely.

Plutarch, *On Common Conceptions (Against the Stoics)* 1081c-d

Plutarch reports the Stoic understanding of "the now," the present moment, that it does not really exist but is part past and part future.

The Stoics do not admit the existence of the shortest element of time, nor do they concede that the now is indivisible, but that which some-one might assume and think of as present is, according to them, partly future and partly past. Therefore, nothing remains of the now, nor is there left any part of the present time, but what is said to exist now is partly spread over the future and partly over the past. . . . In the third, fourth, and fifth books of his *On Parts*, Chrysippus declares that part of the present time is future and part is past.

Origen, *On Principles* 3.1.2

Origen presents Stoic thinking on the cause of a thing's motion.

[2] Of things that move, some have the cause of their motion within themselves, while others are set in motion from the outside alone. So it is that things that are carried are set in motion from the outside alone, things such as pieces of wood and stones and everything that is held together by means of the constitution of their matter alone. . . . Animals and plants, and generally things held together by means of nature and soul, have the cause of their motion within themselves. . . . The Stoics say that fire is the cause of its own motion, and perhaps also springs of water.

And of those things that have the causes of their motion within themselves, the Stoics say that some are moved from themselves, while others are moved by means of themselves. They say "from themselves" of things without a soul, while of those with a soul they say "by means of themselves." Things with a soul move by means of themselves when a presentation occurs that rouses an impulse. In some animals presentations occur that urge them on by a kind of natural impulse to an orderly and regular motion. We see this in the case of spiders when a presentation occurs that rouses an impulse in them to weave webs. . . . And likewise in bees that are roused to form honeycombs.

Alexander of Aphrodisias, *On Mixture*

Alexander explains the nature of the breath that unites and pervades sub-stance and holds the cosmos together.

The whole substance is united by a breath pervading all of it, and by which the cosmos is being held and kept together and is in sympathy with itself. . . . The Stoics attribute its unity to certain bonds and material causes and a certain breath[2] pervading the whole substance. . . . The breath, which consists of fire and air, roams through all the bodies and mixes with all of them, and the existence of each depends on that.

Alexander of Aphrodisias, *On Mixture*

Alexander presents Chrysippus' theory of mixture, including the nature of different kinds of mixture.

Chrysippus' theory of mixture is as follows: he assumes that the whole material cosmos is unified by a breath that wholly pervades it, and by which the cosmos is made coherent and kept together and is made intercommunicating.

And of the compounded bodies some become mixed by juxtaposition when two or more substances are put together in the same place and placed side by side, joining each other, as he says, and preserving in this juxtaposition their proper essence and quality according to their individuality, as happens, for instance, when beans and grains of wheat get mixed with one another.

Some bodies are destroyed together through a complete fusion of their substances and their respective qualities. Such is the case with drugs whose components undergo simultaneous destruction, and, as a result of it, another body emerges.

Certain mixtures, he says, result in a total interpenetration of substances and their qualities, the original substances and qualities being preserved in this mixture. This he calls specifically a mixing of the mixed components. It is characteristic of the mixed substances that they can again be separated, which is only possible if the components preserve their properties in the mixture. . . . This interpenetration of the components he assumes to happen in that the substances mixed together interpenetrate one another such that there is not a particle among them that does not contain a share of all the rest. If this were not the case, the result would not be mixing but juxtaposition.

The supporters of this theory adduce evidence for their belief from the fact that many bodies preserve their qualities whether they are present in smaller or in larger quantities, as can be seen in the case of frankincense. When burned, it becomes greatly rarefied, but for all that it preserves its quality. Further, there are many substances, which, when assisted by others, expand to an extent which they could not do by themselves. Gold, for instance, when mixed with certain drugs, can be spread and rarefied to an extent that is not possible if it is beaten out by itself. Similarly, there are cases where we can be effective together with others, while we cannot when we are alone. And grapevine tendrils that cannot stand up by themselves can do so if they are entangled with one another. Therefore, he says, we should not be surprised that certain substances assist each other by forming a complete union such as to preserve their own qualities while totally interpermeating each other, even if the mass of one is so slight that by itself it could not preserve its quality if spread to such an extent. Thus the ladle of wine mixes with a large amount of water, being assisted by the latter to spread throughout a great volume.

To prove this assertion, the Stoics adduce as clear evidence the fact that the soul has substantiality of its own as has the body containing it. By totally pervading the body it preserves in this mixture its own essence—there is no part of the living body that does not have its share in the soul. And the same holds for the nature of plants and for the physical structure of those things held together by a state or condition.

Alexander of Aphrodisias, *On Fate*

Alexander presents the Stoic theory of "the possible."

The Stoic theory is that "the possible" does not exclude that everything will happen according to fate. And they define the possible event as something that is not prevented by anything from happening even if it does not happen. "There is nothing to prevent the occurrence even of the opposite of what happens through fate. For even though it does not occur, it is still possible." And the fact that the preventing causes are not known to us is the reason for the assumption that there was no hindrance for the things to happen. For these things that are the causes for the opposite things to happen according to fate are also the causes for the non-happening of things themselves, if, as they say, it really is impossible that under the same circumstances the opposite should happen. But because we have no knowledge of things that happen, therefore, so they say, things that do not happen seem possible to us.

Plutarch, *On Stoic Self-Contradictions* 1052c; 1053b-c

Plutarch reports the Stoic view of the development of the cosmos.

[1052c] In the first part of his work *On Providence*, Chrysippus says, "Zeus grows until he consumes everything. As death is the separation of soul from body, and as the soul of the cosmos does not leave it but is growing continuously until it has consumed all matter, one cannot say that the cosmos is mortal." . . . [1053b-c] In the first book of his work *On Providence*, Chrysippus says, "When the cosmos is completely in the fiery state, so, at the same time, are its soul and its leading part. But if what is left over of the soul is changing into the humid state, the cosmos is in a certain way transformed into body and soul, and, therefore, it is composed of both, thus exhibiting another order."

Sextus Empiricus, *Outlines of Pyrrhonism* 3.218

Sextus gives the Stoic teaching that God pervades all.

[218] The Stoics say that God is a pervading breath that pervades even ugly or putrid things.

Sextus Empiricus, *Against the Physicists* 1.11, 60-65, 75-79, 88-94,
101-114, 123-126, 131-135, 137, 211, 332, 336; 2.3, 142, 218, 234[3]
(with a summary of the surrounding text given in italics)

In Against the Physicists, *Sextus presents what natural philosophers have thought about the two basic principles of everything—the active and the passive principles. In so doing, he explores arguments for and against God or the gods and the notion of cause.*

Book 1

1-10 *"Those natural philosophers who seem to have classified most exactly the principles of everything declare that some of these are active and some are material [or passive]." Beginning with Homer, Anaxagoras of Clazomenae, and Empedocles of Acragas, Sextus offers examples of such thinkers who identified both an active or efficient principle and one passive or material.*

[11] When the Stoics declare that there are two principles, God and matter without quality, they assume that God acts and that matter is passive and changed.

12-59 *Sextus goes on to explore both kinds of principles, beginning first with the active principle or God and "how we humans acquired the notion of God." After reporting a number of reasons why humans have come to believe in God or the gods, Sextus moves on to the question of whether God or the gods exist. "That God exists is the view of most of the dogmatists and the common preconception of ordinary people." By contrast "that God does not exist is the view of those who are called 'atheists.'"*

[60] Those who claim that the gods exist endeavor to support their thesis in four ways.[4] First, they argue from the agreement that exists among all human beings. Second, from the orderly arrangement of the cosmos. Third, from the absurd consequences of the denial of the divine. Fourth and last, by refuting the opposing arguments.

[61] Arguing from the common notion of God or the gods, they say that practically all men, both Greeks and non-Greeks, believe in the existence of the divine. And for this reason they are one in sacrificing and in praying and in dedicating lands and temples to the gods. Some humans do this in one way, some in another way, as though all of them trusted in and relied on the existence of some God but did not possess the same preconception about its nature.

But if this preconception had been false, they would not have agreed in this way. Therefore, gods exist.

[62] Moreover, false opinions and extraordinary assertions do not survive longer than those people for whom they were maintained; rather; they come to an end with them. For example, men honor kings with sacrifices and the other rituals by which they approach and pray to the gods. Yet they observe these practices only as long as the kings themselves are alive. And when they are dead, they give them up as though contrary to custom and impious. But the concept of the gods persists from eternity into eternity—a likely view arising from the evidence of what takes place in the cosmos.

[63] Beyond this, even if one should pass over the conjecture of the ordinary individual and trust in those men who are intelligent and endowed with genius, one may see how poetry produces no great or brilliant work in which God is not the one who possesses authority and power over whatever happens—as in the war between the Greeks and the non-Greeks described by the poet Homer. [64] One can see that the majority of natural philosophers are in agreement with the poets. For Pythagoras and Empedocles and the Ionians and Socrates and Plato and Aristotle and the Stoics and perhaps "the philosophers of the garden" too—as the declarations of Epicurus testify—allow for the existence of God. [65] Therefore, just as if we were investigating something that is seen, it would be reasonable for us to trust those with the sharpest sight, and if something that is heard, those with the sharpest hearing, so when we are looking into something contemplated by reason, we should trust no one except those sharpest in mind and reason, such as were any of these philosophers.

66-74 *Sextus next conveys a reply from the opposing side having to do with the common notions all men and poets have about what goes on in Hades. The Stoics concede the point but argue that the notion of the gods is different. "Such, then, is the argument from the common and agreed on opinion about God."*

[75] Let us also examine the argument that is based on the orderly arrangement of the cosmos. The material substance of existing

things, they say, in itself without motion and without form, is bound to be moved and given form by some cause. Accordingly, just as when we behold a very beautiful work in bronze we long to learn who the craftsman is since the bronze material itself is without motion, so when we contemplate the matter of the whole cosmos moving and existing in form and orderly arrangement, we reasonably look for the cause that moves it and gives it many forms.

[76] It is plausible that this cause is nothing other than some power that pervades the whole even as our soul pervades us. This power, then, is either self-moving or moved by some other power. And if it is moved by another power, then that other power is also unable to move unless it is moved by another power. But this is absurd. There exists, therefore, a power that is of itself self-moving, and this power is divine and everlasting. For this power is either in motion from eternity or from some definite point in time. But it is not in motion from a point in time since no cause of its motion exists from a given point in time. So then, eternal is the power that moves matter and arranges it, leading it into births and changes. Consequently, this power is God.

[77] Moreover, that which generates what is rational and wise is certainly itself rational and wise. But the aforementioned power is of such a nature that it makes human beings; therefore, it is rational and wise, which is, in fact, the very nature of the divine. Gods, therefore, exist.

[78] Turning to bodies, some are unified, while some are formed from conjoined things and some from separate things. Unified bodies are those that are controlled by a single state or condition, such as plants and animals. Those formed of conjoined things are such as those that are composed of adjacent things that tend to combine into one main structure—things such as chains and city walls and ships. Those formed of separate things are such as those that are compounded of things that are disjoined and isolated and existing by themselves—things such as armies and flocks and choruses.

[79] Since, then, the cosmos also is a body, it is either a unified body or one formed from conjoined things or from separate things. But it is neither from conjoined nor separate things. . . . These points establish that the cosmos is a unified body.

80-87 The cosmos is shown to be a unified body since it exhibits certain sympathies. Moreover, the nature that manages the cosmos is the best—it is "intelligent, good, and immortal." Such is God; therefore, gods exist.

[88] Cleanthes established the point in this way: "If one nature is stronger or better than another nature, there will be some strongest or best nature. If one soul is better than another soul, there will be some best soul. Accordingly, if one animal is stronger than another animal, there is some strongest animal. For such things will not go on without limit. So then, as a nature is not capable of infinite growth in terms of being stronger or better, neither is a soul nor an animal capable of the same. [89] One animal, however, is stronger than another animal. A horse, for instance, is stronger than a tortoise, a bull is stronger than an ass, and a lion is stronger than a bull. And of all the animals on earth, the human being excels and is the best in terms of bodily disposition and that of the soul.

[90] Yet a human being cannot be the very best animal because, for example, he is bad all of the time, and if not all, then most—for even if he attains virtue, he attains it late and at the setting of life's sun. And human beings are subject to death, and weak, and require countless forms of assistance, such as food and coverings and all the other attention given to the body, which stands over us like some cruel tyrant, demanding its daily tribute and threatening us with disease and death unless we provide for its washing and anointing and clothing and feeding. So it is that a human being is not a perfect animal but imperfect and far removed from the perfect.

[91] But that which is perfect and best will be better than a human being, complete with every virtue and refusing every vice. And this animal will not differ from God. God, therefore, exists."

Such, then, is the view of Cleanthes.

[92] The Socratic philosopher Xenophon[5] also offered an argument for the existence of the gods, though he attributed the proof to Socrates in conversation with Aristodemus.

"Tell me, Aristodemus, are there any people you have admired for their wisdom?"

"Yes," he said.

"And who are they?"

"I have admired Homer for his poetry, Polycleitus for his sculpture, and Zeuxis for his painting."

[93] "Then is it not because of the extraordinary craftsmanship of their productions that you are satisfied with them?"

"Yes, it is," he said.

"If, then, Polycleitus' statue of a man were to come to life, would you not be satisfied with the artist even more?"

"Very much so!"

"So then, if when you saw a statue of a man, you said that it had been fashioned by some artist, when you see a human being well-disposed in soul and well-equipped in body, do you not think that he has been fashioned by some extraordinary mind? [94] And when you further observe the arrangement and function of his parts? For instance, that he has made humans upright. Or that he has given them eyes to see what is visible and ears to hear what is audible. And what use would smell have been if he had not also supplied them with nostrils? Or flavors if he had not made within them a tongue that judges them? And you know that you have in your body a small portion of earth from the great amount of earth that exists, and a little moisture from the great amount of water that exists, and the same with fire and air. But from what source do you suppose you happened to snatch a mind if it alone exists nowhere else?"

Such, then, is Xenophon's argument.

95-100 *Sextus reports how some counter Xenophon's argument, and then he puts it in an alternative form, finishing with: "If there had not been some mind in the cosmos, there would not have been some mind in you. But there is some mind in you. And because of this the cosmos is intelligent. And being intelligent, it is also God."*

[101] And Zeno of Citium, taking Xenophon as his starting point, argues this way: "The thing that emits the seed of something rational is itself also rational. But the cosmos emits the seed of something rational. Therefore, the cosmos is rational." . . .

[102] The plausibility of this argument is manifest. For the origin of motion in every nature and soul seems to come from the leading part. And all the powers that are sent out into the parts of the whole are sent out from the leading part as from a fount or spring, so that every power that exists in the part also exists in the whole because it is distributed from its leading part. Therefore, whatever the part is in terms of power, so the whole must be first. [103] For this reason, if the cosmos emits the seed of a rational animal, it does not do so by agitation as with humans, but by containing the seeds of rational animals. But it does not contain them in the same way that we might speak of the vine containing its grapes, that is, by way of inclusion. Rather, it does so because the generative seeds or principles of rational animals are contained within it. So then, the argument is this: "The cosmos contains the generative seeds or principles of rational animals; therefore, the cosmos is rational."

[104] Once again, Zeno says, "The rational is better than the nonrational. But nothing is better than the cosmos. Therefore, the cosmos is rational. Likewise with the intelligent and that which participates in life and has a soul. For the intelligent is better than the nonintelligent, and that with life is better than that without life. But nothing is better than the cosmos; therefore, the cosmos is intelligent and alive."

[105] Another argument such as this is given by Plato. He writes it this way: "Let us declare the cause by which the framer organized this production and this all. The framer was good, and in the good there is no envy concerning anything. And being like this, he wished that all things would become like him as much as possible. We will be right, then, in accepting from men of wisdom this which is the most powerful principle of generation and order." [106] Then, after going through a few more points, he says, "So it was because of this consideration that he framed mind within soul and soul within body as he organized the all, so that the work he was completing might in its nature be the most beautiful and the best. So then, in accord with the likely account,⁶ we must declare that this cosmos is in truth a living animal with a soul and mind because it has come into existence through the providence of God."

[107] So then, Plato expounded the same argument as Zeno. For this one also says that the all is most beautiful, a work completed in accord with nature, and, in accord with the likely account, it is a living animal with a soul both intelligent and rational.

[108] But Alexinus[7] twisted Zeno's argument in this manner: "The poetical is better than that which is not poetical. And the grammatical is better than that which is not grammatical. And that which is observed in accord with the other arts is better than that which is not. But nothing is better than the cosmos; therefore, the cosmos is poetical and grammatical."

[109] But in reply to this parallel argument, the Stoics say that Zeno has chosen what is absolutely better—that is, the rational is better than the non-rational, the intelligent than the non-intelligent, and the living than the non-living. By contrast, Alexinus has not. [110] For the poetical is not absolutely better than that which is not poetical, and the grammatical is not absolutely better than the non-grammatical. So we observe a great difference between the arguments. For see how a poetical Archilochus is not better than a non-poetical Socrates, and how a grammatical Aristarchus[8] is not better than the non-grammatical Plato.

[111] The Stoics and those who agree with them also endeavor to build an argument for the existence of the gods from the motion of the cosmos. For thanks to many points of observation, everyone agrees that the cosmos is in motion. [112] It is moved, then, by nature or by choice or by a necessary whirling movement. But that it is moved by a necessary whirling movement is not reasonable. For a whirling motion is either disordered or ordered. And if it is disordered, it is not able to move something in an orderly manner. But if it moves something in an orderly and harmonious manner, that thing will be divine and excellent. [113] For it never would have moved the whole in an orderly manner that conserves it if it had not been intelligent and divine. And if it is such, it cannot be a whirling motion—for a whirling motion is disordered and brief in duration. So, as Democritus and those around him said, the cosmos is not moved by a necessary whirling movement. [114] Neither is it moved by a non-perceptive nature insofar as the intelligent nature

is better than this. And we see that these kinds of natures are contained in the cosmos. By necessity, therefore, the cosmos itself must possess an intelligent nature by which it is moved in an orderly manner. And this is doubtlessly God.

115-122 *After expounding a few more arguments for the existence of God, Sextus moves on to explore the third way by which those who "maintain that the gods exist try to establish their thesis"—that is, the argument "from the absurd consequences of the denial of the divine."*

[123] Next, let us examine the nature of the absurd consequences of denying the divine. If gods do not exist, then piety is non-existent. For piety is the knowledge of service to the gods, and there cannot be any service of things non-existent, nor will any knowledge about this service come to be. Just as there cannot be any knowledge of service to hippocentaurs since they are non-existent, so there cannot be any knowledge of service to the gods if they are non-existent. So it is that if the gods do not exist, then piety is non-existent. But piety exists. Therefore, we must say that gods exist.

[124] Again, if gods do not exist, then holiness is non-existent since it is a kind of justice toward the gods. But according to the common conceptions and preconceptions of all human beings, holiness exists. And, accordingly, something holy exists. And so the divine exists.

[125] If, however, gods do not exist, wisdom is done away with since it is "the knowledge of divine and human matters." And just as there is no knowledge of both human and hippocentuarean matters given the fact that humans exist while hippocentaurs do not, so too there will be no knowledge of divine and human matters if humans exist but gods do not. But it is absurd to say that wisdom does not exist. Consequently, it is absurd to think that the gods are non-existent.

[126] And if justice too has been introduced because of the interaction of humans with one another and with the gods, then if gods do not exist, neither will justice unite the two. But the very thought is absurd.

127-130 *Sextus discusses the Pythagorean position that humans share fellowship not only with gods but also with irrational animals since one spirit pervades the whole cosmos like a soul. Hence the Pythagorean counsel against slaying and eating animals. He counters the argument by suggesting that, if true, then we likewise cannot eat plants or chisel stones.*

[131] Why, then, do the Stoics say that humans have a certain just relation and interaction with one another and with the gods? It is not because of the spirit[9] that moves through all things—otherwise there would be some observance of justice between us and non-rational animals. Rather, it is because we possess reason, which extends to one another and the gods. By contrast, the irrational animals have no relation of justice toward us since they have no share in reason. So then, if we perceive justice thanks to the partnership we humans have with one another and we humans have with gods, then if gods do not exist, neither does justice exist. But justice exists. We must say, then, that gods exist.

[132] More: if gods do not exist, neither does prophecy exist since it is the knowledge that observes and interprets the signs given by gods to men. Nor yet do inspiration and astrology, nor divination, nor prediction by means of dreams exist. But it is absurd to do away with so many things already believed in by all men. Therefore, gods exist.

[133] Zeno offered this argument also: "One may reasonably honor the gods. But one may not reasonably honor those who are non-existent. Therefore, gods exist."

Some reply with this parallel argument, saying, "One may reasonably honor wise men. But one may not reasonably honor those who are non-existent. Therefore, wise men exist." But this conclusion was not pleasing to the Stoics since they have never been able to find what they would call a wise man.

[134] In reply to the parallel argument, Diogenes the Babylonian says that the meaning of the second premise in Zeno's argument is this: "But one may not reasonably honor those who are not of such a nature as to exist." For when this premise is accepted, it is clear that the gods are of such a nature as to exist. [135] But if this is so, then

they do now actually exist. For if they had existed at any time, they also exist now, just as, if atoms had existed, they also exist now. For according to the notion of such bodies, they are imperishable and without beginning. . . . But the wise do not have such a nature."[10] . . .

[137] Such, then, are the typical arguments made by the Stoics . . . in favor of the existence of gods.

138-210 *In the sections that follow, Sextus presents the arguments of those who do not believe in the existence of gods. In conclusion, he suggests that one is better off suspending judgment relative to their existence since some argue for and some against their existence, and since the beliefs of ordinary people differ regarding gods.*

He moves on to passive matter and the notion of cause—whether cause exists or not. He explores the arguments of those who argue for its existence and of those who doubt it. While discussing the latter, he observes that . . .

[211] The Stoics declare that "every cause is a body that causes something incorporeal in a body." For example, "the scalpel" is a body, and "the flesh" is a body, and the predicate "being cut" is incorporeal. Again, "the fire" is a body, and "the wood" is a body, and the predicate "being burned" is incorporeal.

212-331 *Sextus describes other arguments regarding cause, including the point that "if there is something that is affected, it is affected either through addition or through subtraction or through alteration and change." Connected to this point, he observes, is "the difficulty concerning the whole and the part." Consequently, he goes on to explore notions of "the whole" and "the part" and "the all."*

[332] Now the philosophers of the Stoic school assume that "the whole" differs from "the all." For they say that the whole is the cosmos, whereas the all is the external void together with the cosmos. In this way, the whole is limited (for the cosmos is limited), but the all is unlimited (for the void outside the cosmos is so). . . .

[336] The Stoics declare that the part is neither other than the whole nor the same. For the hand is neither the same as the human

(for it is not a human) nor other than the human (for it is included in the thought of the human as human).

337-440 Sextus completes his discussion of "efficient principles of the cosmos." He turns his attention next to views about "the primary and most fundamental elements." Some take the view that bodily things are the most fundamental. For instance, Empedocles and the Stoics both hold that there are four elements, "earth and water and air and fire." Others identify incorporeal principles. In the remainder of Book 1, Sextus discusses other ideas and problems, including "the difficulties about bodies."

Book 2

1-2 Sextus proceeds to the "incorporeals" or "intangibles" (as Epicurus calls them) in Book 2, beginning with an investigation of "place" and the related notions of "void" and "room."

[3] The Stoics declare that "void is that which is capable of being occupied by something that exists but is not so occupied. Or it is an interval void of body—or one unoccupied by body. And place is that which is occupied by something that exists and made equal to that which occupies it"—now calling body "something that exists," as is evident from the interchange of the names. And "room," they say, is "an interval partly occupied by body and partly unoccupied."[11]

4-351 In the remainder of Book 2, Sextus presents various arguments regarding the notions of place, motion (about which the Stoics affirm it exists), time (about which the Stoics declare it is "the interval of the motion of the cosmos"), number, and coming into being and perishing. The following are some of the Stoic considerations he reports about these and other points (all in Book 2).

[142] The Stoics . . . say that bodies and places and times are divisible without limit or to infinity. . . .

[218] The Stoic philosophers think that time is incorporeal. For they declare that of the "somethings," some are corporeal or bodies,

and others are incorporeals. They count four kinds of incorporeals, namely, "a thing said" or "a sayable" and void and place and time. And from this it is clear that, in addition to assuming that time is something incorporeal, they also regard it as a thing thought about as self-evident.

[234] The Stoics . . . declare that, of the "somethings," some are corporeal or bodies, and other are incorporeals. They think that time is a certain kind of incorporeal that is thought about as self-evident.

Notes

[1] It may be useful to think of something like tug of war. When a team pulls the rope toward their side, they are simultaneously pulling outward (toward themselves) and inward (away from—which is also in or inward from—the other team).

[2] "Breath" (*pneuma*) may also be given as "spirit." Thus, where you see "breath" in the following texts, you may also wish to read "spirit."

[3] The same as *Against the Mathematicians* 9.11, 60-65, 75-79, 88-94, 101-114, 123-126, 131-135, 137, 211, 332, 336; 10.3, 142, 218, 234.

[4] Sextus shifts between the singular (God) and plural (gods) as if they are interchangeable.

[5] Though it is Xenophon's argument, the Stoics would have used it. Indeed, Zeno of Citium did apparently build on the argument (see 1.101 below). Xenophon (c. 430-354 BC) was a statesman and historian from Athens. Drawing on his experience with the philosopher Socrates, he wrote the *Apology* recounting Socrates' defense, and the *Memorabilia*, *Oeconomicus*, and *Symposium*, works also centered on Socrates and his conversations with others. He also wrote non-Socratic works.

[6] The *eikos logos*, the likely account—that is, the most probable, reasonable account. For the passage, see Plato, Timaeus 29d ff.

[7] Alexinus was a Megarian philosopher. His life coincided with Zeno's.

[8] Archilochus (fl. seventh century BC) was a Greek iambic and elegiac poet. The content of his poems was, to many in the ancient world, morally repugnant. As for Aristarchus (fl. second century BC), the point seems to be that, as head of the Alexandrian Library, he focused on purely literary or grammatical matters whereas Plato was concerned with the soul and virtue in his writings.

[9] Or breath (*pneuma*).

[10] There is an interesting parallel here (relative to the notion or concept of both gods and atoms) to Anselm of Canterbury's much later (eleventh century AD) ontological argument for the existence of God.

[11] Compare to Sextus Empiricus, *Outlines of Pyrrhonism* 3.124.

THIRTEEN

STOIC ETHICS
IN OTHER ANCIENT AUTHORS

IN BRIEF: *Clement first presents various Stoic views regarding the goal of life. Next, Plutarch explains the Stoic position that passion is simply the base manifestation of reason or the leading part of the soul. Third, Sextus Empiricus discusses the virtues as arts. Fourth, Sextus gives an overview of what the Stoics believe regarding what is good, bad, and neither. The good is benefit or that which is not other than benefit. The Stoics do not count bodily goods as goods. Goods either belong to the soul, are external, or are neither. Indifferent things are either preferred or not preferred. Finally, Johannes Stobaeus presents a summary of the Stoic system of ethics, including the nature of good things, the nature of virtue and various virtues, and the nature of passion and the four primary passions (desire, fear, pain, and pleasure).*

Clement of Alexandria, *Stromata* 2.21

Clement presents the views of different Stoics regarding the end or goal of life.

Zeno the Stoic holds that the goal is to live according to virtue. Cleanthes believes it is to live in agreement with nature. And Diogenes holds that the goal is found in acting with sound reason, which he identified as choosing things according to nature. And Antipater, his friend, supposes the goal is found in the continuous and permanent choice of things according to nature and the rejection of things contrary to nature.

Plutarch, *On Moral Virtue* 446f-447a

Plutarch explains the Stoic position that the passions are base opinions or judgments, which is to say that passion is simply the base manifestation of reason or the leading part of the soul.

[446f] Some [the Stoics] say that passion is not different from reason. Neither is there disagreement nor discord between the two. Rather, reason—which is one thing—turns both ways. [447a] And because it is so sudden and swift, the change escapes our notice. We do not see that the same thing in the soul is by nature disposed to desire and to repent, to grow angry and to fear, to be drawn to shameful behavior by pleasure, and, again, to stop the same. And as for desire, anger, fear, and all passions such as these, they are base opinions and judgments, which do not arise in one part of the soul, but are inclinations and surrenders, assents and impulses of the whole leading part of the soul. Generally speaking, they are certain activities that may in a moment be changed this way or that, just as the sudden actions of children have a ferocity and vehemence that is unstable and fickle because of a lack of strength.

Sextus Empiricus, *Outlines of Pyrrhonism* 3.188

[188] The Stoics say that the goods of the soul are certain arts. These are the virtues. And an art, they say, is a system consisting of co-exercised apprehensions. And these apprehensions arise in the leading part of the soul.

Sextus Empiricus, *Against the Ethicists* 3, 22-27, 46, 59-63, 73, 170 *(with a summary of the surrounding text given in italics)*

Sextus explores the Stoic view, along with that of other dogmatic philosophers, of what good is, what evil is, and what is neither. The Stoics declare that the good is benefit (virtue and excellent action) or that which is not other than benefit (the excellent human and the friend). They recognize three kinds of goods, those belonging to the soul, external goods, and some that are neither. Unlike other dogmatic philosophers, the Stoics do not count "bodily goods" as goods. Other things such as health are "indifferent," a classification that, among other things, signifies "that which contributes neither to happiness nor

*to unhappiness." Some indifferent things are "preferred"; some are "rejected"
or "not preferred." Things preferred have considerable "value." Pleasure is a
thing indifferent and not preferred. Finally, practical wisdom ("the knowledge
of things good and evil and neither") exists as an art of life. Only the wise, as
ones who possess virtue and love valuable things, are truly noble and wealthy.*

*1-2 Now that Sextus has addressed logic and physics or natural philoso-
phy (in other works), he turns to ethics, which most philosophers, he observes, analyze in terms of good and evil.*

[3] All of the philosophers who opine about the elements of ethics
in this way—and, most evidently of all, those of the Old Academy
and those of the Peripatetic school, and, in addition, those of the
Stoic School—are used to dividing them up by saying that "of existing things, some are good, and some are bad, and some are between the two." They call the latter "indifferent."

*4-21 Sextus goes on to look at various formulations or classifications re-
garding what exists, including a brief exploration of the word "is," before
turning again to the nature of the good, the bad, and the indifferent.*

[22] Now the Stoics, clinging to the common notions (as they call
them), define the good in this manner: "good is benefit or that which
is not other than benefit."[1] By "benefit" they mean virtue and excellent action, and by "that which is not other than benefit" they mean
the excellent human and the friend. [23] For since virtue is a certain
state of the leading part, and excellent action is an activity in accord
with virtue, they are by all means benefits. And the excellent human
and the friend, once again, belonging themselves to the set of "good
things," cannot be said to be a benefit or not a benefit for the following reason.
[24] The descendants of the Stoics say that the parts are neither
the same as the whole nor different from the whole, even as the hand,
for instance, is neither the same as the whole human being (for the
hand is not the whole human being), nor is it other than the whole
(for the whole human being is thought a human being with the hand

included). Since, then, virtue is a part both of the excellent human and of the friend, and the parts are neither the same as their wholes nor other than their wholes, the excellent human being and the friend are spoken of as "that which is not other than benefit." So it is that every good thing is encompassed by the definition, whether it is directly a benefit or not other than a benefit.

[25] Following on this, they next say that "good" has three senses. They give a separate description for each meaning. In one sense, they say that "good" means that by which or from which there is "benefit." This is the most fundamental good; it is virtue. For from virtue, as from a spring, all benefit naturally flows. [26] In another sense, "good" is that according to which "benefit" is a contingent result. In this way, not only will the virtues be called "good" but also the actions in accord with them, insofar as the benefit results from them. [27] In a third and final sense, "good" means the kind of thing that benefits—a description that embraces the virtues and virtuous actions, friends and excellent human beings, as well as gods and excellent divine powers.

28-45 Sextus notes that "Zeno and Cleanthes and Chrysippus have defined happiness as 'a good flow of life.'" He goes on to observe that assertions such as the good is "the beneficial" or "the choiceworthy for its own sake" or "that which contributes to happiness" fail to explain what the good is in itself but only give its "accidental or contingent qualities." Turning from the good, he briefly explores "the bad" and "the indifferent" before asking whether or not good and evil, or good things and bad things, even really exist. Whatever the case is, different people offer different answers regarding the good just as happens with bodily beauty—Ethiopians see it in one thing, Persians in another. This is true not only for ordinary people but also for the philosophers. The Academics and the Peripatetics identify three kinds of goods—soul goods (for example, virtue), bodily goods (for example, health), and goods external to both soul and body (for example, wealth).

[46] The Stoics, though they too said there are three kinds of good things, they nevertheless grouped them differently. For of these goods, some belong to the soul and some are external, while some

neither belong to the soul nor are they external. They get rid of the bodily kind of goods as not really being good things. The goods that belong to the soul are, they say, the virtues and excellent actions. Those that are external are the friend and the excellent human being and excellent children and parents and like things. And that which is neither of the soul nor external is the excellent human in relation to himself—for it is impossible for him to be either external to himself or his soul since he is composed of soul and body.[2]

47-58 Other philosophers, Sextus says, say bodily goods are the primary goods. Many, he goes on, declare health to be a good; others do not. He gives the Academic Crantor's illustration where each of the goods—wealth, pleasure, health, and courage—presents itself in a theater in the attempt to convince the Greeks that it is the primary good. The Greeks end up awarding prizes in this order: courage, first, followed by health, pleasure, and wealth. Crantor, Sextus observes, "put health in second place."

[59] The Stoics, however, said that health is not a good but an indifferent. They hold that the term "indifferent" has three senses. In one sense, it is said of that for which there exists neither an impulse nor a repulsion, such as the fact that the stars or the hairs of the head are odd or even in number. [60] In another sense, it applies to that for which there exists an impulse and a repulsion—but no more for this thing over that thing. For instance, in the case of two drachma coins that are indistinguishable in stamp and brilliance, when one must choose one of them, there is an impulse for one, but no more for this coin over that coin. [61] In a third and final sense, they say the indifferent is that which contributes neither to happiness nor to unhappiness. They say that health and disease and all bodily things and most external things fall under this meaning since they lead neither toward happiness nor toward unhappiness. For a thing is indifferent if it may be used both well and poorly. And though virtue is used well and vice is used poorly every time, health and bodily things may be used well sometimes and poorly at other times. Because of this, they are indifferent.

[62] Moreover, of things indifferent, they say that some are "preferred" and others are "rejected" or "not preferred," and others are

neither preferred nor rejected. The preferred are those that possess sufficient or considerable "value." The rejected are those with a considerable lack of value. And those things that are neither preferred nor rejected are things such as extending the finger or curling it back and everything like that. [63] Placed among the things preferred are health and strength and beauty, wealth and reputation and like things, but among the rejected are disease and poverty and pain and analogous things.[3]

64-72 The Stoic Ariston of Chios, however, did not accept the idea of "preferred indifferents." Rather, he said there is no distinction between the things that fall between virtue and vice. He suggested instead that a preference for things such as health depends on circumstances rather than on the thing itself. For example, if all healthy men must serve a tyrant while the sick may not, then health is not a preferred thing.[4]

Sextus further explores notions of the good, which, he suggests, should be "good in relation to all men" if it is "good by nature." But there's no such thing. And it is no good, he says, to simply "call good everything that is held by anyone to be good" since some things would be both good and not good at the same time. Take pleasure, for example. Epicurus declares it a good. By contrast, Antisthenes the Cynic, who counted it a bad thing, said, "I would rather be mad than enjoy pleasure."

[73] The Stoics say that pleasure is indifferent and not preferred. But Cleanthes says that it is neither natural nor does it possess value for life. Rather, like a cosmetic brush, it does not naturally exist. By contrast, Archedemus says that, like armpit hair, it naturally exists, but it has no value. But Panaetius says that some pleasures are natural and some are unnatural.

74-169 Sextus concludes that nothing is good by nature—this despite the fact that "Zeno . . . opined that virtue is the good," and others identified other goods. And nothing is choiceworthy in itself. The same applies to evil or bad things. The "Stoics say that folly is bad." Others suggest other evils.

Sextus observes that, according to the skeptics, it is important to "suspend judgement" regarding the existence of good and bad things. This is the key to living a life that flows well and happily. By contrast, the assumption of "the existence of good and bad things by nature" leads to mental disturbance and an unhappy life. "For by always pursuing what he supposes is good by nature and avoiding what he assumes is bad, he will never be free from mental confusion and trouble." But, says Sextus, "if a man declares that nothing is by nature choiceworthy any more than the opposite, then . . . he will live happily and undisturbed." This goes for things such as money, reputation, honor, and pleasure, as well as for things proposed by the dogmatic philosophers. Following the skeptic approach does not mean that one will be entirely happy. Still, the skeptic way results in less perturbation.

The next question is whether there exists an art of life. The dogmatists say there is. Epicurus, Sextus reports, "declared that 'philosophy is an activity that procures the happy life by means of reasoning and discussion.'"

[170] The Stoics unreservedly declare that practical wisdom, which is the knowledge of things good and evil and things neither, exists as an art of life, and that only those who take hold of practical wisdom are noble, rich, and wise. They say this because the man who acquires things of great value is rich, and virtue is of great value, and the wise man alone acquires this. It is the wise man alone, then, who is rich. And the lover of valuable things is noble. But the wise man alone is a lover of valuable things. The wise man alone, then, is noble.

171-257 Sextus observes, however, that once again the dogmatic philosophers propose not one but many arts of life. Against such an art, he offers further evidence, including Stoic writings indicating that Zeno judged there was no shame in Oedipus sleeping with his mother, Jocasta, and that Chrysippus saw nothing wrong with parents having children by their own children or siblings by siblings, and that the Stoics, depending on the circumstance, permitted cannibalism.[5] He further points out that the art of life, even if such a thing exists, cannot be taught. So ends his discussion of "the most essential problems that belong to ethics."

Johannes Stobaeus, *Anthology* 2.5; 2.10

Relative to Stoic ethics, much of what comes below is a repetition of what other

authors had already summarized in antiquity—a point that follows from the
fact that Johannes Stobaeus wrote sometime early in the fifth century AD and
made use of earlier writers and collectors. For this reason, the Cave has not
included everything from the Anthology.⁶ *As for what we have included, Jo-*
hannes Stobaeus covers the nature of good things; good things as various vir-
tues; the nature of virtue and various virtues; and, finally, the nature of
passion and the four primary passions (desire, fear, grief, and pleasure).

[5] What follows are the teachings of Zeno and the rest of the Stoics
regarding the ethical part of philosophy. . . . Zeno says that whatever
has a share in substance exists. And of these things, some are good,
some are bad, and some are indifferent. On the one hand, good
things are these: practical wisdom, justice, moderation, courage, and
everything that is virtue or has a share in virtue. On the other hand,
bad things are these: folly, injustice, immoderation, cowardice, and
everything that is vice or has a share in vice. And indifferent things
are these: life, death, reputation, obscurity, pain, pleasure, wealth,
poverty, sickness, health, and everything like these. . . .

Practical wisdom is knowledge of what one should do, and what
one should not do, and neither. Or it is knowledge of good things
and bad things and of things that are neither that are natural to a
political animal, that is, an animal living in a community. . . . Moderation is knowledge of what is to be chosen and what is to be
avoided and what is neither. And justice is knowledge of the distribution of valuable things to each man. And courage is knowledge
of what is fearful and what is not fearful and what is neither. . . .

Of the virtues, some are primary and some are arranged under
these primary virtues. There are four primary virtues: practical wisdom, moderation, courage, and justice. Practical wisdom has to do
with duties or fitting activities, moderation with human impulses,
courage with situations demanding patient endurance, and justice
with the distribution of things. . . . The goal of every one of these
virtues is life in conformity with nature. . . .

As the health of the body is a good mix of the hot and cold and
the dry and wet in the body, so also is health of the soul a good mix
of teachings in the soul. Likewise, just as strength of the body is

sufficient tension in the sinews, so also is strength of the soul sufficient tension in making judgments and in acting and in not doing so. And just as beauty of the body is due proportion of the limbs relative to one another and to the whole, so also is the beauty of the soul due proportion of reason and its parts relative to the whole and to one another. . . .

The Stoics say that there are many virtues and that they are inseparable from one another. In terms of substance, they are the same as the leading part of the soul. Hence, they declare that every virtue is a body since the intellect is a body, as is the soul. . . .

There is nothing between virtue and vice, for all human beings have inducements from nature toward virtue. And, according to Cleanthes, humans are like half lines of iambic verse, so that if they are incomplete or unfinished, they are base, but if they are brought to perfection, they are excellent. They also say that the wise man does everything in accord with all the virtues. This is so because everything he does is perfect, and so he is not lacking even one virtue. . . .

Moreover, they declare that every base man is mad. Relative to himself and to those things that have to do with himself, he possesses ignorance—the very thing that is madness. And ignorance is the vice opposite of soundness of mind. . . .

[10] The Stoics say that passion is an excessive and disobedient impulse in the choosing or selecting reason, or it is a motion of the soul that is contrary to nature. . . . In terms of kind, the primary passions are these four: desire, fear, grief or pain, and pleasure. . . .

The terms "irrational" and "unnatural" do not mean what they commonly mean. Rather, "irrational" is the same as "disobedient to reason." For every passion is forceful—as those who are in a state of passion often see that it is beneficial not to act in such a way, but they are carried off by the violence of the passion as though by some disobedient horse. And so they are led to do it. . . .

And everyone in a state of passion turns away from reason—but not like those who are deceived regarding one point or another, but in a unique way. For example, those who are deceived by the idea that atoms are the first principles of things, whenever they learn that they do not exist, they turn away from the teaching. But those who are in a state of passion—even if they learn and even if they are taught that they should not give themselves over to grief or fear or, generally speaking, they should not permit any passion in the soul—they nevertheless do not turn away from these, but they are led by the passions into being controlled by their despotic rule.

So then, they say that desire is an appetite that is disobedient to reason. Its cause is the assumption that a good is coming. . . . Fear is a refusal or avoidance that is disobedient to reason. Its cause is the assumption that an evil is coming. . . . Grief is a contraction of the soul that is disobedient to reason. Its cause is the assumption that a new or recent evil is nearby or present. Pleasure is an elation of the soul that is disobedient to reason. Its cause is the assumption that a new or recent good is nearby or present.

NOTES

[1] Compare to Sextus Empiricus, *Outlines of Pyrrhonism* 3.169-170. The term given as "benefit" here (*ōpheleia*) could also be given as "utility," "profit," or "advantage."

[2] Compare to ibid., 3.181.

[3] Compare to ibid., 3.191.

[4] Compare to ibid., 3.192 where, instead of the example of the healthy versus the sick in relation to the tyrant, Sextus mentions the rich and the poor—that one would prefer to be poor if the tyrant were threatening and attacking the rich.

[5] Compare to ibid., 3.207.

[6] For instance, we leave out a long catalogue of virtues subordinate to the primary virtues; how the wise man acts virtuously relative to *symposia* (drinking parties) and sex, and how he is the true lover of music and literature, as well as a good prophet and poet and priest; the nature of the good and good things; various kinds of friendship; the nature of the happy life (Zeno's "living in agreement" or Cleanthes' "living in agreement with nature," as well as other early Stoic formulations); a description of the "indifferent," preferred things, and appropriate actions; the nature and kind of impulses; information relative to the four primary passions and those that fall under each; justice and the law; the differences between and qualities of the virtuous and the base man; that suicide is sometimes appropriate for the virtuous but not for the base; and so on.

POINTS OF WISDOM
& WAYS OF PRACTICE
FROM THE EARLY STOICS

- Plan of Life Following the Early Stoics

- Points of Wisdom from the Early Stoics

- Ways of Practice Following the Early Stoics

PLAN OF LIFE
FOLLOWING THE EARLY STOICS

As with any other plan, a plan of life is made to accomplish many goals or possibly just one significant goal. In the case of the "Plan of Life Following the Early Stoics," the goal is happiness in terms of a life in agreement with nature and in accord with reason and virtue. The following plan consists of the most significant goals and practices inspired by early Stoic philosophy.

> "You, O Zeno, made self-sufficiency your rule, letting go of empty riches. With gravity of deportment—venerable, revered—you discovered a manly doctrine. And with foresight you contended by means of a deliberate plan, the mother of fearless liberty."—Zenodotus the Stoic

1. **Practice philosophy**. Think-observe-do. Remember: the goal of philosophy is to think well (logic), in order to observe the nature of things, including human beings, well (natural philosophy), in order to do well or be happy (ethics).

2. **Guard your mind**. Cultivate your intellect in order to guard your mind. Just as a wrestler acquires moves and trains so as to avoid being thrown in a match, you should learn to reason well and practice sensible thinking so that you will not be thrown in life. Listen and learn from the wise so that you too may be wise.

3. **Be truthful**. Try never to hold mere opinions. Be willing to declare, "I don't know." Withhold assent when necessary. The goal is knowledge—not merely the vapory appearance of knowledge. Ignorance is *not* bliss. Cling to the truth.

4. **Observe nature in order to live in agreement with nature**. Know that by some mind or law the cosmos is graspable by your senses and intelligible to your mind. Know, therefore, that in some manner the cosmos makes rational sense. Accordingly, discover and be

confident in your place in the great scheme of things—both in the whole and in the part. In all things, live in harmony with nature. Most of all, be human!—which is to be rational.

5. **Live according to reason**. Recognize the beneficial role of reason in human life. When natural impulses present themselves, allow reason to shape them skillfully—from natural lumps of clay to noble objects of art. Free from negative passions or emotions, permit the leading part of your soul (the *hēgemonikon*) to guide you. Like a well-walled city, manage your life with reason.

6. **Live according to virtue**. Know that living in agreement with nature and by means of reason is to live in accord with virtue. Be convinced that virtue is the only good, that vice is the only evil, and that things indifferent are *truly* indifferent. Exercise yourself in practical wisdom, courage, moderation, and justice, as well as the subordinate virtues.

7. **Judge well. Assent well**. Practice dealing with sensations and presentations, particularly those that arouse harmful passions or emotions that are contrary to reason—envy, annoyance, anger, lust, fear, and the like. Understand that passions are judgments; they are decisions. When in doubt, withhold assent or judgment. Wait. Ask yourself the following questions: "What is the alternative?" "Do I need to feel this way?" "How else can things be?" "In what other way can I look at things?"

8. **Evaluate well**. Learn the true rather than the apparent value of things. Do not give things a distorted value. Know what is good (the beneficial—virtue and things associated with virtue); know what is bad (the harmful—vice and things associated with vice); and know what is indifferent (that which neither contributes to happiness nor to unhappiness). Do not confuse the good with the indifferent. Of indifferent things, recognize that some are preferred (things that are in accord with nature and have value) and some are rejected (things that are not in accord with nature and have no value). Practice letting

go of preferred indifferents and embracing some non-preferred or rejected indifferents.

9. **Freely accept your life**. In order to be free, voluntarily choose to follow the wagon of fate. Bravely bow to destiny. Stand firm in your station. Do what must be done.

10. **Do your duty**. Determine what is appropriate and do it. Generally speaking, your duty is to be virtuous—to follow reason in conformity with nature. Specifically, your duty is revealed by who you actually are and your actual circumstances—your relationships, where you live, what you do, and so on. Play your role well—the one you've been given, the one you're playing *right now*. Be social. Cultivate friendship. Care for others as you care for yourself—and know that when you care for others, you *are* caring for yourself.

11. **Remember the Cynics**. Keep in mind that according to the Stoics, the Cynic way of life is "a shortcut upon the path of virtue" and so "a shortcut leading to happiness." Therefore, as the Cynics would do, reduce your desires, practice endurance, develop self-control, strive for self-sufficiency, and live simply.*

12. **Call on and admire God**. Knowing that your life and your mind is a participation in the life and mind of God, the active principle in the cosmos, look to God for direction in all things—God, "the origin and leader of nature," the one who guides all things with "the universal rational principle that moves through all things." Ask God to "deliver all human beings from mournful ignorance." With awe and full of admiration, hymn God's law—for "there is no greater honor prize than to hymn the universal law."

To learn more about the ancient Greek Cynics, read the Cave's *The Best of the Cynics: The Lives, Writings & Teachings of the Ancient Cynics*.

EXAMPLE OF A STOA (Exterior)

Though grander in scale, the above reconstructed *stoa* in present-day Athens (called the Stoa of Attalos) gives some idea of what the *Stoa Poikilē*—the painted, covered, and colonnaded walkway where Zeno of Citium developed Stoicism and lectured—was like.

Image—The Classics Cave

POINTS OF WISDOM
FROM THE EARLY STOICS

The following points of wisdom come from the early Stoics. Each begins in italics with a single word or more indicating the point's topic. For more points of wisdom from the early Stoics organized by topic, read The Classics Cave's The Wisdom & Way of the Early Stoics.

Shoot for the goal of life The goal of life is to live in conformity with nature—that is, with our own nature as well as with the nature of the whole cosmos. Accordingly, one holds back from every action forbidden by the law common to all things—that is to say, the right reason that pervades all things and is the same as Zeus, who leads the administration of every existing thing. This very thing is the virtue of the happy man and the good flow of life, when all actions promote the harmony of the divine power dwelling in each man with the will of the administrator of the whole cosmos.

—Diogenes Laertes (DL from now on)

Follow nature and virtue Living in accord with virtue is equivalent to living in accord with the experience of nature as it actually happens.—*Chrysippus of Soli*

Keep in mind the tie of human being to divine being We humans are your offspring, Zeus, having received your voice-image, we alone of all mortals who live and move on earth.—*Cleanthes of Assos*

Know what we humans are (soul and body) Human beings are composed of soul and body.—*Sextus Empiricus*

Realize the ubiquity of mind Mind pervades every part of the cosmos just as the soul pervades every part of us.—*Chrysippus of Soli*

Study philosophy to be virtuous and happy If, then, it is true that all the good and none but the good are happy, what possession is greater than philosophy, or what is more divine than virtue? — *Cato (Cicero)*

Long for philosophy; deliberately choose a noble life If anyone has longed for philosophy, turning away from well-known pleasure that renders effeminate the souls of some of the young, it is clear that he is inclined to nobility of life not only by nature but by deliberate choice. — *Zeno of Citium*

The divisions of philosophy There are three divisions of philosophy, namely, logic, natural philosophy or physics, and ethics. And they begin their teaching with logic. . . . The Stoics liken philosophy to a fertile, all-productive field. Logic is the fence that goes around the field, ethics is the crop, and physics is the soil or the fruit tree. — *DL*

Study dialectic so as not to be thrown Without the study of dialectic, the wise man cannot guard himself in argument so that, as in a wrestling match, he will never be thrown. This is because the study of dialectic enables him to distinguish between truth and falsehood, and to judge well between what is plausible and what is ambiguously expressed. And without the study of dialectic, the wise man cannot methodically ask questions and give answers. — *DL*

How dialectic guards us Dialectic offers a method that guards us against giving assent to any falsehood or ever being tricked by deceptive probability. And it enables us to maintain and to defend the truths that we have learned about good and bad things. . . . Without the art of dialectic any man may be tricked and led away from what is true or actual toward what is false or deceptive. If, therefore, thoughtlessness and ignorance are in all matters faulty and full of misfortune, then the art that removes them is correctly termed "virtue." — *Cato (Cicero)*

Act in accord with nature and reason The goal of life is to act with sound reason in the selection of those things that follow nature. — *DL*

Act in accord with nature and virtue The end or goal of life is to live in agreement with nature, which is the same as living in accord with virtue since nature leads us toward virtue. — *Zeno of Citium*

The good (for human beings) is a kind of fulfillment "The fulfillment or perfection of a rational being *as* a rational being following nature" is another particular definition the Stoics give for the good. Virtue is such a perfection since acts done according to virtue and excellent men are participants in virtue, as are its accompanying byproducts, joy and merriment and like things. — *DL*

Do your duty The goal of life is to live while carrying out every duty, that is, whatever is appropriate. — *Archedemus of Tarsus*

Nature's gifts to plants and animals (including humans) We observe that nature sustains things that spring up from the earth (plants). For these, nature grants nothing more than the ability to nourish themselves and to grow. To animals she gives sensation and motion, together with a kind of appetite or desire that draws them toward health-giving things and withdraws them from destructive things. — *Balbus (Cicero)*

How nature regulates and sustains plants and animals (and humans) The Stoics declare that nature originally made no difference between plants and animals. Nature regulates the life of plants without the use of impulse and sensation, just as certain plant-like processes go on in us. But for animals, impulse was added to this general rule of nature later on. Impulse makes animals pursue what is suitable. Nature's rule for animals is to follow the direction of impulse. — *DL*

Our first impulse (as animals) is to self-preservation The Stoics say that an animal's first impulse is to self-preservation since nature endears the animal to itself from the beginning. — *Chrysippus of Soli*

Know why we (animals) act We Stoics must assert that nature has made the animal so that it is near and dear to itself. As such, it pushes away all that is harmful and pulls near all that is suitable and fitting. — *DL*

Pleasure is not the goal of impulse The Stoics declare false the assertion—

made by some—that the first urge or impulse of animals is directed toward pleasure. By contrast they say that pleasure, if it is anything at all, is a byproduct that never comes until nature by itself has sought and taken those things suitable to the animal's constitution—a byproduct that is comparable to animals that have a cheerful expression and plants that are luxuriant or in full bloom.—*DL*

If pleasure is the goal, many shameful things will follow Pleasure is not to be placed among the primary objects of natural impulse. Many shameful things will occur if we think that nature has placed pleasure among the first objects of desire.—*Cato (Cicero)*

We humans should shape our (animal) impulses by means of reason Impulse makes animals pursue what is suitable. Nature's rule for animals is to follow the direction of impulse. . . . For those beings we call rational, the rational life correctly became the natural life when reason was given to them by means of a more perfect rule. Reason was added to shape impulse as a skilled craftsman.—*DL*

We humans should control our (animal) impulses by means of reason To animals nature gives sensation and motion, together with a kind of appetite or desire that draws them toward health-giving things and withdraws them from destructive things. She gives even more than this to human beings. For them, she added reason, by which the appetites or desires of the soul are controlled—sometimes giving them free rein and sometimes holding them back.—*Balbus (Cicero)*

Follow those impulses that spur you on to fitting, rational, virtuous acts Of actions done in relation to impulse, some are fitting, some are not fitting, and some are neither fitting nor are they not fitting. Those acts that are fitting are the ones that reason within us seizes upon and chooses to do, such as honoring one's parents, brothers, sisters, and homeland, and adapting oneself to and spending time with one's friends. . . . It is always fitting to live in accord with virtue.—*DL*

Virtue is fulfillment Virtue is in one sense the perfection of anything in general, say of a statue. Virtue may be non-intellectual, such as health, or intellectual, such as practical wisdom. —*DL*

Virtue and reason Zeno assigned all the virtues to reason. —*Varro (Cicero)*

Virtue is the only good, noble, beautiful thing Virtue of the soul is the only good. . . . The only beautiful or noble thing is a good thing— this is virtue and whatever participates in virtue. . . . Virtue itself, and whatever participates in virtue, is spoken of as good in three ways: one, as the source from which the benefit results; two, as that according to which the benefit results—for example, the action done according to virtue; and three, as that by the agency of which the benefit results—for example, the excellent man who participates in virtue. —*Athenaeus the epigrammatist and DL (Hecaton, Chrysippus)*

Things indifferent Things that are neither good nor bad are those things that neither benefit nor harm—things such as life, health, pleasure, beauty, strength, wealth, good reputation, and noble birth, as well as their opposites, death, disease, pain, ugliness, weakness, poverty, bad reputation, low birth, and the like. —*DL*

Of indifferent things, prefer things with value Regarding indifferent things, they say that some are preferred and some are not preferred—that is, they are rejected. Those things that have value are preferred, while those that do not have value are rejected. —*DL*

What it means to benefit or harm To benefit is to move or to restrain oneself or something in accord with virtue. To harm is to move or to restrain oneself or something in accord with vice. —*DL*

Choose virtue and be happy Virtue is a harmonious disposition, choice-worthy for its own sake—not from fear or hope or any external motive. Happiness consists in virtue, which is the state of the soul that tends to make the whole of life harmonious. —*DL*

Seek completion in virtue There is nothing between virtue and vice, for all human beings have inducements from nature toward virtue. And, according to Cleanthes, humans are like half lines of iambic verse, so that if they are incomplete or unfinished, they are base, but if they are brought to perfection, they are excellent.—*Johannes Stobaeus*

We truly can become better That virtue can be taught is clear from the case of base men becoming good. . . . The proof that virtue really exists is the fact that Socrates, Diogenes, and Antisthenes, as well as their followers, made moral progress.—*DL and Posidonius of Apamea*

There are primary and secondary virtues Among the virtues, some are primary, and some are subordinate to these. The following are the primary virtues: practical wisdom, courage, justice, and moderation. Specific virtues are magnanimity, self-control, patient endurance, ready-mindedness, and good counsel.—*DL*

There are primary and secondary vices Vice exists as the opposite of virtue. . . . Among the vices, some are primary, and some are subordinate. Folly, cowardice, injustice, and immoderation are primary, and lack of self-control, slow-mindedness, and bad counsel are subordinate.—*DL*

Passions good and bad The Stoics say that there are three good passions: joy, caution, and willing. . . . There are four major kinds of (*bad*) passions: grief, fear, desire, and pleasure.—*DL*

Violent passions are irrational and thus unnatural The terms "irrational" and "unnatural" do not mean what they commonly mean. Rather, "irrational" is the same as "disobedient to reason." For every passion is forceful—as those who are in a state of passion often see that it is beneficial not to act in such a way, but they are carried off by the violence of the passion as though by some disobedient horse. And so they are led to do it.—*Johannes Stobaeus*

Be wise, seek improvement Wise men are genuinely earnest for and attentive to their own improvement, employing a manner of life that hides the base away while making what good there is in things appear.—*DL*

WAYS OF PRACTICE
FOLLOWING THE EARLY STOICS

The following ways of practice, inspired by the early Stoics, are offered with the goal of practice in mind, the application of ancient wisdom and ways to our contemporary lives. The Cave hopes they will serve, in some small measure, as a source of inspiration and motivation. Use them to contemplate your life—where you are now, where you are going, and how you can better get there. For these exercises and practices, and other similar ones, pick up the Cave's forthcoming The Early Stoics Workbook & Journal. *One last note. You will likely find that the space given for responses is not enough. If so, jot your thoughts and practices down in a separate place.*

PRACTICE 1: LIVING WITH IMPULSE

"The Stoics declare that nature originally made no difference between plants and animals. Nature regulates the life of plants without the use of impulse and sensation, just as certain plant-like processes go on in us. But for animals, impulse was added to this general rule of nature later on. Impulse makes animals pursue what is suitable. Nature's rule for animals is to follow the direction of impulse."—Diogenes Laertius

REFLECTION • For the Stoics, human beings are included among "animals"—a word that, in Greek, simply means a "living being" (*zōon*). Accordingly, we can say that "nature's rule for human beings is to follow the direction of impulse." But **what is "impulse"?**—whether for human beings or any other animal? **Name** and **describe** the role or function of **two natural impulses**.

Impulse ("natural impulse") is . . . _____

_____

_____

Natural impulse 1 _____

_____

Natural impulse 2 _____

_____

(Circle)   the following that <u>are not</u> natural impulses

Eating	Driving a car	Sleeping
Playing sports	Praying	Working for pay
Drinking water	Having sex	Drinking wine
Building a house	Talking to a friend	Eating cake

Explain why you circled any that you circled. If you did not circle any, explain what generally makes each natural.

_____

_____

_____

_____

_____

Rectangle	your answer

True   or   False   Natural impulses <u>always</u> lead toward benefit.

Explain your response: _____

_____

_____

_____

THE PAST ▪ Have you ever wanted to say "**No**" to a natural impulse? If so, why? And if so, **how** did you go about saying "No"?

_____

_____

_____

_____

_____

THE FUTURE ▪ Going forward, what is **one impulse** you have that you would like to **control** or **regulate**? **Describe** how you hope to control or regulate it. Then **practice** controlling or regulating it.

_____

_____

_____

_____

_____

PRACTICE 2: USING REASON TO SHAPE IMPULSE

"We observe that nature sustains things that spring up from the earth. For these, nature grants nothing more than the ability to nourish themselves and to grow. To animals she gives sensation and motion, together with a kind of appetite or desire (impulse) that draws them toward health-giving things and withdraws them from destructive things. She gives even more than this to human beings. For them, she added reason, by which the appetites or desires of the soul are controlled—sometimes giving them free rein and sometimes holding them back." —Cicero (Balbus speaking)

"Nature's rule for animals is to follow the direction of impulse. . . . For those beings we call rational, the rational life correctly became the natural life when reason was given to them by means of a more perfect rule. Reason was added to shape impulse as a skilled craftsman." —Diogenes Laertius

Circle your answer. Explain your answer on the lines that follow.

I   agree   or   disagree

that reason exists "to shape impulse as a skilled craftsman."

_____

_____

REFLECTION ▪ Answer the following questions: What is the purpose (or what are the purposes) of reason? Are non-human animals rational? Do non-human animals use reason to "control" themselves, that is, to control their impulses? Can we humans use reason to "shape" or "control" ourselves (our impulses)? Describe one time you used reason to "shape" or "control" yourself—that is, one of your impulses.

What is the purpose of reason? _____

_____

_____

_____

Do non-human animals use reason to "control" themselves, that is to control their impulses?

_____

_____

_____

Can we humans use reason to "shape" or "control" ourselves (our impulses)?

_____

_____

_____

Describe one time you used reason to "shape" or "control" yourself—that is, one of your impulses.

_____

_____

_____

GOING FORWARD ▪ **Explain** how you will use reason to "shape" or "control" yourself relative to one impulse in the future. Be **specific** and **concrete** in terms of the impulse, and why, how, and when you will use reason to shape it.

_____

_____

_____

_____

PRACTICE 3: KNOWING & ACTING IN ACCORD WITH WHAT IS FITTING

"All 'appropriate acts' (or fitting acts) are based on the primary impulses of nature." —Cicero (Marcus Cato speaking)

"Of actions done in relation to impulse, some are fitting, some are not fitting, and some are neither fitting nor are they not fitting. Those acts that are fitting are the ones that reason within us seizes upon and chooses to do." —Diogenes Laertius

AGREE – DON'T AGREE ▪ Relative to "fitting acts" that "reason within us seizes upon and chooses to do" (see the quote above), Diogenes goes on to give the **examples** listed below. **Explain** why you believe each is or is not a "fitting" or "appropriate" act "based on the primary impulses of nature," as Cicero words it. **What other acts** (one or two) would you add to Diogenes' list?

"Honoring one's parents, brothers, and sisters." _____

_____

_____

"Honoring one's homeland." _____

_____

_____

"Adapting oneself to and spending time with one's friends."

_____

_____

"Living in accord with virtue." _____

_____

_____

The one or two act I would add . . . _____

_____

_____

_____

_____

OTHER MATTERS OF INTEREST
RELATED TO THE EARLY STOICS

THE CAST OF SIGNIFICANT STOICS
A QUICK REFERENCE & CHRONOLOGY

THE EARLY STOA
—late fourth through the first half of the second century BC

ZENO OF CITIUM: the son of Mnaseas (or Demeas); born in Citium (Cyprus) c. 335 BC. Inspired by the ideas and example of Socrates, Zeno learned from the Cynic Crates of Thebes as well as other philosophers before setting out to found his own school around 300 BC. He lectured in a covered colonnade called the Painted Colonnade (*Stoa Poikilē*—hence the name Stoic or Stoicism) on the edge of Athens' marketplace. Zeno taught that happiness consists in virtue, which is a life in harmony with nature and thus in accord with reason. He emphasized the significance of learning how to gain true knowledge through dialectic and the importance of studying the nature of the cosmos and human life in order to better know how to live in harmony with nature. Zeno died in 263 BC.

CLEANTHES OF ASSOS: the son of Phanias; born in Assos (northwestern Turkey) c. 331 BC. Cleanthes followed Zeno of Citium as the second head of the Stoic school. Initially a boxer, he turned to Zeno of Citium and philosophy when he moved to Athens. Renowned for his love of hard work, Cleanthes worked as a laborer to support himself. He wrote the *Hymn to Zeus*, which celebrates Zeus as the origin and leader of nature, guiding all things with a universal law. Cleanthes died in c. 232 BC.

CHRYSIPPUS OF SOLI: the son of Apollonius; born in Soli (Cilicia, in south-central Turkey) c. 280 BC. Chrysippus followed Cleanthes as the third head of the Stoic school. He significantly shaped and even reformulated Stoicism during his tenure as chief Stoic. He is known for his development of logic, and particularly for his system of dialectic. He also worked on the problem of fate and human responsibility. He is said to have written some-705 works, none of which wholly survive. Chrysippus died c. 207 BC.

PERSAEUS OF CITIUM: the son of Demetrius; born in Citium (Cyprus) c. 306 BC. Though the nature of his relationship with Zeno of Citium is unclear (whether he was a slave, scribe, or friend), Persaeus lived and studied with him. When, due to old age, Zeno of Citium declined King Antigonus' invitation to visit and instruct him, he sent two men in his place. Persaeus was one of them. He travelled to Macedonia and taught Antigonus' son, Halcyoneus. Persaeus died in the king's service in Corinth in c. 243 BC.

PHILONIDES of Thebes (Greece), **CALLIPUS** of Corinth (Greece), **POSIDONIUS** of Alexandria (Egypt), **ATHENODORUS** of Soli (Cilicia, in south-central Turkey), and **ZENO** of Sidon (Lebanon) were all third century BC students of Zeno of Citium.

ARISTON (ARISTO) **OF CHIOS**: the son of Miltiades; born in Chios (a Greek island) sometime in the third century BC. Ariston was a student of Zeno of Citium. Counted a heterodox Stoic, he focused on ethics, discarding both logic and natural philosophy.

APOLLOPHANES OF ANTIOCH: born in Antioch (southeastern Turkey, near Syria) in the early third century BC, Apollophanes studied with Ariston of Chios in Athens. He emphasized practical wisdom.

HERILLUS OF CARTHAGE: born in Carthage (Tunisia) sometime in the third century BC. Herillus was a student of Zeno of Citium. Considered a heterodox Stoic, he declared that knowledge is the goal of life.

DIONYSIUS OF HERACLEA (THE RENEGADE): the son of Theophantus; born in Heraclea (in Bithynia, in northwestern Turkey) c. 328 BC. Initially the student of Zeno, after a painful illness, he eventually went over to the Cyrenaic school, declaring pleasure to be the goal of life. Dionysius died c. 248 BC.

SPHAERUS OF BOSPORUS (OR OF BORYSTHENES): born c. 285 (or 265) BC. Having studied with Zeno of Citium, Sphaerus became Cleanthes' student upon Zeno's death. He visited the court of Ptolemy in Egypt in place of Cleanthes. Sphaerus died c. 221 BC.

ZENO OF TARSUS: born in Tarsus (south-central Turkey) sometime in the middle of the third century BC, Zeno of Tarsus followed Chrysippus as the fourth head of the Stoic school in 204 BC. Orthodox relative to most Stoic teachings, he seems to have questioned the great conflagration (*ekpurōsis*). Zeno died sometime in the second century BC.

DIOGENES OF BABYLON: born in Seleucia (near Babylon in Iraq) c. 240 BC. Diogenes was the student of Chrysippus and then Zeno of Tarsus, whom he followed as the fifth head of the Stoic school. He is known for his visit to Rome in 155 BC as one of three Athenian philosopher-ambassadors. Diogenes died in 152 BC.

ANTIPATER OF TARSUS: born in Tarsus (south-central Turkey) sometime in the latter half of the third century BC. Antipater followed Diogenes of Babylon as the sixth head of the Stoic school. Antipater died sometime in the latter half of the second century BC.

BOETHUS OF SIDON: born in Sidon (Lebanon), Boethus was the student of Diogenes of Babylon. He flourished in the second century BC.

ARCHEDEMUS OF TARSUS: born in Tarsus (south-central Turkey) sometime in the first part of the second century BC, Archedemus likely studied with Diogenes of Babylon. He wrote *On Utterance* and *On Elements*.

HERACLIDES OF TARSUS: born in Tarsus (south-central Turkey), Heraclides was the follower of Antipater of Tarsus. He flourished in the second century BC.

APOLLODORUS OF ATHENS: born in Athens c. 180 BC, Apollodorus studied with Diogenes of Babylon. He lived in Alexandria for a time, working as a scholar. Apollodorus died sometime after 120 BC.

APOLLODORUS OF SELEUCIA: born in Seleucia (near Babylon in Iraq) sometime in the second century BC. He was a student of Diogenes of Babylon. He is significant as one of Diogenes Laertius' many sources.

THE MIDDLE STOA
—the second half of the second century to the end of the first century BC

PANAETIUS OF RHODES: the son of Nicagoras; born in Rhodes (a Greek island off southwestern Turkey) c. 185 BC. Panaetius was the student of both Diogenes of Babylon and Antipater of Tarsus. He moved to and was influential in Rome mid-second century. He followed Antipater of Tarsus as the seventh head of the Stoic school in 129 BC. Like Zeno of Tarsus, he doubted the great conflagration (*ekpurōsis*). He also questioned the effectiveness of divination. Panaetius died in 109 BC.

POSIDONIUS OF APAMEA: born in Apamea (Syria) c. 135 BC. Posidonius was the student of Panaetius. After living and studying in Athens, he moved to Rhodes. Subsequently, Rhodes became the center of Stoicism. Diogenes Laertius (*Lives* 7.54) includes him with "the older Stoics"—older or earlier, that is, relative to Diogenes Laertius' time (third century AD). Posidonius died c. 51 BC.

HECATON (HECATO) **OF RHODES**: born in Rhodes sometime in the first century BC, Hecaton was the student of Panaetius of Rhodes.

ANTIPATER OF TYRE: born in Tyre (Lebanon) sometime in the first century BC, Antipater introduced Cato the Younger (Marcus Cato) to Stoicism. He died c. 44 BC.

MARCUS PORCIUS CATO (CATO THE YOUNGER): born in 95 BC. Marcus was a Roman statesman who held various political offices in the Roman *cursus honorum* (the typical political career path). One of the earliest Stoics in the Roman Republic, he was perhaps the most archetypical *Roman* Stoic. Cicero uses him as the Stoic voice to "expound the whole system of Zeno and the Stoics" in his *On Ends*. He died in 46 BC.

ARIUS (AREUS) DIDYMUS: born in Alexandria (Egypt) sometime in the first century BC. Focusing on practical moral philosophy, Arius spent time counseling the Roman emperor Augustus. He wrote a consolation for Livia Drusilla (Julia Augusta, the wife of Augustus) on the occasion of the death of her son Nero Claudius Drusus.

ATHENODORUS OF TARSUS: the son of Sandon; born in Tarsus (south-central Turkey) sometime in the first century BC. Like Arius Didymus, he was a court philosopher to Augustus. He was a friend of Cicero.

EUDROMUS: The dates of the Stoic Eudromus are uncertain. He wrote a work titled, *Ethical Elements*.

CRINIS: The dates of the Stoic Crinis are uncertain. He wrote a work titled, *Art of Dialectic*.

THE LATE STOA
—the late first century BC to the last quarter of the fifth century AD
(roughly coinciding with the time of the Roman Empire)

SENECA (THE YOUNGER): the son of Seneca the Elder; born in Corduba (Córdoba, Spain) between 4 BC and 1 AD. Seneca practiced and wrote about Stoicism as a politician and writer. He served as tutor and advisor to the Roman emperor Nero. He is known for his many tragedies, his several consolations, his letters to Lucilius, as well as his essays on many topics, including anger, the shortness of life, tranquility, and happiness. Implicated in the Pisonian conspiracy of 65 AD, Seneca was forced to commit suicide.

MUSONIUS RUFUS: born in Vulsinii (Italy) before 30 AD. Influential in Rome, he was banished a number of times by different emperors, including in 65 AD after the Pisonian conspiracy. Though he did not write down his own works, many of his sayings and discourses survive. He died sometime before 102 AD.

EPICTETUS: born in Hierapolis in Phrygia (western Turkey). Though a slave in Rome for a portion of his life, Epictetus was nevertheless allowed to study philosophy with Musonius Rufus. At some point his master Epaphroditus (who had been Nero's slave) liberated him. When he was banished from Rome c. 90 AD, Epictetus travelled to and settled in Nicopolis in Epirus (Greece), where he opened a school of philosophy. Epictetus is known for his *Discourses* and *Handbook* (*Enchiridion*), which were composed and recorded by his student Arrian (c. 90-160 AD). The longest extant Stoic works, both emphasize ethics. Key points include the idea that we should judge and act based upon what is up to us (such as opinions, beliefs, and desires) versus what is not up to us (such as material possessions, reputation, and status). It is oftentimes our judgment about something that is upsetting rather than the thing itself. It is important to be people of integrity, to live simply, and to put a hold on pleasure, always respecting the faculty of judgment, our ruling principle. And whatever we do, in whatever situation, we should always ask, "What would Socrates or Zeno [of Citium] do?"

HIEROCLES: the Stoic Hierocles wrote the *Elements of Ethics* sometime prior to 150 AD, a work that deals with, among other matters, one's natural relationship to oneself, and one's relationship and duty to others.

MARCUS AURELIUS: born in Rome in 121 AD. Marcus Aurelius spent much of his time as Roman emperor (161-180 AD) defending the Roman Empire against invasions in the east and west. Trained in Stoicism, he is known for his journal of meditations, *To Himself* (often titled, *Meditations*), in which he contends that happiness is knowing that one is part of a good and natural whole, which is ordered and guided by providence or universal reason rather than chance.

The Stoic World: From the Mediterranean to Mesopotamia

The Stoics came from and taught all over the Mediterranean world, including each of the cities pinpointed above.

Note: some modern place names are given for purposes of orientation.

EXAMPLE OF A STOA (Interior)
Though grander in scale (as mentioned a few pages back), the above reconstructed *stoa* in present-day Athens (called the Stoa of Attalos) gives some idea of what the *Stoa Poikilē* —the painted, covered, and colonnaded walkway where Zeno of Citium developed Stoicism and lectured— was like.

Describing the interior of the *Stoa Poikilē*, the ancient Greek travel writer Pausanias reveals that the painting of "the battle of Marathon in the *Stoa Poikilē* was done by Panainos." An ancient scholiast writes, "Mikon painted the battle of the Amazons" therein. The ancient Roman writer Pliny adds Polygnotos of Thasos to the number of artists who painted murals in the *Stoa Poikilē*. We're told he painted "for nothing" whereas Mikon did so "for a fee."*

Image—The Classics Cave

*For more, see J.J. Pollitt, *The Art of Ancient Greece: Sources and Documents* (New York: Cambridge University Press, 1990).

THE VIRTUES & VICES

*The following virtues and vices appear in the various sources included in this volume. Definitions are those provided by the same. If a virtue or vice is not defined, that is because it remains undefined in the sources.**

PRIMARY VIRTUES

Practical wisdom (*phronēsis*) is the knowledge of good and bad things and what is neither; it has to do with duties or fitting activities; it is knowledge of what one should do, and what one should not do, and neither.

Courage (*andreia*) is the knowledge of what is fearful and what is not fearful and what is neither; it has to do with situations demanding patient endurance (*karteria*).

Moderation (*sōphrosunē*) is the knowledge of what is to be chosen and what is to be avoided and what is neither; it has to do with human impulses.

Justice (*dikaiosunē*) is the knowledge of the distribution of valuable things to each man; it has to do with the distribution of things.

SECONDARY VIRTUES

Good counsel (*euboulia*), which is the knowledge by which we see what to do and how to do it if we are to act in a useful and profitable manner, and **understanding** (*sunesis*) follow upon practical wisdom.

Good order or **discipline** (*eutaxia*) and **propriety** or **decorum** (*kosmiotēs*) follow upon moderation.

Unshakeable determination (*aparallaxia*) and **vigor** (*eutonia*) follow upon courage.

Equality (*isotēs*) and **fair-mindedness** (*eugnōmosunē*) follow upon justice.

Magnanimity (*megalopsuchia*) is the knowledge or habit that makes one superior to whatever commonly happens to base and excellent men.

Self-control (*enkrateia*) is an unbeatable disposition relative to those things that are in accord with right reason or a habit that is never conquered by pleasure.

Patient endurance (*karteria*) is the knowledge or habit that suggests what we must—and what we must not—abide by and endure, and what is neither.

Ready-mindedness (*anchinoia*) is a habit that discovers the appropriate thing to be done at any moment.

Frugal, thrifty: (*euteles*); simple, frugal (*litos*).

Self-sufficiency, independence (of others) (*autarkeia*).

Love of hard work (*philoponia*); **diligent**, industrious (*philoponos*).

PRIMARY VICES

Folly (*aphrosune*). **Cowardice** (*deilia*). **Immoderation** (*akolasia*). **Injustice** (*adikia*).

SECONDARY VICES

Lack of self-control (*akrateia* or *akrasia*). **Slow-mindedness** (*bradunoia*). **Bad counsel** (*kakoboulia*).

DIALECTICAL VIRTUES

Dialectic (*dialektikos*) enables one to distinguish between truth and falsehood, and to judge well between what is merely plausible (*pithanos*) and what is ambiguously expressed.

Freedom from rashness or **deliberateness** (*aproptosia*) is the knowledge of when one should assent to something or not.

Discretion or **levelheadedness** (*aneikaiotes*) is a strong rational stance relative to what merely seems to be so as not to be taken in by it.

Irrefutability (*anelenxia*) is strength in arguments so that one is not drawn over by the argument to the opposite side.

Earnestness or **absence of frivolity** (*amataiotes*) is the habit of referring presentations to right reason.

* For the broader context and a deeper understanding of how the Greeks thought about virtue, see the Cave's *Arete: Excellence or Virtue: What the Ancient Greeks Thought and Said about Arete.*

THE PASSIONS*

A passion or an emotion is a judgment or a decision. There are both good passions and bad passions. A good passion is a motion in line with reason. A bad passion is a motion or excessive impulse of the soul that is contrary to nature and reason.

GOOD PASSIONS

Joy (*chara*) is the opposite of pleasure; it is sensible elation, that is, elation backed by good reason.

Caution (*eulabeia*), that is, discretion or circumspection, is the opposite of fear. It is avoidance backed by good reason, or the reasonable turning of one's course. (For example, even though the wise man will never fear anything, he will nevertheless act with caution.)

Willing (*boulēsis*) is reasonable appetite, that is, appetite backed by good reason.

SUBORDINATE GOOD PASSIONS

Gladness (*terpsis*), **merriment** (*euphrosunē*), and **cheerfulness** (*euthumia*) fall under joy.

Respect or **modesty** (*aidōs*) and **religious purity** (*hagneia*) fall under caution.

Goodwill (*eunoia*), **kindliness** (*eumeneia* or *eumenēs*), **being welcoming** (*aspasmos*), and **brotherly love** (*agapē*) fall under willing.

BAD PASSIONS

Grief or pain of the mind (*lupē*) is a contraction of the soul contrary to reason.

Fear (*phobos*) is the expectation of something bad or unfortunate.

Desire or longing (*epithumia*) is an appetite (*orexis*) that is contrary to reason.

Pleasure (*hēdonē*) is an elation that is contrary to reason that arises from getting and amassing what seems to be choiceworthy.

SUBORDINATE BAD PASSIONS

under grief

Pity (*eleos*) is the pain felt at undeserved suffering.

Envy (*phthonos*) is the pain felt when one sees the goods of other people.

Jealousy (*zēlos*) is the pain felt when someone has a thing that one desires.

Rivalry (*zēlotupia*) is the pain felt when someone possesses what one has.

Heaviness (*achthos*) is a pain that weighs us down.

Annoyance (*enochlēsis*) is a pain that confines us and gives us a sense of a lack of room.

Distress (*ania*) is a pain brought on by anxious rumination that lasts and increases.

Anguish (*odunē*) is a difficult pain.

Confusion (*sunchusis*) is an irrational pain of the mind that wears one out and prevents one from viewing the situation as a whole.

under fear

Terror (*deima*) is a fear that produces fright.

Shame (*aischunē*) is the fear of a bad reputation.

Hesitation (*oknos*) is the fear that one will have to act.

Consternation (*ekplēxis*) is fear due to a presentation of some unusual occurrence.

Panic (*thorubos*) is fear after a rush of sound.

Mental agony (*agōnia*) is fear of some uncertain event.

under desire

The **state of want** or **lacking** (*spanis*) is the failure of desire, when desire does not reach its object but is nevertheless attracted to it in vain, stretching out to it.

Hatred (*misos*) is the growing and lasting desire for things to go badly for someone.

Love of strife (*philoneikia*) is desire connected with partisanship or a philosophical school.

Anger (*orgē*) is the desire for revenge against the one who appears to have done one an undeserved injury.

Erotic love or **desire** (*erōs*) is a desire that is not present in excellent men. It is the effort to win affection due to the visible presence of beauty.

Spiritedness (*thumos*) is the first stirring of anger.

Wrath (*mēnis*) is a longstanding and vengeful anger, ever-waiting for its chance to act.

under pleasure

Enchantment (*kēlēsis*) is pleasure that charms the ear, casting a spell over it.

Joy in the misfortune of others (*epikairekakia*) is *schadenfreude*, the pleasure that comes when bad things happen to other people.

Delight (*terpsis*) is, as it were, a turning of the soul. It is a certain stimulus for the soul toward loosening or letting go.

Relaxation (*diachusis*) is the breaking down of virtue.

*Not included are the additional passions mentioned by Cicero: disparagement, mourning, sadness, woe, lamenting, apprehension, despair, timidity, dread, faintness, bewilderment, awe, rage, enmity, discord, ardent longing, ostentation.

THE GOOD, THE BAD & THE INDIFFERENT

The good is that which is beneficial. The bad is that which is harmful. The good both produces and is happiness, whereas the bad both produces and is unhappiness. As virtue, the good is in step with nature and reason; as vice, the bad is not.

Indifferent things neither contribute to happiness nor to unhappiness (such as good and bad things do). Some do no more benefit than harm; some can be used both well and badly.

GOOD THINGS (the **beneficial**)

Virtue or **virtues**, including the primary virtues (practical wisdom, courage, moderation, justice) and secondary or subordinate virtues (such as good counsel, patient endurance, magnanimity, self-control).

Things that **participate in virtue** or the virtues, such as virtuous acts, as well as wise friends and an excellent homeland (one governed well or wisely).

BAD THINGS (the **harmful**)

Vice or **vices**, including the primary vices (folly, cowardice, immoderation, injustice) and secondary or subordinate vices (such as a lack of self-control, slow-mindedness, bad counsel).

Things that **participate in vice** or the vices, such as vicious acts, as well as foolish friends and a non-excellent homeland (one governed poorly or foolishly).

INDIFFERENT THINGS

Indifferent things include bodily and external things, including life and death, health and disease, working senses and non-working senses, strength and weakness, pleasure and pain, beauty and ugliness, wealth and poverty, noble birth and low birth, and a good and bad reputation.

VALUE: a thing has value if it is in accord with nature, or it produces something else that is so, and it is deserving of choice.

PREFERRED THINGS
(are in accord **with nature** and have **value**)

Life, health, working senses, bodily wholeness, strength, beauty, wealth, noble birth, a good reputation, natural ability, and moral progress.

REJECTED OR NOT PREFERRED THINGS
(are **not** in accord **with nature** and have **no value**)

Death, disease, non-working senses, disability, weakness, pleasure, pain, ugliness, poverty, low birth, a bad reputation, lethargy, lack of natural ability, and lack of skill.

THE **DIVINE PERSPECTIVE** REGARDING ALL THINGS

"For you, Zeus, what is unpleasant is pleasant. In this manner you have joined together all noble things with things ignoble, so that there is one everlasting rational principle in all things."

—*Hymn to Zeus*, Cleanthes of Assos

GLOSSARY
OF ENGLISH WORDS & GREEK EQUIVALENTS
that appear in the writings related to the early Stoics

*For the **virtues** and the **passions**, see the above pages devoted to each.*

The **active** (principle): *to poioun* (τὸ ποιοῦν).

Administration (of the cosmos) *dioikēsis* (διοίκησις).

Advantage, profit, use: *onēsis* (ὄνησις).

Animal, living being: *zōon* (ζῷον).

Apparition, phantom; a seeming (thing): *dokēsis* (δόκησις).

Assent, approval: *sugkatathesis or sunkatathesis* (συγκατάθεσις).

Assumption: *hupolēpsis* (ὑπόληψις)

Bad, evil: *kakos* (κακός).

Base, thoughtless: *phaulos* (φαῦλος).

Beautiful; noble: *kalos* (κάλος); **beauty**: *kallos* (κάλλος).

Benefit, advantage, profit, utility: *ōpheleia* (ὠφέλεια).

Body: *sōma* (σῶμα).

Breath, current; spirit; a blowing, a wind: *pneuma* (πνεῦμα).

Canon; rule, standard, measure: *kanōn* (κανών).

Concept, conception; notion: *ennoia* (ἔννοια).

Condition, state: *hexis* (ἕξις).

Constitution, construction, structure: *sustasis* (σύστασις).

Corporeal (corporeal substance); body: *sōma* (σῶμα); **incorporeal**: *asōmatos* (ἀσώματος).

Cosmos; the world or universe; order: *kosmos* (κόσμος).

Criterion; a means for judging, a standard, measure: *kritērion* (κριτήριον).

Decision, judgment; separating, distinguishing: *krisis* (κρίσις).

Definition; boundary, limit: *horos* (ὅρος).

Desire, yearning, longing: *epithumia* (ἐπιθυμία)

Destiny, necessity: *anankē* (ἀνάγκη).

Destructible, perishable: *phthartos* (φθαρτός); **indestructible**, imperishable: *aphthartos* (ἄφθαρτος).

Dialectic; conversational: *dialektikos* (διαλεκτικός).

Direct apprehension: *katalēpsis* (κατάληψις); **apprehending presentation** (implied): *katalēptikos* (καταληπτικός).

Disgust, aversion; repulsion: *aphormē* (ἀφορμή).

Disposition; arrangement: *diathesis* (διάθεσις).

Duty, what is fitting or appropriate: *kathēkon* (καθῆκον). **Duties**, appropriate actions: *kathēkonta* (καθήκοντα).

Element: *stoicheion* (στοιχεῖον); the **four elements** are **fire:** *pur* (πῦρ); **water:** *hudōr* (ὕδωρ); **air:** *aēr* (ἀήρ); and **earth:** *gē* (γῆ).

To **endear,** to be endeared; to be near and dear; to be made friendly: *oikeioō* (οἰκειόω); **one's own;** suitable, fitting: *oikeios* (οἰκεῖος).

Ethical (part of philosophy); moral: *ēthikos* (ἠθικός).

Excellent; earnest, serious: *spoudaios* (σπουδαῖος).

Experience; acquaintance with: *empeiria* (ἐμπειρία).

A **failure,** fault, error, sin: *hamartia* (ἁμαρτία) or *hamartēma* (ἁμάρτημα).

Fate: *heimarmenēn* (εἱμαρμένην).

Fluid; wet, moist: *hugros* (ὑγρός).

Freedom, liberty: *eleutheria* (ἐλευθερία); free: *eleutheros* (ἐλεύθερος).

Generated, originated; with a beginning: *genētos* (γενητός); **ungenerated,** unborn, uncreated, unoriginated; without beginning: *agenētos* (ἀγένητος).

Goal (of life), end; purpose: *telos* (τέλος).

God: *theos* (θεός). Gods: *theoi* (θεοί).

Good: *agathos* (ἀγαθός).

Good flow (of life): *euroia* (εὔροια).

The **great conflagration;** the great reversion and conversion of all things into fire (God-as-fire): *ekpurōsis* (ἐκπύρωσις). Related to *ekpuroō* (ἐκπυρόω): to burn to ashes, consume utterly.

Habit; a possession: *hexis* (ἕξις).

Happiness: *eudaimonia* (εὐδαιμονία). **Happy:** *eudaimōn* (εὐδαίμων). **Unhappiness,** misfortune: *kakodaimonia* (κακοδαιμονία).

Heaven, sky: *ouranos* (οὐρανός).

Human being; man: *anthrōpos* (ἄνθρωπος); **human form,** in the form of a human: *anthrōpormorphos* (ἀνθρωπόμορφος).

Ignorance: *agnoia* (ἄγνοια).

Impression: *tupōsis* (τύπωσις); **alteration,** difference, change: *alloiōsis* (ἀλλοίωσις); **modification:** *pathos* (πάθος).

Impulse: *hormē* (ὁρμή).

Indestructible, incorruptible, immortal: *aphthartos* (ἄφθαρτος).

Indifferent, neither good nor bad: *adiaphoros* (ἀδιάφορος).

To **infer;** to draw a conclusion: *perainō* (περαίνω).

Intellect; understanding; thought: *dianoia* (διάνοια).

Intelligence, understanding, thought: *noēsis* (νόησις).

Judgment, decision; separating, distinguishing: *krisis* (κρίσις).

Knowledge; science: *epistēmē* (ἐπιστήμη).

Law: *nomos* (νομός).

Leading part (of the soul); ruling part; ruling principle: *hēgemonikon* (ἡγεμονικόν).

To **live according to virtue**: *kat' aretēn zēn* (κατ᾽ ἀρετὴν ζῆν).

To **live in agreement with nature**: *homologoumenōs tēi phusei zēn* (ὁμολογουμένως τῇ φύσει ζῆν); to live in conformity with nature: *akolouthōs tēi phusei zēn* (ἀκολούθως τῇ φύσει ζῆν).

Living, alive, having life in one; ensouled: *empsuchos* (ἔμψυχος).

Logical (part of philosophy); rational: *logikos* (λογικός).

Maker; skilled workman, handicraftsman; the Maker: *dēmiourgos* (δημιουργός)—from *dēmiourgeō* (δημιουργέω): to do work; fabricate.

Matter; wood; a forest: *hulē* (ὕλη).

Mind: *nous* (νοῦς).

Nature: *phusis* or *physis* (φύσις). **Natural** (part of philosophy); physics, natural philosophy: *physikos* or *phusikos* (φυσικός).

Notion, thought-object: *ennoēma* (εννόημα).

Opinion, judgment, belief, conjecture; reputation: *doxa* (δόξα).

To **manage** (a house): *dioikeō* (διοικέω); **orderly arrangement** (of the cosmos): *diakosmēsis* (διακόσμησις); **administration** (of the cosmos) *dioikēsis* (διοίκησις).

Pain, suffering: *algēdōn* (ἀλγηδών).

Passion; emotion: *pathos* (πάθος).

The **passive** (principle) *to paschon* (τὸ πάσχον).

To **pervade**; to extend: *diēkō* (διήκω).

Phantom appearance, vision; a mere image: *phantasma* (φάντασμα).

Philosophy: *philosophia* (φιλοσοφία). **Philosopher**; lover of wisdom: *philosophos* (φιλόσοφος). To **do** or **study philosophy**: *philosopheō* (φιλοσοφέω).

Place: *topos* (τόπος).

Pleasure, delight, enjoyment: *hēdonē* (ἡδονή).

Practice, custom; habit of life, way(s) of life: *epitēdeuma* (ἐπιτήδευμα).

Preconception; a natural concept: *prolēpsis* (πρόληψις).

Preferred: (*proēgmena*) (προηγμένα); **rejected**, not preferred: *apoproēgmena* (ἀποπροηγμένα).

Presentation; appearance: *phantasia* (φαντασία).

Principle; origin, first cause: *archē* (ἀρχή).

Proof; affording proof, demonstrative: *apodeiktikos* (ἀποδεικτικός).

Proposition: *axiōma* (ἀξίωμα).

Providence; foreknowledge: *pronoia* (πρόνοια).

Quality: *poios* (ποῖος); **without quality**: *apoios* (ἄποιος).

Real thing or object: *pragma* (πρᾶγμα); **existing thing**, real thing: from *huparchō* (ὑπάρχω).

Reason; discourse; argument; account; statement; word: *logos* (λόγος); **right reason**; straight reason: *orthos logos* (ὀρθός λόγος).

Reasonable, sensible: *eulogos* (εὔλογος); to **act with sound reason**; to act rationally: *eulogisteō* (εὐλογιστέω).

Rhetorical; oratorical: *rhētorikos* (ῥητορικός); **rhetoric**, the art of speaking: *rhētorikē* (ῥητορική).

Room; space: *chōra* (χώρα).

Seed: *sperma* (σπέρμα); **generative principle**, rational seed: *spermatikos logos* (σπερματικός λόγος).

Sensation; perception by the senses: *aisthēsis* (αἴσθησις); **sense-based**; of or for perception by the senses: *aisthētikos* (αἰσθητικός).

Soul; life: *psuchē* or *psychē* (ψυχή).

Stoic: *stōikos* (στωικός).

Substance: *ousia* (οὐσία).

Suitable: *artios* (ἄρτιος).

Syllogism; reasoning: *sullogismos* or *syllogismos* (συλλογισμός).

Tendency; liability, proneness to a thing; evil proclivity; in medicine, an illness to which people are commonly liable, such as a cold: *euemptōsia* (εὐεμπτωσία).

Tension: *tonos* (τόνος)

Wise, a wise man: *sophos* (σοφός).

Theological (part of philosophy): *theologikos* (θεολογικός).

Thing said, a sayable: *lekton* (λεκτόν).

Thing signified: *sēmainomenon* (σημαινόμενον).

Time: *chronos* (χρόνος)

Training, exercise, practice: *askēsis* (ἄσκησις).

Truth, reality: *alētheia* (ἀλήθεια); **true**, unconcealed: *alēthēs* (ἀληθής).

Turned aside, turned around, perverted, distorted: *diastrephō* (διαστρέφω); **distortion**, perversion, twisting, distortion (of the limbs): *diastrophē* (διαστροφή).

Utterance; the sound of the voice; an articulate sound: *phōnē* (φωνή).

Value, worth; the worth or value of a thing: *axia* (ἀξία).

Vice, badness: *kakia* (κακία).

Virtue, excellence; goodness: *aretē* (ἀρετή); **virtuous**: *enaretos* (ἐνάρετος).

Void, empty, emptiness: *kenos* (κενός).

Way, path, road: *hodos* (ὁδός).

The **whole** or the **entirety** (the cosmos): *to holon* (τὸ ὅλον); the **all** or the **totality** (the cosmos with the external void): *to pan* (τὸ πᾶν).

Work, toil; suffering, pain: *ponos* (πόνος).

Zeus; the father of gods and men: *Zeus* (ζεύς).

SOURCES & FURTHER READING

The Classics Cave's rendition of Diogenes Laertius' writing about the early Stoics (Parts 1 and 2) was made using the Greek text found in R.D. Hicks' translation of Diogenes Laertius' *Lives of Eminent Philosophers* (1925), as well as the Greek texts and other immensely helpful tools found at the Perseus Digital Library. Otherwise, the Cave checked its own version against the translations of C.D. Yonge (1853) and R.D. Hicks (1925), as well as the more recent one of Brad Inwood and Lloyd P. Gerson (2008). The Greek text for the Cave's translation of *The Hymn of Cleanthes* (Interlude) is from E.H. Blakeney's *The Hymn of Cleanthes* (1921). The Latin for Cicero (his various works) is from the Perseus Digital Library. Renditions of Cicero's work were made with an eye on or were taken directly from (with modifications) the versions, sometimes in the public domain, of H. Rackham's translations of *On Ends* (1914), *On the Nature of the Gods* (1933), *Academica* (1933), and *On Fate* (1942), and J. E. King's translation of the *Tusculan Disputations* (1927). The Greek text for Johannes Stobaeus' *Anthology* (Part 4) is from Augustus Meineke's *Ioannis Stobaei: Eclogarum, Physicarum et Ethicarum* (1864). The Greek text for the works of Sextus Empiricus is from R.G. Bury's translation of *Outlines of Pyrrhonism* (1933), *Against the Logicians* (1935), and *Against the Physicists* and *Against the Ethicists* (1936) (against which the Cave checked its own version). As for other selections in Part 4, the Cave utilized the Greek texts and consulted the English translations found at the Perseus Digital Library, as well as other readily and publicly available resources, including those in the public domain. When suitable, the Cave used public domain translations with little to no alteration. See endnotes for more.

FURTHER READING

Becker, Lawrence C. *A New Stoicism*. Revised ed. Princeton: Princeton University Press, 2017.

Bourke, Vernon J. *Graeco-Roman to Early Modern Ethics*. Vol. 1 of *History of Ethics*. Mount Jackson: Axios Press, 1968.

Buzaré, Elen. *Stoic Spiritual Exercises*. Morrisville: Lulu, 2011.

Copleston, Frederick. *Greece and Rome: From the Pre-Socratics to Plotinus*. Vol. 1 of *A History of Philosophy*. Westminster: Newman Press, 1946.

Dudley, Donald R. *A History of Cynicism—From Diogenes to the 6th Century A.D.* Strand: Methuen & Co. Ltd, 1937.

Gottlieb, Anthony. *The Dream of Reason: A History of Western Philosophy from the Greeks to the Renaissance*. New York: W.W. Norton & Company, 2016.

Grafton, Anthony, Glenn W. Most, and Salvatore Settis, eds. *The Classical Tradition*. Cambridge: The Belknap Press, 2010.

Hadot, Pierre. *What Is Ancient Philosophy?* Translated by Michael Chase. Cambridge: The Belknap Press of Harvard University Press, 2002.

Hicks, R.D. *Stoic and Epicurean*. New York: Scribner, 1910.

Hierocles the Stoic: "Elements of Ethics," Fragments, and Excerpts. Translated by David Konstan. Commentary by Illaria Ramelli. Atlanta: Society of Biblical Literature, 2009.

Inwood, Brad, ed. *The Cambridge Companion to the Stoics*. Cambridge: Cambridge University Press, 2003.

———. *Stoicism: A Very Short Introduction*. Oxford: Oxford University Press, 2018.

Inwood, Brad, and Lloyd P. Gerson. *The Stoics Reader: Selected Writings and Testimonia*. Indianapolis: Hackett Publishing Company, 2008.

Irvine, William B. *A Guide to the Good Life: The Ancient Art of Stoic Joy*. Oxford: Oxford University Press, 2009.

Kenny, Anthony. *Ancient Philosophy*. Vol. 1 of *A New History of Western Philosophy*. Oxford: Oxford University Press, 2004.

Lipsius, Justus. *On Constancy*. Translated by Sir John Stradling. Edited, introduced, and noted by John Sellars. Exeter: Bristol Phoenix Press, 2006.

Long, A.A. *Hellenistic Philosophy: Stoics, Epicureans, Sceptics*. 2nd ed. London: Duckworth, 1986.

Meyer, Susan Sauvé. *Ancient Ethics: A Critical Introduction*. Abingdon: Routledge, 2008.

Murray, Gilbert. *The Stoic Philosophy*. New York: The Knickerbocker Press, 1915.

Musonius Rufus: Lectures & Sayings. Translated and introduced by Cynthia King. Edited by William B. Irvine. CreateSpace, 2011.

Pigliucci, Massimo. *How to Be a Stoic: Using Ancient Philosophy to Live a Modern Life*. New York: Basic Books, 2017.

Robert, Donald. *Stoicism and the Art of Happiness*. London: Hodder & Stoughton, 2013.

Salzgeber, Jonas. *The Little Book of Stoicism: Timeless Wisdom to Gain Resilience, Confidence, and Calmness*. Independently published, 2019.

Sambursky, Samuel. *Physics of the Stoics*. Princeton: Princeton University Press, 1959.

Seddon, Keith. *Epictetus' Handbook and the Tablet of Cebes: Guides to Stoic Living*. London: Routledge, 2005.

Stockdale, Jim. *Thoughts of a Philosophical Fighter Pilot*. Stanford: Hoover Institution Press, 1995.

Will you help the Cave? Here's how . . .

- **Buy** a book. **Join** a club. **Sponsor** the Cave. **Give** a donation.
- **Talk** to friends and family about Cave books and the free online Cave content at the Cave (www.theclassicscave.com).
- Leave a **positive review** online—if possible, **five stars** with a **brief remark** about what you liked. This truly helps!
- **Write us** at contact@theclassicscave.com to let us know how you've benefited from our work. This inspires us to do more!

THE CLASSICS CAVE is a small, shoestring operation, on fire to spread the wisdom and ways of ancient Greek literature. We **rely on you**, the friend of the Cave, to let people know how you liked and benefited from what we're doing. We also **depend on you** to **improve our books**. Did you see something that requires editing? Something we got wrong? Something we need to add? Despite our great effort and care to get everything right, it happens. So please **let us know** by emailing us at contact@theclassicscave.com. Otherwise, **visit** the Cave to benefit from our ever-growing collection of free online content at www.theclassicscave.com. And don't forget to **support our mission** to spread the wisdom and ways of ancient Greek literature by **buying** and **reading** Cave Books, **enjoying** Cave Gear, **joining** The BAGL Club or AAGS, or by **sponsoring** or **giving** to the Cave. **Thanks!**

Read and enjoy more from the **early Stoics**!

If you benefited from *The Best of the Early Stoics*, you may wish to pick up another Cave book related to the early Stoics or Stoicism. Visit the Cave at www.theclassicscave.com.

www.theclassicscave.com

Pick up a **CAVE book** . . .

from HOMER . . .

from the CYNICS . . .

From EPICURUS . . .

www.theclassicscave.com

 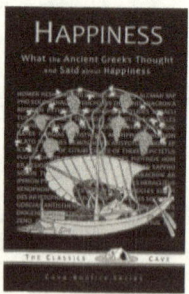